Perspectives in Creativity

Perspectives in Creativity

Edited by

Irving A. Taylor
Lakehead University

J. W. Getzels
University of Chicago

 Aldine Publishing Company, Chicago

ABOUT THE EDITORS

Irving A. Taylor received his undergraduate training in Art and Psychology at the University of Houston. He completed graduate work in Social Psychology at the University of Houston and received his Ph.D. in Social Psychology from New York University. Dr. Taylor has served as Director of the Creativity Program, Center for Creative Leadership and is currently Professor of Psychology at Lakehead University.

Jacob W. Getzels received his undergraduate training in English and Comparative Literature at Brooklyn College and completed graduate work in this area at Columbia University. He received his Ph.D. in Social Relations from Harvard University and is currently R. Wendell Harrison Distinguished Service Professor, Departments of Education and of Behavioral Sciences, The University of Chicago.

First published 1975 by
Aldine Publishing Company
529 South Wabash Avenue
Chicago, Illinois 60605

ISBN 0–202–25121–7 clothbound edition
Library of Congress Catalog Number 74–22645

Printed in the United States of America

To Jan and P.K.P.J.

Contents

vii

Preface

CERTAIN HISTORIC EVENTS—whose significance may be recognized only in retrospect—mark paradigmatic shifts in a field of inquiry. The shifts make possible the identification of new problems and provide the concepts and methods needed to explore, if not yet ultimately to solve, the problems. Issues that had formerly gone unrecognized, or if recognized had seemed unamenable to inquiry, become subjects of systematic study.

In higher mental functioning, the work on genius by Galton was such an event; the invention of the intelligence test by Binet was another; the longitudinal investigation of giftedness by Terman yet another. J. P. Guilford's formulation of creativity in his presidential address at the American Psychological Association meeting in 1950 may also have been such an event.

In that address, he observed that in the preceding quarter-century there had appeared in the psychological literature fewer than 200 studies on the subject of creativity. A decade and a half later, in 1965, more than 100 such studies appeared in the single year. Indeed, it has been estimated that the number of studies on creativity for the year and a half 1965–1966 equalled that of the preceding five years, which in turn equalled that of the preceding ten years, which in *its* turn equalled that of the preceding hundred years.

Now, a quarter-century after the address, it seems an appropriate time to take stock, to make at least a partial inventory as it were, of the work in the field. We asked a number of people identified with the psychological study of creativity—some who had preceded Guilford, but chiefly those who had followed him—to write autobiographically of their engagement with the area.

We especially asked those with the longest involvement to write not only about what they had found, as they might for a journal article, but to relate more personally what they had thought and done. In effect, we asked them for an intellectual history of their work: How had they gotten started? How had their ideas developed? What in their thinking had remained the same? What had changed? What had been their successes? Their failures? Where should further inquiry proceed? Or should it? In short, what were their *perspectives* in creativity.

As will be apparent from the varying and sometimes contradictory perspectives of the contributors, to say nothing about the perspectives of those it was impossible to include but whose work is reviewed, many of the concepts, methods, and findings remain matters of disagreement. This is all to the good. The orderly expression of differences is the prime characteristic of a field of inquiry that is alive and well—a field that is not already foreclosed by dogma but still in a dynamic state open to conceptual and methodological transformation.

Guilford began his address with the statement, "I discuss the subject of creativity with considerable hesitation, for it represents an area in which psychologists generally, whether they be angels or not, have feared to tread." The chapters in this book represent the thought and work of some people who, whatever their fears, did venture to tread in the area.

The introductory chapter—a survey of the study of creativity from the nineteenth century to the present, with emphasis on the past twenty-five years—provides a context for the subsequent chapters. In the next chapter, J. P. Guilford describes the development of the field of creativity from the perspective of the Structure of Intellect model during the quarter-century since his 1950 address. Concurrent with Guilford's work was the broad research program of Donald W. MacKinnon and his colleagues at the Institute of Personality Assessment and Research, which is described by Dr. MacKinnon in chapter 3. J. W. Getzels and Mihalyi Csikszentmihalyi recount in the following chapter how, though starting with a conception of creativity as a problem-solving process, they were driven through their work with artists to a conception of creativity as also, and perhaps primarily, a problem-finding process. In the fifth chapter, Frank M. Andrews describes his investigations with the Remote Associates approach of the social and psychological factors underlying creative production in scientific laboratories.

The first five chapters tend to reflect programmatic-empirical perspectives. Although there are of course overlaps, the ensuing three chapters tend to reflect rather more individual-clinical perspectives. In chapter 6, Frank Barron examines the problem of creativity and alienation, and sketches various techniques he has used to increase empathic feelings in order to reduce meaninglessness and free the imagination. Anne Roe's studies of artists and scientists are already classics; in chapter 7, she relates how she began her work on creativity and describes her initial studies of the sources and development of paintings as reported by twenty artists. In the following chapter, Salvatore Maddi writes critically regarding the widely-held belief that social integration and a permissive environment are conducive to creative endeavor, and explores a number of contrary motivations and conditions underlying creativity.

The final group of chapters reflects perspectives of a rather more applied sort, although the applications are placed within a theoretical and empirical context. In chapter 9, Calvin Taylor and Richard Ellison describe the development of the Utah program of assessment and intervention from its initial focus on creativity in science and technology to the more recent focus on creativity of children in the classroom. Next, Sidney Parnes discusses his work on "brainstorming," setting forth how the original emphasis on imagination evolved to the present emphasis on a balance between imagination and judgment, freedom and discipline. In the following chapter, George Prince tells of the development of "synectics" since its early formulation and recounts its application to creative production in industry through the recognition of three human needs: to accomplish objectives, to believe in one's competence, and to be in touch with one's nonlogical feelings and anxieties. In chapter 12, E. Paul Torrance examines recent criticism of the work on creativity in the schools and describes his own efforts in devising diagnostic tests and educational methods; he indicates how the work has had and will continue to have a beneficial influence on education. In the thirteenth chapter, Irving A. Taylor sets forth a theory of transactualization and delineates how it operates as a systematic approach to the investigation of creative processes with implications for leadership. The final chapter briefly recapitulates the development of the study of creativity and offers some speculations regarding possible future lines of inquiry.

The editors wish to thank the Center for Creative Leadership for providing the facilities for a symposium by the contributors on the Future Implications of Creativity Research in May, 1973, assisted by Gerald Austin, Dorothy Sutton, Julia Rogers, Shirley Haworth, as well as Norma Kay, who also devoted considerable time and effort in checking references, editing, and preparing an initial index, which was completed by Tom Managhan, and Betty Everhart, who assisted in the final preparation of the manuscript.

I.A.T.
J.W.G.

Contributors

Frank M. Andrews, Director of the Survey Research Center, Institute for Social Research; Associate Professor, Department of Psychology, University of Michigan. Co-author, with Donald C. Pelz, of *Scientists in Organizations: Productive Climates for Research and Development.*

Frank Barron, Professor of Psychology, University of California, Santa Cruz; Research Psychologist, Institute of Personality Assessment and Research, University of California, Berkeley. Author of *Creative Person and Creative Process* and *Artists in the Making.*

M. Csikszentmihalyi, Associate Professor, Department of Behavioral Sciences, University of Chicago. Co-author, with J. W. Getzels, of "The creative artist as explorer" in J. McV. Hunt (Ed.) *Human Intelligence.*

Robert L. Ellison, Research Director, Institute for Behavioral Research in Creativity, Salt Lake City, Utah. Co-author, with C. W. Taylor, of "Predicting Creative Performance from Multiple Measures," in *Widening Horizons in Creativity,* C. W. Taylor (Ed.).

J. W. Getzels, R. Wendell Harrison Distinguished Service Professor in the Departments of Education and of Behavioral Sciences, University of Chicago. Co-author of *Creativity and Intelligence: Explorations with Gifted Students.*

J. P. Guilford, Professor Emeritus, Department of Psychology, University of Southern California, Los Angeles; President of the American Psychological Association, 1950. Author of *The Nature of Human Intelligence* and *Intelligence, Creativity and Their Educational Implications.*

Salvatore R. Maddi, Professor, Department of Behavioral Sciences, University of Chicago. Co-author of *Functions of Varied Experience;* author of *Perspectives on Personality: A Comparative Approach.*

Donald W. MacKinnon, Professor Emeritus of Psychology, and formerly

Director of the Institute of Personality Assessment and Research, University of California, Berkeley; Research Psychologist, IPAR, and President, Western Psychological Association, 1963–1964. Co-author of *Experimental Studies in Psychodynamics and Assessment of Men.*

Sidney J. Parnes, Professor of Creative Studies, State University College, Buffalo, New York; President, Creative Education Foundation; Director, Creative Problem-Solving Institute. Author of *Creativity: Unlocking Human Potential;* co-editor of *A Source Book for Creative Problem-Solving.*

George M. Prince, Chairman, Transactional Awareness, Inc.; Chairman, Synectics, Inc., Cambridge, Massachusetts. Author of *The Practice of Creativity: A Manual for Group Problem Solving.*

Anne Roe, formerly Director, Center for Research on Careers, 1963–1966. Author of *The Making of a Scientist;* "A Psychological Study of Eminent Psychologists and Anthropologists, and a Comparison with Biological and Physical Scientists."

Calvin W. Taylor, Professor, Department of Psychology, University of Utah. Author of *Climate for Creativity;* co-editor of *Scientific Creativity: Its Recognition and Development.*

Irving A. Taylor, Professor of Psychology, Lakehead University, Ontario, Canada, formerly Director of Creativity Program, Center for Creative Leadership. Author of "Nature of the Creative Process" in *Creativity: An Examination of the Creative Process,* P. Smith (Ed.), and "Similarities in the Structure of Extreme Social Attitudes."

E. Paul Torrance, Chairman and Professor of Educational Psychology, University of Georgia. Author of *Dimensions of Early Learning: Creativity,* and *Encouraging Creativity in the Classroom.*

1. A Retrospective View of Creativity Investigation

Irving A. Taylor

PSYCHOLOGY, AS A SCIENCE for less than 100 years, has devoted its energies to various aspects of human life, pursuing implications of resulting theories. From these theories, many hypotheses about human behavior have been derived and empirically tested either under laboratory conditions or in the complex arena of everyday life. In modeling their science after the physical sciences, psychologists have generally devoted their attention to relatively less complex modes of behavior such as sensation, perception, motivation, and learning. Although they have been interested in creativity and have utilized their own creative abilities throughout the history of psychology, psychologists have only recently focused their attention on the creative process itself. A large-scale attempt to understand this complex human capability has occurred only during the last quarter century.

Frequently cited for his part in stimulating interest in this area is J. P. Guilford (1950), who indicated in his presidential address to the American Psychological Association that less than .2 percent of the literature in psychology was devoted to creativity. He (1970) reported that by 1969 creativity investigation had increased to 1.4 percent—a sevenfold increase. Although creativity investigation is still not firmly entrenched as a major area of study in psychology, this highly neglected field of investigation is clearly gaining momentum.

The present chapter will survey the literature, indicating salient features and highlighting important issues in creativity investigation. The survey will not be exhaustive as others have provided adequate surveys from various points of views (e.g., Golann, 1963; Mackler and Shontz, 1965; Dellas and Gaier, 1970; Guilford, 1970; Torda, 1970; Bloomberg, 1973). My purpose will be to examine the literature within a systematic framework, and provide a context for the subsequent chapters of this book. This chapter has

1

been organized around the following questions: What is creativity? What are the systematic approaches to its study? What are the important areas of research? How is creativity assessed? Can creativity be developed? Finally, Why the growing concern with creativity?

What Is Creativity: Origins and Perspectives

Definitions of creativity are often misleading; they say too much and too little. They may, however, provide a point of departure for more extended and systematic investigation. Early definitions of creativity tended to be unitary in nature and they frequently indicated sources or origins of creativity, such as vitalism, nativism, empiricism, emergentism, serendipity, romanticism, physiology, culture, interpersonal relations, and personal (I. Taylor, 1973b).

Morgan (1953) listed 25 definitions of creativity which he extracted from the literature. Most of these definitions imply that creativity involved the development of something unique. Earlier, Spearman (1931) had generated interest in the area with his book *Creative Mind*. There he defined creativity as "the power of the human mind to create new content—by transferring relations and thereby generating new 'correlates'—extends its sphere not only to representation in ideas, but also to fully sensuous presentations" (p. 148). The Gestalt psychologists defined creativity as an action that produces a new idea or insight through imagination rather than through reason or logic. Thurstone (1962) similarly assumed "that the creative act is characterized by the moment of insight which is often preceded by nonverbalized prefocal thinking," and that creative thinking "is normally followed by explicit and deductive thinking in testing the new idea" (p. 52). As early as 1900 Ribot described creativity as a process of association by which mental states become joined together so that one state tends to invoke the other.

These early definitions are unifactory in nature, a practice which some current investigators continued. Mednick (1962), following the associationistic tradition of Ribot, defined creativity as a forming of associative, and largely mutually remote, elements into new combinations. Many contemporary investigators such as Barron (1969) and May (1959) simply defined creativity as the ability to bring something new into existence. Others, such as Fromm (1959), have described it as the ability to see or to be aware and to respond. Schachtel (1959) somewhat similarly described it as the art of viewing the familiar fully in its inexhaustible being. Others have analogized creativity in terms of biological processes (Gerard, 1946; Eccles, 1958; Sinnott, 1959; Gutman, 1967; Mumford, 1970, pp. 378–93).

Some researchers, most notably Guilford (1967a), view creativity as inherent in all persons, qualitatively similar at all levels, and therefore their concern is with quantitative differences relative to general population norms. Others, such as Ghiselin (1958), have postulated two kinds of creativity: the creativity manifested in those who devote their lives to creative ends, and the creativity manifested by the general population. This generally implied distinction, that there is a qualitative difference between the general population and those devoting their entire lives to creative ends, was the probable basis for selecting and observing highly creative individuals in several face-to-face studies.

Several earlier investigators postulated multilevels of creativity, particularly Freud's (1933) primary and secondary processes and Jung's (1946) differentiation between the type of creativity that transcends the boundary of psychologically intelligible material and the other type which does not. Maslow (1954) suggested two levels or distinct types of creativity. There is first the little-understood talent-type creativity, exemplified by such unique individuals as Mozart. Such geniuses display innate capabilities characterized by a complex and unique drive. The second is the self-actualized creativity, akin to the naïve creativeness of unspoiled children, a potential given to all human beings at birth. Five levels or dispositions to creativity, apparently related to different stages of individual development, were identified by I. Taylor (1959) which were expressive, technical, inventive, innovative, and emergentive creativity.

Many investigators have attempted to formulate criteria within their definitions of creativity. Newell, Shaw, and Simon (1963) have suggested the following criteria, one or more of which must be satisfied to be considered creative: (1) a product that has novelty and value either for the thinker or the culture; (2) a product that is unconventional in the sense that it requires modification or rejection of previously accepted ideas; (3) a product resulting from high motivation and persistence, either over a considerable span of time or at a high intensity; (4) a product resulting from the formulation of a problem which was initially vague and ill-defined (p. 780). I. Taylor (Taylor and Sandler, 1972) has suggested the following criteria for identifying a creative product: generation, reformulation, originality, relevancy, hedonics, complexity, and condensation.

According to Murray (1959), creativity is a process that results in a composition that is both new and valuable. Stein (1956) had similarly suggested that creativity is "that process which results in a novel work that is accepted as tenable or useful or satisfying by a group at some point in time" (p. 172). The last part dealing with acceptance is an historic point of view calling attention to the fact that societies and their values undergo change. It suggests that there is no absolute way to define creativity and that which is regarded as creative in one culture at one point in time may not be in another. Chambers (1969) defined creativity as a process in which new and unique products emerge from the interaction of the organism and its environment, involving the dimensions of level, field, and type.

Other investigators have also stressed the importance of viewing creativity as emerging from the interaction between the person and the environment. Rogers (1959), for example, defined creativity as an "emergence in action of a novel relational product, growing out of the uniqueness of the individual on the one hand, and the materials, events, people, or circumstances of his life on the other" (p. 71). Torrance (1962b) saw creative thinking "as the process of sensing gaps or disturbing, missing elements; forming ideas or hypotheses concerning them; testing these hypotheses; and communicating the results, perhaps modifying and retesting the hypotheses" (p. 16). Synectics, developed by Gordon (1961), defined the creative process as the mental activity in problem-stating, problem-solving situations where artistic or technical inventions are the result, thus stressing both problem formulation and problem solving as parts of the creative process.

Several current definitions are multifactor or multiprocess in nature. I. Taylor (1973b) has described the processes of creativity as a system involving a person who shapes or designs his environment by transforming basic problems into fruitful outcomes facilitated by a stimulating climate. The multifactor or multiprocess conception of creativity is reflected in the following description by MacKinnon: "It involves a response or an idea that is novel or at the very least statistically infrequent. But novelty or originality, while a necessary aspect of creativity, is not sufficient if a response is to lay claim to being a part of the creative process; it must also to some extent be adaptive to reality. It must serve to solve a problem, fit a situation, or accomplish some recognizable goal. And thirdly, true creativeness involves a sustaining of the original insight, an evaluation and elaboration of it, a developing of it to the full." MacKinnon goes on to indicate that creativity involves "a process that is extended in time and characterized by originality, adaptiveness, and realization." (see chapter 3.)

These diverse definitions indicate points of agreement and points of divergence. Sometimes these definitions serve as points of departure for systematic investigation. Frequently, however, they are not taken seriously, and there is often little continuity between the definition proffered and the ensuing theory and research. If one is to gain a better understanding of creativity, therefore, one should examine the systematic approaches, theories, and researches that have been developed, particularly during the past quarter century.

Systematic Approaches to Creativity

The greatest degree of divergency in creativity investigation is apparent in the formulation of various systems and approaches. It would seem that these divergent approaches take on the major characteristics of the creative process itself. Although any attempt to categorize the various approaches can be misleading, since a great deal of overlapping occurs, for convenience the following systems will be examined: psychoanalytic, humanistic, trait-factorial, holistic, and associationistic.

PSYCHOANALYTIC

Freud (1910, 1924, 1947) was the first to suggest clearly a dynamic theory of the creative act. He was probably the first to undertake serious work on man's ability to create. To Freud, the process of sublimation provided the energy for all cultural accomplishments, including creativity. Imaginative creation like daydreaming was asserted to be a continuation and substitute for childhood play. Creative production was seen as the result of unconscious conflicts of drives and needs sublimated through the ego's effort into outcomes useful to both the creator and society. Freud's early writings generated in others a continuing interest in artistic creativity, largely from studies of poets, artists, and writers. Sublimation was seen as the basic process by which sexual energy was transformed into socially acceptable forms. Creativity was also seen as a substitute for achieving satisfaction and thus avoiding the hardships of reality. The creative individual turns from reality to fantasy, where he gives full play to his erotic wishes. If successful, he molds his fantasies into a new reality which becomes creative. Creative behavior is then an overt manifestation of sublimation, an unconscious process through which libidinal or aggressive energies are converted into culturally sanctioned behaviors. Since Freud also identified psychopathology as having an identical origin, a theoretic link was postulated between creativity and mental illness, although Freud did make a distinction between the two phenomena.

One additional aspect of Freud's conception of creativity was his belief that the manifest artistic formulation was a restructuring of archaic unconscious images after these had been accepted as conscious symbols and after the symbols had been reformulated within contemporary acceptable modalities. The creative process thus originated within and not outside the person, and the creation mirrors unconscious imagery after it has been processed through the ego.

The prolific writings of Freud generated a host of subsequent investigations. The most important of these were psychoanalytic variations formulated by his disciples, Adler, Jung, and Rank.

For Jung (1971), "the unsatisfied yearnings of the artist reach back to the primordial image in the unconscious which is best fitted to compensate the inadequacy and one-sidedness of the present" (p. 321). The creator, in raising his image from the deepest unconsciousness, brings it into relation with conscious values, transforming it until it can be accepted by the minds of his contemporaries (Jung, 1959). Jung emphasized the concept of the collective unconscious, a storehouse of racial memories handed down from the distant past in the form of archetypes. Man consistently strives to develop from a less complete stage to a more complete one, aiming toward individuation, the most complete differentiation and harmonious blending of all man's characteristics.

Adler's (Ansbacher and Ansbacher, 1956) concept of the individual's creative power was one of his major achievements as a personality theorist. His emphasis was on the uniqueness of persons as evident in each individual's life style rooted in his specific inferiorities. Compensation for these inferiorities led to creative achievement. Adler, like Jung, posited an innate pattern of behavior striving for positive growth and self-actualization. For Adler, however, as opposed to Freud and Jung, creativity sprang from man's consciousness rather than from his unconsciousness. All other aspects of man are subordinated to the creative power of the individual. Even personality is created from man's constitutional disposition and experience. Creativity was viewed as supreme usefulness, and those who are more creative are more useful for purposes of serving a social function.

Rank (1932, 1945) was more concerned with art and creativity than other early psychoanalysts. He believed that the individual was able to reach his highest level of development by realizing an independent will through which he could resolve his guilt feelings and integrate his personality. He identified this person as the creative type or artist, and attributed to him the highest level of creative functioning. The artist's motivation resulted from the need to externalize his personality into artistic acts.

A more recent psychoanalytic position has been developed by Kris (1952), who proposed the concept of "regression in the service of the ego," suggesting that in the creative act the artist is in a state in which the ego is temporarily reduced. During this time the ego uses regressive material for its own creative purposes. Central to creativeness, then, is a relaxation of the ego for creative functions as revealed in fantasy, dreams, states of intoxication, and fatigue. Such functional regression is especially prominent in and characteristic of the process of inspiration. For Kris, creativity occurs when there is free interplay between preconscious and conscious, an active and autonomous functioning rather than one in which unconscious impulses are most active.

Fairbairn (1938) and Grotjahn (1957) have suggested another psychoanalytic proposition, that creation is a "restitution for destructive impulses." The process involved is one of atonement for original aggressive trends. The creative transformation is an attempt at restitution or restoration, through fantasy for example, to alleviate guilt and anxiety. Through identification the audience joins with the creator in his original emotions of destruction and restoration.

Another psychoanalyst to be considered is Kubie (1958) who wrote about neurotic distortion in the creative process. The preconscious ego functions occupy a central place for artistic creativity in Kubie's model, which holds that creative productivity is not compatible with psychopathology.

HUMANISTIC

The roots of humanism stem largely from the positive aspects of psychoanalytic approaches. One of the major concepts related to creativity in humanism is self-actualization, which is considered to be the motivating drive for creativity. Humanists frequently hold an optimistic and positive view of man, which includes the belief that everyone possesses creative potential. Goldstein (1939), though not generally considered a humanist, was an important proponent of self-actualization. He assumed that there was only one drive, the drive of self-actualization. Normal behavior involves a continual change of tension which enables and impels the organism according to its nature to actualize itself in further activities.

Maslow (1954) and Rogers (1963) have been the leading contemporary proponents of self-actualization, although Rogers prefers to use the concept, "fully functioning person." Other investigators have used concepts similar to self-actualization. Fromm (1941), for example, talked about productive orientation; Lecky (1945) referred to unified self-consistent personality; Snygg and Combs (1949), the preservation and enhancement of the phenomenal self; Horney (1950), the realization of self; Riesman (1950), the autonomous person; May (1953), existential being; Allport (1955), creative becoming and functional autonomy.

According to Fromm (1959), one experiences creativity only after reaching some degree of inner maturity when projection and distortion are reduced. In being creative it is important to accept oneself at face value, neither rejecting "evil" parts of oneself, nor evaluating different experiences as they occur. Creativity for Fromm requires flexibility between rational and emotional, objective and subjective experiences. His central view is that one should accept human sensuality, for with this acceptance one is brought to a state of awareness and to a readiness for creativity. Rejection of sensual orientation reduces the capacity to be alive and creative.

An implication of the humanistic position according to Moustakas (1967) is that the creative person leads his life in the present with a forward thrust into the future, experiencing change and transformation in a state of "becoming," or a basic drive to create one's own life through self-determination.

Maslow (1959) drew early attention to an important Jungian feature of the creative process, the integration and resolution of dichotomies and the fusion of primary and secondary processes. Healthy, creative people are able to be childlike at one time and when appropriate, grownup, rational, and critical. The creative person may be both childlike and mature at the same time. People in general, according to Maslow, are afraid to learn about their inner processes and thereby do not become self-actualized. Creative people, however, override this fear and the rigid structuring of social norms, thereby expressing and integrating aspects of themselves which contribute to their integrity, wholeness, and creativity. For Maslow, self-actualization seems to be synonymous at times with health itself, representing the expression of the fullest humanness or "being" of the person. Self-actualizing creativity may be an essential characteristic of humanness, stressing first the personality rather than its achievements. The self-actualizing personality may express boldness, courage, freedom, spontaneity, perspicuity, and self-acceptance. Achievements such as problem solving and product making are secondary to the self-actualizing creativity of the personality. Maslow also pointed out that self-actualizing creative people are independent, autonomous, and self-directed.

According to Rogers (1959), "the mainspring of creativity appears to be the same tendency which we discover so deeply as the curative force in psychotherapy—*man's tendency to actualize himself, to become his potentialities.* By this I mean the directional trend which is evident in all organic and human life—the urge to expand, extend, develop, mature—the tendency to express and activate all the capacities of the organism, to the extent that such activation enhances the organism or the self" (p. 72). The mainspring for creativity, then, is self-actualization, including openness to experience, internal locus of evaluation, and the ability to toy with elements and concepts. The external conditions that facilitate creativity include the acceptance of the individual as of unconditional worth, a climate in which critical evaluation is absent, and support for psychological freedom. The underlying theme stressed by Rogers—keynoting other humanists—is the desire of the individual to achieve fully his potential through interaction with a supportive environment.

Humanists share with psychoanalytic investigators the view which posits man in conflict with his society. Freud regarded the creative impulse as having a psychopathological source. The humanists, however, view the creative impulse as stemming from man's essential health. They often subscribe to the belief that human beings are basically good but corrupted by societal demands. Although there has been research of a general nature in this area, the evidence provided by Maslow and other humanists involving self-actualization and creativity has been sketchy.

TRAIT-FACTORIAL

Trait theory diverges markedly from other approaches. Traits are distinct characteristics of an individual, and the trait approach emphasizes individual differences. The statistical techniques of factor analysis are frequently used to identify traits, and factorial approaches are used to isolate separate intellective factors. These factors are derived largely from batteries of tests constructed on theoretical considerations and are usually administered to a large number of subjects. The statistical procedures of factor analysis reveal intercorrelations among tests organizing into factors those tests which are highly related to one another. The factor underlying a group of correlated tests is then given a name. Investigators may try to design a test that measures only one factor.

An early exponent of trait theory was Galton, who in his book *Hereditary Genius* (1870) proposed that mental capacities are inherited and follow certain laws of transmission which can be determined by observation. Cattell (1903) later did a statistical study of eminent men, the first of a series of such studies. Cattell believed that innate characteristics were more potent than social tradition or physical environment. Spearman's book, *Creative Mind* (1931), generated further interest in the trait approach to creativity, although his description of the creative process appears to be associationistic. He believed that knowing is accomplished through three generative principles: tendencies to experience, to see a relationship, and to generate correlates. Creativity, he believed, was related to the last principle, that of displacing a relation from one idea to another idea and thereby generating a further correlative idea which might be entirely novel.

Roe's (1946, 1953*a*, 1953*b*) influential and pioneering research in this field examined the distinguishing characteristics of eminent scientists and artists. Thurstone (1950) also generated early interest by indicating that many intelligence tests do not measure certain factors which are closely related to creativity. Subsequent researchers investigating the personality traits of creative individuals have included MacKinnon (1961*a*), Barron (1961), and Cattell (1959). Their studies, usually involving direct observation of highly creative men and women in such fields as mathematics, physics, biology, architecture, and painting, will be discussed in a subsequent section.

The most notable contemporary proponent of the trait-factorial approach to creativity is Guilford (1959). Using factor analytic techniques, he and his associates at the Psychological Laboratory at the University of Southern California have identified 120 factors of intellectual ability and have developed marker tests for many of them. Guilford has embodied these factors in a three-dimensional theoretic model of intelligence called the "structure of intellect" (SI). Inherent in this model is Guilford's assumption that intelligence is not a single, monolithic factor, but that many primary and independent intellectual factors, some unmeasured by IQ tests, make up the domain of human intellectual ability.

The three dimensions of Guilford's SI model are: contents, composed of information in the environment discriminated by the organism; operations, the intellectual processing of various kinds that occurs in relation to that information; and products, the forms that the information takes after processing. Cognition, the immediate recognition of previously stored information, and divergent production, the generation of information based upon variety and quantity of output, are basic to Guilford's model.

Guilford has contributed two important hypotheses concerning creativity: that creativity may involve processes different from intelligence, and that creativity is a multidimensional variable. In describing primary traits related to creativity, Guilford (1959) has included the following: a generalized sensitivity to problems; fluency of thinking involving such factors as word fluency, associational fluency, expressional fluency, and ideational fluency; flexibility of thinking, involving spontaneity (figural and semantic) and figural adaptive flexibility; originality; redefinition, which has figural, symbolic, and semantic factors; and semantic elaboration. Guilford and his associates hold that creative talents are largely outside the realm of intelligence as it is ordinarily measured, and that they are widely distributed in different degrees throughout the population, that is, not confined to a few gifted individuals.

HOLISTIC

Duncker (1926) was one of the earliest investigators of creativity to adapt a holistic or Gestalt point of view. The early Gestalt psychologists Köhler (1929), Koffka (1935), Wertheimer (1945), and Lewin (1935) related creativity to "insight." Wertheimer, in his provocative book *Productive Thinking,* described creative thinking as occurring in a field which becomes focal but not isolated. This is followed by a deeper structural view of the field, resulting in changes in functional meaning, grouping, and organizing until gaps in a problem are resolved. This involves a process of closure in which a field is restructured to restore harmony and obtain equilibrium. It is not a piecemeal operation, but rather one in which each step is subsumed or affected by the whole situation. For Lewin, similarly, the whole situation involves the self and the world with no fixed divisions.

More recent holistic investigators are Schachtel (1959) and Arnheim (1954). Schachtel's theoretical system combines elements of psychoanalysis, humanism, and cognitive approaches and therefore can be called holistic, or at least eclectic. He related creativity to two stages: autocentricity, the self-centered stage of the infant; and allocentricity, the object-centered stage of the mature person. Autocentricity involves a mode of perception with minimal differentiation. A child reaches the stage of allocentricity when he can experience objects independent of his underlying wishes and fears. This openness to the object world is a prerequisite for creativity. His allocentric encounters may alternate between global attention in which the object is perceived as a whole and selective attention in which the various facets of the whole are actively grasped. Openness is a key organizing concept in Schachtel's approach to creativity, but the openness is to the outer rather than the inner experiences, although object exploration is intrinsically motivated. For Arnheim (Peterson, 1972), originality involves getting back to the origin, to the roots of one's experience, the way it smells, tastes, and feels. Earlier, Arnheim (1947) stated that perceptual preference for balance, symmetry, and dynamic richness are expressed in creative art forms. A creative contribution, then, is made through simplification, preference for balanced, regular, symmetrical patterns, and enrichment of the structure.

ASSOCIATIONISTIC

According to one group of investigators, the ability to think creatively is a matter of utilizing a variety of associations accessible to an individual. Unusual recombination of these bonds results in creativity. Ribot (1900), a forerunner of the modern associationistic approach to creativity, described the process as one in which mental states became joined in such a way that one state tends to evoke the other. Unlike association by contiguity, which often results in stereotyped responses, associations by resemblance—either direct or through a mediating idea, as in analogical thinking—are the bases for creative association. In the creative process, complementary processes of association and disassociation occur by spontaneously causing images to associate into groups through imagination. With regard to mechanical invention, Ribot posited four phases—the germ, incubation, flowering, and completion.

Mednick (1962) and his colleagues (for example, Andrews, 1962) are the leading contemporary associationists concerned with creativity. Mednick described "the creative thinking process as the forming of associative elements into new combinations which either meet specified requirements or are in some way useful. The more mutually remote the elements of the new combination, the more creative the process or solution" (p. 221). Any condition of the organism which brings the necessary associative elements into additional contiguity will increase the probability of a creative solution. For Mednick, three types of creative associations are serendipity, similarity, and mediation. The number of ideas brought into contiguity account for individual differences in the degree of creativity. Individual differences also involve need for associative elements, associative hierarchy, number of associations, cognitive or personality styles, and selection of creative combinations.

Mednick's straightforward theory has stimulated a growing body of research in which creativity is characterized by the combining of mutually distant associative elements of thought. Creative individuals solve problems by juxtaposing a number of ideas not previously related to one another. Creativity is thus a matter of novel arrangements of temporarily contiguous, unusual associations to a given stimulus. Mednick has operationally defined the creative process as the distribution of the individual's associations around ideas which he has called the associative hierarchy of responses.

Koestler's (1964) approach to creativity may be considered in certain respects associationistic in nature. In his book *The Act of Creation,* he suggested that creativity involved "the displacement of attention to something not previously noted, which was irrelevant in the old and is relevant in the new context; the discovery of hidden analogies as a result of the former; the bringing into consciousness of tacit axioms and habits of thought which were implied in the code and taken for granted; the uncovering of what has always been there" (pp. 119–120).* He coined the word "bisociation" to make a distinction between routine skills of thinking which occur on a single plane and the creative act, which operates on more than one plane. In the latter, transitory states of instability occur where the balance of emotion and thought is disturbed.

Creativity Research

The complexity of the processes involved make research in creativity especially difficult. In general, several areas of research can be identified. These include: (1) the creative personality; (2) creative problem formulation; (3) the creative process; (4) creative products; (5) creative climates; (6) creativity and mental health; and (7) creativity and intelligence.

THE CREATIVE PERSONALITY

A great deal of research has focused on identifying the characteristics of the creative personality, usually from a trait point of view. About a century ago, Galton (1874) researched outstanding scientists and reported that half possessed to an appreciable degree the following characteristics: energy, health, steady pursuit of purpose, business habits, independence of views, and a strong innate taste for science. For Galton, "genius" referred to an automatic activity of the mind, that is, inspiration, as distinguished from an effort of the will. He further described the personality of the genius as enthusiastic, having rapid, fluent, firm mental associations, and vivid imaginations, and driven rather than in control.

Roe (1946, 1953a, 1953b) was an early pioneer in investigation of eminent people, especially highly creative painters and scientists. Her research, begun in the 1940s, stimulated other investigators in laboratories around the country. On the basis of data obtained from Rorschach, TAT, and biographical material, she found curiosity, persistence, high energy level, and need for independence to be salient characteristics of research scientists. Both painters and scientists were found to have a strong motivation to succeed, a characteristic she attributed to basic insecurity. Implicit in her early studies was the assumption that mental health affects creativity by providing motivation for the highly creative person. Willingness to work hard seemed to be the most general characteristic of the samples she studied.

Roe (1972), incidentally, reported differences involving age and productivity in scientists, an area investigated also by Lehman (1953, 1966a, 1966b)

*Copyright © Arthur Koestler, 1964.

and Dennis (1958, 1966). In terms of sex, Helson (1961, 1966, 1967, 1968) has noted differences in creativity for females as compared to males.

By far the most frequently cited research concerning the characteristics of the creative personality stems from the work of MacKinnon (1960, 1961a, 1961b) and his associates at the Institute for Personality Assessment and Research (IPAR). Their initial concern was with the highly effective person, but they subsequently focused on examining highly creative persons such as research scientists, writers, mathematicians, and architects. The picture of the highly creative architect, for example, emerged as self-confident, flexible, self-accepting, having little concern with social restraints or others' opinions, and strongly motivated to achieve, primarily in situations requiring independent thought and action. Perceptual openness, indicating a greater awareness and receptiveness both to the outer and inner world, differentiated between the more creative and less creative architects.

According to MacKinnon, highly creative persons stress their inventiveness, independence, individuality, enthusiasm, determination, and industry, while the less creative stress virtue, good character, rationality, and concern for others. Being more self-accepting, highly creative persons are able to speak frankly and in a more unusual way about themselves. Their openness to experiences allows them to struggle with the opposites of their nature striving for a more effective reconciliation, tolerating increasing amounts of tension as they strive for creative solutions to problems which they set for themselves (MacKinnon, 1960). In the IPAR studies which used extensive assessment techniques, high creatives were found to be strongly interested in aesthetic and theoretical matters, and tended to be highly intuitive and introverted.

Barron (1953) found in his early research that highly creative persons have a preference for cognitive complexity. One of the stylistic variables emerging was a preference for rich, dynamic, asymmetrical information as opposed to the simple and symmetrical. This was found to be true of creative artists as well as research scientists, architects, and writers. In terms of values, Barron (1952) found that creative subjects approved of the modern, experiential, primitive, and sensual, while they disliked the aristocratic, traditional, and emotionally controlled. Other variables related to complexity as opposed to simplicity included personal tempo, verbal fluency, impulsiveness, expansiveness, originality, sensuality, sentience, aesthetic interest, and femininity in men (Barron, 1953). Using a composite score based on a variety of measures of originality, Barron (1963a) showed that creative persons tended to reject suppression as a mechanism for the control of impulse. He (1961) also observed that highly creative writers were more frequently in trouble psychologically than people in general, but they had greater ego strength and more resources for coping with their problems. Creative people, according to Barron, are accurate, sharp observers, have high sexual drive, and are more vigorous and nervous than others; they bind high levels of tension, receive pleasure from discharging these tensions, and can temporarily avoid distinction between self and object.

For Barron (1963a), the "moral attitude" is a motivational characteristic of the creative. It is a personal commitment to the aesthetic and philosophic meaning expressed in their work. No genuinely creative act can result without this firm commitment, which entails an exceptionally strong need to find order where none appears and is considered to be a highly motivating factor (Barron, 1963b). Barron subsequently initiated a ten-year multifaceted research program in aesthetic education summarized in his book, *Artists in the Making* (1972).

Crutchfield (1961), a colleague of MacKinnon and Barron, described creative individuals as being more flexible and fluent, having more unique perceptions and cognitions, and being more intuitive, empathic, and perceptually open than the general population. R. B. Cattell and his associates (Cattell and Drevdahl, 1955; Cross, Cattell, and Butcher, 1967) using a factorial analytic approach, found that creative artists and writers demonstrated ego strength, dominance, self-sufficiency, sensitivity, introversion, desurgence, and radicalism.

A number of research programs on creativity and the creative personality have been stimulated by the important Utah Conference series initiated by C. Taylor (e.g., 1956, 1958, 1959, 1964a, 1964b, 1972; Taylor and Williams, 1966). Taylor's work, empirically based and criteria oriented, has focused on career creative performers utilizing a variety of target subjects. He has studied creative persons both as criteria and predictors and has focused his attention on multiple talents including academic, creative, planning, communicating, forecasting, and decision-making abilities (C. Taylor, 1968).

The early work of Maddi (1965), involving the motivation of creative persons, emphasized the importance of curiosity, novelty seeking, and avoidance of boredom for the creative person. Although he first viewed stimulus seeking or curiosity as motivation for the creative person, he later (see chapter 11) stressed the strenuousness involved in creative work and criticized the actualizationists for failing to take this into account. Maddi has examined three sources of creativity: creativity arising from unconscious conflicts in the life of the individual, creativity resulting from resolution of these conflicts, and creativity resulting from attempts to avoid alienation. In his early study (1965) he had reported that frustration of need states did not necessarily inhibit creativity.

Torrance and Dauw (1965) have also probed the motivation for creativity and suggest that there is a great striving and need for excellence and greater attention for unusual, unconventional achievement, indicating a strong desire to discover and use one's potential. I. Taylor (1973b) in several exploratory researches on creative motivation reported that there is a tendency for creative people to want to shape or design their environment rather than to be shaped by it. In their study of young art students at the Art Institute of Chicago, Getzels and Csikszentmihalyi (1968) found that these subjects did not differ on cognitive measures, but differed on measures of value and personality from normative college students. Getzels and Jackson (1962) found that highly creative students have personality structures that are congruent with recognized mature creatives, although less sharply delineated.

CREATIVE PROBLEM FORMULATION

Although various investigators have noted the importance of creative problem formulation as a research area, very little research has been conducted in this area. Lowenfeld (1962), for example, commented on the role of problem formulation or, more specifically, sensitivity to problems. According to Lowenfeld, creative persons are unusually sensitive to what they see, hear, and touch; they respond readily to the "feel," the texture qualities and characteristics of materials that are generally hidden to less sensitive persons. The importance of sensitivity, of being able to feel the problems of other people, other cultures, races, and nations is stressed by Lowenfeld.

Many other investigators, such as philosophers of science, general semanticists, and anthropologists have similarly called attention to the importance of problem formulation, although not always in the context of investigating creativity.

I. Taylor (1972b) investigated the relationship between creativity and problem formulation as an abductive process as described by Peirce (Fann, 1970). In general, some preliminary observations indicated that those high in creativity tend to gravitate to generic problems similar to the "generative notion" described by Langer (1942). Generic problems are the genotypes of related manifest phenotypes. To use a medical analogy, the relationship between genotype and phenotype is similar to the relationship between underlying pathology and its resulting symptoms; that is, creative people tend to relate to the underlying problem and less creative people to its superficial observable manifestations.

Most noteworthy in terms of research on problem formulation is the early paper of Getzels (1964) and the subsequent investigation by Getzels and Csikszentmihalyi (1966). Getzel's interest in the area of problem finding grew out of his thoughts about creative thinking, in which he differentiated between the nature of "presented" and "discovered" problems. To differentiate, the central question is "How are new problems discovered?" rather than the more conventional question "How are presented problems solved?" Observing how artists formulate their problem before they begin to work, Csikszentmihalyi and Getzels (1971) found that originality was highly related to problem finding and discovery orientation. For Getzels, the first step in creative activity involves discovering and formulating the problem itself, which may provide half the solution. Getzels believed that creativity investigators should turn their attention to and examine problem finding in addition to problem solving. Johnson (1946) in this regard has noted the essential point that the formulation of a problem determines the formulation of the answer.

CREATIVE PROCESS

Whether a problem is presented or discovered, creative processes are required to reach creative solutions or products. These processes, which entail the capacity to transform or find new and unexpected relations between bits of information, may allow men to transcend the usual view of psychological behavior as a stimulus-response function. This ability for solving problems may be characterized by novelty, unconventionality, and persistence.

Early in the century Poincaré (1913) described his own processes of mathematical creation. The creative processes of other highly creative persons have been described in their own words in a stimulating book edited by Ghiselin, *The Creative Process* (1952). In 1926 Wallas suggested four stages in forming a new thought: preparation, incubation, illumination, and verification. Although these terms have become commonplace, few investigators have empirically investigated these steps in the creative process. A few (Patrick, 1935, 1937, 1938, 1941; Eindhoven and Vinacke, 1952), however, did attempt to determine experimentally whether these steps could be identified and whether they ran sequentially as Wallas suggested. Some of the concepts were found to be relevant but the sequence of steps was more varied than originally described.

From her investigations of eminent men, Roe concluded, "Creativity, as seen in both artists and scientists, does not come from any sudden inspiration invading an idle mind and idle hands, but from the labor of a driven person" (see chapter 5). Fulgosi and Guilford (1968) examined short-term incubation using a task involving divergent production. They found that "the incubation time interval of 20 minutes demonstrated a significant gain in quantity of responses over performances with no interval, while the 10 minute interval yielded very little gain, but increases in relative quality—evidenced by an increased number of remote responses—were more clearly seen in tests without the incubation interval" (p. 132).

Osborn (1953) operationalized a procedure to facilitate creative thinking frequently called "brainstorming" which utilizes personal interaction. According to Osborn, "Most of us can work better creatively when teamed up with the right partner because collaboration tends to induce effort, and also to spur our automatic power of association. On this latter point, Thomas Carlyle wrote: 'The lightning spark of thought, generated in the solitary mind, awakens its likeness in another mind.' " (p. 72). Parnes (1962a), who has developed brainstorming into a successful program for the development of creativity called the Creative Problem-Solving Institute, has used a powerful analogy to describe the creative problem-solving process in groups: "Let us consider the stimulation of a group in another way: When you look into a kaleidoscope, you see a pattern. If you manipulate the drum of the kaleidoscope, you begin to get countless patterns. If you then add a new piece of crystal to the kaleidoscope, and hold the drum still, you see a slightly different pattern. Now if you manipulate the drum, with the new stone included, you have a tremendous number of new possible patterns" (p. 285). The following five-step procedure for developing creativity is provided in the annual basic course of the Institute: fact-finding, problem-finding, idea-finding, solution-finding, and acceptance-finding (Parnes, 1967).

Gordon (1961) has developed another, and in many ways similar, program for developing creativity called "synectics." He indicates the following as phases involved in problem solving: (1) the problem as given; (2) making the strange familiar; (3) the problem as understood; (4) operational mechanisms; (5) the familiar made strange; (6) psychological states; (7) states integrated with problem; (8) viewpoint; and (9) solution or research target. Synectics makes considerable use of analogy and metaphor in creative problem solving in a pragmatic program designed to develop inventive ability. It has subsequently been developed further as a method for creative problem solving for management by Prince (1970). I. Taylor (Taylor and Sandler, 1973) has focused on transformation techniques such as reversals in developing the creative process.

For Stein (1956) creativity is a process of formulating and testing hypotheses and communicating the results, and occurs through processes of social transaction. Barron (1964) has described the nature of the creative process in his studies on the relationship of ego diffusion to creative perception: "In the sequence of related acts which taken together as a process result in the creation of something new, there occur consistently a rhythmic alternation and occasionally a genuine resolution or synthesis of certain common antinomies. By this I mean that certain apparently contradictory and contrary principles of action, thought, and feeling, which usually must be sacrificed one to the other, are instead expressed fully in the same sequence, the dialectic leading at special moments to an unusual integration" (p. 81).

MacKinnon (1971) has utilized an ingenious technique for examining the creative process. He implanted a repressed emotional complex in hypnotized subjects so as to study the nature of symbol formation. This provided a powerful technique for examining symbolic transformations of elements in the unconscious into the kind of fantasy which we recognize as part of the creative process.

CREATIVE PRODUCT

Ghiselin (1958) has pointed out that a creative product is "intrinsically a configuration of the mind, a presentation of constellated meaning, which at the time of its appearance in the mind was new in the sense of being unique, without a specific precedent" (p. 36). Sprecher (1959) stated, "A truly creative product or contribution has the characteristic of being itself creative in the sense that it *generates additional creative activity*" (p. 294). He pointed out that many creative findings lead to new problems which require new solutions which in turn lead to new discoveries. The amount of activity a creative product *generates* can be considered as an important but frequently undervalued criterion, and is probably related to a large extent to divergent production.

Many researchers have directed their energies to identifying a variety of criteria which characterize a creative product. Jackson and Messick (1965) contributed important insights regarding creative product criteria, and most investigators would agree with their statement, "No matter what other positive qualities it might possess, then, we generally insist as a first step that a product be novel before we are willing to call it creative" (p. 312). This criterion, also referred to as originality, statistical infrequency, or unusualness, has to do with the newness of a product.

Jackson and Messick also suggested criteria having to do with the "correctness" and the "goodness" of a person's response. The former is similar to the concept of relevancy, the latter to the concept of hedonics. The criterion of *correctness* has to do with the degree to which certain objectives have been satisfied, and the criterion of *goodness* to the worth or value of a person's response to the product. Guilford (1957) has elaborated on the distinction between the "correct" and the "good." Where correctness may be used as a criterion primarily in scientific products, less logical standards such as "good" are used to evaluate artistic products, although this distinction may not be fully supported by further examination. According to Jackson and Messick (1965), "To be appropriate a product must fit its context; it must 'make sense' in light of the demands of the situation and the desires of the producer" (p. 313).

Transformation is another important criterion of a creative product. This criterion involves the extent to which the product reformulates a situation or field. It is concerned with "the power to transform the constraints of reality. Some objects combine elements in ways that defy tradition and that yield a new perspective" (Jackson and Messick, 1965, p. 315). According to Horner (1968), a creative product that does not adapt to the demands of its time may actually facilitate change by incorporating the structure of the new and unique outcome. According to Ghiselin (1958), "The mind in its major creative action assumes responsibility for making and remaking the universe of meaning sustained by the culture in which it moves" (p. 43). Products embodying the potential for transformation are likely to stimulate viewers, thus altering their conventional way of perceiving.

An additional criterion proposed by Jackson and Messick (1965) is condensation, in which the product unifies a great deal of information and expresses it in a highly condensed form. Products which appear simple at first glance may on further examination contain highly complex information as, for example, Einstein's $E = MC^2$ formulation. Concentrated information can be a highly imaginative and powerful characteristic of creative products. Condensation summarizes essences which can be expanded and interpreted in a multiplicity of ways. In evaluating the characteristics of creative products, I. Taylor (Taylor and Sandler, 1972) has developed a Creative Product Inventory which profiles a product in terms of the several criteria mentioned above; that is, its generative power, transformation power, degree of originality, relevancy, hedonics, complexity, and condensation.

CREATIVE CLIMATE

What constitutes a creative climate? What conditions facilitate and stimulate creativity? Environmentalists such as Torrance have sought to specify situational factors functionally related to creativity and to isolate important variables which foster or inhibit creative expression. Torrance (1967) suggested that a situation should provide the following as important factors in increasing a person's productivity, largely in an educational setting: respect unusual questions, respect unusual ideas, show that ideas have value, provide opportunities and credit for self-initiated learning, and allow performance to occur without constant threat of evaluation.

Maddi (1965) assumes an opposing view and suggests that creativity will occur regardless of climate or setting. Torrance and Gupta (1964) have shown in field experiments, however, that materials designed to provide experiences in creative thinking prove powerful enough to make differences in creative development. It is altogether possible that the way creative abilities develop and function is strongly influenced by the way environment supports a person's creative needs. C. Taylor has edited a book, *Climate for Creativity* (1972), based on one of the Utah Conferences in which the participants identified a host of environmental factors both favorable and unfavorable to creativity. Andrews has examined "factors which affect the likelihood of a new idea crossing the hurdle-filled gap and being developed into an innovative output" (see chapter 10), and also factors contributing to a stimulating laboratory for scientists.

Sensory stimulation is another important variable related to facilitating creativity. I. Taylor (1972a) found that exposure to intensive Simultaneous Sensory Stimulation over a short period of time can facilitate openness and creative divergent production. Schachtel (1959) has noted the impact of sensory stimuli on the individual, and Murphy (1947) has indicated the importance of sensory stimulation and enrichment as providing an impetus for creative growth.

RELATIONSHIP BETWEEN CREATIVITY AND MENTAL HEALTH

There are generally two views posited as to the relationship between creativity and mental health. Earlier views, particularly those stemming from Freudian psychoanalysis, held that creativity stemmed from conflict and neurotic tendencies. In 1891, Lombroso (Stein and Heinze, 1960) saw genius as a "degenerative psychosis of the epileptoid group," and believed that "the coincidence of genius and insanity enables us to understand the astonishing unconsciousness, instantaneousness, and intermittence of the creations of genius" (pp. 351–52).

According to Bellak (1958), both those who are creative and those who are mentally disturbed show the quality of ease of ego regression, although the former are able to synthesize and to increase the adaptive capacities. May (1959) quarreled with current psychoanalytic theories because of their implicit or explicit associations of creative persons with neurotic patterns. He pointed out that "regression" indicates a reductive approach, reducing creativity to neurotic processes, and he urged the view that creativity be related to health and not to disease or neurosis.

Many contemporary investigators have taken a similarly strong position in regard to relating creativity to mental health. Foremost have been Maslow (1959), Rogers (1959), and Fromm (1959), who have asserted that creativity occurs in the well adjusted. Self-actualization, which Maslow relates to creativity, is a process of realizing and completing one's self by an integration within and between one's self and the world. By this process, the person becomes unified, more open to experience, and more open to experience, and more fully functioning. Maslow strongly contended that creativity is inversely related to mental illness and emphatically stated that the most healthy people are the most creative, and reported a great overlap in the descriptions of healthy and creative individuals. He suggested that creative individuals may not be dependent on conformistic adjustment but are able to experience freedom and independence from constraining restrictions of others.

Maslow felt that there had been insufficient research in the relationship of psychotherapy and creativeness. He believed that through such research an obvious relationship between creativity and health would be found which would provide a foundation on which to construct a theory of creativity (1972).

Barron (1958) has stated that although the creative person may appear to be unbalanced, he may in fact be healthier than the average. The imbalance may result because of the differences between himself and the social majority since his sensitivity, high energy level, and ability for complex synthesis set him apart. Findings of MacKinnon (1961b) and others at IPAR have indicated that there is no empirical evidence to support the assumption of a necessary relationship between creativity and neurosis. The studies at IPAR have shown that creative persons are superior on ego strength scales, which would presumably provide creatives with adequate mechanisms to handle problems.

The question may still be raised as to what extent certain types of creativity and creative processes are related to mental health, and what types of processes are more inclined to dispose the person toward neurotic patterning. Future research may indicate that creativity is not clearly related to either mental health or illness.

RELATIONSHIP BETWEEN CREATIVITY AND INTELLIGENCE

According to Guilford (1970), Terman ruled creativity out of the realm of intelligence in his first Stanford-Binet test. Guilford, however, believed that creative thinking ability may be an important aspect of intelligence, and in his work at the Aptitude Research Project he has brought creativity within the domain of intelligence. Wallach (1971) has asked, "Why have psychologists developed an interest over the last two decades or so in the possibility of distinguishing between creativity and intelligence?" (p. 1) He indicated that an answer lies in the nature of our society, its values and goals. By examining what these values and goals fail to emphasize, Wallach and many other investigators have concluded that a relationship holds between creativity and intelligence at the lower intellective levels, but not at the higher levels. An analysis of earlier data of Wallach and Kogan (1965) revealed that creative thinking is independent of the conventional realm of intelligence and is a pervasive and unitary dimension. Using Guilford-derived creativity tests and intelligence tests, correlations among creativity factors were about .5, and correlations among intelligence measures were also about .5. However, the average correlation between creativity and intelligence was about .1.

Thurstone (1950), who was a research assistant in Thomas Edison's laboratory, presented provocative material which stimulated others to examine possible creativity factors not included in the usual standard intelligence tests. In an analysis of intelligence tests, Thurstone and one of his students, C. Taylor (1947), moved away from the "right or wrong answer" approach and identified two fluency factors, fluency of ideas and verbal versatility.

Several investigators, including Getzels and Jackson (1962), Torrance (1962b), and Guilford (1967b), obtained results in their researches that also indicated a valid distinction between creativity and the traditional concept of general intelligence. They cited relatively low correlations between measures of IQ and creativity. Getzels and Jackson (1962), using tests derived from the Guilford battery, attempted to show that creativity and intelligence were separate constructs. However, they pointed out that this does not mean that there is no relationship between creativity and intelligence over the whole range of these two variables. A certain amount of intelligence, they suggested, is required for creativity. Torrance (1962b), using a more elaborate experimental design, presented data to support a similar-finding.

MacKinnon (1961a) and his associates in their study of creative achitects found that when they were ranked according to degree of creativity, the correlation between creativity and IQ was −.08. In this regard, MacKinnon stated that this does not mean that there is no correlation over the whole range of creativity between creativity and intelligence, but suggests that while a certain amount of intelligence is required for creativity, beyond that point being more or less intelligent is not critically related to the level of creativeness. According to MacKinnon (1962a), the data suggest that "if a person has the minimum of intelligence required for mastery of a field of knowledge, whether he performs creatively or banally in that field will be crucially determined by nonintellective factors" (p. 493). Barron (1961) reported similar results in his study of creative writers, and observed that a commitment to creativity may already be selective for intelligence. He (1963a) suggested that over a total range of intelligence and creativity, a low correlation of about .4 exists, but that beyond an IQ of 120 intelligence may be a negligible factor in creativity. On the other hand, Mednick and Andrews' (1967) data did not support the idea that creativity and intelligence are relatively independent processes among the very bright, but are more closely related at lower levels of intelligence.

It should be pointed out, however, that even such critics as Thorndike (1966) and McNemar (1964), who so severely criticized investigations in this area, did agree that there were some bases for differentiating between creativity and intelligence in some respects. Thorndike, for example, pointed out that the data suggested that "there is some reality to a broad domain, distinct from the domain of the conventional intelligence test to which the designation of 'divergent thinking' or 'creative thinking' might be applied" (p. 52). McNemar implied a partial differentiation by suggesting "at the high IQ levels there will be a very wide range of creativity, whereas as we go down to average IQ, and on down to lower levels, the scatter for creativity will be less and less" (p. 879).

The Assessment of Creativity

Terman (1906) concluded that inventive qualities were outside the realm of intelligence, based on his experience with an ingenuity test. Dearborn as early as 1898 found relative independence between tests of "productive imagination" and intelligence. Chassell (1916) subsequently devised tests for originality, providing relative values so as to rank individuals for originality. Before 1950, Chassell (1916), Andrews (1930), and Welch (1946), to mention a few, were able to replicate Terman's findings. Since the prevailing notion then was that intelligence is a monolithic ability, there was no desire to envision intelligence broadly, as Guilford (1968) subsequently did, as embracing several components, some of which would not necessarily have to correlate with others. The first Stanford revision of the Binet scales, therefore, omitted scales relevant to the creative potential. In Terman's selection of scales, tests of ingenuity did not differentiate between extreme groups which had been ranked for brightness versus dullness, and as a result tests of creative qualities or ingenuity have been excluded over the years from intelligence scales.

The most elaborate battery of tests to assess creativity was developed by Guilford and his associates. Though many of these tasks were originally developed by Thurstone, Guilford has modified these tests through the years and developed them within the framework of his structure of intellect (SI) with its 120 possible factors, most of which have now been discovered through factor analysis (twenty were first identified by Thurstone and his associates). Guilford (1959) has attempted to identify SI factors through analytic methods making use of a cubical model of intellectual abilities, each dimension representing a mode of variation among the factors. The three-way classification model includes the kind of material and content of thought, varieties of activities or operations performed, and the variety of resultant products. Guilford developed tests for many of the intellectual domains of divergent production and some for transformational abilities. According to Guilford, the discovery of SI functions has made it possible to observe the processes involved in retrieving information from memory storage in divergent and convergent production operations.

After several years of basic research, Torrance selected and developed tests or activities for measuring creative thinking. Several additional years were spent in developing and revising his *Norms Technical Manual* (1966). His tests, "Thinking Creatively with Words," each contain seven activities, and the tests, "Thinking Creatively with Pictures," each contain three activities, thus allowing for measures of both verbal and figural creativity.

The Remote Associates Test (RAT) (1967) developed by Mednick (1962) measures ability to think creatively on associative interpretations, a process of seeing relationships between seemingly mutually remote ideas and forming them into new associative contributions in accordance with specified criteria. The RAT utilizes a series of three words drawn from remote association clusters, and the subject is required to find a fourth word which could serve as an associative link between them. Although the RAT has been employed by many investigators (for example, Andrews, 1962, 1965), because of its convergent nature it has been criticized as being more a measure of intelligence than creativity which is frequently assumed to be divergent in nature. Mednick has pointed out, however, that creativity involves not only divergent thinking but also the ability to converge on appropriate and fruitful solutions.

Several other techniques used for assessing creativity might be noted. C. Taylor, Ellison, and Tucker developed the Alpha-Biographical Inventory (Institute for Behavioral Research in Creativity, 1968) composed of 300 multiple-choice items to assess potential for scientific creativity. The Welsh Figure Preference Test (1959), which includes the Barron-Welsh Art Scale, requires reaction to 400 figures of varying dimensions. Empirical evidence indicates that the Art Scale may be a promising nonverbal measure of creative potential since it has had some success in correlating independent criterion measures of creativity. The Adjective Check List (Gough and Heilbrun, 1965) contains several hundred adjectives of self-descriptions or descriptions of individuals by one or more observers. The Myers-Briggs Type Indicator (Myers, 1962) is a test of cognitive styles based largely on Jungian theories of psychological attitudes, functions, and types. I. Taylor (1973a) has developed a Creative Behavior Disposition Scale which evaluates attitudinal dispositions toward various types of creativity. Other tests which have been found useful in assessing creativity are the Minnesota Multiphasic Personality Inventory (Hathaway and McKinley, 1943), the California Psychological Inventory (Gough, 1957), the Allport-Vernon-Lindzey Study of Values (1951), and the Strong Vocational Interest Blank (Strong, 1943) used by MacKinnon (1962b) in his study of architects.

MacKinnon believes that "so-called tests of creativity" have a certain face validity, but that they leave "unilluminated the personological context in which the process goes on" (see chapter 3). He suggests that thought be given to how the creative process occurs over long periods of time utilizing a variety of observations of introspective and experimental techniques for a more appropriate assessment of creativity.

Can Creativity Be Developed?

While assessment involves important problems which have not yet been resolved, such as identifying external criteria for validation purposes, differentiating creativity from other mental processes, and the larger problem of assessing such a complex process in structured situations, the development of creativity invites a whole new list of questions. An initial one can be raised as to whether creativity can actually be developed. During exposure to developmental techniques for increasing creativity, a great deal of valuable observation as to how creativity occurs is possible, and may provide a successful context for assessing creativity. Creativity is often not responsive to conscious efforts to initiate or control it since it is highly unpredictable and is resistant to scheduling. At some point, however, some conscious discipline and control is beneficial and necessary. It is difficult to know whether developing creativity is like building a muscle or following a recipe.

The complexities involved in creativity development would indicate that there is no one direct approach and that different methods and techniques may profit one person but not another. McPherson (1964, p. 132) has classified current training programs for creativity into four groups: (1) those which are designed to develop sensitivity to problems; (2) those which are directed to cognitive development problem-solving techniques; (3) those which provide individuals with knowledge as to factors which hinder or block creativity and those which facilitate it; and (4) those which prepare individuals to accept and support their innovative ideas.

Osborn (1953) stimulated much thought concerning techniques for developing creativity which has led to a highly successful development program, the Creative Problem-Solving Institute at Buffalo, currently directed by Parnes. Osborn suggested four basic rules for brainstorming: (1) criticism is ruled out—adverse judgment of ideas must be withheld; (2) "free-wheeling" is welcome—the wilder and freer the idea the better; (3) quantity of ideas is wanted—the larger the number of ideas presented the greater the probability that good ideas will occur; and (4) combination and improvement of ideas are sought—suggestions as to how the ideas of others can be improved or joined together into still better ideas. The purpose of brainstorming is to free a person from the usual inhibitions and blocks to his creative processes. Individuals and groups are asked to express ideas spontaneously and quickly until a sufficient number of ideas are expressed which are then judged.

Parnes (1962b) stated that "recent research does seem to warrant the postulate that the gap between the individual's innate creative talent and his lesser actual creative output can be narrowed by deliberate education in creative thinking. . . . The evidence of the current research does point to a definite contradiction of the age-old notion that creativity cannot be developed" (p. 191). Parnes has developed an eclectic approach for nurturing creative behavior by incorporating and synthesizing as much as possible from the growing literature on creativity. The emphasis at Buffalo has shifted to a stronger balance between imagination and judgment, between spontaneity and implementation. In terms of society's present and future needs, it should be noted that brainstorming has been one of the first organized systems for producing ideas, demonstrating that it is possible to increase creativity. D. Taylor, Berry, and Block (1958) presented evidence that individuals working alone could solve problems better than groups utilizing methods of brainstorming. These findings do not reduce the importance of increasing creativity through group problem-solving methods but only show that individual creativeness is better than group brainstorming.

Synectics, another important approach to developing creativity, was initiated by Gordon (1961) and subsequently developed by Prince (1970). The word "Synectics" was coined by Gordon from Greek words which mean "joining together" of apparently different and irrelevant elements. Largely a method utilizing invention and widely used by management groups, it was developed to increase the probability of successfully stating and solving problems. Synectics attempts to study the creative process while it is in motion. The process essentially involves making the strange familiar, and making the familiar strange. It operates largely through the use of personal analogy, which requires psychological identification with important components of the problem; direct analogy, which requires looking for comparable processes in a field different from the one in which one is working; symbolic analogy, requiring the use of poetic images and symbolism; and fantasy analogy, which requires the use of wish fulfillment ignoring laws governing the universe. According to Prince, Synectics succeeds to the degree that a climate is created that makes stimulating demands without threat and explicitly appreciates such processes as wishing and imaging. He has been concerned with developing those processes which allow for cooperation and joint accomplishment as well as satisfaction. The degree to which people can successfully work together will be determined by the use of power or effective ways of sharing power and changes of one's self-concept or image. Support is provided so that people can feel free to try and to risk failure.

Torrance (1962b) has instituted highly workable methods for enhancing and developing creativity, particularly in his programs for gifted and deprived children. He has suggested the following specific conditions as essential in developing creativity: reward diverse contributions, help creative persons recognize the importance of their own talents, avoid exploitation, accept limitations, develop minimum skills, make use of opportunities, develop values and purposes, hold to purposes, avoid equating divergence with mental illness or delinquency, reduce overemphasis on sex roles, learn to be less obnoxious without sacrificing creativity, reduce isolation, learn to cope with anxiety, fears, hardships, and failure. Torrance believes that creative abilities are more subject to modification than are those measured by intelligence tests, and urges that educational programs build upon this strength. Torrance and his associates have developed a variety of instructional media which facilitate creative development. These materials can be used with elementary school children, for example, without damaging socialization processes that occur at this level.

The creative development program initiated by I. Taylor (1972b) focuses on: (1) transposing one's ideas into the environment; (2) formulating basic or generic problems; (3) transforming ideas through reversals and analogies; (4) generating outcomes with creative characteristics; and (5) facilitating these processes through exposure to direct sensory stimulation.

According to C. Taylor (1968), research has shown that we have talents of many different types, not just "general intelligence." He has suggested a grouping of talents based on world-of-work needs. Six important types of talents include academic, creative, planning, communication, forecasting, and decision making. He urges that these talents be cultivated within the school curriculum.

Growth of Interest in Creativity

There are many factors which delayed the growth of interest in creativity investigation. It is a general observation that creative individuals may be perceived as threatening and disruptive to a prevailing system or organization. The status quo is threatened because every creative act may transcend the established order and may appear eccentric to others. Toynbee (1964) has highlighted the high premium our society places on conformity in terms of efforts to standardize human behavior through both egalitarianism and conservatism. He points out that both work against creativity and that "in combination, they mount up to a formidable repressive force" (p. 8). There is general agreement among creativity investigators that society tends to conduct its affairs in ways that dampen rather than encourage creativity. What is in question, according to Mumford (1970), is the development of a system which has become so detached from human needs that the process goes on automatically with perhaps the sole goal of maintaining the complete apparatus in a power-making, profit-yielding state.

What forces, then, have brought creativity investigation into prominence? Rogers (1959) and others point out that, with the kaleidoscopic changes that occur at a geometric rate, development of genuine, creative adaptation may represent the only way for constructive continuity. As Rogers states, "Unless man can make new and original adaptations to his environment as rapidly as his science can change the environment, our culture will perish. Not only individual maladjustment and group tensions but international annihilation will be the price we pay for a lack of creativity" (p. 70). The development of our complex society has produced alienation of man from himself and from his fellow man. The importance of developing creative behavior from the social point of view then becomes urgent.

Barron points out factors which have fostered creativity investigations. These factors, he believes, have resulted from a maximum of social forces outside of psychology, and they have included the forces of radical change in social mores and the need for individuals to develop their own personal potentials (see chapter 12). According to Guilford (1959), we are in mortal struggle for the survival of our way of life, and world-shaking incidents have moved us out of our lethargy and complacency. We now recognize the factors of boredom, the challenge of space, the need to transcend daily life as defined in established configurations, and a prevailing need to search for the excellence of man. There is also a present tendency to develop hidden self-awareness and a general need for more information about the positive aspects of human nature. Artists, writers, and scientists according to Bruner (1967) are seeking an answer to the nature of their acts.

This growth of interest in creativity has not been without its criticism, some of which is justified. Some scientists have felt that the rise of creativity investigation is a threat to other established areas of investigation, such as general intelligence. Anyone examining the literature in the field becomes aware of great diversity and the need for theoretic synthesis and integration. Many are concerned with the semantic ambiguities which make reading the creativity literature a difficult problem. Words like "innovator," "creator," "divergent thinker," "original thinker" are frequently used interchangeably. Also many studies tend to deal with relatively small samples, and many criticisms have been directed to limited or faulty research designs. Some writers have criticized the lack of precision in the reporting of results, and some have noted that certain researchers tend to be anecdotal. Another deficiency in creativity investigation has been the absence of replicative, follow-up, and longitudinal studies. A frequent criticism is that there has been a failure to establish acceptable criteria for creativity, a problem fundamental to all aspects of creativity research. Some critics have frowned on the implications that creativity is a cardinal virtue providing a new social model by which humans are to be measured.

No one questions the immense benefits resulting from creative endeavors. According to Guilford (1967a), it should have been the responsibility of psychology in the past to reach an understanding of creativity, but psychologists were more concerned with simpler processes, and apparently lacked the courage to tackle the complex problems of studying creativity. Barron has pointed out that "what creativity research has done is to reopen some of the doors that were closed to psychology when it self-consciously separated itself from philosophy" (see chapter 12).

If we seek to improve our society we will need to understand the process of innovation and creativity and expand its applications into all fields of endeavor. According to Torrance (1962a), developing creativity is important from the standpoint of personality development and mental health to improve the effectiveness in the acquisition of information, and to apply knowledge to daily personal and professional problems. He further indicates that it is imperative to identify, develop, and utilize creative talents upon which the future of our civilization depends.

Insight into creative processes can also increase human effectiveness and efficiency. Utilizing our active intelligence can assist in the control of difficult problems, problems that are perhaps solvable only through creative means. For, as Toffler (1970) has stated, "By making imaginative use of change to channel change, we can not only spare ourselves the trauma of future shock, we can reach out and humanize distant tomorrows" (p. 430).

References

Allport, G. W. *Becoming: Basic considerations for a psychology of personality.* New Haven: Yale University Press, 1955.

Allport, G. W., Vernon, P. E., and Lindzey, G. *Study of Values: Manual of directions.* Rev. ed. Boston: Houghton Mifflin, 1951.

Andrews, E. G. The development of imagination in the preschool child. *University of Iowa Studies of Character,* 1930, *3*(4).

Andrews, F. M. *Creativity and the scientist.* (Doctoral dissertation, University of Michigan) Ann Arbor, Mich.: University Microfilms, 1962, No. 63–306.

Andrews, F. M. Factors affecting the manifestation of creative ability by scientists. *Journal of Personality,* 1965, *33,* 140–152.

Ansbacher, H. L., and Ansbacher, R. R. (Eds.), *The individual psychology of Alfred Adler.* New York: Basic Books, 1956.

Arnheim, R. Perceptual abstraction and art. *Psychological Review,* 1947, *54,* 66–82.

Arnheim, R. *Art and visual perception: A psychology of the creative eye.* Berkeley: University of California Press, 1954.

Barron, F. Personality style and perceptual choice. *Journal of Personality,* 1952, *20,* 385–401.

Barron, F. Complexity-simplicity as a personality dimension. *Journal of Abnormal and Social Psychology,* 1953, *48,* 163–172.

Barron, F. The psychology of imagination. *Scientific American,* 1958, *199,* 150–166.

Barron, F. Creative vision and expression in writing and painting. In *Proceedings of the Conference on "The Creative Person."* Berkeley: University of California, University Extension, 1961.

Barron, F. *Creativity and psychological health: Origins of personality and creative freedom.* Princeton, N.J.: Van Nostrand, 1963. (*a*)

Barron, F. The needs for order and for disorder as motivation in creative activity. In C. W. Taylor and F. Barron (Eds.), *Scientific creativity: Its recognition and development.* New York: Wiley, 1963. (*b*)

Barron, F. The relationship of ego diffusion to creative perception. In C. W. Taylor (Ed.), *Widening horizons in creativity.* New York: Wiley, 1964.

Barron, F. *Creative person and creative process.* New York: Holt, Rinehart & Winston, 1969.

Barron, F. *Artists in the making.* New York: Seminar Press, 1972.

Bellak, L. Creativity: Some random notes to a systematic consideration. *Journal of Projective Techniques,* 1958, *22,* 363–380.

Bloomberg, M. Introduction: Approaches to creativity. In M. Bloomberg (Ed.), *Creativity: Theory and research.* New Haven, Conn.: College & University Press, 1973.

Bruner, J. The conditions of creativity. In H. E. Gruber, G. Terrell, and M. Wertheimer (Eds.), *Contemporary approaches to creativity.* New York: Atherton, 1967.

Cattell, J. McK. A statistical study of eminent men. *Popular Science Monthly,* 1903, *62,* 359–377.

Cattell, R. B. The personality and motivation of the researcher from measurements of the contemporaries and from biography. In C. W. Taylor (Ed.), *The* third (1959) University of Utah Research Conference on the Identification of Creative Scientific Talent. Salt Lake City: University of Utah Press, 1959.

Cattell, R. B., & Drevdahl, J. E. A comparison of the personality profile (16 PF) of eminent researchers with that of eminent teachers and administrators, and of the general population. British Journal of Psychology, 1955, 46, 248–261.

Chambers, J. A. Beginning a multidimensional theory of creativity. Psychological Reports, 1969, 25, 779–799.

Chassell, L. M. Tests for originality. Journal of Educational Psychology, 1916, 7, 317–329.

Cross, P. G., Cattell, R. B., and Butcher, H. J. The personality patterns of creative artists. British Journal of Educational Psychology, 1967, 37, 292–299.

Crutchfield, R. The creative process. In Proceedings of the Conference on "The Creative Person." Berkeley: University of California, Extension Division, 1961.

Csikszentmihalyi, M., and Getzels, J. W. Discovery-oriented behavior and the originality of creative products: A study with artists. Journal of Personality and Social Psychology, 1971, 19, 47–52.

Dellas, M., and Gaier, E. L. Identification of creativity: The individual. Psychological Bulletin, 1970, 73, 55–73.

Dennis, W. The age decrement in outstanding scientific contributions: Fact or artifact. American Psychologist, 1958, 13, 457–460.

Dennis, W. Creative productivity between the ages of 20 and 80 years. Journal of Gerontology, 1966, 21, 1–8.

Duncker, K. A qualitative (experimental and theoretical) study of productive thinking (solving of comprehensible problems). Pedagogical Seminary and Journal of Genetic Psychology, 1926, 33, 642–708.

Eccles, J. C. The physiology of imagination. Scientific American, 1958, 199, 135–146.

Eindhoven, J. E., and Vinacke, W. E. Creative processes in painting. Journal of General Psychology, 1952, 47, 139–164.

Fairbairn, W. R. D. Prolegomena to a psychology of art. British Journal of Psychology, 1938, 28, 288–303.

Fann, K. T. Peirce's theory of abduction. The Hague: Martinus Nijhoff, 1970.

Freud, S. The relation of the poet to day-dreaming. In Collected papers. Vol. II. London: Hogarth, 1924. (Originally published in 1908.)

Freud, S. Three contributions to the theory of sex. New York: Nervous and Mental Disease Publishing Company, 1910.

Freud, S. Civilization and its discontents. New York: Cope & Smith, 1933.

Freud, S. Leonardo da Vinci: A study in psychosexuality. Trans. by A. A. Brill. New York: Random House, 1947.

Fromm, E. Escape from freedom. New York: Farrar and Rinehart, 1941.

Fromm, E. The creative attitude. In H. H. Anderson (Ed.), Creativity and its cultivation. New York: Harper, 1959.

Fulgosi, A., and Guilford, J. P. Short-term incubation in divergent production. American Journal of Psychology, 1968, 81, 241–246.

Galton, F. Hereditary genius: An inquiry into its laws and consequences. New York: D. Appleton, 1870.

Galton, F. English men of science, their nature and nurture. London: Macmillan, 1874.

Gerard, R. W. The biological basis of imagination. Scientific Monthly, 1946, 62, 477–479.

Getzels, J. W. Creative thinking, problem-solving, and instruction. In E. Hilgard (Ed.), Theories of learning and instruction. 63rd Yearbook of the N. S. S. E., Part I. Chicago: The University of Chicago Press, 1964.

Getzels, J. W., and Csikszentmihalyi, M. Portrait of the artist as an explorer. *Transaction*, 1966, *3*, 31–35.

Getzels, J. W., and Csikszentmihalyi, M. The value-orientations of art students as determinants of artistic specialization and creative performance. *Studies in Art Education*, 1968, *10*, 5–16.

Getzels, J. W., and Jackson, P. W. *Creativity and intelligence: Explorations with gifted students.* New York: Wiley, 1962.

Ghiselin, B. (Ed.) *The creative process.* Los Angeles: University of California Press, 1952.

Ghiselin, B. Ultimate criteria for two levels of creativity. In C. Taylor (Ed.), *The second (1957) University of Utah Research Conference on the Identification of Creative Scientific Talent.* Salt Lake City: University of Utah Press, 1958.

Golann, S. E. Psychological study of creativity. *Psychological Bulletin*, 1963, *60*, 548–565.

Goldstein, K. *The organism: A holistic approach to biology: Derived from pathological data in man.* New York: American Book, 1939.

Gordon, W. J. J. *Synectics: The development of creative capacity.* New York: Harper, 1961.

Gough, H. G. *California Psychological Inventory manual.* Palo Alto, Calif.: Consulting Psychologists Press, 1957.

Gough, H. G., and Heilbrun, A. B. *The Adjective Check List manual.* Palo Alto, Calif.: Consulting Psychologists Press, 1965.

Grotjahn, M. *Beyond laughter.* New York: McGraw-Hill, 1957.

Guilford, J. P. Creativity. *American Psychologist*, 1950, *5*, 444–454.

Guilford, J. P. Creative abilities in the arts. *Psychological Review*, 1957, *64*, 110–118.

Guilford, J. P. Traits of creativity. In H. H. Anderson (Ed.), *Creativity and its cultivation.* New York: Harper, 1959.

Guilford, J. P. Creativity: Yesterday, today, and tomorrow. *Journal of Creative Behavior*, 1967, *1*, 3–14. (a)

Guilford, J. P. *The nature of human intelligence.* New York: McGraw-Hill, 1967. (b)

Guilford, J. P. *Intelligence, creativity and their educational implications.* San Diego: Knapp, 1968.

Guilford, J. P. Creativity: Retrospect and prospect. *Journal of Creative Behavior*, 1970, *4*, 149–168.

Gutman, H. The biological roots of creativity. In R. L. Mooney and T. A. Razik (Eds.), *Explorations in creativity.* New York: Harper, 1967.

Hathaway, S. R., and McKinley, J. C. *Minnesota Multiphasic Personality Inventory.* Minneapolis, Minn.: University of Minnesota Press, 1943.

Helson, R. Creativity, sex, and mathematics. In *Proceedings of the Conference on "The Creative Person."* Berkeley: University of California, University Extension, 1961.

Helson, R. Personality of women with imaginative and artistic interests: The role of masculinity, originality, and other characteristics in their creativity. *Journal of Personality*, 1966, *34*, 1–25.

Helson, R. Sex differences in creative style. *Journal of Personality*, 1967, *35*, 214–233.

Helson, R. Generality of sex differences in creative style. *Journal of Personality*, 1968, *36*, 33–48.

Horner, A. J. Genetic aspects of creativity. In G. Bühler and F. Massarik (Eds.),

The course of human life: A study of goals in the humanistic perspective. New York: Springer, 1968.

Horney, K. *Neurosis and human growth*. New York: W. W. Norton, 1950.

Institute for Behavioral Research in Creativity (IBRIC). *Manual for Alpha Biographical Inventory*. Salt Lake City: IBRIC, 1417 So. 11th East, 1968.

Jackson, P. W., and Messick, S. The person, the product, and the response: Conceptual problems in the assessment of creativity. *Journal of Personality*, 1965, *35*, 309–329.

Johnson, W. *People in quandaries*. New York: Harper, 1946.

Jung, C. G. *Psychological types*. New York: Harcourt, Brace, 1946.

Jung, C. G. The archetypes and the collective unconscious. In *Collected works*. Vol. 9, Part I. Princeton, N.J.: Princeton University Press, 1959.

Jung, C. G. On the relation of analytical psychology to poetry. In J. Campbell (Ed.), *The portable Jung*. New York: Viking, 1971.

Koestler, A. *The act of creation*. New York: Macmillan, 1964.

Koffka, K. *Principles of Gestalt psychology*. New York: Harcourt, 1935.

Köhler, W. *Gestalt psychology*. New York: H. Liveright, 1929.

Kris, E. *Psychoanalytic explorations in art*. New York: International Universities Press, 1952.

Kubie, L. S. *Neurotic distortion of the creative process*. Lawrence, Kans.: University of Kansas Press, 1958.

Langer, S. *Philosophy in a new key*. Cambridge, Mass.: Harvard University Press, 1942.

Lecky, P. *Self-consistency: A theory of personality*. New York: Island Press, 1945.

Lehman, H. C. *Age and achievement*. Princeton, N.J.: Princeton University Press, 1953.

Lehman, H. C. The most creative years of engineers and other technologists. *The Journal of Genetic Psychology*, 1966, *108*, 263–277. (*a*)

Lehman, H. C. The psychologist's most creative years. *American Psychologist*, 1966, *21*, 363–369. (*b*)

Lewin, K. *A dynamic theory of personality: Selected papers*. New York: McGraw-Hill, 1935.

Lombroso, C. *The man of genius*. London: Walter Scott, 1891. (M. I. Stein and S. J. Heinze. *Creativity and the individual: Summaries of selected literature in psychology and psychiatry*. Glencoe, Ill.: Free Press, 1960.)

Lowenfeld, V. Creativity: Education's stepchild. In S. J. Parnes and H. F. Harding (Eds.), *A source book for creative thinking*. New York: Scribner's, 1962.

MacKinnon, D. W. The highly effective individual. *Teachers College Record*, 1960, *61*, 367–378.

MacKinnon, D. W. Creativity in architects. In *Proceedings of the Conference on "The Creative Person."* Berkeley: University of California, Extension Division, 1961. (*a*)

MacKinnon, D. W. The study of creativity. In *Proceedings of the Conference on "The Creative Person."* Berkeley: University of California, Extension Division, 1961. (*b*)

MacKinnon, D. W. The nature and nurture of creative talent. *American Psychologist*, 1962, *17*, 484–495. (*a*)

MacKinnon, D. W. The personality correlates of creativity: A study of American architects. In G. S. Nielsen (Ed.), *Proceedings of the XIV International Congress of Applied Psychology, Copenhagen, 1961*. Copenhagen: Munksgaard, 1962. (*b*)

MacKinnon, D. W. Creativity and transliminal experience. *Journal of Creative Behavior*, 1971, *5*, 227–241.

Mackler, B., and Shontz, F. C. Creativity: Theoretical and methodological considerations. *The Psychological Record,* 1965, *15,* 217–238.

Maddi, S. R. Motivational aspects of creativity. *Journal of Personality,* 1965, *33,* 330–347.

Maslow, A. H. *Motivation and personality.* New York: Harper, 1954.

Maslow, A. H. Creativity in self-actualizing people. In H. H. Anderson (Ed.), *Creativity and its cultivation.* New York: Harper, 1959.

Maslow, A. H. A holistic approach to creativity. In C. W. Taylor (Ed.), *Climate for creativity.* New York: Pergamon, 1972.

May, R. *Man's search for himself.* New York: W. W. Norton, 1953.

May, R. The nature of creativity. In H. H. Anderson (Ed.), *Creativity and its cultivation.* New York: Harper, 1959.

McNemar, Q. Lost: Our intelligence? Why? *American Psychologist,* 1964, *19,* 871–882.

McPherson, J. H. Environment and training for creativity. In C. W. Taylor (Ed.), *Creativity: Progress and potential.* New York: McGraw-Hill, 1964.

Mednick, M. T., and Andrews, F. M. Creative thinking and level of intelligence. *Journal of Creative Behavior,* 1967, *4,* 428–431.

Mednick, S. A. The associative basis of the creative process. *Psychological Review,* 1962, *69,* 220–232.

Mednick, S. A. *Remote Associates Test.* Boston: Houghton Mifflin, 1967.

Morgan, D. N. Creativity today. *Journal of Aesthetics,* 1953, *12,* 1–24.

Moustakas, C. *Creativity and conformity.* New York: Van Nostrand Reinhold, 1967.

Mumford, L. *The myth of the machine: The pentagon of power.* New York: Harcourt Brace Jovanovich, 1970.

Murphy, G. *Personality: A biosocial approach to origins and structure.* New York: Harper, 1947.

Murray, H. A. Vicissitudes of creativity. In H. H. Anderson (Ed.), *Creativity and its cultivation.* New York: Harper, 1959.

Myers, I. B. *Manual (1962): The Myers-Briggs Type Indicator.* Princeton, N.J.: Educational Testing Service, 1962.

Newell, A., Shaw, J. C., and Simon, H. A. The process of creative thinking. In H. E. Gruber, G. Terrell, and M. Wertheimer (Eds.), *Contemporary approaches to creative thinking.* New York: Atherton, 1963.

Osborn, A. F. *Applied imagination: Principles and procedures of creative problem solving.* Rev. ed. New York: Scribner's, 1953.

Parnes, S. J. Can creativity be increased? In S. J. Parnes and H. F. Harding (Eds.), *A source book for creative thinking.* New York: Scribner's, 1962. (a)

Parnes, S. J. Do you really understand brainstorming? In S. J. Parnes and H. F. Harding (Eds.), *A source book for creative thinking.* New York: Scribner's, 1962. (b)

Parnes, S. J. *Creative behavior workbook.* New York: Scribner's, 1967.

Patrick, C. Creative thought in poets. *Archives of Psychology,* 1935, *26,* 1–74.

Patrick, C. Creative thought in artists. *Journal of Psychology,* 1937, *4,* 35–73.

Patrick, C. Scientific thought. *Journal of Psychology,* 1938, *5,* 55–83.

Patrick, C. Whole and part relationship in creative thought. *American Journal of Psychology,* 1941, *54,* 128–131.

Peterson, J. R. Eyes have they, but they see not: A conversation with Rudolf Arnheim about a generation that has lost touch with its senses. *Psychology Today,* 1972, *6*(1), 55–58.

Poincaré, H. Mathematical creation. In H. Poincaré, *The foundations of science.* New York: Science Press, 1913.

Prince, G. M. *The practice of creativity: A manual for dynamic group problem solving.* New York: Harper, 1970.

Rank O. *Art and artists.* Trans. by C. F. Atkinson. New York: Knopf, 1932.

Rank, O. *Will therapy and truth and reality.* Trans. by J. Taft. New York: Knopf, 1945.

Ribot, T. The nature of creative imagination. *International Quarterly,* 1900, *1,* 648–675, and *2,* 1–25.

Riesman, D., Glazer, N., and Denny, R. *The lonely crowd.* New Haven, Conn.: Yale University Press, 1950.

Roe, A. Artists and their work. *Journal of Personality,* 1946, *16,* 1–40.

Roe, A. *The making of a scientist.* New York: Dodd, Mead, 1953. (*a*)

Roe, A. A psychological study of eminent psychologists and anthropologists, and a comparison with biological and physical scientists. *Psychological Monographs,* 1953, *67* (2, Whole No. 352). (*b*)

Roe, A. Maintenance of creative output through the years. In C. W. Taylor (Ed.), *Climate for creativity.* New York: Pergamon, 1972.

Rogers, C. R. Toward a theory of creativity. In H. H. Anderson (Ed.), *Creativity and its cultivation.* New York: Harper, 1959.

Rogers, C. R. The concept of the fully functioning person. *Psychotherapy,* 1963, *1,* 17–26.

Schachtel, E. G. *Metamorphosis.* New York: Basic Books, 1959.

Sinnott, E. W. The creativeness of life. In H. H. Anderson (Ed.), *Creativity and its cultivation.* New York: Harper, 1959.

Snygg, D., and Combs, A. W. *Individual behavior.* New York: Harper, 1949.

Spearman, C. *Creative mind.* New York: D. Appleton, 1931.

Sprecher, T. B. Committee report on criteria of creativity. In C. W. Taylor (Ed.), *The third (1959) University of Utah Research Conference on the Identification of Creative Scientific Talent.* Salt Lake City: University of Utah Press, 1959.

Stein, M. I. A transactional approach to creativity. In C. W. Taylor (Ed.), *The 1955 University of Utah Research Conference on the Identification of Creative Scientific Talent.* Salt Lake City: University of Utah Press, 1956.

Strong, E. K., Jr. *The vocational interests of men and women.* Stanford, Calif.: Stanford University Press, 1943.

Taylor, C. W. A factorial study of fluency in writing. *Psychometrika,* 1947, *12,* 239–262.

Taylor, C. W. (Ed.) *The 1955 University of Utah Research Conference on the Identification of Creative Scientific Talent.* Salt Lake City: University of Utah Press, 1956.

Taylor, C. W. (Ed.) *The second (1957) University of Utah Research Conference on the Identification of Creative Scientific Talent.* Salt Lake City: University of Utah Press, 1958.

Taylor, C. W. (Ed.) *The third (1959) University of Utah Research Conference on the Identification of Creative Scientific Talent.* Salt Lake City: University of Utah Press, 1959.

Taylor, C. W. (Ed.) *Creativity: Progress and potential.* New York: McGraw-Hill, 1964. (*a*)

Taylor, C. W. (Ed.) *Widening horizons in creativity.* New York: Wiley, 1964. (*b*)

Taylor, C. W. Be talent developers as well as knowledge dispensers. *Today's Education,* December 1968, 67–68.

Taylor, C. W. *Climate for creativity.* New York: Pergamon, 1972.

Taylor, C. W. and Williams, F. E. (Eds.) *Instructional media and creativity.* New York: Wiley, 1966.

Taylor, D. W., Berry, P. C., and Block, C. H. Does group participation when using brainstorming facilitate or inhibit creative thinking? *Administrative Science Quarterly,* 1958, *3,* 23–47.

Taylor, I. A. The nature of the creative process. In P. Smith (Ed.), *Creativity: An examination of the creative process.* New York: Hastings House, 1959.

Taylor, I. A. The effects of sensory stimulation on divergent and convergent thinking. *Abstract Guide of the XXth International Congress of Psychology,* Tokyo, 1972, 364. (*a*)

Taylor, I. A. A theory of creative transactualization: A systematic approach to creativity with implications for creative leadership. *Occasional Paper,* Buffalo, N.Y.: Creative Education Foundation, 1972, No. 8. (*b*)

Taylor, I. A. The measurement of creative transactualization: A scale to measure behavioral dispositions to creativity. Paper presented at the meeting of the Southeastern Psychological Association, April 1973. Published by *Journal of Creative Behavior,* 1974, *8*(2), 114–115. (*a*)

Taylor, I. A. Psychological sources of creativity. In Z. A. Piotrowski (Chm.), Psychological origins of creativity: A clinical analysis. Symposium presented at the meeting of the American Psychological Association, Montreal, August 1973. (*b*)

Taylor, I. A., and Sandler, B. E. Use of a creative product inventory for evaluating products of chemists. *Proceedings of the 80th Annual Convention of the American Psychological Association,* 1972, *7,* 311–312.

Taylor, I. A., and Sandler, B. E. Developing creativity in research chemists. *Proceedings of the 81st Annual Convention of the American Psychological Association,* 1973, *8,* 585–586.

Terman, L. M. Genius and stupidity: A study of some of the intellectual processes of seven "bright" and seven "stupid" boys. *Pedagogical Seminary,* 1906, *13,* 307–373.

Thorndike, R. L. Some methodological issues in the study of creativity. In A. Anastasi (Ed.), *Testing problems in perspective.* Washington, D.C.: American Council on Education, 1966.

Thurstone, L. L. *Creative talent.* (University of Chicago Psychometric Laboratory Report No. 61) Chicago: University of Chicago, 1950.

Thurstone, L. L. The scientific study of inventive talent. In S. J. Parnes and H. F. Harding (Eds.), *A Source book for creative thinking.* New York: Scribner's, 1962.

Toffler, A. *Future shock.* New York: Random House, 1970.

Torda, C. Some observations on the creative process. *Perceptual and Motor Skills,* 1970, *31,* 107–126.

Torrance, E. P. Developing creative thinking through school experiences. In S. J. Parnes and H. F. Harding (Eds.), *A source book for creative thinking.* New York: Scribner's, 1962. (*a*)

Torrance, E. P. *Guiding creative talent.* Englewood Cliffs, N.J.: Prentice-Hall, 1962. (*b*)

Torrance, E. P. *Torrance Tests of Creative Thinking: Norms-technical manual.* Princeton, N.J.: Personnel Press, 1966.

Torrance, E. P. Give the "devil" his dues. In J. G. Gowan, G. D. Demos, and E. P. Torrance (Eds.), *Creativity: Its educational implications.* New York: Wiley, 1967.

Torrance, E. P., and Dauw, D. C. Aspirations and dreams of three groups of creativity gifted high school seniors and comparable unselected group. *Gifted Child Quarterly,* 1965, *9,* 177–182.

Torrance, E. P., and Gupta, R. *Development and evaluation of recorded programmed experiences in creative thinking in the fourth grade.* Minneapolis: Bureau of Educational Research, University of Minnesota, 1964.

Toynbee, A. Is America neglecting her creative minority? In C. W. Taylor (Ed.), *Widening horizons in creativity.* New York: Wiley, 1964.

Wallach, M. A. *The intelligence/creativity distinction.* New York: General Learning Press, 1971.

Wallach, M. A., and Kogan, N. *Modes of thinking in young children: A study of the creativity-intelligence distinction.* New York: Holt, Rinehart & Winston, 1965.

Wallas, G. *The art of thought.* New York: Harcourt Brace, 1926.

Welch, L. Recombination of ideas in creative thinking. *Journal of Applied Psychology,* 1946, *30*, 638–643.

Welsh, G. S. *Welsh Figure Preference Test: Preliminary manual.* Palo Alto, Calif.: Consulting Psychologists Press, 1959.

Wertheimer, M. *Productive thinking.* New York: Harper, 1945.

2. Creativity: A Quarter Century of Progress

J. P. Guilford

1975

Introduction

MY IMPRESSION IS THAT on this unique occasion we are expected to survey, each from his own point of view, man's progress in explorations of creativity during the past quarter century, to offer some evaluations, and to make some extrapolations into the future. Having done this sort of thing three times in recent years (Guilford, 1965, 1967*b*, 1970), I shall find it a bit difficult to avoid redundancy.

AREAS OF DEVELOPMENT

Taking a broad view of the domain with which we are concerned, I see three areas in which developments can be considered. Probably the most vigorously investigated have been problems of creative disposition, to determine the characteristics of those who exhibit to greater degrees different forms of creative production. It is generally agreed that productions are creative if they have qualities of novelty about them—novelty within the history of the individual's behavior, and probably also within the social context. So long as we maintain the role of scientist, we are not concerned with whether or not the products are socially valuable. The technologist is likely to add that specification.

Creative dispositions have been studied from different directions. The aspect with which I have been most concerned is that of intellectual abilities or functions. This does not mean that I have not recognized the importance of other qualities, in the form of motivational and temperamental traits.

The picture of creativity-related intellectual abilities has pointed directly to another important area, that of creative-thinking processes. As so often happens, technology outruns scientific foundations. As long as forty years ago, special strategies for generating novel ideas had been developed and

37

were being taught. Methods that have been more fruitful have survived, and can now be accounted for in terms of basic psychological principles. What we know now could serve as a basis for other strategies and tactics that could be taught.

The broadest, and most heterogeneous, area to be considered is concerned with determiners of creative disposition and creative production. The role of heredity was first considered almost a hundred years ago by Galton, in his studies of genius. There has been very little attention to this problem in recent times, using experimental approaches. On the other hand, there has been much attention to environmental or biographical factors. The relation of creative disposition to IQ, or academic aptitude, has been extensively investigated. Some efforts have been made to remove some of the pressures for conformity in education and to encourage the employment of general and special educational procedures aimed at development of creative skills.

CONSEQUENCES OF DEVELOPMENTS

Besides considering progress in these various areas, it is important for us at this time to see the needs for further investigations, and to decide in which directions the more promising and significant progress lies. It is important, also, to note whether what we already know about creativity is being exploited as it should be toward the development of a more creative society.

INTELLECTUAL BASIS FOR CREATIVE PRODUCTION

The human mental abilities that contribute to potential for creative production, and the mental functions that go with them, I consider to be an important part of human intelligence, when that construct is conceived as broadly as it should be. Since much of what follows depends upon features of my structure-of-intellect (SI) model, for the uninitiated reader, especially, some explanation of that model is in order.

One of the earliest conceptions of intelligence among the Romans equated it to information. To this day, that connection persists in some governmental affairs. In my conception, the connection is also a good one for psychology, except that intelligence is not the information itself but rather a collection of abilities or functions for processing information. Abilities differ with respect to kinds of information, and to kinds of operations we perform with information. I define information as that which we discriminate. Information comes in chunks or items, and every item is different in some way from all other items. No discrimination, no information.

Items of information differ in two ways: substantive differences, or *content,* and regarding form, or *product.* All items of information are constructed by our brains, and the constructs are products. The content categories are like codes or languages. The individual products are like words within those languages.

Kinds of Content. To be more specific, four major kinds of content are recognized. One of them is *figural,* which is generated rather immediately from input from the sense organs as what we call perception. The most important kinds in this category are visual-figural and auditory-figural. It takes different abilities to process these two kinds of information.

Perceptions lead to thoughts, and we have another kind of information called *semantic* in the SI model. It should be said, however, that thoughts in the form of images would be figural, for they more or less duplicate perceptions. This leaves "imageless thoughts" for the semantic category. But there is still a multitude of items of semantic information.

A third kind of content is called *symbolic*. It is composed of signs or labels that commonly stand for items of other kinds of information. Letters, words, and numbers are the most familiar examples. Symbolic information is the language of the mathematician, but, of course, it is shared by anyone who speaks or reads. It is the important medium of communication.

The fourth kind of content is given the label *behavioral,* because it is concerned with mental events. We can be aware to some extent of what the other fellow is feeling or thinking, or what he intends to do, by means of cues that we obtain from his behavior. Some writers call this mode of communication "body language." Abilities for dealing with this kind of information determine how well we understand other people and how well we can deal with them. The limited "intelligence" represented by an IQ has no provision for this kind of ability. Abilities concerned with behavioral information may be said to compose a "social intelligence."

Products of Information. Within each of the content areas of information we find the same six kinds of products or brain-produced constructs. The basic kind of construct is a *unit.* A unit, like a thing, can stand by itself. It can be analyzed into other units, however, as when the parts of a tree—trunk, branches, twigs, leaves—are constructed as separate units.

Units can be grouped because they are similar, and we have *classes* (or class ideas), another kind of product. Units can be connected in other ways, giving still other kinds of products. One broad kind of connection is seen when one unit suggests another, as when lightning suggests thunder. This somewhat casual, but logical, kind of connection is called an *implication.* It has commonly been known as an "association," but the term "implication" better suggests its logical nature. Other instances of implications are describable as expectations or as predictions, which takes the concept beyond the idea of association.

A more definitive connection between two units is a *relation,* as when we know that "wet" is the opposite of "dry," and "cornea" is a part of the "eye." When more than two things are connected, we have a *system,* such as an organized sentence, a paragraph, a story, or a scientific theory. Any temporal or spatial sequence or arrangement is a system. One of the most interesting products is a *transformation,* which is any kind of change in an item of information, including redefinitions and substitutions. We shall see that transformations have special significance for creativity.

Intellectual Operations. There are five known basic operations that we perform with information. One operation is just knowing it, which means structuring it, and which I have called *cognition.* Technically, we may say that it is a matter of coding, within any one of the content areas and in the form of one of the kinds of products.

Information that we obtain can be put into storage, in an operation that can naturally be called *memory.* That is as far as the SI meaning of "memory" goes. Getting information out of storage involves two kinds of operation—*divergent production* and *convergent production.* These operations mean the retrieval of stored information for use when it is thought to be needed. The difference between the two is that divergent production is a broad search, usually in an open problem, in which there are a number of possible answers. I also sometimes say that it is the generation of logical alternatives. Fluency of thinking is the name of the game. Convergent production, on the other hand, is a focused search, for, from the nature of the given information or problem, one particular answer is required. I sometimes say that it is the generation of logical imperatives. Actually, the difference between the two productive operations is a relative one, depending upon the degree of restraint or limitation upon the desired answer. One may also indulge in a guessing approach to a convergent problem, which means divergent production on the way to convergent production.

In such a case, especially, there must be decisions as to which answers are best, if not *the* best. This brings in the fifth kind of operation of *evaluation,* or judging the suitability of information. There is a comparing of the known or produced information in the light of certain logical criteria, such as identity, similarity, and consistency. Information that we have cognized or produced is constantly under evaluative checking for satisfaction of requirements.

The Structure-of-Intellect Model. From what I have just been saying about kinds of information and of operation, it might be concluded that there should be broad intellectual abilities, each in line with one of the categories. There is some indication that this is true. But research has indicated much more clearly that each ability or function is concerned with only one kind of content, one kind of product, and one kind of operation. Each little cube or cell in Figure 2.1 represents such a combination. Thus, we can say that there is a certain ability for cognition of semantic units,

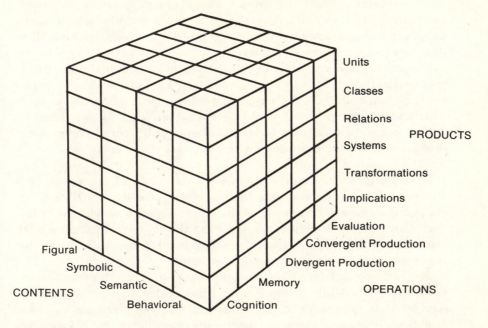

FIGURE 2.1.

which is a fancy name for knowing word meanings, an ability measured by a good vocabulary test. Incidentally, this ability dominates common verbal IQ tests. Another ability would be memory for semantic transformations. An example of this activity would be your putting into memory storage a pun you have just heard so that you could tell the joke later. A pun is a good example of a semantic transformation. Still another ability would be convergent production of a symbolic implication, as in answering questions like $7 \times (4 + 2) = ?$, where the answer, 42, is implied by the given information.

RELEVANCE OF THE SI MODEL FOR CREATIVE POTENTIAL

All the intellectual abilities contributing to creative potential should be found represented somewhere in the SI model. Let us consider the three facets or dimensions of the model in turn.

Informational Content and Creativeness. Consideration of the common fields of creative performance will show that they correspond to the SI categories of content. Creators specializing in visual-figural information include producers of visual art in any form, architects, engineers, and inventors. Creators in auditory-figural information are composers, arrangers, and stylistic performers of music. In the symbolic category we find mathematicians and cryptographers. The semantic list is a bit longer:

writers, speakers, teachers, scientists, and planners. Creative performers specializing in behavioral information are salesmen, politicians, teachers, parents, policemen, lawyers, judges, and probation officers, not that all in these groups are necessarily creative.

If a person shines creatively in two or more fields of everyday activity, it may be that those fields all emphasize the same kind of content, or the person is high in abilities in more than one content area. Being high in more than one content category would be desirable especially in science or drama. But the informational-content categories do seem to present some limitations upon the extensiveness of a person's creativeness.

SI Operations and Creativeness. Of the five kinds of operations, it is apparently generally recognized that divergent production (DP) has the most to do with creative behavior. In order to give more realism to this operation, let us take a few examples, selected from typical tests in the DP category. All examples are from the semantic-content area. The information processed may be in any kind of product.

In a common task for DP of semantic units, we give a problem like the following: Name all the things you can think of that are white and edible. The search is to be made within a class with the two given specifications. It may elicit responses such as: sugar, salt, snow, bread, flour, foam, and milk.

In a task requiring the production of alternative class ideas, we may present a list of perhaps ten familiar words that can be classified in several different ways by regrouping, with at least three words to a class. Some individuals may produce only one set of classes while others produce several.

For a task of producing alternative relations, we may ask in what different ways a father and daughter are related. For example, they are parent and child, of opposite sex, one is older, stronger, and wiser than the other, and so on.

Tasks given as tests for production of systems often require the composition of sentences. We may ask the person to write as many sentences as he can in each of which three different words are all used, for example, desert, food, and army. He has to interrelate the three concepts in various ways.

A common task for producing alternative transformations asks the examinee to suggest clever titles for a given short story, as if he were writing newspaper headlines. To be clever, a title almost has to involve a transformation, such as by allusion to something well known or by a pun.

A test for producing alternative implications presents a pictorial symbol, such as a bell, and asks for all the possible occupations or kinds of jobs that this symbol might suggest for a person who wears it on his clothing. It should be added that all DP tests are standardized by applying a working-time limit to each problem or set of problems.

As stated earlier, divergent production is the generating of logical alternatives to fit a cognized situation. When I say "logical," in this connection, I mean two things. On the one hand, the information produced is in the form of products, all six kinds of which I regard as logical constructs, basic to a "psycho-logic." This conception of products is clearest in the cases of the products of classes, relations, and implications, but it can be defended in the cases of units, systems, and transformations (Guilford, 1974). All the SI products are forms of mental constructs or informational structures that have logical properties.

The other meaning of "logical" here is expressed by using the definitive synonym "relevant." Relevance means that there is some reasonable kind of connection between the stimulus information, or input, and the produced information, or output. In this connection, I must comment on the proposition that is sometimes expressed, to the effect that the creative person is "open to the irrational in himself." If this means being "illogical," I do not accept the proposition, for I believe that all intellecual performance is "logical" in the broad sense I have mentioned, and is therefore "rational." When someone says that certain information-processing behavior is "irrational," he' is displaying failure to see connections that are relevant to the person in question.

What I think the proposition under question really means is that the more creative person is ready to make and to accept more remotely connected output as being relevant. It is also said of the more creative person that he is more ready to take risks; he is not afraid of being wrong; he is willing to try out "long shots."

There is considerable evidence of various kinds to support the alleged relevance of divergent production for successful creative thinking. I have assembled much of that evidence elsewhere (Guilford, 1967a). Evidence has continued to accumulate. Furthermore, differential effects are being demonstrated, showing that different DP abilities or functions are relevant, depending upon the kind of informational content and informational product featured in the immediate task. In the SI model there are twenty-four places for DP abilities, all of which have been demonstrated by factor analysis at least once. This statement applies when only the six *visual*-figural abilities are taken into account. Theoretically there should also be six *auditory*-figural DP abilities. These auditory-DP abilities represent an unexplored area.[1]

When we view the creative performance in the larger context of problem solving, we find that all the other SI operations play their roles. Cognition is involved in seeing that a problem exists and in structuring the problem so that it is understood. The known structure of the problem serves as a search model, with which one explores his memory file (or pile), and possibly also his immediate environment, to find what is needed for a solution or to produce a solution from the information he retrieves.

Searching the memory store has already been identified in the form of divergent and convergent production. These operations play key roles, for without them there is no solution. The operation of evaluation plays a number of roles throughout problem-solving episodes. There are evaluative checks on conceptions of the problem as well as on solutions that are produced. And throughout the whole process there is at least short-term memory, a recording of informational events that have transpired, so that we need not repeat our errors and we can remember our more promising attempts.

Contributions of Transformations. Perhaps fully as important for creativeness as the divergent-production functions is another segment of the SI model that contains the transformation abilities. Although the horizontal transformation layer of the model intersects with the divergent-production column, most of the transformation abilities involve other kinds of operations—cognition, memory, convergent production, and evaluation. In our processes of problem solving, we can see, or cognize, that transformations occur, as in visualizing changes in perceived figures or in revising meanings connected with words. We can remember these changes and later retrieve them, as in divergent and convergent production. And we can reach decisions regarding the adequacy or suitability of the change, in the operation of evaluation.

The chief role of transformations in our creative thinking is that they provide needed flexibility. How often do we persist in trying to solve the wrong problem? There is no headway until our conception of the problem is revised. How often do we persist in trying to use an old solution because it worked before but will not work under even slightly altered conditions? Sometimes a very simple transformation is the key to an important invention, as when the eye of the needle was moved from the blunt end where it had always been to the sharp end where it is needed in the sewing machine.

OTHER TRAITS RELEVANT FOR CREATIVENESS

What is true of the multivariate nature of intellectual talents is probably also true of nonintellectual qualities. No one person possesses all the favorable qualities. His stronger motivational traits direct his interests and determine to some extent his sources of satisfaction. His temperamental characteristics may help to determine his strategies, and, in general, the way in which his talents are employed. The joint effects of intellectual and nonintellectual qualities may well be observable in what have been called "cognitive styles" or "cognitive attitudes."

Unfortunately. there is no well-recognized taxonomy of either motivational or temperamental traits, as there is in the intellectual domain. The best we can do is to note the more characteristic qualities that seem to be related to creative production. The relevant traits have been observed either from the study of socially recognized creative producers or of those who score high in divergent-production tests. The sources of such information are scattered. In the quick review that follows, the traits are differentiated as motivational and temperamental. The former include needs, interests, and attitudes; and the latter, some qualities describing the manner or style of behavior.

Motivational Qualities. Creative people are reported to be generally highly motivated, and to show a high energy level, with effective work habits. The behavioral signs are often described by saying "dedicated to his work" or "persistent in intellectual tasks." But such qualities are likely to be true of all successful people, especially creative or not. In both cases, these qualities are likely to mean that the person has found work that he likes and that gives him satisfaction. As symptoms of creative disposition, therefore, these qualities are ambiguous. Their absence would be more decisive than their presence.

The more creative person is said to have a high level of curiosity. I interpret this quality as a need to know, a desire to learn or to accumulate information. The person with curiosity seeks to have a well-stocked memory store, which he needs in productive thinking. It is no wonder that distinguished creative people often point out the need for a large stock of information.

Along with the need to know, there is likely to be also an interest in reflective thinking, from which satisfaction is derived. Probably most satisfying are the achievements in productive thinking, divergent and convergent. In some of my own research, incidentally, we found that there is a real difference in degree of interest in these two kinds of thinking, and there is a small negative correlation between the two interests.

There are some other qualities that also have intellectual implications, especially where transformations are concerned. The more creative adolescents are said to be less tied to reality, which suggests more readiness to let transformations occur, or even to seek them (Getzels and Jackson, 1962). There is said to be an unusual appreciation of humor and facility for producing humor. I suggest that this probably refers to the variety of humor that depends upon transformations. We have some evidence that associated with at least one DP ability is the need for adventure. This need may also account for the tendency toward risk-taking. A need for variety can also be tied to the high curiosity level. Often reported is a higher level of tolerance for ambiguity. Sometimes there is said to be a preference for disorder, in visual forms, at least. Both these qualities suggest that ambiguous or disordered situations present welcome challenges to the confident, creative thinker. There is also probably a desire to resolve the ambiguity and to organize the disordered information. In both cases, systems of some degree of complexity are to be produced. Much creative production is involved with the organization of new systems.

Other qualities may be summed up in the word "individuality." The creative person is a self-starting creature, with a strong need for autonomy and self-direction. The adolescent shows interests in unconventional careers. There is need for recognition from others for personal accomplishments, yet the standards of evaluation are likely to be the creator's own; he is said to possess independent judgment. In this same area we may cite the commonly low level of sociability and the high level of self-sufficiency. Unlike his peers, he is unwilling to accept things as they are; he seeks improvements. He commonly says or thinks, "There must be a better way." His showing of self-confidence reflects a high evaluation of himself. This quality may go so far as to include self-assertiveness, if not aggressiveness, but this is by no means universal. Rejecting some conventional standards, the creative boy may show some feminine interests, and the creative girl may show some masculine interests. The creative man shows some aesthetic interests, which, of course, are not commonly regarded as being masculine.

From scattered sources (e.g., Kallick, 1962) we gain impressions that those with higher creative potential differ in various other ways from those with lower potential. Individuals with high potential indulge in reading as a favorite pastime. They are more likely to report that they are frequently surprised or puzzled. They think that children should be taught to be different; those with low potential think that children should be taught to conform. The highs think that daydreaming can be fun; the lows think it can be useful. The highs know that they are bright and think that they can control their own destinies; they feel destined for great things.

One description sometimes applied to the creative person is that he is exceptionally "aware of his own impulses." I do not know what this means. It has little communication value except for the initiated.

TEMPERAMENTAL QUALITIES

Some temperamental qualities of creative persons were touched upon in the discussion of interests, above; for example, the higher levels of self-sufficiency and self-confidence. One quality that could be added here is introversion, what I have called "thinking introversion," which is probably included within the concept of pleasure in thinking also mentioned above. Creative people are sometimes said to be impulsive, and this may be limited to the sphere of thinking activities. It could be an aspect of risk-taking, which was associated above with the trait of need for adventure.

More broadly speaking, the creative person is said to be neither neurotic nor psychotic. The old saying that linked genius with madness is apparently not true. A neurotic condition tends to retard or inhibit thinking. A psychotic condition, although freeing the person to some extent from reality, also yields socially irrelevant responses.

Creative-Thinking Processes

The processes of creative thinking were touched upon in the discussion of divergent-production and transformation abilities, particularly, in connection with the intellectual aspects of creative disposition. Although the abilities or functions in those categories appear to be at the heart of operations of creative thinking, many other functions make their contributions, and they can also be described in terms of concepts of the SI model.

A larger view of the subject gives us a comprehensive picture of problem solving. There is something creative about all genuine problem solving. Although it is easiest to see problem-solving events in the work of the scientist and technologist, they also abound in everyday personal affairs, and we can say that the artist, of whatever kind, also solves problems. In his case, the problems are concerned with self-expression and communication.

For a general picture of problem-solving events, I have presented an operational model, in which all the SI operations play roles, and any kind of informational content and product may be involved (Guilford, 1966, 1967a). Cognition operates in seeing that a problem exists and in analyzing and structuring the problem, setting up what Duncker called a "search model." Earlier I used the term "search" in defining productive thinking, either divergent or convergent. Both are concerned with searching the memory store for needed information. Along the way, information is evaluated, bringing in another kind of SI operation—evaluation. Evaluated (and accepted or rejected) are conceptions of the problem as well as the information retrieved from storage, and any transformations or new construction made of it. The SI operation of memory, which is concerned only with the putting of information into storage and must therefore be distinguished from the memory store, comes into play in keeping a running account of steps in the problem-solving event. Without this record, we should be helpless.

It is stometimes said that the creative person is "in close touch with his unconscious." This is another of those cryptic, ambiguous statements that mean many things to different people. Attributing certain behavioral processes to an "unconscious" has no explanatory value whatsoever, and is like sweeping things under the rug. At its worst, an animistic conception is introduced. If the expression has any meaning at all, I think it should mean facility in retrieving information from memory storage, which implies divergent- and convergent-production operations. Let us fully admit that a considerable part of thinking activity is unconscious, in the sense that the thinker cannot observe all the steps. It is often said that he "sees the tip of the iceberg." To say that something is unconscious does not relieve us of the responsibility of finding out what the processes are. This we must infer from what we *can* observe, mostly as outsiders. The discovery of the SI functions has enabled us to make a good beginning in this enterprise.

Determiners of Creative Disposition

HEREDITY

In considering the question of how creative people "got that way," for other aspects of personality, we look to possible hereditary and environmental sources. Although Galton found that genius tended to "run in families," in his study the hereditary and environmental sources were confounded, and no uncontested conclusions could be drawn. Most studies of hereditary contributions to intellectual abilities have been done with IQ tests. In terms of SI categories, IQ tests have been much restricted to the operation of cognition, to semantic content, and to the products of units and systems. Because a strong hereditary effect upon IQ is often reported, to the extent that creative performance depends upon IQ, it is accordingly dependent upon heredity. Studies of direct effects of heredity upon divergent-production abilities have been very rare, as yet. Barron's study, the only one I know of, utilizes twins and seems to show some direct relationship, but it is apparently much weaker than that for IQ (Barron, 1970), and it may vary from one DP ability to another.

We have the common observation that creative persons come from homes of higher socioeconomic levels, which could mean that either the heredity behind the homemakers or the nurture that the home provides is the determiner, or both. The other unknown is whether the effect is directly exerted on DP abilities or indirectly through consequences on IQ.

BIOGRAPHICAL CIRCUMSTANCES

Biographical features that are associated with socially recognized genius have been studied by Goertzel and Goertzel (1962). Among the parents of geniuses they found a higher incidence of respect for learning and an encouragement of investigation and independent thinking in their children. Again, some of this may have contributed indirectly through effects on abilities represented in the IQ. The parents had strong opinions, which might suggest rigidity, but, on the other hand, they supported minority causes. Fathers, often reported to be unrealistic, were inclined to be dreamers and were often either failures economically or had widely fluctuating fortunes. Some mothers were ambitious and domineering, and others were described as "smothering mothers," who showered their sons with love and affection. The child's home was often a troubled one, with conflicts between parents. There were quite a number of children with physical handicaps, thus providing support for Adlerians. There were an unusual number of deaths in the family, with accompanying traumas. In spite of the parents' respect for learning, the children frequently disliked school, and tutoring at home was common.

It seems to me that the general picture is one of families in which the children encountered unusual numbers of problems to be solved. In their efforts to solve the problems, the children had unusual exercises in creative thinking. They thus developed problem-solving skills. There were conditions that otherwise encouraged individualism, and motivation to make better lives for themselves.

Things Still To Be Done

From this sketchy review of what we know about creativity, what is implied about future needs? In our present-day, enormously complicated human milieu, problems of all kinds arise on every hand. Failure to solve some of them, or postponement of attempts to solve them, may even spell disaster. Are we and our leaders equipped to undertake solutions? What does it take to make better problem solvers?

As a people who have been "going West" for nearly 400 years, Americans have had unusual numbers of problems to solve, and they have generally risen to the occasion. America is recognized historically as a leader in mechanical inventions, and the founding fathers of the United States were also innovative in bringing into the world new forms of government. But the innovations needed to make our social, economic, and legal systems serve us better have been slower to come than those providing for a superb gadgetry. One reason is that while our patent system has richly rewarded the inventor, there has been no comparable system of rewards for innovative social ideas. As Torrance has often said, to get creative behavior, we must reward it. Can we institute any better assurances of rewards for new and workable social ideas that is comparable to that provided by our patent system?

IMPLICATIONS FROM KNOWLEDGE OF CREATIVE DISPOSITIONS

Knowledge of the characteristics of the more creative person can start us on several roads. If we are concerned with identifying children and youths who have unusual promise, we can assess those qualities that appear to be contributory to future success. Because of the multivariate nature of creative dispositions, we should be able, furthermore, to forecast in which areas the person's talents and inclinations are greatest. We would describe him by means of an individual profile with respect to relevant abilities and other traits. We could probably see in which directions his development could be the most rapid, and also detect some characteristics that, if not given special educational attention, would become unnecessary handicaps.

Assessment of Creative Potential. We are already prepared to do a great deal in the assessment of creative-thinking potential. As elsewhere, I argue strongly against a policy of giving an individual a single value to indicate his level of creative talent, as I have argued against the use of a single score to indicate level of intelligence. In either case, such information is ambiguous. Furthermore, by this approach, much potentially useful information is lost.

Now there will be those who are disappointed in the amount of prediction of a creative-production criterion that can be obtained from a test of any one ability, and they will continue to look for "the philosopher's stone," a single test that will predict at a substantial or high level. They will be doomed to disappointment. The prediction of creative performance of any kind is a multivariate affair, requiring the properly weighted combination of a number of predictors. Jones (1960), Elliott (1964), and others have demonstrated that weighted combinations of only a few DP tests can predict performance criteria as well as academic aptitude tests predict achievement (grade-point averages) of college students.

As in most areas of trait measurement, we lack all the knowledge and the instruments that we need. In the intellectual domain, all of the divergent-production abilities in the SI model have been demonstrated by factor analysis, with tests available for many of them. Most of the transformation abilities have also been demonstrated, with tests available for some. There are also tests for abilities in other SI categories, abilities that are contributory to learning and to problem solving.

Having rejected the use of an over-all creativity score, I now retreat a little in saying that there may be some meaningful composite scores, short of an all-inclusive one. Although my associates and I in research have always rotated axes in factor analysis orthogonally, we did not necessarily believe that all the SI abilities are mutually independent. We didn't have faith in any of the methods of oblique rotation, which are in common use to find correlations between first-order factors. There may well be higher-order divergent-production factors and abilities. If so, my guess is that the second-order factors would be along the lines of the content categories; that is, a visual-figural-divergent-production factor, a semantic-divergent-production ability, and so on. A third-order factor in common to all the DP abilities might also be a fair hypothesis. Indications for higher-order factors along the lines of the product categories are not so clear.

Theoretically, I should say that the higher-order DP factors would depend upon how much the tested population had generalized its DP abilities. G. W. Ferguson (1956) was probably right when he suggested that aptitude factors arise by generalizations of specific practiced skills. The skill in performing any task may be thought to have at least two components. One is a specific affair, unique to the particular task, and there are one or more others of a more general nature, shared with other tasks that are similar to it psychologically.

Limited experimental research has tended to show that drills in certain selected tasks are followed by gains in performance in other tasks that feature the same common-factor ability, but not in tasks for other factors. Generalization in intellectual ability seems limited within operation, content, and product boundaries. One way in which broader generalizations might be effected would be to make the learner aware of the parallels across SI boundaries, so that he applies what he learns in a task that is salient for one SI ability to tasks involving parallel abilities. Perhaps some of these parallels are sensed by individuals, without their being taught, and such transfers occur automatically, thus producing high-order factors.

Assessment of Other Qualities. It is commonly recognized that, in general, assessment of traits of motivation and temperament is in a less satisfactory state than assessment of intellectual traits. Although there have been factorial definitions of many variables of needs, interests, and attitudes, and also in the domain of temperament (Guilford, 1959), and some definitive instruments of measurement are available, there has been limited information regarding predictive validity against creative-production criteria. Obtained validity indices have generally shown low relationships with criteria of performance for single trait scores. Again, multiple predictions are needed. Much tedious validation effort will be needed in order to determine which traits and their tests are relevant.

PROMOTING CREATIVE DEVELOPMENT

Knowledge of the traits that enter into creative disposition should help not only to identify and locate potential creative talent but also to give us clues to promote development in creative directions. This is more true of abilities than of other traits, for, as pointed out earlier, the abilities directly suggest certain creative processes. It is not so clear how we should go about improving traits of motivation and temperament, and whether, if we succeeded, gains in creative performance would automatically follow.

Special Training in Creative Thinking. It has been repeatedly demonstrated that exercises designed to increase success in creative thinking have the effect of raising status in the relevant SI abilities. Torrance's (1972) recent review of studies of effectiveness of various methods of training for creative thinking gives the palm to Alex Osborn's procedures, as described in his book *Applied Imagination* (Osborn, 1963). These procedures have a solid foundation of theory in the creative aspects of the SI model. This is another instance of technology outrunning basic knowledge, in this case, owing to the rare insights of Alex Osborn.

Results of training experiments also support the multivariate view of creative potential. For any given type of training, certain SI abilities show improvements while others do not. In a grand educational experiment at the college level, Parnes and Noller (1972) have found that abilities, some outside the divergent-production and transformation categories as well as some within those categories, are affected, much as one should expect, knowing the kinds of exercises given the students.

From this it should follow that in the educational setting, one should give due regard to the SI abilities probably involved in the behavior skills to be achieved, and he should select his pre- and post-test instruments accordingly, if there is to be evaluation of the generalized effects of the training. There is evidence (Forehand and Libby, 1962) that perhaps even more important than drill in thinking exercises is the step of imparting knowledge of the nature of creative thinking. Information concerning the SI model and the problem-solving model that is based upon it (Guilford, 1967a) should be useful in this situation.

Considering the special creative-thinking courses known to me, I should say that they fall short of offering a full curriculum. Use of the two models just mentioned would help to evaluate courses as to comprehensiveness. When the goal is aimed at better problem solving, the range of SI abilities involved is much greater. It is quite natural that the courses should stress semantic content, for that is the kind of information in most common use in our verbal civilization. But I suspect that there is an unexpressed expectation that training in this area will transfer automatically to other areas of information. From what we know about transfer effects, that training would do little for the visual artist or the creative musician, for the mathematician or the politician, unless the analogies are pointed out, and some exercise is given in transfer.

Of all the content categories, that of behavioral information is probably most neglected in exercises in creative thinking, yet in that area are some of the most significant everyday problems. They are encountered not only by politicians, whom I have mentioned, but also by all those who need to influence or control people—parents, teachers, policemen, attorneys, judges, probation officers, social workers—the list is a long one. If these are the kinds of people we are to make more creative thinkers, we should do better by giving attention to solving behavorial problems.

It is not clear, but I am sure that not all the SI informational products are given due attention. Brainstorming sessions may emphasize units of information unduly. Solutions to problems in daily life may call for new relations or implications, as when a scientist is attempting to decide what the connection is between two things or two variables, or when generating alternative hypotheses to account for some phenomenon. A detective also needs the generation of such products. The need to produce systems is obvious in much creative work, systems such as melodies, story plots, or scientific theories. The unique importance of transformations was emphasized earlier.

In the larger context of problem solving, we need to consider functions outside the category of divergent production. Some attention is given to evaluation, in some instances, but probably not enough. Some attention is given to seeing problems, but the nature of that step is not often realized. Analytical studies have led to the conclusion that seeing that a problem exists is a matter of cognition of implications. We size up an object or a situation and we are aware of a shortcoming of some kind. I once addressed an organization of engineers, who wanted to know how they could more readily translate discoveries in basic science into useful inventions. I pointed out that they must improve their skills in seeing implications. They could start with the nature of the scientific finding and its properties and ask themselves, how, by virtue of these attributes, it leads to new uses. Or they could start with a collection of human needs, needs that could possibly be collected in public polling; they should define those needs in terms of specific requirements, which might lead to things that fit those specifications.

Remembering that productive thinking depends very heavily upon stored information, in a course on problem solving we might give some attention to memory training. This should emphasize how information is put into storage, for how it is stored will make a difference in how efficient the retrieval can be. Things can be retrieved more readily if they are properly organized and labeled, for we get at them by using appropriate cues. The activity is analogous to looking for a book in a library. Organization of the memory store depends upon how items of information are put into storage, and this means the manner in which the information is learned. In order to tag information in a useful way, full advantage must be taken of the logical constructs of classes, relations, implications, and systems—the SI products. But to be left with flexibility, information needs to be in cross classifications, hierarchies, and other alternative systems. The simple moral for education is that attention should go well beyond the teaching of isolated units.

Creative Education in General. The special approaches to development of creative thinking have never been known to achieve miracles. But, if by any approach we could lift the population's problem-solving skills by a small amount on the average, the summative effect would be incalculable. The special methods of training have been usually applied outside the academic setting. To have any widespread effect on the population, they would need to be utilized within the academic world. But in that connection, the somewhat specialized procedures should be expanded, as suggested earlier. Educational practices should be revamped from the bottom to the top, giving attention to creative problem-solving skills. For this purpose, many suggestions can be made. Many of these ideas have already been recommended and have been put into effect in places, but this reorganization should become more nearly universal.

Some general principles are agreed upon. The student's role must be a more active one. He should be given not only opportunity to pursue learning as a goal, but also personal responsibility for learning. The teacher's role should be to stimulate and to guide, providing a favorable climate and the necessary tools. As much as possible, the student should discover what he learns; he should not just wait for the teacher to tell him the information. Education must be more individualized, each child progressing at his own rate, his goal being to make progress, and when he puts forth the effort, progress should be forthcoming. He should have immediate and adequate feedback information, as the basis for reinforcement that rests on intrinsic, rather than extrinsic, motivation.

In the past, the goal of education has been too much directed toward the stockpiling of information. A well-stocked memory store is, of course, a necessary asset in creative problem solving. But information is by no means sufficient. Viewed in one way, stockpiling of information contributes to exercise of the SI operations of cognition and memory. This emphasis neglects the productive-thinking and evaluative functions that are so important for creativity. Skills must be developed for *using* information as well as for *storing* it. Instruction should be problem-centered. The student should encounter many problems; problems that are difficult enough to be challenging to him but not so difficult as to discourage effort. Creative behavior should be rewarded. Intrinsic rewards are best. Skills in evaluation should not be overlooked, but personal criticism should be kept at a minimum. If special weaknesses appear, special exercises should be prescribed. Students should be taught to be flexible in their thinking. In a fast-moving, fast-changing world, the individual must be ready to alter information and habits. Requirements of new problems render both information and skills rapidly out of date.

The setting and the climate for creativity in schools must be favorable. The school administration must be for it, the teachers must be for it, and parents must at least acquiesce. The school housing should be adapted to creative learning. The curriculum should be designed to offer different kinds of problems. The teacher's lesson plans should be adapted to this kind of learning—programming teaching operations with enough flexibility to take advantage of student-initiated trends.

While I am on the subject of education, I cannot refrain from adding some unique suggestions. Using the structure-of-intellect model as the frame of reference, I recommend that every student be given the chance to show what he can do with respect to all the intellectual functions. Each child is thus likely to find areas in which he can do relatively well, and in which learning can be more rapid and more rewarding. He is thus also likely to find areas of stronger interests. Assessments of the status of the student in various SI abilities would also be informing for teachers and counselors.

I also frequently recommend that as early as the child is ready for it, he be given information regarding the nature of his own intellectual resources.

As suggested earlier, this step should be an important basis for effecting transfers of learning, and the broadening of skills. Incidentally, I have been told by a teacher who has tried it, that his group of Negro children in grades four to six could be given some degree of understanding of the SI model and could apply it effectively in their own learning. As related by Robert Rose, of the San Bernardino, California Schools, after such treatment, the children showed very unusual gains in achievement tests and in IQ.

NEEDED BASIC RESEARCH

We know something about what the creative problem solver does in the act of thinking, but we need to know more. We know that a key activity in productive thinking, divergent or convergent, is retrieval of information from memory storage, but we do not know as much as we should about the process of retrieval itself, and the conditions that are favorable or unfavorable. Psychologists have lavishly investigated learning, including the putting of information into storage, while neglecting the process of recall. And when recall has been investigated, it has usually been what I call "reproductive" recall rather than "transfer" recall, which is so likely to be needed in productive thinking (Guilford, 1967a). In transfer recall, an item of information is retrieved in connection with some new cue, not the one in connection with which it was learned.

We need to know more about transformations, which have been almost entirely neglected except incidentally by Gestalt psychologists. Why are some people more ready than others to revise their conceptions? The answer is not to be found in a general personality trait of flexibility versus rigidity. Our research has found that even within the realm of thinking, there is more than one trait of this nature. Even each of the 20 transformation abilities in the SI model has its measure of independence. We may ask some general questions, however. Are there principles to be found to account for particular kinds of changes in information? Can transformations take place in information while it is in storage, or only when it is retrieved? Progress in making fruitful investigations, as usual, depends upon our ability to ask significant questions about the phenomenon.

The last question asked regarding transformations leads to the more general question about the role of *incubation* in problem solving. I doubt that any recognized creative person would deny the fact that incubation occurs and is frequently helpful. This phenomenon, of course, is an observed progress during times when one is not actively pursuing solutions. In experimental studies of the matter over long periods of time, it would be difficult to exert the controls one should desire. A study of short-term incubation (over a period of minutes) has been done (Fulgosi and Guilford, 1968), using a divergent-production task (Consequences). Positive effects upon performance in the task were found to increase during the first 20 minutes. In a second study, it was found that the effects decreased during the next 40 minutes. The possibility of experimental investigation of incubation has thus been demonstrated.

THE USE OF BIOGRAPHICAL INFORMATION

One use that has been made of biographical features found to be associated with creative performance in later life is found in Calvin W. Taylor's (IBRIC, 1968) Alpha Biographical Inventory. This purely empirical method has value in identifying youth and adults who have higher probabilities of exhibiting creative behavior. It is useful in selection of personnel in industrial settings and in spotting students with talents that are overlooked by ordinary academic-aptitude tests. It is a "shotgun" approach, lacking basic psychological theory, however, and hence would not be very useful in research where well-defined variables are needed.

Can use be made of any particular biographical features, such as those mentioned by Goertzel and Goertzel (1962)? I doubt that anyone would be heartless enough to recommend the institution of precarious and troubled homes in order to make a child more creative. Nor would one recommend the infliction of a physical handicap. We could tell a mother, perhaps, to be either dominating or loving. But if my interpretation of the effects of the troubled homes is correct, all we would need to do is to see to it that the child has numerous problems to solve. The problems should be paced at a level appropriate for the child at his level of development—problems neither too easy nor too difficult. This would take considerable attention and ingenuity on the part of the parents, who should not only contrive natural problems but also arrange for appropriate rewards for successful solutions. In more general terms, we need to train parents how to be teachers and how to take advantage of situations for teaching as events arise. The right kind of teaching parents could be the most important key to the development of a creative, problem-solving society. A problem-solving society should also be high in status with respect to mental health.

Expectations from Drugs. Probably because of its alleged "mind-stretching" effects and its production of bizarre hallucinations, LSD has received the most attention as a possible augmentor of creative thinking, with lasting as well as temporary consequences. A well-controlled experiment designed to test lasting effects (at least to six months) was conducted by the McGlothlins and Cohen (1967). A large number of different kinds of tests of creative-thinking abilities, of attitudes, and of behavior of different kinds were used in this connection. There was no significant gain in any creative-thinking test, either short-term or long-term in duration. There was a significant increase in self-observed aesthetic interests, and more incidence of attention to art and music, but no improvement in productive performances in those areas. Perhaps the aesthetic interest came from the startling sensory effects of the drug.

Effects of Psychotherapy. There may have been some experimental studies of effects of psychotherapy upon creative production, but I do not happen to be acquainted with any of them. As in studies of other effects of therapy, it may be very difficult to demonstrate positive results experimentally. It is known that individuals who score high on divergent-production tests are inclined to have slightly lower scores on neurotic tendency or emotional immaturity, consistent with the common observation that neurotics are less creative.

Probably the most that can be expected is that therapy would remove some of the blocks that may exist in the way of creative production. An anecdotal bit of evidence comes from E. G. Boring, one of our distinguished psychologists, who underwent psychoanalysis with the hope of performing more creatively as a scientist. From his own evaluation, the results were very disappointing (Boring, 1940). In such an instance, one may conclude either that there were no blocking impediments, or that therapy did not succeed in removing them.

Summary

A survey of psychological research on creativity, with new theory and new methods, during the past quarter century shows substantial progress in several areas—dispositions of the more creative individuals and some of the apparent determiners, the basic nature of creative thinking, and procedures for improving creative performances. The multivariate nature of the contributing qualities of creative persons has been well established, and it involves both intellectual and nonintellectual traits.

Episodes of creative problem solving involve a great many different intellectual functions that are represented in the structure-of-intellect model. Thus, creative abilities are a part of intelligence, not something apart from it. Most critically involved, particularly at the stage of generating ideas, are the divergent-production abilities or functions and those involving transformations of information. The former provide an abundance of alternative ideas; the latter a flexibility in the structuring of information so that alterations and adaptations can occur.

Various procedures for improvement of potential for creative thinking have been tried experimentally. The most successful methods can lay claim to theoretical bases in structure-of-intellect concepts. Teaching individuals the nature of those concepts has also been found to be effective. There is insufficient scientific evidence as yet to lead us to expect much in the way of creative benefits from psychotherapy or the use of drugs.

Further research is needed on basic problems, especially on the process of retrieval of information (recall) from memory storage, which is at the heart of creative thinking. More should be learned regarding the phenomena of transformations, their nature, and their determiners. Experimental investigation of the phenomenon of incubation has been barely started.

Note

1. For a condensed history of the research on discoveries of divergent-production abilities, and other abilities, see Guilford and Hoepfner (1971).

References

Barron, F. Heritability of factors in creative thinking and esthetic judgment. *Acta Geneticae Medicae et Gemellogie,* 1970, *19,* 204–208.

Boring, E. G. Was this analysis a success? *Journal of Abnormal and Social Psychology,* 1940, *35,* 4–10.

Elliott, J. M. Measuring creative abilities in public relations and in advertising work. In C. W. Taylor (Ed.), *Widening Horizons in creativity,* pp. 396–400. New York: Wiley, 1964.

Ferguson, G. A. On transfer and the abilities of man. *Canadian Journal of Psychology,* 1956, *10,* 121–131.

Forehand, G. A. and Libby, W. L., Jr. *Effects of educational programs and perceived organizational climate upon changes in innovative administrative behavior.* Chicago: University of Chicago Center for Progress in Government Administration, 1962.

Fulgosi, A. and Guilford, J. P. Short-term incubation in divergent production. *American Journal of Psychology,* 1968, *81,* 241–246.

Getzels, J. W. and Jackson, P. W. *Creativity and intelligence.* New York: Wiley, 1962.

Goertzel, V. H. and Goertzel, M. C. *Cradles of eminence.* Boston: Little Brown, 1962.

Guilford, J. P. Creativity. *American Psychologist,* 1950, *5,* 444–454.

Guilford, J. P. *Personality.* New York: McGraw-Hill, 1959.

Guilford, J. P. Implications of research on creativity. In C. Banks and P. L. Broadhurst (Eds.), *Studies in psychology presented to Cyril Burt.* London: University of London Press, 1965.

Guilford, J. P. Intelligence: 1965 model. *American Psychologist,* 1966, *21,* 20–26.

Guilford, J. P. *The nature of human intelligence.* New York: McGraw-Hill, 1967. (a)

Guilford, J. P. Creativity, yesterday, today, and tomorrow. *Journal of Creative Behavior,* 1967, *1,* 3–14. (b)

Guilford, J. P. Creativity: Retrospect and prospect. *Journal of Creative Behavior,* 1970, *4,* 149–165.

Guilford, J. P. Psychology with act, content, and form. *Journal of General Psychology,* 1974.

Guilford, J. P. and Hoepfner, R. *The analysis of intelligence.* New York: McGraw-Hill, 1971.

IBRIC. *The alpha biographical inventory.* Greensboro, N.C.: Prediction Press, 1968.

Jones, C. A. Some relationships between creative writing and creative drawing of sixth grade children. Doctoral dissertation, Pennsylvania State University, 1960.

Kallick, M. A construct validation of a creativity questionnaire and certain theoretical considerations. Master's thesis, University of Akron, 1962.

McGlothlin, W., Cohen, S., and McGlothlin, M. S. Long lasting effects of LSD on normals. *Archives of General Psychiatry,* 1967, *17*, 521–532.

Osborn, A. F. *Applied Imagination.* New York: Scribner, 1963.

Parnes, S. J. and Noller, R. B. Applied creativity: The creative student project: Part II. *Journal of Creative Behavior,* 1972, *6*, 164–186.

Torrance, E. P. Can we teach children to think creatively? *Journal of Creative Behavior,* 1972, *6*, 114–143.

3. IPAR's Contribution to the Conceptualization and Study of Creativity

Donald W. MacKinnon

BEFORE PSYCHOLOGISTS COULD turn in any very effective way to the study of creativity—as they have done in the last twenty-five years—psychology itself had to change. The neglect of so complex a phenomenon as creativity by a psychology newly born in 1879 with Wundt's founding of the first psychological laboratory in Leipzig is understandable. In its early attempts to establish itself as an empirical and experimental science, psychology focused its attention upon the simpler aspects of consciousness and behavior for the study of which there were manageable techniques. Later when behaviorism became the dominant emphasis in American psychology the climate was even less congenial to such complex topics as that of creativity. For the early behaviorists, the human nature of man and his personality lay outside the domain of scientific discourse and research. The model of man which they constructed was the model of man as a machine. Furthermore, a psychology that paid little or no attention to persons and to which the concept of personality was largely foreign could hardly tackle the concept of creativity.

It remained for Freud and the early psychoanalysts to bring the person as an object of study into psychology. But it was the sick person not the well one that became the focus of attention. Psychopathology is vivid; it cries out for treatment and care. So, understandably, over the years there has been a continuing emphasis upon research into the nature of human emotional and mental distress, in the attempt to find some cure for them. But the model of man developed by the psychoanalysts was a medical model and unfortunately their theory of personality was one that generalized pathology to all of man's functioning. Psychoanalysis told us what makes men break down but gave us little insight into the forces that enable a person to overcome adversity, to realize his potentialities, and to develop his creativeness to the full.

60

Two publications of major importance for the development of a third kind of psychology (that has been variously called personology, humanistic psychology, and the Third Force) were Gordon W. Allport's *Personality: A psychological interpretation* in 1937 and Henry A. Murray's *Explorations in personality* in 1938. These two works in a most impressive way introduced the topic of personality in its normal and more favorable manifestations into academic psychology. There were other events that changed the nature of psychology and the objects of its study and thus laid the groundwork for the more recent preoccupation with the topic of creativity: the demonstration by the Gestalt psychologists that complex processes of thought and action could be brought into the laboratory and submitted to experimental manipulation and measurement; the reintroduction into psychology of the concepts of self (McDougall) and ego (Allport) and the development of an ego-psychology; the demonstration by Henry Murray and his associates at the Harvard Psychological Clinic of the possibility of gaining an understanding of personality through the use of a multiplicity of assessment techniques; the application of such techniques in the assessment of the effective functioning of man (the Assessment Program in the Office of Strategic Services) and Guilford's originative presidential address to the American Psychological Association in 1950 entitled "Creativity."

The changes wrought in psychology since the late 1930s have been noted by Sanford (1963) to be an increased awareness of the complexity of personality; a decreasing accent upon motives, accompanied by an increasing emphasis upon cognitive variables as the significant variables of personality; an increasing holistic orientation; and a trend toward thinking about higher things. And certainly one of the higher things that has increasingly drawn the attention of psychologists is man's creativeness.

IPAR'S Study of Personal Effectiveness

The Institute of Personality Assessment and Research (IPAR) was established on the Berkeley campus of the University of California in 1949 with the specific purpose of thinking about and investigating higher things. Made possible by a grant from the Rockefeller Foundation, the Institute had as its objective the development and use of psychological assessment techniques in the study of effectively functioning persons. Its research task would be to develop techniques and procedures for the assessment of personality and to utilize the assessment procedures as research techniques to shed light on two long neglected questions: (1) What are the characteristics of persons who are highly effective in their personal lives and professional careers? and (2) How are such effectively functioning persons produced in our society?

The stimulus for the establishment of such an institute had been the experiences of several psychologists in the assessment program of the

Office of Strategic Services (1948).[1] It was in this program that, for the first time, large numbers of highly effective persons were intensively studied by psychologists and psychiatrists who, to their surprise, discovered again and again that persons of the most extraordinary effectiveness had had life histories marked by severe frustrations, deprivations, and traumatic experiences. By the then generally accepted theory of personality development they should have been psychiatric casualties, but they were not. Those of us who were members of the OSS assessment staff had had it vividly impressed upon us how little we knew about the development of personality and especially how ignorant we were about the factors that make it possible for a person to profit from adversity to realize his potentialities, and in the long run to become a truly effective and creative person. It was to investigate such phenomena as these that IPAR was established.

The staff's first task was to conceptualize an effective person and to formulate a set of hypotheses about the development and functioning of such persons which could be submitted to empirical test,[2] and one of our first assumptions was that a variable of creativity, although at that time we called it originality, would be a crucial factor in effective functioning.[3]

In summarizing IPAR's hypotheses about the role of originality in the personality structure of the highly effective or successful person, Barron wrote:

> In addition to these personal characteristics, the successful person will be original and creative. This will show itself in a greater tolerance for unusual ideas and formulations in his field, and will generally issue in original and constructive work. The original person will be facile in perceiving equivalences in the patterning of experience. This feeling for metaphor may lead to a reconstruction of experience in a novel fashion: invention, in the broader sense of that term. The original person is at home to asymmetry, or even positively prefers it to symmetry. It is often the unfinished, the implicit, the connoted, and the suggested, which have the greatest charm for him. He has independence of judgment and freedom of perception, so that he need not resort to stereotypes nor depend upon conventional categories. He can tolerate ambiguities and perplexities, and is able to settle for probability rather than certainty. In spite of being quite open-minded and tolerant in some respects, however, he may be rather judgmental in others. If his idea immediately recommends itself to his own sense of reality or beauty, he may persevere in it and adhere to it in a relatively inflexible manner—he is certain, then, of his own rightness.
>
> What is referred to here as originality is, perhaps, better spoken of as generativity or constructiveness. It involves *adding something of one's own* to the elements of experience, making a new pattern which would not otherwise have come into being. This may show itself not only in artistic or scientific creation, but in more general patterns of living and in all sorts of personal interactions, from a casual conversation to an international conference. Thus seen, it is closely related to what might be called sensitiveness, ethical, emotional and esthetic.
> [1950, pp. 5–6]

The Institute's first study was of 80 graduate students at Berkeley each of whom was judged to have demonstrated some degree of effectiveness since he was presumably within a year of obtaining his Ph.D. and hopefully would in his subsequent career demonstrate more. Three criterion variables were conceptualized: P (potential success), O (originality), and S ("all around" personal soundness). It was our thought that the potential success of a student, i.e., "the likelihood that he would in future years contribute significantly to his field in some manner or another," would be a function of his originality ("freshness of vision and creativity of thought") and his all-around soundness ("general effectiveness as a *person,* rather than as a professional individual. The emphasis is upon the attributes of personality and character, such as maturity, balance, integrity, judgment, and the like, which make for soundness in various areas of life."). Ratings of P, O, and S were made for each student by two or more of his professors who knew him best.[4]

Prior to the seeing of any students each staff member filled out an adjective check list[5] to describe an "ideally original person." A compositing of the most frequently checked adjectives yielded the staff's a priori "stereotype" of an original person. When this was later compared with the adjectives checked most frequently to describe those students seen in assessment who had been given the highest and lowest ratings on originality by their professors, there was considerable congruence between the two lists, but there were notable differences too.

Where we had expected to find original students rather free, spontaneous and unconventional (in our stereotype we had checked more often individualistic, spontaneous, daring, independent) in reality the more original students were seen as serious, organized, and rational (we checked more often civilized, reliable, quiet, responsible). Conversely, our stereotype of the unoriginal student included such adjectives as apathetic, dull, stolid, and commonplace, but we found ourselves checking such adjectives as emotional, restless, stubborn, and defensive to describe those who had received low ratings on originality. In this sample at least, the original students conveyed much more a picture of professional responsibility than of carefree bohemianism (Gough, 1950).

This unexpected finding might be due to a serious misconception on our part of the traits of highly original graduate students, or it might be the result of a bias in our sample of graduate students, most of whom were being trained in the sciences, and particularly the physical sciences. Thus the question was raised in our minds, "Do these adjectival descriptions apply chiefly to persons who are original in a special way, i.e., as physical scientists, or are the descriptions true more generally?" With data from only one sample it would not be possible to answer the question, but we were sensitized to the requirement, if we were to undertake further studies of originality, of having subjects drawn from a diversity of fields. Any new study would have to control systematically for field of specialization, or major academic interest. Only then could it be known whether, for example, original artists are very different from original physicists, and original social scientists different from both.

In an attempt to develop, in addition to faculty ratings, a measure of originality, the responses of the graduate students to a battery of seven "free-expression" tests consisting of fairly unstructured stimulus materials, providing subjects an opportunity to create freely their own responses, were examined. The subjects' responses on all of these tests were rated for originality. Finding very low intercorrelations among all of these measures, Schimek (1954) concluded that originality cannot be considered a generalized factor in such performances. Arguing that the most valid index of originality is likely to be a subject's most original responses in areas where he is most proficient, rather than his average performance on a group of unrelated procedures, Schimek took as a subject's originality score, the composite of the ratings he had received on two procedures only, those on which he had obtained his highest average ratings of originality.

Originality so measured proved to be significantly correlated with intellectual competence and self-assurance (drive, self-assertion, dominance), but not with intelligence test scores, and not with personal soundness. Schimek confirmed as well a finding by another staff member, that preference for complex and asymmetrical designs goes along with originality. Barron (1952) had advanced the notion that artistic perception should be related to originality in any field of intellectual endeavor and, in work with Welsh (Barron and Welsh, 1952), developed a measure of aesthetic preference that is now known as the Barron-Welsh Art Scale. In the IPAR study of graduate students and in subsequent studies, originality has consistently been found to be associated with preference for complex rather than simple perceptual fields, as measured by this test.

It is interesting to look back and discover the degree to which our early study of originality in graduate students foreshadowed the later findings in our studies of highly creative mature professionals.

An item analysis of the personality inventory items checked more often as true or self-descriptive by those high on Schimek's measure of O than by those who scored low revealed differences that were summarized as follows:

> The Highs are verbally fluent, show intellectual curiosity and an apparent richness of inner life. They emphasize self-discipline, self-reliance and have a somewhat defensive need for privacy. They are not gregarious, and do not care too much about social conventions or the opinions and feelings of other people, or at least wish they did not. They are willing to admit fears and unconventional tastes. The dominant impression for this group is that of personal autonomy, individual values, and intellectual independence.
>
> The Lows do not have much tolerance for novel or ambiguous situations, they prefer adhering to established customs. They seek emotional reassurance

by identifying with in-group and authority figures, and by being "one of the crowd." Great emphasis is put upon external signs of social approval and conformity. Noticeable physical handicaps are strongly denied. Along with this tough-minded and somewhat self-righteous appearance the Lows also feel inadequate, insecure and misunderstood; they are jealous of people who are different or better off than they, and secretly envy them for being able to "get away with it."

The over-all impression suggests that this group does not have the emotional strength to be different or to face disapproval—much less to be creative. They exhibit some of the characteristics of the "authoritarian personality." [Schimek, 1954, p. 44]

It may be noted that the assessment staff's impression of those who were high or low on originality, or on an intermediate level of originality as measured by free-response tests, was congruent with the subject's own impressions of themselves.

When the originality of graduate students was estimated by faculty ratings, the picture of the original student was somewhat different from that which emerged when performance on free-response tests was taken as the measure of their originality. Those high on faculty-rated originality appeared to be the more scholarly type in a single field of endeavor, efficiently self-disciplined, and socially somewhat inflexible and withdrawn. Those high on the free-response measure of O represented the more artistic type, fluent, witty and with many simultaneous interests. The former revealed a "tough-minded" type of object-oriented creativity, dealing by preference with non-human topics; the latter a "tender-minded" type of creativity showing a predilection for direct involvement with feelings and interpersonal relations. The data suggested to us that originality is not a homogeneous trait and that several types of original and unoriginal people would eventually have to be distinguished, and further that special attention would have to be given in any future research to the criterion measures which would be used to identify creative persons.

Early efforts of the IPAR staff were directed not only to the conceptualization of originality but also to the development of instruments to measure it. An examination of the correlates of rated originality in the graduate student study was the basis of Gough's development of a 44-item self-report scale to identify personality factors such as independence of mind, skepticism, self-confidence, and analytical fluency, which enter into research originality. This scale was labeled O–I (Gough, 1952, 1954). He also developed a cluster of 32 adjectives which had been found empirically to correlate with ratings of originality in the study of graduate students. This measure was designated O (Originality) (Gough, 1952). Later (Gough, 1957b) he came to conceptualize five dimensions that he believed were among the most important of the personological determinants of originality:

O–1. Intellectual competence. The capacity to think, to reason, to comprehend and to know.

O–2. Inquiringness as a habit of mind. An unending curiosity about things, about people, and about nature; an inner spur toward resolution and discernment.

O–3. Cognitive flexibility. The ability to shift and to adapt, and to deal with the new, the unexpected, and the unforeseen.

O–4. Esthetic sensitivity. A deep-seated preference for the appreciation of elegance of form and of thought, of harmony wrought from complexity, and of style as a medium of expression.

O–5. Sense of destiny. This includes something of resoluteness and (naturally) of egotism, but over and above these a belief in the foregone certainty of the worth and validity of one's future and attainment. [Ibid., p. 9]

Brief measures of each of these dimensions were developed consisting of five 20-item nonoverlapping, inventory scales O–1, O–2, O–3, O–4, O–5, and O–T, the sum of the five scales. These scales which have shown significant correlations with creativeness in later studies have been collected into a single testing pamphlet along with an additional scale called "P–4" which is designed to measure the motivational components of personal success and constructive achievement. This test is titled the Differential Reaction Schedule (DRS) (Gough, 1955, 1957c).

In the Institute's study of leadership in Air Force officers initiated in 1954 (MacKinnon et al., 1958), it was possible, on the basis of earlier work, to administer a fairly large battery of tests of originality. Among these, eight measures were combined on an a priori basis by Barron (1955) to yield a composite score of originality for each subject. Before examining the personality correlates of this composite measure of originality, he formulated five major hypotheses concerning the differences between subjects who are regularly original and those who are not.

The five hypotheses, confirmed in this study, were that "original persons: (1) prefer complexity and some degree of apparent imbalance in phenomena, (2) are more complex psychodynamically and have greater personal scope, (3) are independent in their judgments, (4) are more self-assertive and dominant, and (5) reject suppression as a mechanism for control of impulse" (Ibid., pp. 482–83).

In this study, Barron also developed a 49-item self-report scale to measure the disposition toward originality in verbal expression or *Verbal Originality* (O–B) (Barron, 1965).

In the same sample of Air Force officers, Barron (1957) was able to study the variables of personality associated with originality when intelligence was partialled out. They were (a) disposition toward integration of diverse stimuli; (b) energy, fluent output and involvement; (c) personal dominance and self-assertion; (d) responsiveness to impulse and emotion; (e) expressed femininity of interests; and (f) general effectiveness of performance. He also identified two contrasting groups—one high on originality, low on intelligence; the other high on intelligence, low on originality—and discovered that they described themselves quite differently on the Adjective Check List (ACL) (Gough and Heilbrun, 1965).

Those high on originality but low on intelligence described themselves as: affected, aggressive, demanding, dependent, dominant, forceful, impatient, initiative, outspoken, sarcastic, strong, suggestible. Those high on intelligence but low on originality saw themselves as: mild, optimistic, pleasant, quiet, unselfish. Contrasting these self-descriptions with the generally favorable staff descriptions of subjects who were both original and intelligent, he hypothesized "that intelligence represents the operations of the reality principle in behavior, and is responsible for such characteristics as the appropriate delay of impulse expression and the effective organization of instinctual energy for the attainment of goals in the world as it is. To use another of the distinctions proposed by Freud in his theory of the mental apparatus, primary process thinking to the exclusion of the secondary process marks the original but unintelligent person, secondary process thinking which carries ego-control to the point where the ego is not so much strong as muscle-bound marks the intelligent but unoriginal person, and easy accessibility of both primary process and secondary process marks the person who is both original and intelligent" (Barron, 1957, p. 739). He was then led to speculate that in the effectively original person there may be "an ability to regress very far *for the moment* while being able quite rapidly to return to a high degree of rationality, bringing with him the fruits of his regression to primitive and fantastic modes of thought (a variant of the phenomenon termed 'regression in the service of the ego' by Lowenstein and Kris)" (Barron, 1957, p. 739).

In all of the work thus far reviewed, IPAR, whether it knew it or not, was tooling up conceptually and methodologically for its extensive study of creativity which, supported by a grant from the Carnegie Corporation of New York, began in 1956 (IPAR Staff, 1955).

IPAR's Study of Creativity

In undertaking to study creativity our first task was to decide what we would consider creativity to be. This was necessary, first, because the meanings of creativity have been so numerous, and, second, because only with an agreed-upon conception of what creativity is would we be in a position to know what kinds of persons we would want to study.

We quickly agreed that true creativeness fulfills at least three conditions. It involves a response or an idea that is novel or at the very least statistically infrequent. But novelty or originality, while a necessary aspect of creativity, is not sufficient if a response is to lay claim to being a part of the creative process; it must also to some extent be adaptive to reality. It must serve to solve a problem, fit a situation, or accomplish some recognizable goal. And thirdly, true creativeness involves a sustaining of the original insight, an evaluation and elaboration of it, a developing of it to the full.

Creativity, we thought, involves a process that is extended in time and characterized by originality, adaptiveness, and realization. Conceiving creativity accordingly had important consequences for our researches: we would not study creativity while it was still potential but only after it had come to expression in clearly identifiable creative products. In other words, we would, at least at the beginning, limit our researches to the study of persons who had already demonstrated a high level of creative work.

We did not feel compelled to define creativity more precisely. For some, creativity is the ability to bring something new into existence. Others have argued that creativity is not an ability, but rather the psychological process or processes by which novel and valuable products are fashioned. Still others in discussing creativity stress not the process but the product. Indeed, definitions of creativity range all the way from the concept of creativity as nothing more than novel problem-solving to conceiving of it as the full realization and expression of all an individual's unique potentialities. Actually, we thought it ill-advised to find the single best definition among these rather specific conceptions of creativity since creativeness properly carries all of these meanings and many more besides.

It appeared, at least to me (MacKinnon, 1970), that creativity is best conceived of as a multifaceted phenomenon rather than as a theoretical concept to be precisely defined. Creativity might then be thought of as something like the title of a book—in other words, a rubric under which a number of related topics quite naturally fall.

One advantage of considering creativity in this way, especially for one who would study creativity in its broadest aspects, is that an enormously complex phenomenon is broken down into its distinguishable aspects or facets, each of which is more manageable and more amenable to research than is the global concept of creativity.

Considered in this manner there are four major facets of creativity: (1) the creative product, (2) the creative process, (3) the creative person, and (4) the creative situation. Each of these aspects of creativity can be formulated as a question to which empirical research can provide at least some answers.

The major questions to be asked are: (1) What are creative products? What qualities and characteristics identify them, distinguishing them from more commonplace productions? (2) What is the nature of the creative process? What are the qualities and kinds of psychological processes by means of which the new, of whatever kind, is brought into existence? (3) What are the traits and characteristics of creative persons that mark them off from their less creative peers? (4) What are the characteristics of the creative situation, the life circumstance, or the social, cultural, and work milieu which facilitate and encourage the appearance of creative thought and action?

THE CREATIVE PRODUCT

The creative product is a domain of research that has been largely neglected. However, there is a sense in which we know most about creative products since they are the manifest and tangible expressions or resultants of creative activity. Indeed a thorough examination of them should permit us to make certain inferences concerning the nature of the creative process, and certainly it is only through their existence that we identify creative persons, distinguishing them from their less creative peers and from those others whose creative potential has not yet found expression.

To speak of the creative product as though there were only one kind of product is a great oversimplification. Creative products range from such concrete and tangible objects as a piece of sculpture or a physical invention to such intangibles as leadership or providing educational and business climates which permit those in them to express to the full their creative potential. Some have even spoken of the person as a product; for example, the individual who makes his own being and life a work of art. We assumed that the agreement among experts concerning the creativeness of a product would be greater for those products that are relatively public and permanent; and this influenced our decisions concerning the groups of creative persons we would study.

In undertaking our studies of creativity we turned to the experts in several fields of creative endeavor, asking them to nominate for us their outstandingly creative coworkers. In so far as they were able to carry out this assignment, and especially in so far as they were able to do so with a high degree of agreement, that is, reliabilities as high as +.84, they were evaluating not so much the persons whom they nominated as the products these persons had created.

We are here concerned with the problem of the criteria for creativity, and it is clear that all too often investigators have settled for obviously crude and fallible quantitative criteria rather than struggle with the more difficult task of coming to agreement upon acceptable qualitative criteria. In short, it would appear that the explicit determination of the qualities which identify creative products has been largely neglected just because we implicitly know—or feel we know—a creative product when we see it.

It was considerations such as these that led us to assume that if those who nominated creative persons for our study were to do so adequately, it would be necessary to direct their attention, first, to the products of the creative subjects which justified their nominations as creative, and second, to the meaningful and easily differentiated aspects or dimensions of these products.

Thus, for example, in our study of architects the task set for the five professors of architecture who served as a nominating panel was for each of them working independently to nominate the forty American architects who in his judgment were the forty most creative architects in the country. To lessen the likelihood of multiple frames of reference being used they agreed that in making their nominations each panel member would use the following definition of creativity in architecture: originality of thinking and freshness of approaches to architectural problems; constructive ingenuity; ability to set aside established conventions and procedures when appropriate; a flair for devising effective and original fulfillments of the major demands of architecture: technology (firmness), visual form (delight), planning (commodity), and human awareness and social purpose.

By incorporating into our definition of creativity the three traditionally recognized demands of architecture: firmness, commodity, and delight (Sir Henry Wotton, 1624), and adding a fourth of our own, human awareness and social purpose, we sought to obviate a possible source of error in nominating architects for study. If the task had been simply to list the forty most creative architects in the country the danger would have been that prestige and reputation, in some cases doubtless well earned but in other instances questionable, might have determined inordinately the nominations that were made. Requiring of panel members that they consider the degree to which each nominated architect had *in his designed buildings* actually shown creativeness in meeting each of the four specified facets of architecture forced them to think more in terms of products than of persons. For each nominated architect, nominators were asked to rate that architect's creativeness on each of the four dimensions of architectural practice. No overall rating of creativeness was requested.

To insure further that the nominations would be based on specific accomplishments and innovations rather than on prestige and notoriety, each panel member had the further and final task of writing a summary evaluation of the work of each architect whom he nominated, and a statement as to what specific work or works justified his nomination as one of the most creative architects in the country.

Another assumption made by us was that the validity of ratings would be maximized by describing the rating variables in the idiom of the field, architecture, rather than in the jargon of psychology. Thus in a conference preceding the actual making of nominations, the mutually agreed-upon meanings of the four facets of architectural creativity were worked over until acceptable to all nominators.

An even more detailed analysis of the distinguishing marks of creative products as a basis for the identification of creative persons has been Helson's (1970) study of works of fantasy and imagination written for children. Among the differentiated variables descriptive of the books which were rated or ranked by judges were five formal dimensions, sixteen stylistic characteristics, nine themes, ten needs, and eight types of interpersonal relationships which were emphasized in the fantasies.

Regardless of the degree to which our criteria for creativity have been differentiated, we have, in all of our studies, assumed that the identification of more or less creative persons had to be based firmly upon an evaluation of their products by experts, and not by us or by so-called tests of creativity. Indeed, whether one chooses to study the creative person, the creative process, or the creative situation, one must, we assumed, identify them through a critical assessment of products created by a given person, through a given process, and in a given situation. Fallible as the consensus of experts concerning the creativeness of products inevitably is, there was, we felt, no better method of identifying the several aspects of creativity which we would study. In this sense, the study of creative products is the basis upon which all research on creativity rests and until this foundation is more solidly built all such research will leave something to be desired.

THE CREATIVE PROCESS

In applying in 1955 to the Carnegie Corporation of New York for support of our projected studies of creativity we noted that the researches of the Institute, focused upon the personality structure of the original person, had ignored almost completely the study of the processes whereby fresh insights arise, inventive solutions are achieved, and new media for the artistic expression of mood and feeling are discovered. The assessment of personality, typically crowded into at most a few days of observation, provides neither the appropriate atmosphere nor the leisure for adequately studying the creative process.

Regardless of how creative a person may be, one cannot count upon his being able to manifest his creativeness upon demand, at a given time, or in a given assessment situation. And that is precisely what so-called tests of creativity require of a subject. It is, of course, possible to administer a variety of tests that have a certain face validity as tests of creativity, and we have done just that but have never taken the performance of our subjects on such tests as the criterion of their creativeness.

Few would doubt that the psychological processes involved in thinking of unusual or original uses and consequences (Kettner, Guilford, and Christensen, 1959) are like those involved in thinking of original ideas in any field of creative endeavor. Analysis of the processes elicited by such tests of creativity can shed some light on the nature of the creative process, but it leaves unilluminated the personological context in which the process goes on—the interests and values, the needs and aspirations, and the gnawing tensions of unsolved problems—and it ignores the extended time dimension of creative striving and the societal context which may facilitate or inhibit the process.

The creative act may be of brief duration, but more often it is a protracted affair. The moment of insight and inspiration may be sudden and brief, but it comes usually after a prolonged searching. To observe the whole span of creative thought and action would require considerable periods of time; for such a study subjects would have to be available not for brief periods of assessment but for months and possibly years of observation.

We did give thought, of course, to how the creative process might be studied over long periods of time with a variety of observational, introspective, and experimental techniques. Though few of these projected studies were actually made—our research energies were directed mainly to the study of creative persons—they have a certain historical interest and still appear as worthy of being carried out as when they were first formulated by us.

For example, one might hope to find a few highly creative persons who would be willing to introspect upon their own on-going creative processes and allow clinically trained personologists to discover aspects of the process upon which they might be themselves unable to report. But, valuable as self-reports would be, perhaps even more revealing would be the free associations of creative persons to the significant and germinal ideas in the chain of their creative thinking. The relation of dream content over time to the vicissitudes of the creative process could also be studied.

A modification of this design was carried out by Barron (1969) in his study of creative writers. Although it was not possible to observe their creative processes over time, in a specially designed interview Barron sought from his subjects retrospective accounts of the biography of one of their creative products—that is, a sonnet, a novel, a short story. There is, however, one serious drawback in studies such as these: the highly personal nature of the insights and understanding which are gained all too often preclude their publication.

A further technique which might be used with those subjects who would be willing to cooperate and be capable of so doing would be the induction of hypnosis in order to obtain in hypnotic trance reports on those phases of the creative process which normally go on outside of awareness.

Anther technique for studying the nature of symbol formation is that of implanting in hypnotized subjects a repressed emotional complex by suggesting to them that they have committed an act which has made them feel guilty and troubled. The suggestion further is given to the subjects that the guilt-producing incident has been forgotten but that they will dream about it the following night. This experiment was actually performed (MacKinnon, 1971). The dreams produced were widely different: in one, there was no reworking of the content of implanted complex, only a reliving of the suggested experience in the dream; another consisted mainly of unpleasant affect with the subject experiencing a troubled and depressed mood the following day; in a third, there was an imaginative and symbolic working over of the latent content of the complex. Since the content of the repressed complex was known to the experimenter, he was able to see the relation between it and the form in which it was expressed in the subjects' dreams. Differences in the transliminal experience of giving conscious expression to repressed unconscious content were shown to be related in a meaningful way to the subject's psychological type and to the psychic function—intuition, sensation, thinking, and feeling, as conceptualized by Jung (1923) and measured by the Myers-Briggs Type Indicator (Myers, 1962)—which he uses in dealing with his inner life. One is thus provided with a powerful technique for studying the symbolic transformations of elements of the repressed unconscious into that type of active fantasy which we recognize as creative process.

It has been frequently observed that between the period of undertaking the solution of a difficult problem and the final arrival at the solution there is interposed a period of turning away from the problem to other pursuits and concerns. We noted that two major hypotheses have been advanced concerning the role and function of such an "incubation" period in arriving at a creative solution. One interprets the incubation period as permitting the operation of certain unconscious processes. The other interpretation conceives of the passage of time away from direct attention to the problem as permitting the "unfreezing" of a fixated way of seeing the problem or its elements. Experiments can be done to determine the relative weight of these and still other alternatives. Such experiments are only now being conducted at IPAR by Robert M. Olton, Jr.

The role of *accident* in the creative and inventive process has rightly been emphasized in the anecdotal literature. There can be little doubt that the "chance" occurrence of an event at the appropriate time during the creative process may be signally important in providing the cue or the material necessary for the creative act. For research, the implications of this are that study should be made (1) of the conditions under which such accidents are more and less likely to occur, and (2) of the conditions under which such accidents, if they *do* occur, are more likely to result in the desired creative effect. A related phenomenon is the use of incidental cues in problem solving. The conditions under which such cues are likely to be used have been studied by Crutchfield (1961), and individual and sex differences in the use of incidental cues have been investigated by Mendelsohn and Griswold (1964, 1966, 1967) and by Mendelsohn and Lindholm (1972).

Related to, but more general than, the last point, is the critical importance of *timing* of events in the creative process. It would appear almost certain that the ontogeny of an idea or other creative product, like the developmental history of any organic whole, is characterized by lawfulness, and that it is subject to experimental and observational study, particularly with respect to the phase-sequence of events.

For investigations of the relation between the more conscious ego functions and more primitive layers of the personality, a relation which to some observers has appeared crucial for an understanding of the creative process, there are at hand, we noted, two techniques. One would involve the administration of a mind-altering drug, and the other a marked reduction of the stimulation of the exteroceptors. Both procedures induce marked personality changes, though both the degree and quality of change varies greatly from person to person. The relation of these changes to other aspects of the personality has not been adequately studied, and cannot be until those who are subjected to such treatment are first thoroughly assessed. Both procedures offer exciting possibilities for the investigation of the consequences of bombarding the ego with primitive impulse and imagery. Is the more creative person one who can give himself over more completely to ordinarily unconscious forces and still retain some degree of ego-control? Barron (1957) had already found some evidence in support of this notion and obtained more in his study of creative writers and artists (Barron, 1961, 1962, 1963, 1972).

Much has been written of the affective life of the highly creative person. It seemed clear to us that there is a connection, albeit a mysterious one, between affectivity and the creative process. In the arts, the great productions appear to be exquisite attempts to resolve an internal turbulence. In the sciences, the important theoretical efforts seem to be personal cosmologies as much as anything else (witness Einstein, the prime example; Sherrington, Cannon, Born, Schrodinger, and others). The validity of the creative product thus is almost (but not quite) incidental to the forces driving its expression. And the forces are largely affective.

There seems to be, we noted, an element of the primitive, the naïve, the unsophisticated, in the creative person, an ability not to be invariably "reality-oriented" or rather, to recognize that much of what we consider objective is only consensual. In what ways and, in particular, with what degree of compartmentalization is the creative person "child-like"? Is he affectively appropriate but cognitively unusual? Or is his entire personality tinged by his unique perceptions and expressions?

Considerations such as these, we further noted, point to the need for studying the inner workings and the inner experience of creative individuals as well as investigating their purely cognitive abilities. In particular, ways of objectifying internal experience must be used. For the study of affective response in such individuals, physiological measures in conjunction with situational variation, seem indicated as a means of operationalizing inner states. The extent to which creative individuals feel feeling, their reactions to stimulus-reduced environments which thrust them back upon themselves, the amplitude and frequency of their fluctuations of mood and directedness—these are problems of moment which, with difficulty, are experimentally accessible.

The discussion of the creative process thus far has taken no cognizance of the possibility that there may be different kinds of creative process. To what extent are the creative processes of mathematicians, musicians, physicists, painters, and entrepreneurs alike, and to what degree and in what respects different? Are different kinds of imagery, of metaphor and analogy, used in these quite different fields? Is the use of geometric symbols more appropriate to the solution of certain problems than the employment of algebraic symbols, or is the preference for one rather than the other determined by personal and temperamental factors? In what respects is the creativity of a sick and tortured person the same as the creativity of a calm and placid individual, and in what ways different? Some of these questions about different kinds of creative process become in a larger context questions about variations in style of creative work, different types of consciousness, indeed different types of creative persons, since cognitive processes are not purely cognitive in character but are vitally embedded in the total complex of personality.

THE CREATIVE PERSON

We began our researches on creativity with the assumption that there are different kinds of creativity: artistic creativity in which products are clearly expressions of the creator's inner states, his needs, perceptions, motivations, and the like; scientific and technological creativity in which operations are performed on some aspect of the environment which results in novel and appropriate products but to which the worker adds little of himself or of his style as a person (although this description is more appropriate for technological and inventive activity than for more theoretical scientific work); and hybrid forms of creativity such as architecture in which the creative products are both an expression of the architect and thus a personal statement and at the same time an impersonal meeting of the demands of an external problem. If workers in each of these domains were studied, it would be possible to say something about the characteristics of creative persons across several fields of endeavor and also to delineate the ways in which creative persons in one field are different from creative persons in other areas, and, sampling widely in each of the fields, to discover what distinguishes creative persons in any field from those who are relatively uncreative. As representative of artistic creativity we studied novelists, poets, and essayists; as representative of scientific and technological creativity research, scientists, engineers, and inventors; and as representative of creativity that is at once artistic and scientific, mathematicians and architects.

We assumed that creative persons would be intelligent and often highly so, and found that indeed they are (Barron, 1965; MacKinnon and Hall, 1972). But we assumed also that intelligence alone would not make for creativity. Intelligence as measured by an intelligence test, we had already learned, must be distinguished from the effectiveness with which a person uses whatever intelligence he has. The effective use of intelligence, we hypothesized, depends in large measure upon the mechanisms of defense which an individual employs, and more specifically upon his eschewing the mechanisms of repression and suppression; and this also was confirmed (MacKinnon, 1962; Barron, 1965). The effective use of intelligence, and especially its creative use, we assumed would be related to traits of personality, to attitudinal and motivational variables, to cognitive styles, interests, and values in clearly specifiable ways.

In view of the often asserted closeness of genius and insanity and our own earlier finding that originality was not positively related to personal soundness, we assumed that creative persons might have somewhat more psychopathology but also would be characterized by higher ego-strength (Barron, 1953a) than those less creative and sought to test this hypothesis with the Minnesota Multiphasic Personality Inventory (MMPI) (Hathaway and McKinley, 1943) and with life-history interviews. Psychopathology was found in creative persons but also evidence of ego-strength, and the courage to be open to experience, especially of the inner life.

The finding that creative men earn high scores on the Mf (feminine interest) scale of the MMPI confirmed our expectation, derived from the writings of Jung (1928), that they would give a more integrated expression to the feminine side of their nature than less creative men. And this along with other findings tended to confirm a broader hypothesis about creative persons, one also derived from Jungian theory, namely, that creative persons would show more reconciliation of the opposites of their nature than would less creative persons.

Assuming that creatives would differ from noncreatives in their preference for the opposed attitudes and psychological functions conceptualized by Jung (1923), we administered the Myers-Briggs Type Indicator (Myers, 1962). Our assumptions that creatives would tend to be introverted and to show a preference for intuition over sensation, and for perception over judgment were confirmed. We were less clear as to whether thinking or feeling would be preferred by our creative subjects. Actually a preference for thinking or for feeling turned out not to be related to creativity but to the type of materials or concepts with which the creative person deals: writers prefer feeling; mathematicians, research scientists, and engineers prefer thinking; architects split fifty-fifty in their preference for one or the other of these two functions.

Building upon Barron's earlier works with aesthetic preference, it seemed likely that creative subjects would show a perceptual preference for the complex and asymmetrical, and they did. Building upon Crutchfield's

(1951, 1955) and Barron's (1953*b*) studies of independence of judgment it was hypothesized that creative persons would show considerable independence and need for autonomy, and on several measures of these traits they scored high.

It seemed likely that creative persons in the fields chosen for study would show a distinctive pattern of interests as had graduate students (Gough, 1953) and military officers (MacKinnon et al., 1958) who had scored high on originality. With only slight variation from group to group, creative persons have shown interests similar to those of psychologists, author-journalists, lawyers, architects, artists, and musicians, and unlike those of purchasing agents, office men, bankers, farmers, carpenters, veterinarians, policemen, and morticians, as these are assessed by the Strong Vocational Interest Blank (Strong, 1943). We have interpreted such a pattern of interests to mean that "creative persons are relatively uninterested in small details or in facts for their own sake, and more concerned with their meanings and implications, possessed of considerable cognitive flexibility, verbally skillful, interested in communicating with others and accurate in so doing, intellectually curious, and relatively disinterested in policing either their own impulses and images or those of others" (MacKinnon, 1962, p. 490).

It also seemed likely that creative persons would have a distinctive pattern of the values conceptualized by Spranger (1928) and measured by the Allport-Vernon-Lindzey Study of Values (1951). Theoretical and aesthetic values are most highly prized by the creative persons in our studies. Among creative research scientists the theoretical value is highest with the aesthetic value almost as high, among creative architects the order is reversed, and among creative mathematicians the two values are high and approximately equally strong.

In line with our expectation that creative persons would more often than not be introverted, we assumed that they would in other ways show a distinctive pattern of social relations. Among architects, for example, on the FIRO-B (Schutz, 1958) the more creative subjects revealed a desire not to be included in the activities of others nor to include them in theirs, along with a desire to be free from the control of others while themselves exercising control over others.

Despite our expectation of some psychopathology in our creative subjects, in our theorizing we favored the view that "creative expression is an integral facet of the personality . . . the highest and most distinctive manifestation of it" (Gough, 1964, pp. 5–6). Accordingly we assumed that creative persons would reveal a favorable profile of traits on the California Psychological Inventory (Gough, 1957*a*), an instrument designed to tap and to meaasure the more positive aspects of personality. Across samples, they tended to do just that.

Our hypothesis that creativeness is more an expression of health than of disease, a manifestation of the person at his best, receives some support in our study of architects from our finding that multiple regression equations limited to three scales from each of seven personality inventories yielded significant cross-validated correlations with ratings of creativity for inventories measuring the more favorable aspects of personality but not for the MMPI which measures psychopathology. Specific cross-validated coefficients were as follows: SVIB, .55; CPI, .47; MBTI, .42; FIRO-B, .41; ACL, .38; Study of Values, .38; and MMPI, .20[6] (Hall and MacKinnon, 1969).

We assumed that the staff's perceptions of the more creative subjects would differ from its perceptions of those less creative. Three techniques for recording staff impressions of our subjects were employed: the Adjective Check List (Gough & Heilbrun, 1965), the Q-sort method (Block, 1961), and trait rating. As predicted, creative persons were seen as quite different from relatively uncreative persons (e.g., Barron, 1965; MacKinnon, 1967).

In general and across samples the more creative persons were seen as ingenious, imaginative, courageous, original, artistic, clear-thinking, insightful, interests wide, versatile, intelligent, individualistic, preoccupied, complicated. Adjectives more often used to describe the less creative persons were appreciative, considerate, conventional, obliging, sympathetic, lazy, easygoing, shy, dull, inhibited, weak.

A similar picture of creative persons is seen in the staff's composite Q-sort description of them. In three samples, for example, the following items received average Q-sort values of either 9 or 8 on a 9-point scale:

Thinks and associates to ideas in unusual ways; has unconventional thought processes.
Is an interesting, arresting person.
Genuinely values intellectual and cognitive matters.
Appears to have a high degree of intellectual capacity.

In addition, there were of course differences in placement of Q-items for the several samples, most of which make good sense (Barron, 1965).

Attributes which we assumed would, in general, bear some relation to creativity can be gleaned from an examination of the traits which we undertook to rate for each subject after the assessment weekend and without knowledge, it goes without saying, of his creativeness as judged by the experts. There was some slight variation in the lists of traits rated for each sample, but the one used with creative architects is typical. The trait ratings significantly correlated with rated creativity were: originality .61, aesthetic sensitivity .53, sense of destiny .53, ideational responsiveness .45, cognitive flexibility .44, inquiringness as a habit of mind .44, independence .44, sense of personal identity .43, intellectual competence .40, cathexis of intellectual activity .38, critical judgment .37, social acuity .31.[7] Trait ratings not significantly related to the criterion in this sample were: dominance .28, behavioral output .28, breadth of interests .28, likability .22, personal soundness .17, impulsivity .17, responsibility .13, warmth .07, masculinity −.10, and rigidity −.22 (MacKinnon, 1967).

We also assumed that creative persons would see themselves both as individuals and as professionals in a manner different from those of less creative talent, and sought to test this hypothesis with the ACL, with a specially developed Q-sort deck of statements describing talents, skills, interests, values, modes of working, work habits, and so on, which subjects could sort to describe themselves in their professional roles (Gough and Woodworth, 1960), and with life-history and professional field interviews. The ACL and the professional Q-sort deck can be used to describe oneself as one is or as one would wish ideally to be, as a person and as a professional worker. Differences in self-imagery between creative persons and persons of lesser creativity have been found and reported in almost all of the IPAR studies (e.g., MacKinnon, 1963).

Beyond the generality of traits possessed in common by those who are creative, we assumed that stylistic, typological, and sex differences would also be found among creative persons. Gough and Woodworth, for example, hypothesized that stylistic differences as well as those of competence would be found among practitioners in any field of creative endeavor. For their study of research scientists they prepared, in collaboration with consultants in physics and engineering, a research scientist Q-sort deck consisting of 56 short statements describing aspects of scientific work and modes of approach to research which their subjects sorted to describe themselves as scientists.[8] In this study eight different types of researcher were identified and labeled: (1) methodologist, (2) initiator, (3) zealot, (4) artificer, (5) diagnostician, (6) esthetician, (7) independent, and (8) scholar. The types are here ranked according to their mean score on the criterion: the scientist's creativeness and general competence as an industrial researcher as ranked by his supervisors and peers. One might wonder, however, what the rank order of judged creativeness of these types might have been had these scientists been working in an academic setting and had the criterion measures been collected there.

Reference has already been made to the relevance of Freudian theory and of Jung's theory and typology to differences in creative functioning. It seemed likely that a congruence in personality traits between subjects differing in the level of their creativeness and Rank's (1945) typology of the average or normal man, the conflicted or neurotic person, and the artist or man of will and deed would exist. Such congruence has been found for architects (MacKinnon, 1965), for college women (Helson, 1968b), for mathematicians (Helson and Crutchfield, 1970a), and for writers of fantasy for children (Helson; 1973a, 1973b).

As for sex differences in creativity, we had noted in our proposal to the Carnegie Corporation that a problem of special interest arises from the seldom disputed fact that far fewer women than men attain distinction for their originality in the arts, sciences, and business enterprises. Whether this difference is due largely to social and cultural factors, to differences in role-expectations and role-possibilities, or to more basic psychological and biological differences is a problem on which we would hope to shed some light by embarking for the first time upon a program of research that would study women as thoroughly with the multiform techniques of assessment as men have been studied.

In the early stages of her study of creativity in women, Helson (1961, 1965, 1966a, 1966b, 1967a, 1968a) was looking for a way to investigate whether the creative process was different in men and women. She came upon an essay by Erich Neumann (1954) in which he gave a phenomenological description of two types of consciousness which he called patriarchal and matriarchal. Although the conceptualization of these types was much influenced by Neumann's studies of the development of consciousness in patriarchal and matriarchal cultures over the course of human history, he also noted that they were analogous to male and female procreative roles. Patriarchal consciousness he described as purposeful, assertive, objective, and analytical, concerned with mechanical or logical causation. In matriarchal consciousness the psyche is filled with an emotional content over which it "broods" until an organic growth is "realized." It reflects unconscious processes, sums them up, and guides itself by them. It is more interested in the meaningful than in facts or dates, and is oriented toward organic growth.

Helson (1967b) embodied some of Neumann's ideas in her adaptation of the research scientist Q-sort deck of Gough and Woodworth for a study of research style in some 90 men and women mathematicians. Her first finding was that there was a significant association between creativity and "sex-appropriateness" of creative style. In other words, creative male mathematicians tended to describe their approach to research as purposive, assertive, analytical, etc.; creative women mathematicians described their approach in terms of emotional brooding, reception of ideas from the unconscious, etc.; and the less creative men and women mathematicians each tended, less sharply, in the opposite direction.

Subsequent studies have helped to extend, qualify, and clarify what is involved in this intriguing but complex pattern (Helson, 1968b). For example, Neumann was careful to distinguish patriarchal and matriarchal from male and female. He thought that there was a special relationship between the matriarchal and the creative, but that among the creative male geniuses of history, one could identify both patriarchal and matriarchal types. Helson and Crutchfield (1970a, 1970b) studied research style among creative mathematicians, all of whom were male. A cluster analysis produced six clusters, several of which seemed to describe aspects of the patriarchal and matriarchal syndromes. They then identified types of professional style, in which patriarchal and matriarchal features were prominent, and went on to show that the types were related to personality characteristics, descriptions of parents, and to various features of home background.

In a study of literary fantasy, Helson (1970; 1973*a*; 1973*b*) has adduced evidence that the creative product reflects the motive-pattern that produced it, and that three main types of fantasy—heroic, tender, and comic—correspond to what Neumann would call the patriarchal, matriarchal, and "early masculine" types of consciousness.

Having accumulated a considerable body of data on the characteristics of creative persons we have sought increasingly to relate these data to major theories of personality. Several examples of this interest have already been mentioned. One was the paper by MacKinnon (1965) in which he showed how findings from the study of architects gave a good fit to Rank's theory of the adjusted, conflicted, and creative types, or stages, in man's relationship to society. Others are the recent papers by Helson (1973*a*, 1973*b*) who showed how the Rankian stages may be integrated with stages in the development of the relation between the ego and the unconscious as described by Jung.

THE CREATIVE SITUATION

In considering the creative situation, the problem is to discover those characteristics of the life circumstances and the social and cultural and work milieu which facilitate or inhibit the appearance of creative thought and action.

To speak of a creative situation is to imply that creativity is not a fixed trait of personality but something that changes over time, waxing and waning, being facilitated by some life circumstances and situations and inhibited by others. Although such an assertion would be accepted by almost everyone, much less agreement can be found for statements which specify the types of situation or life circumstance or conditions of work that facilitate or inhibit creativity. Such disagreement merely underscores the continuing need, despite a considerable body of research findings, for research to determine what kinds of situations contribute most significantly to the encouragement of what kinds of creativity in what types of individuals at what periods in his life. The problem almost certainly has to be phrased in this manner, for it is not likely that all persons will find the same situation equally conducive to creative effort, nor that what is best for them at one age will be equally facilitative at another time.

In the personal history and professional field interviews conducted with our subjects, we have inquired about their early experiences in the home, in school, and in the community, about those persons who nurtured their interests and shaped eventually their professional identities; and we have explored as thoroughly as we could the conditions of work carried out alone and with others which, on the one hand, have hampered, and on the other hand, have facilitated their creative efforts.

Each question asked in our interviews implicitly stated an hypothesis concerning the effects of life history events and current circumstances in facilitating or inhibiting creative potential.

Despite wide diversity, the biographies of our creative subjects revealed several recurrent themes: an early development of interest in and sensitive awareness of their inner experience, and of their ideational, imaginal, and symbolic processes, such introversion of interest often stemming from an unhappiness or loneliness in childhood due to sickness, a lack of siblings or companions, a natural shyness, etc.; the possession of special skills and abilities which the child enjoyed exercising and the expression of which was encouraged and rewarded by one parent or the other or some other adult; aesthetic and intellectual interests of one or both parents similar to those of the child; an unusual freedom for the child in making his own decisions and exploring his universe whether granted by the parents or asserted and demanded by the child—in other words, an early and unusual amount of independence both in thought and action; a lack of intense closeness between parent and child so that neither overdependence was demanded nor a feeling of rejection experienced—in short, a kind of parent-child relationship that had a liberating effect on the child; a lack of anxious concern for the child on the part of the parents; the presence of effective adults of both sexes, not necessarily the father or the mother, with whom identification could be made and who offered effective models for the development of ego-ideals; frequent moving during the early years, often from abroad to this country, providing both personal and cultural enrichment for the child; and freedom from pressure to establish prematurely one's professional identity.

Many of these circumstances and interpersonal experiences would have been predicted to be found in the life histories of creative persons because of their congruence with the factors which according to Rank's (1945) theory make for the realization of creative potential and individuality, according to Erikson's (1950) theory are crucial for fullest development of ego, and according to White's (1959) theory sustain and nurture the fullest development of competence. It must be noted, however, that such favorable early life histories have not been found for all creative subjects or for all of our creative samples. More pathology of early life circumstances appears in the life histories of creative writers than in the biographies of creative architects, mathematicians, and research scientists. In Helson's (1973a) study of writers of fantasies for children, for example, a relationship between certain types of childhood pathologies and types of literary genre was discovered for male authors: the heroic and tender patterns appear to have originated in compensation for father-deprivation and mother-deprivation respectively; the comic pattern appears to reflect conflict between admiration for the father and reluctance to take his role.

In general, there was a continuity of traits and interests and personality structure in the life histories of creative subjects (Brooks, 1963). But there were discontinuities, too (Parloff et al., 1968).

In our research proposal to the Carnegie Corporation we also noted that the role of interpersonal and social relations in facilitating and inhibiting creativity could also be studied under experimentally controlled conditions. An assessment community offers an ideal setting for such investigations. Subjects who have been thoroughly studied by a multiplicity of assessment techniques can be assigned to groups of known composition, with subsequent observation of the effects of variation in interpersonal relationships and group structures upon the creativity both of individuals in the groups and of the groups *qua* groups in solving problems either undertaken by them or assigned to them. One hypothesis that might thus be tested is that the formal properties of productive groups will match in major respects the formal properties of personality structure of creative persons. A first small step in the direction of investigating some of these problems was made by Bouchard (1966) in his doctoral research: "Personality, Problem-Solving Procedure, and Performance in Small Groups," a line of investigation which he has continued to pursue since leaving IPAR.

In planning our research we noted that in the case of subjects who can be studied over considerable periods of time, it should be possible to relate fluctuations in creativity to changing life conditions. Such data would not be obtained entirely through the medium of interviews but also through observation of the subjects in the natural milieu of their daily lives, with special reference to the conditions under which they study or work. There would be the possibility also of investigating through experimental manipulations the extent to which individuals who have not previously been distinguished by their creativity can be trained to be more creative and original.

Two projects in the domain of nurturing creativity have been the Productive Thinking Project developed by Crutchfield (1969) and his associates (Covington, Crutchfield, Davies, and Olton, 1972), and Barron's (1972) program of basic research in aesthetic education.

Building upon his insights into creative persons as they revealed themselves in the IPAR studies and upon his own earlier analysis of the creative process, Crutchfield (1961, 1969) conceptualized four sets of skills involved in productive thinking: *problem discovery and formulation, organizing and processing of problem information, idea generation,* and *evaluation of ideas.* In addition to these sets of skills, Crutchfield conceptualized a metaskill or *master thinking skill* which makes possible the effective coordination, integration, and utilization of the several specific skills. Then, in cooperation with his associates, he constructed an educational program to nurture the development and use of these skills in creative thinking (Covington et al, 1972). *The Productive Thinking Program,* consisting of sixteen booklets of self-instructional lessons, plus supplementary exercises, is designed for fifth- and sixth-grade children. In practice it has proved highly effective. Trained children, as compared with matched controls, on subsequent testing "excel in being sensitive to puzzling facts, in asking relevant information-seeking questions, in generating ideas of high quality, in seeing problems in new ways, in planning a systematic attack on problems, in evaluating ideas, and in achieving actual solutions to problems" (Crutchfield, 1969, p. 68). And these effects have been shown to be long lasting.

Building upon his early interest in aesthetic sensitivity and his demonstration of its relation to creativity, Barron initiated in 1968 a multifaceted basic research program in aesthetic education. Questions around which the research was organized were: "(1) the interrelationships among such factors as esthetic sensitivity, esthetic judgment, acuity of visual perception, esthetic literacy, valuation of the esthetic, and talent for esthetic expression; (2) developmental changes in these capacities with age and educational experience; (3) sex differences and age-sex interactions in the development and use of these capacities; (4) influence of educational background and social class upon them; (5) the role of personality traits and motives in shaping esthetic creativeness and responsiveness" (Barron, 1967, p. 1). The results of the research have been presented in several papers but most importantly in the book, *Artists in the Making* (Barron, et al., 1972).

If IPAR's theoretical assumptions about the nature of the creative product, the creative process, the creative person, and the creative situation, which have guided us in our researches, appear rather modest they nevertheless express an attitude toward research in personality and creativity which has shaped our work over the past quarter century. The restraint in developing elaborate theories which I urged twenty years ago is, I believe, still appropriate in 1973 as we pursue our efforts to conceptualize and to investigate the multifaceted phenomenon that we call creativity.

To conclude, let me repeat what I have said before about our progress in studying personality:

> I am concerned lest we move too rapidly in personality research from the practical, empirical, and intuitive, to the abstract, rigorous, and formal, with the risk, to which Lewin (1940) called our attention, of building logical superhighways which turn out to be dead ends leading nowhere.
>
> We need hunches and hypotheses concerning the significant phenomenal variables of personality and inferences from behavior to the underlying dynamics of the person. I propose that it is better in personality research today to settle for something less than full-blown theoretical models, namely hunches and working hypotheses. I would urge that we set lower goals and expend as much energy in pursuing them as is now spent, in my opinion, prematurely and fruitlessly in the pursuit of goals too fanciful for the present state of personality research.

But lest I am thought to be championing a raw empiricism I would like to remind you that *ledge,* the second element in the word *knowledge* means sport. Knowledge is the result of playing with what we know, that is, with our facts. A knowledgeable person in science is not, as we are often wont to think, merely one who has an accumulation of facts, but rather one who has the capacity to have sport with what he knows, giving creative rein to his fancy in changing his world of phenomenal appearances into a world of scientific constructs. [MacKinnon, 1953, p. 145]

Notes

1. These psychologists, then or later at the University of California, Berkeley, who took the lead in establishing the Institute were Nevitt Sanford, Edward C. Tolman, Robert C. Tryon, and Donald W. MacKinnon.

2. Staff members who contributed to the formulation of these hypotheses were Frank Barron, Richard S. Crutchfield, Erik H. Erikson, Harrison G. Gough, Robert E. Harris, Donald W. MacKinnon, Nevitt Sanford, and Ronald Taft. The early research hypotheses of IPAR were recorded in two IPAR memoranda, Gough (1949) and Barron (1950) .

3. The development of my own conceptualization of creativity and my ideas about how various aspects of it can be brought under empirical study have been so intertwined and shaped by my colleagues' thinking that any report of my own work has, at the same time, to be a review of the accomplishments of the entire staff of the Institute of Personality Assessment and Research on the Berkeley campus of the University of California.

4. The correlates of all-around personal soundness will not be reviewed here. The interested reader can find them reported in Barron (1954) , and the findings with regard to originality will be reported only in so far as they stimulated IPAR's interest in the study of creativity and influenced our later thinking about it.

5. This was an earlier version (see Gough, 1950) of the (now published) Adjective Check List (Gough and Heilbrun, 1965).

6. For $N = 62$, $r_{p.05} = .25$; $r_{p.01} = .32$.

7. For $N = 40$, $r_{p.05} = .31$; $r_{p.01} = .41$.

8. The professional Q-deck first developed by Gough and Woodworth (1960) in their study of research scientists in industry was subsequently modified for use with the other creative samples studied at IPAR.

References

Allport, G. W. *Personality: A psychological interpretation.* New York: Holt, 1937.

Allport, G. W., Vernon, P. E., and Lindzey, G. *Study of values: Manual of directions.* Rev. ed. Boston: Houghton Mifflin, 1951.

Barron, F. Hypotheses of the Institute of Personality Assessment and Research. *IPAR Memorandum.* Berkeley: University of California Institute of Personality Assessment and Research, 1950.

Barron, F. Personality style and perceptual choice. *Journal of Personality,* 1952, *20,* 385–401.

Barron, F. An ego-strength scale which predicts response to psychotherapy. *Journal of Consulting Psychology,* 1953, *17,* 327–333. (a)

Barron, F. Some personality correlates of independence of judgment. *Journal of Personality,* 1953, *21,* 287–297. (b)

Barron, F. Personal soundness in university graduate students: An experimental study of young men in the sciences and professions. *No. 1 University of Cali-*

fornia Publications Personality Assessment and Research. Berkeley: University of California Press, 1954.

Barron, F. The disposition toward originality. *Journal of Abnormal and Social Psychology,* 1955, *51,* 478–485.

Barron, F. Originality in relation to personality and intellect. *Journal of Personality,* 1957, *24,* 730–742.

Barron, F. Creative vision and expression in writing and painting. In *Proceedings of the Conference on "The Creative Person,"* presented October 13–17, 1961, University of California Alumni Center, Lake Tahoe, California. Pp. II–1 to II–19. Berkeley: University of California, University Extension.

Barron, F. The creative writer. *California Monthly,* 1962, *72,* 11–14, 38–39.

Barron, F. Diffusion, integration, and the enduring attention in the creative process. In R. W. White (Ed.), *The study of lives: Essays on personality in honor of Henry A. Murray,* pp. 234–248. New York: Atherton Press, 1963.

Barron, F. The psychology of creativity. In *New directions in psychology II,* pp. 1–134. New York: Holt, Rinehart & Winston, 1965.

Barron, F. Basic research in esthetic education. Research proposal submitted to U.S. Office of Education Bureau of Research by the Institute of Personality Assessment and Research, University of California, Berkeley, 1967.

Barron, F. *Creative person and creative process.* New York: Holt, Rinehart & Winston, 1969.

Barron, F., et al. *Artists in the making.* New York: Seminar Press, 1972.

Barron, F., and Welsh, G. S. Artistic perception as a factor in personality style: Its measurement by a figure preference test. *Journal of Psychology,* 1952, *33,* 199–203.

Block, J. *The Q-sort method in personality assessment and psychiatric research.* Springfield, Ill.: Charles C. Thomas, 1961.

Bouchard, T. J., Jr. Personality, problem solving procedure, and performance in small groups. Unpublished doctoral dissertation, University of California, Berkeley, 1966.

Brooks, J. B. The behavioral significance of childhood experiences that are reported in life history interviews. Unpublished doctoral dissertation, University of California, Berkeley, 1963.

Covington, M. V., Crutchfield, R. S., Davies, L. B., and Olton, R. M. *The Productive Thinking Program: A course in learning to think.* Columbus, Ohio: Charles E. Merrill, 1972.

Crutchfield, R. S. Assessment of persons through a quasi group-interaction technique. *Journal of Abnormal and Social Psychology,* 1951, *46,* 577–588.

Crutchfield, R. S. Conformity and character. *American Psychologist,* 1955, *10,* 191–198.

Crutchfield, R. S. The creative process. In *Proceedings of the Conference on "The Creative Person,"* presented October 13–17, 1961, University of California Alumni Center, Lake Tahoe, California. Pp. VI–1 to VI–16. Berkeley: University of California, University Extension.

Crutchfield, R. S. Nurturing the cognitive skills of productive thinking. In L. J. Ruben (Ed.), *Life skills in school and society,* pp. 53–71. Washington, D.C.: National Education Association, Association for Supervision and Curriculum Development, 1969.

Erikson, E. *Childhood and society.* New York: W. W. Norton, 1950.

Gough, H. G. Research hypotheses for the IPAR assessment of university graduate students. *IPAR Memorandum,* Berkeley: University of California Institute of Personality Assessment and Research, 1949.

Gough, H. G. Predicting success in graduate training: A progress report. *IPAR Research Bulletin*. Berkeley: University of California Institute of Personality Assessment and Research, 1950.

Gough, H. G. Outline of a proposed chapter: Originality in graduate students. *IPAR Memorandum*. Berkeley: University of California Institute of Personality Assessment and Research, 1952.

Gough, H. G. Some theoretical problems in the construction of practical devices for the early identification of high level talent. Paper read before Social Science Research Council Conference on "Non-intellectual determinants of achievement," April 17, 1953, Princeton, New Jersey. (Mimeo)

Gough, H. G. Some general areas of assessment which should be considered in the study of any group. Consultant's memorandum submitted to the Educational Testing Service, Princeton, New Jersey, 1954. (Mimeo)

Gough, H. G. *Differential Reaction Schedule*. Berkeley: University of California Institute of Personality Assessment and Research, 1955.

Gough, H. G. *California Psychological Inventory manual*. Palo Alto, Calif.: Consulting Psychologists Press, 1957. (*a*)

Gough, H. G. Imagination—undeveloped resource. *Proceedings, First Conference on Research Developments in Personnel Management*, pp. 4–10. Los Angeles: University of California, Institute of Industrial Relations, 1957. (*b*)

Gough, H. G. Researchers' summary data for the Differential Reaction Schedule. *IPAR Memorandum*. Berkeley: University of California Institute of Personality Assessment and Research, 1957. (*c*)

Gough, H. G. Identifying the creative man. *The Journal of Value Engineering*, 1964, *2*, 5–12.

Gough, H. G., and Heilbrun, A. B., Jr. *The Adjective Check List manual*. Palo Alto, Calif.: Consulting Psychologists Press, 1965.

Gough, H. G., and Woodworth, D. G. Stylistic variations among professional research scientists. *Journal of Psychology*, 1960, *49*, 87–98.

Guilford, J. P. Creativity. *American Psychologist*, 1950, *14*, 469–479.

Hall, W. B., and MacKinnon, D. W. Personality inventory correlates of creativity among architects. *Journal of Applied Psychology*, 1969, *53*, 322–326.

Hathaway, S. R., and McKinley, J. C. *Minnesota Multiphasic Personality Inventory*. Minneapolis, Minn.: University of Minnesota Press, 1943.

Helson, R. Creativity, sex and mathematics. In *Report of Proceedings for Conference on "The Creative Person."* Berkeley: University of California, University Extension, 1961.

Helson, R. Childhood interest clusters related to creativity in women. *Journal of Consulting Psychology*, 1965, *29*, 352–361.

Helson, R. Narrowness in creative women. *Psychological Reports*, 1966, *19*, 618. (*a*)

Helson, R. Personality of women with imaginative and artistic interests: The role of masculinity, originality, and other characteristics in their creativity. *Journal of Personality*, 1966, *34*, 1–25. (*b*)

Helson, R. Personality characteristics and developmental history of creative college women. *Genetic Psychology Monographs*, 1967, *76*, 205–256. (*a*)

Helson, R. Sex differences in creative style. *Journal of Personality*, 1967, *35*, 214–233. (*b*)

Helson, R. Effects of sibling characteristics and parental values on creative interest and achievement. *Journal of Personality*, 1968, *36*, 589–607. (*a*)

Helson, R. Generality of sex differences in creative style. *Journal of Personality*, 1968, *36*, 33–48. (*b*)

Helson, R. Sex-specific patterns in creative literary fantasy. *Journal of Personality,* 1970, *38,* 344–363.

Helson, R. The heroic, the comic, and the tender: Patterns of literary fantasy and their authors. *Journal of Personality,* 1973, *41,* 163–184. (*a*)

Helson, R. Heroic and tender modes in women authors of fantasy. *Journal of Personality,* 1973, *41,* 492–512. (*b*)

Helson, R., and Crutchfield, R. S. Creative types in mathematics. *Journal of Personality,* 1970, *38,* 177–197. (*a*)

Helson, R., and Crutchfield, R. S. Mathematicians: The creative researcher and the average Ph.D. *Journal of Consulting and Clinical Psychology,* 1970, *34,* 250–257. (*b*)

IPAR Staff. Proposal for a study of creativity. Submitted to the Carnegie Corporation of New York. Berkeley: University of California Institute of Personality Assessment and Research, 1955.

Jung, C. G. *Psychological types.* New York: Harcourt, Brace, 1923.

Jung, C. G. *Two essays on analytical psychology.* New York: Dodd, Mead, 1928.

Kettner, N. W., Guilford, J. P., and Christensen, P. R. A factor-analytic study across the domains of reasoning, creativity, and evaluation. *Psychological Monographs,* 1959, *73*(9, Whole No. 479).

Lewin, K. Formalization and progress in psychology. *University of Iowa Studies in Child Welfare,* 1940, *16,* 9–42. No. 3.

MacKinnon, D. W. Fact and fancy in personality research. *American Psychologist,* 1953, *8,* 138–146.

MacKinnon, D. W. The nature and nurture of creative talent. *American Psychologist,* 1962, *17,* 484–495.

MacKinnon, D. W. Creativity and images of the self. In R. W. White (Ed.), *The study of lives: Essays on personality in honor of Henry A. Murray,* pp. 250–278. New York: Atherton Press, 1963.

MacKinnon, D. W. Personality and the realization of creative potential. *American Psychologist,* 1965, *20,* 273–281.

MacKinnon, D. W. Assessing creative persons. *Journal of Creative Behavior,* 1967, *1,* 291–304.

MacKinnon, D. W. Creativity: A multi-faceted phenomenon. In J. D. Roslansky (Ed.), *Creativity,* pp. 17–32. Amsterdam/London: North-Holland Publishing Co., 1970.

MacKinnon, D. W. Creativity and transliminal experience. *Journal of Creative Behavior,* 1971, *5,* 227–241.

MacKinnon, D. W., Crutchfield, R. S., Barron, F., Block, J., Gough, H. G., and Harris, R. E. An assessment study of Air Force officers, Part I: Design of the study and description of the variables. Lackland Air Force Base, Texas: Wright Air Developmental Center, Personnel Laboratory, April, 1958. *Technical Report* WADC-TR-58-91 (I), ASTIA Document No. AD 151 040.

MacKinnon, D. W., and Hall, W. B. Intelligence and creativity. In Colloquium 17: The measurement of creativity. *Proceedings, XVIIth International Congress, International Association of Applied Psychology.* Brussels: EDITEST, 1972.

Mendelsohn, G. A., and Griswold, B. B. Differential use of incidental stimuli in problem solving as a function of creativity. *Journal of Abnormal and Social Psychology,* 1964, *68,* 431–436.

Mendelsohn, G. A., and Griswold, B. B. Assessed creative potential, vocabulary level, and sex as predictors of the use of incidental cues in verbal problem solving. *Journal of Personality and Social Psychology,* 1966, *4,* 423–431.

Mendelsohn, G. A., and Griswold, B. B. Anxiety and repression as predictors of the use of incidental cues in problem solving. *Journal of Abnormal and Social Psychology*, 1967, *6*, 353–359.

Mendelsohn, G. A., and Lindholm, E. P. Individual differences and the role of attention in the use of cues in verbal problem solving. *Journal of Personality*, 1972, *40*, 226–241.

Murray, H. A., et al. *Explorations in personality*. New York: Oxford University Press, 1938.

Myers, I. B. *Manual (1962): The Myers-Briggs Type Indicator*. Princeton, N.J.: Educational Testing Service, 1962.

Neumann, E. On the moon and matriarchal consciousness, *Spring*, 1954. (Analytical Psychology Club of New York).

OSS Assessment Staff. *Assessment of men*. New York: Rinehart, 1948.

Parloff, M. B., Datta, L., Kleman, M., and Handlon, J. H. Personality characteristics which differentiate creative male adolescents and adults. *Journal of Personality*, 1968, *36*, 528–552.

Rank, O. *Will therapy and truth and reality*. (Trans. by J. Taft). New York: Knopf, 1945.

Sanford, N. Personality: Its place in psychology. In S. Koch (Ed.), *Psychology: A study of science*. Vol. V. New York: McGraw-Hill, 1963.

Schimek, J. G. Creative originality: Its evaluation by use of free-expression tests. Unpublished doctoral dissertation, University of California, Berkeley, 1954.

Schutz, W. C. *FIRO: A three-dimensional theory of interpersonal behavior*. New York: Rinehart, 1958.

Spranger, E. *Types of men*. (Trans. by Paul J. W. Pigors.) Halle (Saale), Germany: Max Wiemeyer, 1928.

Strong, E. K., Jr. *The vocational interests of men and women*. Stanford, Calif.: Stanford University Press, 1943.

White, R. W. Motivation reconsidered: The concept of competence. *Psychological Review*, 1959, *66*, 297–333.

Wotton, H. *The elements of architecture*. London: John Bill, 1624.

4. From Problem Solving to Problem Finding

J. W. Getzels and M. Csikszentmihalyi

How DID WE COME to study the creativity of *problems* when we began by studying the creativity of *solutions?* How did we reach the conclusion that the creative act involves problem finding as much as it does problem solving (if the two processes can be separated at all), and to hold the hypothesis that creative problems may be as fruitful a subject of study as creative solutions?

We did not come to these considerations, which were vastly surprising to us, by following the prevailing fashion in research, or the suggestions contained in the prevailing literature. Quite the contrary. The emphasis in the literature and in research pointed the other way. There was an abundance of conceptual and empirical work on *problem solving*—literally a dozen theoretical books and hundreds of experimental articles—but virtually no systematic work on *problem finding*, the posing and formulating of problems.

Nor did we get to these considerations through any common sense notions of the relative importance of skill in problem finding and problem solving. Indeed, at first the very notion of problem finding as a human skill sounds absurd. Does not human skill lie in avoiding problems rather than in finding problems, or, if the problems are unavoidable, in solving them? In fact, need one *find* problems? Is not the world already teeming with dilemmas and problems wherever one turns—at home and in business, in economics and in technology, in the arts and in the sciences?

The world is of course teeming with dilemmas. But problematic situations do not present themselves automatically as *problems* capable of solution, to say nothing of *creative* solution. They must be formulated in creative ways if they are to be moved to creative solutions. As Einstein put the issue with regard to science, "The formulation of a problem is often more essential than its solution, which may be merely a matter of mathematical or experimental skill. To raise new questions, new possibilities, to regard old problems from a new angle, requires creative imagination and marks real advance in science" (Einstein and Infeld, 1938, p. 92). And, we would maintain, in art, society, education, and all other aspects of behavior no less than in science. But we are somewhat ahead of the account of how we came to be studying creativity as a problem-finding process, when we had begun by studying creativity as a problem-solving process, which was surely the more natural thing to do.

Changing Conceptions of the Human Being and of Intellect

Two conceptual strands are intertwined in the development of our ideas regarding creativity. One consists of the historical changes affecting conceptions of the human being. The other includes changes in the conceptions of human intellect. The outcome of our empirical and theoretical work in creativity must be placed in the context of these changes even at the risk of delaying the report of what we actually did.

CHANGING CONCEPTIONS OF THE HUMAN BEING

Consider briefly two familiar models of what human beings are like. A half century ago the prevalent model of the human being was a cognitively empty organism responding more or less randomly to stimulation, and connecting specific responses to specific stimuli through the effect of pleasure or pain. The organism would do nothing to learn or think if it were not forced into such activity by primary drives like hunger and thirst, or by externally applied motives like reward and punishment. This description is of course the oversimplification necessary for so brief a sketch. But the essential point regarding this conception of the human being remains: an ideationally empty and cognitively passive organism reacting more or less blindly to stimuli through the operation of rewards and punishments.

Competing with this formulation was an apparently dissimilar and more complex model. According to the latter the first conception did not account for all observed behavior, or for that matter, not even the more significant aspects of human behavior. The individual did not experience his world as discrete stimuli but rather in configurations, and far from being an empty organism psychologically, the human being was a cauldron of needs, values, conflicts, cognitive styles, repressions, and other conscious, subconscious, and unconscious forces which determined his thought and behavior.

Although the two conceptions were dissimilar in manifest respects, there was also a crucial and perhaps more important latent similarity between them. Both conceptions rested on the same underlying *paradigm,* to use

Kuhn's term: they were founded on a combination of the homeostatic model of self-maintenance and the drive theory of behavior.

Briefly stated, according to this paradigm the optimum state of the organism is one of rest, and the organism is said to act in such a way as always to return to the optimum state of rest and equilibrium. Hunger produces tensions driving the organism to seek food, and it ceases to seek food when it has eaten; conflict produces tensions driving the organism to seek relief, and it ceases to seek relief when the conflict is settled; lack of closure produces tensions driving the organism to seek closure, and the organism ceases to seek closure when the gap is filled. A problem produces tensions driving the organism to think, and it ceases to think when the problem is resolved.

This homeostatic tension-reduction conception of the human being led to the view that the individual is essentially passive, accommodative, or at most only reactive. He behaves or thinks in response to a presented stimulus, a felt drive, an experienced conflict, an encountered problem, and then he acts primarily in such way as to return to the presumed natural state of balanced rest. The individual himself will not seek out stimuli, search for conflicts, or discover problems for solution on his own initiative.

In due course, this paradigm of the human being was challenged, at least as it applied to cognitive processes. Learning, thinking, problem solving, curiosity may indeed seem means for reducing certain drives, decreasing certain tensions; but that is not the only way to see them, and perhaps not even the primary way. They may also be seen as ends in themselves. The organism can act to increase as well as to decrease tension and stimulation. Problems—intellectual problems as well as others—which had formerly been looked upon as noxious events to be avoided could be looked upon from the vantage point of this altered paradigm of the human being, as pleasurable events to be sought after.

Once pointed to, the evidence for the altered view was available in so many sources—animal as well as human—that in retrospect it is surprising the view was not more firmly established sooner. As Robert White (1959) argued, one of the most obvious features of animal behavior is the tendency to explore the environment, and curiosity has done in many a cat. Harry Harlow (1954) showed experimentally that monkeys who were viscerogenically sated—that is, they were not hungry, thirsty or otherwise driven by any recognizable drive or lack—learned to unassemble a puzzle for no other apparent reason than the "privilege of unassembling it." The behavior of the animals reduced no recognizable primary drive, provided for no identifiable lack, decreased no observable tension or stimulation; far from trying to avoid problems and reduce tension or stimulation, the animals seemed to seek stimulation through dealing with the problems.

With respect to human beings, it was increasingly argued that the central factor in their development was not the satisfaction of hunger or thirst or some other primary drive, but effective interaction with the environment. As White (1959) observed, a child whose bodily needs have all been satisfied does not, as the homeostatic model of the organism and the drive-reduction theory of behavior would suggest, remain at rest. On the contrary, it is just then that the child's play and exploration are most active and creative. Later in life, there are such common human activities as reading mystery stories, doing crossword puzzles, skin-diving, exploring caves, climbing mountains, traveling to strange places, all of which provide pleasure by raising the level of stimulation rather than by reducing it. Such activities are not readily explicable by the typical concepts of equilibrium models of behavior, as Hebb and Thompson (1954) pointed out. Moreover, carefully controlled experiments have demonstrated that the human being must have a varied sensory input or stimulation if he is to function normally. When he is deprived of such experiences, both his physical and intellectual processes deteriorate (Bexton, Heron, and Scott, 1954).

Most important of all in the present context, a conspicuous portion of human behavior is devoted to what can be classified only as art, science, play, or just "curiosity"—activities which by no stretch of the imagination can be said to contribute to bodily maintenance through the reduction of primary drives or attaining states of rest (Berlyne, 1966). Such behavior is not accommodative or reactive to problems in the usual sense. Rather, problems seem to be sought out because the person needs to deal with what is novel, to exercise initiative, to express his unique character—in a word, to create.

The paradigm of behavior founded in mechanical models of homeostasis neglected a crucial and readily observed characteristic of the human being: his disposition to seek pleasure through encountering problems, raising his level of stimulation, asserting his individuality, acting upon the environment rather than merely reacting to it. To be sure, there are the viscerogenic drives such as hunger and thirst to be satisfied by satiation and a return to equilibrium, but the new model called our attention to needs to be gratified by stimulation—needs for excitement, novelty, and the opportunity to deal with the problematic. In short, from the point of view of the altered paradigm the human being is not only a *stimulus-reducing* or *problem-solving* organism but also a *stimulus-seeking* or *problem-finding* organism (Getzels, 1964; Mackworth, 1965).

CHANGING CONCEPTIONS OF INTELLECT

One strand in the development of our ideas regarding creativity, then, was the changed view of the human being, from only a stimulus-reducing or problem-solving organism, to a stimulus-seeking or problem-finding organism. The second strand closely intertwined with the first was a change in the conception of human intellect, and more specifically the altered view of the relation between intelligence as reflected in the pervasive IQ metric and other processes of intellectual behavior.

The Dominance of Intelligence. Perhaps the greatest obstacle to the emergence of creativity as an autonomous focus of study, one which is still with us albeit in attenuated form, was the historical status of creativity in the shadow of the reigning concept of intelligence, buttressed by the manifest success of intelligence testing. During the first half-century, it was generally held that creativity presented no special issue since the concept of intelligence was sufficient to explain any aspects of mental functioning, and the intelligence test could measure anything that passed through the mind. This was the view with which nearly all of us grew up, not only professionally but implicitly from the day we took the first IQ test.

There is no question that the IQ metric, whatever the current controversies surrounding it, is one of the most productive inventions to come from psychological science. Yet two questions could be raised, at least with the wisdom of hindsight. Was the tacit identification of creative thinking with IQ the result of an explicit theoretical position? And was the identification based on empirical observation? The answer to both questions appears to be negative. It was rather the result of a coincidence of factors which makes the development of a field or discipline at once unpredictable, fascinating, and often frustrating.

As a matter of fact, that the sort of mental functioning which produces works of the highest level of originality might be different from the one needed to resolve set problems had been recognized for a long time and was never really forgotten. Both before and after the invention of the IQ metric, the distinction between purely "rational" thinking and "creative" thinking served as a counterforce to the dominant thesis of monolithic intelligence. Writing two centuries ago, for example, Gerard (1774) noted: "A person . . . may possess reason to perfection, and yet be totally destitute of invention, originality, and genius" (p. 36)—a distinction which was preserved in the theoretical if not the empirical literature. Dewey (1917), Mead (1917), Knowlson (1920), Hirsch (1931), Patrick (1946), to mention only a few, held that creativity entailed a cognitive process not completely synonymous with the one ordinarily encompassed in the concept of intelligence. Through the years there were even sporadic research studies (e.g., Dearborn, 1898; Colvin, 1902; Chassell, 1916) suggesting the possibility of an empirically-founded discrimination. By 1922, when the intelligence test in its standard form was already being widely applied in all sorts of decisions from the education of children to the selection of soldiers and the placement of workers, Simpson could say in the prestigious *American Journal of Psychology:*

> Tests devised to ascertain either native intelligence or acquired knowledge are certainly valuable. [However] there are no elements in them to extract from the mind of the individual his powers of creative productivity and his tendencies toward originality. If his creative ability is expressed in many of these tests, the methods of scoring have failed to take it into consideration. It is evident that we

need tests designed to give us more direct and dependable information upon this essential element of progress—creative imagination. [Simpson, 1922, pp. 234–235]

Why then did it take so long to establish creativity on a relatively autonomous conceptual and empirical footing? And why did so much of the work in the field of creativity take the circuitous form it did?

We have already referred to one of the basic reasons, namely that any notion of an active, creative mind came into conflict with the stimulus-response orthodoxy. The concept of intelligence as instrumentalized in the prevailing tests accorded with the paradigm of the human being as essentially a stimulus-reducing or problem-solving organism. The intelligence test was measuring with apparent precision mental functioning through reactions to standard stimuli requiring subjects to respond to already formulated problems posed by the test. In contrast, those holding to the view that creativity was not synonymous with what intelligence tests measured were arguing that "thought is not a means of solving the problems of this world as they arise, but a great process of realization in which the world is forever transcended" (Mead, 1917, p. 196). The intelligence test became the bastion of the tough-minded empiricists in the new science, while the "creative mind" remained the subject for anecdotal discourse of Hegelian romantics, Bergsonian evolutionists, and tender-minded and scientifically suspect antibehaviorists.

There was also a practical reason for the dominance of intelligence: it was applicable to every person, while creativity, it was believed, was the prerogative of only the few. Intelligence and its measurement were readily integrated into the social system through the use of the IQ metric in educational, military, and commercial institutions. Creativity had only a small constituency and no market. At a deeper level, the elitist connotation of creativity as the characteristic of the rare genius contributed to excluding creativity from the mainstream of systematic psychological investigation.

Concurrent with these circumstances was another reason for the eclipse of creativity as a field of research: there were no creativity instruments to put beside the intelligence tests. The history of western science testifies to the crucial generative effect of a new tool or operational process in the conceptual development of a discipline; rigorous empirical research requires instrumental measurement and manipulation. It was one thing for writers to quote anecdotally the familiar passages from great genius positing that creative accomplishment is the result of mental processes quite distinct from ordinary problem solving; it was another thing to be able to *do* something with their formulations. The anecdotal accounts of genius did not provide a method for measuring and manipulating the phenomena to which they were pointing. It was not surprising that researchers turned to the issues of mental functioning about which they could *do* something. This led to studying intelligence, which could be measured and manipulated by reference to the objective touchstone provided by the IQ test—something that was not available for creativity.

The Emergence of Creativity. The conceptual and social conditions that precluded the emergence of creativity as an autonomous field of study changed by mid-century. In the affluent years following World War II, the United States appeared to be on the way to an economy of surplus rather than scarcity. If one may apply Maslow's hierarchy of needs, we were no longer confined to satisfying only the psychological and safety needs but could also look forward to satisfying the "need to know" and "aesthetic needs" (Maslow, 1954). In Maslow's terms, as the conditions of man free him from exclusive pressure to insure biological preservation—that is, to react to the self-maintenance problems thrust upon him by environment—discontent and restlessness develop to satisfy curiosity, to know, to explain, to understand, and more generally not only to react to the environment but to act creatively upon it.

At the same time, scientific discoveries were increasingly affecting every aspect of daily life—from the already visible beneficial effects of radium and penicillin, to the exhilarating prospect of space exploration, to the dread implications of atomic explosives. These developments conveyed a clear message: in the future, power may depend more on the creative use of mind than on the brute control of matter.

To put the circumstances another way, creative thought had proved itself able to redefine and extend the older notions of food, fuel, space, weaponry, material resources, and human potential. The term creative ceased to be the exclusive province of dissident artists, aesthete, romantics, academics, and pure scientists. It entered into the common parlance even of the hardheaded businessman. The Chicago telephone directory for 1930, for example, listed two businesses with names beginning with "Creative"; by 1950, the number increased to 11; by 1966 it jumped to 45; and in 1972, the directory lists 80. In 1957, when the Soviet Sputnik surprised the United States, creativity became a word to conjure with in the halls of Washington as well. For good or for ill, creativity was taking its place with intelligence in the social system.

Concomitantly, the mechanistic paradigm founded in the combination of the equilibrium or homeostatic model of self-maintenance and the drive or tension reduction theory of behavior was breaking down, and less mechanistic paradigms were taking its place. To put the shift in the sharpest and simplest terms, the Watsonian learning-theory model of a passive organism reacting to the environment was giving way to the Piagetian developmental-theory model of an active organism imposing itself upon the environment. The ideological boundaries between the behavioristic paradigm and the alternate cognitive paradigms were blurred; psychology was becoming a broader and more eclectic discipline. The soverign status of intelligence which had been defined, measured, and codified by two generations of investigators no longer loomed so large over the field of mental functioning. It became possible for other conceptions, and notably for creativity, to emerge out of the shadow of intelligence as foci of study in their own right. But two major obstacles remained: the lack of a clear conceptual distinction between creativity and intelligence, and the lack of an operational approach specific to creativity.

There are certain historic events which, though unrecognized at the time, mark paradigmatic changes and became landmarks in a field of study. Guilford's presidential address of 1950 to the American Psychological Association is such an event (Guilford, 1950). Not only was it an "official statement," but it pointed the way to removing the conceptual and operational obstacles at once. The concept of "divergent thinking" provided a dialectical foil to the reigning notion of intelligence, and the tests that he and his associates had developed provided a usable methodology within the altered conceptual framework.

An outburst of work on creativity followed. In the presidential address, Guilford had called attention to the fact that there had been fewer than two hundred psychological studies of creativity in the preceding quarter century. Within a decade, almost that number were appearing in a single year. Indeed, it has been estimated that the number of studies for the 18 months of 1965 and 1966 equaled that of the preceding five years, which in turn equaled that of the preceding 10 years, which in *its* turn equaled that of the preceding 100 years (Parnes and Brunelle, 1967). Creativity emerged as a field of study with a vengeance.

Divergent Thinking, Intelligence, and Creativity: A Study with Children

It was in this heady climate of conceptual, social, and instrumental change that the first author and a colleague, P. W. Jackson, jointly undertook a series of studies to explore the relationship between divergent thinking, intelligence, and creative performance (Getzels and Jackson, 1962). The focus of the investigation, which began at mid-century, was to examine two groups of adolescents attending a laboratory school. One included students at the top 20 percent in IQ compared with the same-age peers, but below the top 20 percent in the summative score of five divergent thinking measures. Their mean IQ was 150, with a range from 139 to 179 (N = 28; 17 boys, 11 girls). The other group included students at the top 20 percent in the divergent thinking measures but below the top 20 percent in IQ. Their mean IQ was 127, with a range from 108 to 138 (N = 26; 15 boys, 11 girls).

The findings for the entire population of students from which the comparison groups were drawn showed that the measures of divergent thinking and intelligence were positively related but that the correlations were generally low. Manifestly, the sample was not a "normal" one but Torrance soon replicated the findings with eight different samples, comprising a selective school similar to the one in the original study, four elementary schools, including a parochial and a rural school, a public high school, and two samples of graduate students (Torrance, 1960).

Other findings also were novel and unexpected. For example, despite the 23-point difference in IQ, the two groups performed at the same level of achievement on a number of standardized achievement tests. This result was replicated by Torrance in six of his eight schools; only in the parochial and the rural schools were there contra-indications. The parents of the two groups differed on a number of important variables, the parents of the high divergent group being less protective and less critical of their children, less defensive about themselves, and more interested in subjective, internal qualities than in external qualities of achievement (Getzels and Jackson, 1961). These results did not go unchallenged. Yet it is surprising how many of the original findings still stand, so that even the most widely questioned of the initial results—the creativity-intelligence relationships—was confirmed or at least not significantly disproved.

However, the most fruitful clues for understanding the *process* rather than only the *correlates* of creativity, we can see now in retrospect, were contained in an aspect of the study that hardly attracted any notice at the time, the aspect dealing with the *creative performance* of the two groups.

Children in both groups completed two tasks of a creative nature. One task was verbal: to write stories to six need:achievement type stimulus pictures. The other task was nonverbal: to make a drawing appropriate to the title, "Playing Tag in the School Yard." The performance of the two groups on both tasks was startingly different, and, as we look back, the mere statement of the results did not do the data justice.

The original report did not enter into the controversy regarding the meaning of fantasy, and whether fantasy is or is not the "royal road to the unconscious," and hence to the deeper and more stable aspects of personality. Nor shall we do so here. Suffice it to reiterate for present purposes that story-telling and picture drawing are creative processes and have special merits for observing possible distinctive characteristics of the two groups.

We first scored the stories conventionally for the single variable need: achievement. There was no difference whatsoever between the two groups. We then analyzed the total stories. The differences were striking. The stories of the high divergent-thinking group were significantly richer than the stories of the high IQ group in *stimulus-free themes, unexpected endings, humor, incongruities,* and *playfulness* (Getzels and Jackson, 1962, p. 39).

Here, for example, in response to the picture-stimulus perceived most often as a man seated in an airplane, are two stories by a high IQ student and a high divergent-thinking student:

The high IQ subject: "Mr. Smith is on his way home from a successful business trip. He is very happy and he is thinking about his wonderful family and how glad he will be to see them again. He can picture it, about an hour from now, his plane landing at the airport and Mrs. Smith and their three children all there welcoming him home again."

The high-divergent-thinking subject: "This man is flying back from Reno where he has won a divorce from his wife. He couldn't stand to live with her anymore, he told the judge, because she wore so much cold cream on her face at night that her head would skid across the pillow. He's now contemplating a new skid-proof face cream."

Or here is another set of responses to a stimulus-picture perceived most often as a man working late (or very early) in an office.

The high IQ subject: "There's ambitious Bob down at the office at 6:30 in the morning: Every morning it's the same. He's trying to show his boss how energetic he is. Now, thinks Bob, maybe the boss will give me a raise for all my extra work. The trouble is that Bob has been doing this for the last three years, and the boss still hasn't given him a raise. He'll come in at 9:00, not even noticing that Bob had been there so long, and poor Bob won't get his raise."

The high divergent-thinking subject: "This man has just broken into this office of a new cereal company. He is a private eye employed by a competitive firm to find out the formula that makes the cereal bend, sag, and sway. After a thorough search of the office he comes upon what he thinks is the current formula. It turns out that it is the wrong formula and the competitor's factory blows up. Poetic justice!" [Getzels and Jackson, 1962, pp. 39–40]

The stories were written in group sessions, often more than 100 adolescents in the same room, with a maximum writing time of four minutes per story. "Skid-proof face cream"! "Cereal that will bend, sag, and sway"! We said at the time: "It is the ability to restructure stereotyped objects with ease and rapidity—almost 'naturally'—that seems to us to be the characteristic mark" of the one group of students as against the other. The high divergent group tended to free themselves from the stimulus, using it largely as a point of departure for self-expression; the high IQ group tended to focus on the stimulus, using it as the invariant for self-expression. For the high IQ students the problem was essentially one of following up on what others had given him. If the picture stimulus is of a man in an airplane, he tells a story about travel; if the picture stimulus is of a man in an office, he tells a story about work. For the high divergent-thinking subject, the problem was one constructing something that he wants to give. The picture may be of a man in an airplane, but the story he wants to tell is about a divorce; the picture stimulus may be of a man alone in an office, but the story he wants to tell is of a private eye in a cereal factory. Moreover, the high IQ subject employed predetermined categories, the high divergent-thinking subject employed categories that he himself originates. Cereal does not only snap, crackle, and pop, it can also bend, sag, and sway. Face cream does not only skid, it can also be skid-proof.

The same effect was found in the drawings (Getzels and Jackson, 1962,

p. 42f.). Even a cursory look through the production of the two groups showed unmistakable and compelling differences. When the stories were analyzed as stimulus-free or stimulus-bound, 39 percent of the stories by the high IQ group but 75 percent of the stories by the high divergent-thinking group were classified as stimulus-free (p < 05); when the drawings were similarly analyzed, 14 percent of the drawings by the IQ group but 50 percent of the drawings by the high divergent group were classified as stimulus-free (p < 02). For example, one drawing by a high divergent-thinking student portrays a prison yard with guards apparently chasing ("playing tag with") the prisoners. Another drawing by a divergent-thinking student portrays a group of fantastic fish (a "school" of fish), or space objects following one another. A third drawing, a quite elaborate one, seems to represent a play on the word tag—ghosts are tagging the school building with various labels ("tags").

The divergent-thinking student seemed to use the directions to "draw a picture appropriate to the title 'Playing Tag in the School Yard' " as a point of departure rather than a point of conventional focus for his drawing—or sometimes lack of drawing. One of the high divergent subjects, for example, returned what seemed at first glance only a blank sheet of paper, until one noticed that some words had been added to the title. The space within the picture frame had been left white as it had been, but the title had been changed to "Playing Tag in a School Yard—*During a Blizzard.*" Very few of the drawings by the high IQ group had the same nonliteral quality. Instead, they stayed close to the problem posed in the directions, or perhaps better to the part of the directions which said "draw a picture appropriate to the title 'Playing Tag in a School Yard' " and neglected the part which said "you may draw any picture you like—whatever you may imagine for this theme."

At the time of the study, the differences in the stories and drawings were explained in terms of Guilford's distinction between convergent and divergent thinking. He had written regarding the two types of tests:

> In tests of convergent thinking there is almost always only one conclusion or answer that is regarded as unique, and thinking is to be channeled or controlled in the direction of that answer. . . . In divergent thinking, on the other hand, there is much searching about or going off in various directions. . . . Divergent thinking . . . [is] characterized . . . as being less goalbound. There is freedom to go off in different directions. . . . Rejecting the old solution and striking out in some new direction is necessary, and the resourceful organism will more probably succeed. [Guilford, 1957, pp. 6, 9]

In retrospect, there was a crucial issue that was not dealt with in the empirical work or in the indicated formulation. Clearly, the divergent-thinking students were "rejecting old solutions and striking out in some new directions." Yet, after rejecting the old solutions, what is the process—

what are the mechanisms—through which one strikes out towards *new* solutions? A solution is a response to a problem: an old solution is presumably a response to an old problem. Tò what is a *new* solution a response? Is it possible that the high divergent-thinking students who were rejecting the old solutions were rejecting also the old problems and discovering *new problems* which triggered the new solutions? If this is the case—and we believe now that it is at least partly the case—then the process of rejecting old problems and developing new problems is a central issue in creativity, well worth more careful examination.

Presented Problems, Discovered Problems, and Creativity

We did not come to the preceding questions immediately after completion of the work itself. Nor did we come directly to the study of problem finding which we shall report in the next section. In 1962, the first author was asked to do a chapter on "Creative Thinking, Problem Solving, and Instruction" for the 63rd Yearbook of the National Society for the Study of Education entitled *Theories of Learning and Instruction* (Getzels, 1964). After reading the widely-used *Taxonomy of Educational Objectives,* he found himself composing a segment entitled "On the Nature of Problems in Learning: Types of Cognitive Problems" as follows:

> The *Taxonomy of Educational Objectives* suggests a classification of intellective problems in the classroom by *type of learning objective,* and *skill required* as follows: knowledge, requiring recall; comprehension, requiring understanding of what is communicated; application, requiring the use of abstractions in concrete situations; analysis, requiring the dissecting of what is communicated; synthesis, requiring the organization of a pattern from separate parts; evaluation, requiring the judgment of the subject against a standard of appraisal.
>
> This suggested classification deals with *presented* problems. It omits from consideration and seems not to recognize in the classroom a significant group of problems we may call *discovered* problems. A different and perhaps more general classification to include *both presented and discovered problems* may be made if we look at the issues in terms of what is *known* and what is *unknown* in the problem-situation. [Getzels, 1964, pp. 240–241]

Eight types of problem situations were distinguished, varying in terms of how much of the problem is given at the start, how much of the method for reaching a solution is already available, and how general is the agreement as to what constitutes a good solution. At one extreme there are *presented problem situations* where the problem has a known formulation, a routine method of solution, and a recognized solution; here a person needs only to follow established steps to meet the requirements of the situation. At the other extreme, there are *discovered problem situations* where the problem does not yet have a known formulation, a routine method of solution, and a recognized solution; here the person must identify the problem itself, and there are no established steps for satisfying the requirements of the situation.

Within these extremes, it is possible to differentiate systematically among a number of problem situations varying in what is known and unknown, and the corresponding mental processes which are primarily engaged in each situation, from rote memory to creative imagination. The elements of the analytical model may be summarized schematically as in Table 4.1.

TABLE 4.1.   *Types of Problem Situations and Mental Functions*

Problem Situation	Problem		Method of Solution		Solution		Primary Mental Function Engaged
type-case	*others*	*individual*	*others*	*individual*	*others*	*individual*	
1	+	+	+	+	+	−	Memory
2	+	+	+	−	+	−	Reason
3	−	−	−	−	−	−	Imagination

+ known
− unknown

In type-case 1 at one extreme, the problem is generally known, it is known to "others" and also known to the individual (the problem-solver); the method of solution is also known to both; but the solution needs to be known by the individual. For instance, in Wertheimer's classic task of finding the area of a rectangle, the "others" (experimenter, teacher, etc.) assert that the area of a rectangle is side *a* multiplied by side *b*, and the individual is required to solve the problem: What is the area of a rectangle when *a* is 3 and *b* is 4? Here the problem is given—it is presented—and there is a standard method of solution known to others and presumably to the individual as well. All he has to do is plug the given data into the known formula to find the solution that is also already known and permits of no deviation. The mode of thought required is primarily memory and retrieval. This process has been well-investigated both theoretically and empirically.

Consider now type-case 2. To continue with the illustration, the "others" do not begin by giving the formula or assuming that the individual knows the formula. They begin instead, as in Wertheimer's instance, by posing the problem: How would you go about finding the area of a rectangle? Here the problem is still presented, but no standard method for solving it is known to the problem-solver, although it is known to others. The primary mode of thought is no longer memory or retrieval. The individual must reflect upon the presented problem until he reaches a solution, one which matches the solution already known to others. The primary mode of thought required is reasoning and rationality. A substantial amount of theoretical and empirical work has been devoted to this type of thinking as well.

What about type-case 3 at the other extreme? To use the example of the rectangle once more, suppose the "others" say something like: How many important questions can be asked about a rectangle? Or: Formulate a problem about a rectangle and solve it. Here it is the general task that is presented but the specific question or problem must be discovered by the problem-solver himself. In contrast to the preceding presented problem situations, this is a discovered problem situation. The problem-solver must become a problem-finder. And the problems he finds may range all the way from "How would one determine the distance around a rectangle?" or "What is the area of a rectangle?" to "Are there dimensions of a rectangle that make it more pleasing to the eye than other dimensions?"

The problem-solver become problem-finder must feel there is a problem in the object or event, he must formulate the problem, and then attempt to devise appropriate methods for solving it. That is, the problem-solver himself must pose the problem before he can begin to envisage a method toward its solution, and when the solution is obtained—*if* it is obtained— he may have no immediate criterion for its ultimate correctness. Not only the solution but the problem itself must be discovered by the problem-solver; and in fact when he reaches a solution, he cannot compare it against a predetermined standard of right or wrong. He can accept or reject the solution only on the basis of a critical, relativistic analysis—as is the case with works of art. The primary mode of thought required here is what has been called, for want of a more precise term, imagination and creativity. There has been very little theoretical and almost no empirical work relevant to this case.

It need hardly be pointed out that problem solving and problem finding are not as discontinuous as the necessarily schematic representation of the model implies. Nonetheless, at least two things are clear. First, finding a problem—functioning effectively in the discovered problem situation— may be a more important aspect of creative thinking and performance than solving the problem once the problem has been found and formulated. We have already cited Albert Einstein on the importance of problem finding in science. We may cite Wertheimer (1959) with respect to the more general case:

> The problem with its solution function as parts of a large expanding realm. Here the function of thinking is not just solving an actual problem but discovering, envisaging, going into deeper questions. Often in great discoveries the most important thing is that a certain question is found. Envisaging, putting the productive question is often more important, often a greater achievement than solution of a set question. [p. 141]

Second, there are some individuals, like pure scientists and fine artists, who prefer—and of course it is not only a matter of conscious preference— to work in discovered problem situations rather than in presented problem situations. They do not wait for others to assign to them the task of identifying problems; they cannot help being constantly sensitive to previously unidentified problems.

Indeed, this attitude toward problem situations may be the essential difference between the scientist and the technician; the difference is surely not that the one is more technically proficient or better informed than the other. Similarly, this may be the essential difference between the original artist and the copyist; the difference is not in the ability to draw, the graphic talent or craftsmanship per se. Many copyists are more "talented" than fine artists. Rather, it is that the one applies his talent in a discovered problem situation, the other in a presented problem situation. The latter's work may be judged for whether it is right or wrong—does it or does it not match the original. The former's work cannot be judged by this criterion, but is appraised by the very criteria that are automatically defects in the other's case, originality and creativity.

Problem Finding and Creativity: a Study with Artists

Shortly after the model of *presented* and *discovered* problems was formulated, we decided to embark on a substantial empirical study of creativity. In retrospect, it is clear that what happened at this point is a classic instance of the paradoxical lack of congruence between theory and practice which so often accompanies research.

The model suggested a new paradigm for approaching creativity. Yet when we started to collect data we automatically reverted to the already established paradigms. Instead of asking the crucial questions about how discovered problems are found, we proceeded along the familiar route of searching for correlations between personal characteristics on the one hand, and creative achievement on the other.

This phase of the research was surely not useless. Indeed, many significant findings emerged, a number of which have since been reported in the literature (e.g., Getzels and Csikszentmihalyi, 1966; 1968a; 1968b). Yet the conceptual and empirical dimensions were out of phase. It was a case of the empirical hand not knowing what the theoretical hand was doing, and it took us two years of work and reflection to realize the obvious—namely, that the questions we were answering were not the ones we should have been asking.

CORRELATES OF CREATIVITY

The initial studies had been done with children. We now wanted to study a sample of adults actively involved in some form of creative production.

Accordingly we approached the School of the Art Institute of Chicago, one of the leading art schools in the country, for collaboration. They provided this fully. We obtained access to several hundred young artists, all preparing for careers where creativity is a central issue. Of the 321 second- and third-year students, 266 took at least one of the three batteries of instruments which we gave, and 179 students, which then formed our "core sample," completed all tests. The three batteries included speed and power intelligence tests; convergent and divergent thinking tests; measures of perceptual ability; values instruments like the Allport-Vernon-Lindzey Study of Values; personality tests like the 16 PFQ; projective techniques like the Sentence Completion and the TAT; autobiographical and family questionnaires. In all, the three batteries took some six hours of student time. In addition, we had for our use the school records including course grades and teacher ratings. We accumulated sufficient information to answer the widest range of questions that could be asked within the usual correlational paradigm.

We do not wish to focus here on the results of this phase of our work. Our present interest lies elsewhere. Still, a word or two regarding three sets of findings are of some interest and perhaps some pertinence.

One set of data deals with the comparison of art students with other students of the same age and sex. Such analysis seemed useful, since characteristics differentiating future artists from college students should be indicative of the qualities needed to perform in a milieu requiring creativity. A number of the results were clear-cut and highly informative.

The art students did not differ significantly from the norms of any of the cognitive measures. Again and again, their scores on the mental tests coincided with national college averages. But the future artists differed significantly from the norms on virtually all measures of values and personality. For example, the art students of both sexes differed from the respective college norms on four of the six Allport-Vernon-Lindzey values at the .001 level or beyond; and they differed from their respective college norms on 10 of the 16 personalistic factors on the 16 PFQ at the .01 level or beyond.

More specifically, future artists of both sexes were higher than the norms in aesthetic value and lower in economic and social values. The mean aesthetic score of both sex groups was higher than that of any comparable group found in the literature; the mean social score was lower than that of any comparable group; and the magnitude of the theoretical values, second only to the aesthetic values, called attention once more to the accumulating evidence for the coexistence in creative populations of these values, which are often considered incompatible (Getzels and Csikszentmihalyi, 1968a).

With respect to personality, not only did both male and female future artists differ significantly from the respective norms on 10 of the 16 PFQ factors, but on six they differed jointly in the same direction, that is, on factors A, F, G, M, Q1, and Q2. The pattern outlines a personality profile that may be summarized as follows: young artists, compared to college students of their age and sex, are socially reserved, introspective, alienated, imaginative, radical, and self-sufficient. In addition, males tended to score higher than the norms on feminine characteristics, while females to score higher on masculine characteristics. When Cattell's weighted creativity scores were computed, the core sample of 179 art students attained a mean "general creativity" score corresponding to the 89th percentile on the college norms (Csikszentmihalyi and Getzels, 1973).

A second set of data involved a comparison between students specializing in various fields of art. Students at the Art School are differentiated with regard to four "fields of specialization": fine art, advertising art, industrial art, and art education. Systematic differences were found in the values and personality characteristics among the four groups. If particular values are in fact a significant part of the motivational structure of art students, as the preceding data would suggest, then it is reasonable to expect differences in values among the groups of students in the four fields of specialization. Fine art students should have higher aesthetic values, advertising art and industrial art students higher economic values, and art education students higher social values. This was found to be the case. What was perhaps most noteworthy was that the same three values which showed the greatest differences among the fields of specialization were exactly the same values which differentiated both male and female art students from their respective college norms, despite the severe restriction of range because of the already extreme scores for the sample as a whole. These three values then—aesthetic, economic, and social—would seem to be crucial to understanding individuals engaged in the arts. These values not only distinguish the art student group as a whole from the normative college students, but also tend to distinguish among different subgroups within the total art group itself (Getzels and Csikszentmihalyi, 1968b). More especially, the young fine artists were characterized by very high aesthetic values and personality factors like alienation, imaginativeness, unconventionality, and self-sufficiency.

The third set of data involved the correlations between the various test scores and creative achievement. Grades in studio art courses and ratings on originality given by the teachers provided ready-made criteria of achievement to which the effects of the many test scores could be related. A number of systematic relations between the cognitive, perceptual, values, and personality scores and creative achievement were found. But it was also immediately obvious that creative achievement in art school is a very complex matter, depending among other things on the student's sex and field of specialization. What held for one sex was often reversed for the other sex, and what held in one field of specialization was often reversed in another. For example, the creative achievement of female students, and especially of those in applied art, was positively related to their performance on the cognitive and perceptual tests. This was not the case for the male students, for whom in fact the same correlations were sometimes negative. The creative achievement of male students, and especially of those in fine art, was much more closely related to their values and personality characteristics, relationships which tended to disappear for the female students (Getzels and Csikszentmihalyi, 1966).

We need not enter here into the intricacies of the specific results. However, an instance or two may be instructive. For male fine art students the correlation between economic values and the cumulative art grade was −.47 ($p < .01$), while the correlation between the same two variables for the female fine art students was −.01, a difference between the two sexes which was itself statistically significant. Or again, the correlation between spatial visualization and the art grades for the male fine art students was −.32, but for the female applied art students, it was +.52 ($p < .01$). In short, highly significant relationships between cognitive, perceptual, values, and personality characteristics of students and their creative achievement were observed, but these relationships varied with the specific context in which the creative activity was pursued. In art school, sex and field of specialization apparently define significantly different contexts.

When this phase of the study was completed, we were quite exhilarated with the results. We had obtained a reasonably consistent picture of how the cognitive and affective characteristics of individuals committed to a creative field differed from other individuals of the same sex and age, how these characteristics were associated with the pursuit of different areas of specialization within the art field, and how the characteristics were related to creative achievement, at least as defined in an art school.

Yet as we stepped back and surveyed the results, we were struck with the thought that they had not gotten us much closer to the direct understanding, or even the description, of creative production. We knew something more about the *correlates* of creative performance than when we started, yet we did not know much more about the *processes* of creative performance. To be sure, there was that .47 correlation between low economic values and creative achievement for male fine art students, for example—a correlation almost as high as that between intelligence and academic achievement. But what did this say about the way in which the creative work was achieved?

At this point, some things that had seemed forgotten throughout the research were again recalled. We remembered that one of the main reasons for selecting a sample of art students was that the production of a work of art is potentially more open to observation and description than that, say, of a poem or of a mathematical equation. We remembered too the original formulation of the presented- and discovered-problems model of thinking. And we remembered what Einstein had said about the crucial importance of the problem in creative work, and the distinction he made between the ordinary scientist, whom he likened to a detective, and the creative scientist: "For the detective, the crime is given, the problem posed: Who killed Cock Robin? The [creative] scientist must, at least in part, commit his own crime [find his own problem] as well as carry out the investigation" (Einstein and Infeld, 1938, p. 76). It seemed to us that the same holds true not only in scientific work but in all creative endeavor. We realized that if we wished to come to grips with the process of creativity, we had to find a way to observe the process of creative production in art from its beginning when the problem was found, to its end when the problem was executed in a finished drawing.

PROBLEM FINDING AND CREATIVITY

The results of the first attempts to describe how a fine artist paints a picture were thoroughly bewildering. Everyone seemed to have his own pattern of work. Some worked rapidly, some slowly, some daubed flecks of color on the canvas with a brush, others seemed to smear heavy smudges of paint on the canvas with a trowel. Some artists claimed that what they enjoyed most was the smell of the pigment, some enjoyed squeezing the tubes of paint more than anything else, still others declared that what they wanted most was to develop a "new image of universal man," and some said they painted because it was simply the most satisfying thing to do.

Watching the artists work at their easels and talking to them provided literally hundreds of observations to focus on, but none that seemed to provide leverage into the central issue. The observations suggested a multitude of theoretical models that could be used to interpret what we were seeing and hearing, but all the theoretical viewpoints that were considered—ranging from Freud to Piaget, from ego psychology to symbolic interactionism—seemed to obscure the very phenomenon we wished to study.

Finally we recognized the obvious. If we had arrived conceptually at problem finding as a crucial phase of the creative process, we had to devise a way to operationalize problem finding so that it might be observed in actual creative production—in this case, the drawing of a picture.

Drawing a picture may be seen as a process of solution to a problem. Although this "problem" is often not consciously formulated by the artist, it may be assumed that without some source of problematic feelings the artist would have nothing to do. It may be assumed further that if the artist begins a painting as a process of personal discovery of an aesthetic problem, his work will be relatively more original than if he begins a painting to fit a standard aesthetic problem. In a sense, in the first case he is working with what we have called a "discovered problem," in the second with a "presented problem."

It is possible to observe how a problem is *solved*. But how is one to observe how a problem is *found*? More specifically, how is one to tell whether a person approaches the task of drawing a picture as a discovered problem or a presented problem? There is of course no way to do this directly. But it occurred to us that a studio situation could be set up where it was possible to make some strong inferences regarding individual differences among the art students in problem finding as they begin an artistic task. We could then examine the finished product to see whether there are sytematic relationships between the quality of the problem and the quality of the solution, in this case the finished drawing.

Once we formulated *our* problem in these terms, the rest was relatively straightforward, and we proceeded to the second unanticipated phase of the study. We took over a studio at the art school, furnished it with two tables, an easel, paper, and a variety of dry media. On one table we placed some 30 "still-life" objects collected from the studio classrooms. We then asked each of the 31 male fine art students from the original sample, one at a time, to compose a still-life on the second table using as many of the objects as he wished, and then to make any drawing of the still-life. There were no limitations as to time; we only asked that the artist continue until he felt satisfied with what he had done. We watched each artist as he went about his work—from composing the still-life problem to completing the actual drawing (Csikszentmihalyi and Getzels, 1971).

Despite the apparent artificiality of the situation, it was in fact quite similar to the setting in which the young artists usually worked. In the interviews that followed the experiment, 72 percent of the 31 artists stated that the situation was not different from the free-creative setting to which they were accustomed; 14 percent said that although unconstraining, the situation was more similar to a studio class than to a free-creative setting; the remaining 14 percent said they felt some degree of constraint in the situation.

During the course of the work, an observer took notes and photographs of each young artist's behavior. It soon became evident that there were readily identifiable individual differences in the way the artists proceeded, even before they turned to their drawing. The differences at this predrawing stage of the process could be classified into three categories.

One category was the number of objects handled. Some of the artists handled as few as two objects, others as many as nineteen. Our presumption was that in order to discover a more original problem, one had to consider a great number of possible stimuli. If one came to the situation with an already set or standard problem—say, to make a drawing of a "startling vanishing point," as in fact some did—less exploration would be needed. Of course, in normal practice an artist does not touch and move objects around as our subjects were required to do. But he still has to weigh visual stimuli, emotions, or ideas in his mind. We assumed, since one cannot look into the "black box" itself, that behavior such as handling the objects in the experiment reflects mental operations involved in considering inner stimuli, just as the manifest behavior in the Vygotsky test, for example, is similarly taken to reflect mental operations.

A second category was the kinds of interactions the young artists had with the objects. Some simply picked up the objects, took them over to the second table, and immediately began to draw. Other artists rolled the objects in their hands, threw them in the air, held them against the light, smelled them, bit into them, felt their texture, moved their parts, turned them upside down, and so on. Again, we presumed that in order to discover a more original problem, one had to explore the greatest number and variety of problematic elements. If one came to the situation with an already set problem, such exploration was less necessary. And again, the observed behavior was assumed to reflect underlying mental processes analogous to the observed behavior. A person who selects an object-stimulus for creative work after intensive rather than cursory exploration is also likely to utilize inner-stimuli—thoughts, emotions, sense impressions—only after probing into their deeper and more profound qualities.

A third category was the uniqueness of the objects selected by the young artists. Some of the objects, like the leather-bound book, the bunch of grapes, the white wooden ball, were chosen by so many of the artists that they became "clichés" in this sample. Other objects were used by only one or two of the students. That is, some of the artists seemed to seek out original objects, others seemed to choose only the most popular ones. Our presumption was that a person who uses only popular stimuli would be more likely to compose a design conforming to a "presented" than to a "discovered" problem, and the consequent drawing would be less original. To be sure, a great artist can create an utterly original painting with the most hackneyed of objects. But other things being equal, we assumed that the more stereotypic the objects the more conventional the problem, the more unique the objects the more creative the problem is likely to be.

These three variables—the number of objects handled, the quality of interaction with the objects, and the uniqueness of the objects selected for drawing—seemed to reflect, at least within the limits of the experiment, characteristic ways in which a person approaches an unstructured aesthetic task as a presented or a discovered problem situation. Since these behaviors occurred before the artists started to draw we referred to them as problem-finding or discovery orientation at the stage of *problem formulation*. The hypothesis, if we may dignify our conjecture by this term, was that the individuals who considered more problematic elements at this stage, explored the problematic elements more thoroughly, and selected the less common among them, were likely to formulate a visual problem which was creative and would result in a more original drawing.

This was the central point of the inquiry. However, we also pursued the issue in two other ways. We made similar behavioral observations of problem finding or discovery orientation while the artists were actually at the drawing board, and we interviewed the artists in the same regard after they finished the drawing.

With respect to behavior at the drawing board, the *problem solution* stage, the differences were as sharp as those seen at the problem formulation stage. Some artists, for instance, changed their position, changed the materials they used, and changed the composition of the objects. Others worked straight through without any changes whatsoever. Inspection of the photographs taken while the artists were at work revealed that some of the drawings were completely structured after as little as 11 percent of the total drawing time had elapsed, while the final structure of other drawings was not recognizable until 74 percent of the time had elapsed. The differences were not a function of haste or deliberateness in the execution of the drawings; there were no differences in the total elapsed time between the drawings that had been structured early and later. We assumed that this kind of delay in closure was evidence that the artist was still keeping the problem open—in a sense, still problem finding—even while he was drawing.

With respect to the interviews after the drawing had been completed, we attempted to find out if the artists themselves mentioned any concern for problem finding or discovery. Four ratings were derived from the interviews: concern with problem finding or discovery in general, such concern during the problem formulation stage of the experiment, during the problem solution stage, and retrospectively after the experimental problem had been "solved," that is, after the drawing was completed (Csikszentmihalyi and Getzels, 1970).

In all then, we had 3 behavioral measures of problem finding at the stage of problem formulation, 3 at the stage of problem solution, and 4 ratings derived from the interviews. The intercorrelations of the 6 behavioral and 4 interview scores showed that although for the most part of the 10 variables were related, they were not redundant. Of the 56 possible intercorrelations, all but 2 (and these insignificantly) were positive, and 22 were statistically significant at least at the .05 level. Some of the variables were very strongly related. For instance, the rating in amount of concern for problem finding at the stage problem formulation from the interviews was correlated .68 ($p < .0005$) with the behavioral score in intensity of exploration of the objects at the stage of problem formulation, and it was correlated .55 ($p < .005$) with the observer's score of changes in the problem structure and content at the stage of problem solution. Therefore in addition to the separate item scores, problem-finding subtotals were derived, as well as a total score, which was a linear combination of the 10 variables.

This provided us with a tentative method for quantifying problem-finding activity, or more specifically, for measuring whether the approach to an aesthetic task is more in terms of a discovered or of a presented problem situation. The method had high reliability, apparent face-validity, and reasonable internal consistency.

But did it work? Would a systematic relationship be found between our measures of problem finding (or discovery orientation) and an external criterion of the quality of the resulting solution, that is, the completed drawing?

What was needed next was a satisfactory criterion for judging the quality of the drawings. No contemporary criterion for assessing a work of art is foolproof. Only time is the ultimate judge, and even then the verdict is not without variable appeal. To do best under such circumstances, we resolved to proceed as galleries and museums do; by recourse to an "expert jury." Two panels of experts were assembled: five artist-critics, who had previously served on juries for art shows, and five teachers from the art school, who were unaware that the works they were to judge were by students from their school. Each judge was asked to rate the 31 drawings produced in the experiment on three dimensions: craftsmanship or technical skill, originality, and overall aesthetic value. If a judge asked us to define the dimensions, he was told to define them as he would if he were judging an art show.

The ratings produced many interesting patterns, which are reported in detail elsewhere (Getzels and Csikszentmihalyi, 1969). Suffice it to say here that the averaged ratings of the two panels were reliable and highly intercorrelated: craftsmanship ratings by artists and teachers, $r = .75$; originality, $r = .72$; overall aesthetic value, $r = .73$ ($p < .001$ in each case).

The general test of the problem-finding model and method we had devised lay in the nature of the relationship between the ratings of the drawings given by the judges and the scores collected during the experiment. The *crucial* test lay more specifically in the relationship between the ratings in originality of the drawings by the panel of artist-critics and the problem-finding behavior scores at the stage of problem formulation, that is, *before the drawings were begun*. The data are presented in Table 4.2.

TABLE 4.2.   *Correlations Between Problem-Finding Variables at Problem-Formulation Stage, and Evaluation of the Artistic Products by Five Artist-Critics*

Problem-Finding Variables at Problem-Formulation Stage	Dimensions of Evaluation		
	overall aesthetic value (total 5 raters)	originality (total 5 raters)	craftsmanship (total 5 raters)
Manipulation	.48****	.52****	.16
Exploration	.44***	.58*****	.34*
Unusualness	.35*	.42***	.22
Total	.40**	.54****	.28

NOTE: Adapted from Csikszentmihalyi and Getzels, 1971.
  $N = 31$
  *$p < .05$
  **$p < .025$
  ***$p < .01$
  ****$p < .005$
  *****$p < .0005$

It is readily apparent that the results follow the expected direction. Each of the behavioral variables of problem finding is significantly related to the ratings in originality and in overall aesthetic value; one of the problem-finding variables is related to craftsmanship. Similar effects were found in the relationships between problem finding at the problem solution stage of the drawing and from the interviews. In all, of the ten behavioral and interview variables, eight correlated with the originality ratings, seven with the overall aesthetic value ratings, and three with the craftsmanship ratings. When the common variance between originality and the other two ratings was partialled out, overall aesthetic value and craftsmanship ceased to be positively related to the total problem-finding or discovery-orientation scores, while with overall aesthetic value and craftsmanship partialled out originality continued to be highly related to problem finding and discovery-orientation (Csikszentmihalyi and Getzels, 1971).

One further observation is in order, based on data not yet completely analyzed. The preceding results provided encouraging confirmation for the fruitfulness of the problem-finding model. But we wanted to put the model to a more severe test. We wanted to know whether the problem-finding variables measured in the experimental setting would relate to the long-term artistic success of the art students who had been our subjects. If such relationships were to be found, then the problem-finding model and method would have stood a stern test of its relevance for the study of creativity.

In order to evaluate the long-term success of the 31 art students, we sought them out seven years after the experiment, or five years after their graduation from the Art School. Fifteen of the students had abandoned art completely, seven were marginally involved, and nine had achieved various levels of artistic eminence; to our gratification, the work of one had already been bought for the permanent collection of one of the leading art museums. A success scale was constructed based on the ratings given by gallery owners, art critics, and our own knowledge of the artist's achievement.

These success scores were found to be highly correlated with a number of the problem-finding variables. For instance, they correlated .45 ($p < .005$) with the object manipulation variable during the problem-formulation stage of the experiment, and .48 ($p < .005$) with the delay in closure variable, as measured by the film strips, at the problem-solution stage. The success scores correlated .41 ($p < .01$) with the total behavioral problem-finding and interview discovery-orientation score obtained seven years earlier.

It might be appropriate to reiterate our general view of the problem-finding and discovery-orientation variables lest there be some misunderstanding. The experimental conditions seem to have brought out into the open and made observable a process which normally goes undetected whenever an artist is involved in the production of a work of art. Under ordinary circumstances the artist does not inspect, touch, or manipulate concrete objects before he decides what to paint, but he does consider, weigh, and analyze feelings or sensory material. We have assumed for present purposes that the two processes—the manifest and the latent—reflect one another, and we used the former as an index of the latter. Surely, one should not extrapolate from the argument any implication that touching many objects, choosing unique objects, and so on, "causes" originality.

Finally, we can do no better to summarize our approach to problem finding in human thought than to cite a remark attributed to Gertrude Stein: "The question of questions and not answers is very interesting. . . . Suppose no one asked a question. What would the answer be?"

Conclusion

Fifteen years after our interest in creative problem solving as a subject for systematic study was engaged, and almost exactly ten years after we started our first investigation with artists, we have come to a reasonably firm resolution of the issues that had been problematic for us at the beginning. The resolution pointed to the centrality of problem finding in the creative process. This concern with problem finding was translated into a viable model of problem finding and into a method of investigation. The method has been applied, and the results have confirmed the fruitfulness of the conceptual model. Problem finding appears to be a crucial component of creativity, and what is more, it can be observed and assessed with satisfactory reliability and validity.

The initial success, however, is at best only an auspicious beginning. The limitations of our work are not difficult to see. We have looked at problem finding only in the context of the artistic process, and even then we have dealt with only a very small sample. Many questions remain. Is problem finding equally central in other fields where creativity is at issue? Can the problem-finding and discovery-orientation processes be similarly investigated in, say, mathematics and physics, or poetry and politics? Can measures be developed to indicate whether one approaches the daily dilemmas of life as "presented" or "discovered" problem situations? These are some of the questions that we now feel need to be answered. Until they are, the general usefulness of the model and method we have described must remain a *problem*.

References

Berlyne, D. E. Curiosity and exploration. *Science,* 1966, *153,* 25–33.
Bexton, W. H., Heron, W., and Scott, T. H. Effects of decreased variation in sensory environment. *Canadian Journal of Psychology,* 1954, *8,* 70–76.
Chassell, L. M. Tests for originality. *Journal of Educational Psychology,* 1916, *7,* 317–328.
Colvin, S. S. Invention versus form in English composition: An indicative study. *Pedagogical Seminary,* 1902, *9,* 393–421.

Csikszentmihalyi, M. and Getzels, J. W. Concern for discovery: An attitudinal component of creative production. *The Journal of Personality*, 1970, *38*, 1, 91–105.

Csikszentmihalyi, M., and Getzels, J. W., Discovery-oriented behavior and the originality of artistic products: A study with artists. *Journal of Personality and Social Psychology*, 1971, *19*, 1, 47–52.

Csikszentmihalyi, M., and Getzels, J. W. The personality of young artists: A theoretical and empirical exploration. *British Journal of Psychology*, 1973, *64*, 1, 91–104.

Dearborn, G. V. A study of imagination. *American Journal of Psychology*, 1898, *5*, 183–190.

Dewey, J. (Ed.) *Creative intelligence: Essays in the pragmatic attitude.* New York: Holt & Co., 1917.

Einstein, A., and Infeld, L. *The evolution of physics.* New York: Simon & Schuster, 1938.

Gerard, A. *An essay on genius.* London: W. Strahan, 1774.

Getzels, J. W. Creative thinking, problem-solving, and instruction. In E. Hilgard, (Ed.) *Theories of learning and instruction,* 63rd Yearbook of the N.S.S.E., Part I. Chicago: University of Chicago Press, 1964.

Getzels, J. W., and Csikszentmihalyi, M. The study of creativity in future artists: The criterion problem. In O. J. Harvey, (Ed.) *Experience, structure, and adaptability,* 349–368. New York: Springer, 1966.

Getzels, J. W., and Csikszentmihalyi, M. On the roles, values, and performance of future artists: A conceptual and empirical exploration. *Sociological Quarterly,* 1968, *9*, 516–530. (*a*)

Getzels, J. W., and Csikszentmihalyi, M. The value-orientations of art students as determinants of artistic specialization and creative performance. *Studies in Art Education,* 1968, *10*, 1, 5–16. (*b*)

Getzels, J. W., and Csikszentmihalyi, M. Aesthetic opinion: An empirical study. *Public Opinion Quarterly,* 1969, *33*, 34–45.

Getzels, J. W., and Jackson, P. W. Family environment and cognitive style: A study of the sources of highly intelligent and of highly creative adolescents. *American Sociological Review,* 1961, *26*, 3, 351–359.

Getzels, J. W., and Jackson, P. W. *Creativity and intelligence: Explorations with gifted students.* New York: Wiley, 1962.

Guilford, J. P. Creativity. *American Psychologist,* 1950, *5*, 444–454.

Guilford, J. P. A revised structure of intellect. *Reports of the Psychological laboratory,* No. 19. Los Angeles: University of Southern California, 1957.

Harlow, H. F. Motivational forces underlying behavior. In Kentucky Symposium, *Learning theory, personality theory, and clinical research,* pp. 36–53. New York: Wiley, 1954.

Hebb, D. O., and Thompson, W. R. The social significance of animal studies. In G. Lindzey (Ed.), *Handbook of social psychology,* pp. 532–561. Vol. 1. Reading, Mass.: Addison-Wesley, 1954.

Hirsch, N. D. M. *Genius and creative intelligence.* Cambridge, Mass.: Sci-Art Publishers, 1931.

Knowlson, T. S. *Originality, a popular study of the creative mind.* Philadelphia: Lippincott, 1920.

Mackworth, N. H. Originality. *American Psychologist,* 1965, *20*, 51–66.

Maslow, A. *Motivation and personality.* New York: Harper, 1954.

Mead, G. H. Scientific method and individual thinker. In J. Dewey (Ed.) *Creative intelligence,* pp. 176–227. New York: Holt & Co., 1917.

Parnes, S. J., and Brunelle, E. A. The literature of creativity (Part I). *Journal of Creative Behavior*, 1967, *1*, 52–109.

Patrick, C. Creative thinking. In P. L. Harriman (Ed.), *Encyclopedia of psychology*, pp. 110–113. New York: Philosophical Library, 1946.

Simpson, R. M. Creative imagination. *American Journal of Psychology*, 1922, *33*, 234–235.

Torrance, E. P. Educational achievement of the highly intelligent and the highly creative: Eight partial replications of the Getzels-Jackson study. *Research Memorandum BER-60-18*. Bureau of Educational Research, University of Minnesota, 1960.

Wertheimer, M. *Productive thinking*. Enlarged edition. New York: Harper & Row, 1959.

White, R. Motivation reconsidered: The concept of competence. *Psychological Review*, 1959, *66*, 297–333.

5. Social and Psychological Factors which Influence the Creative Process

Frank M. Andrews

An Orientation to the Creative Process

ONE CAN DIFFERENTIATE between a person's *creative ability* and the *innovativeness* of his output.[1]

The first is a quality of the person—different from, but analogous to, intelligence. Mednick (1962) has proposed that the creative process involves bringing together ideas which are not usually associated with one another —that is, making "remote associations." "Creative ability" is this capacity for making remote associations which are *useful*.

Creativity ability is assumed to be reasonably stable for any individual over a 5–10 year period, though it may show short-run fluctuations—perhaps related to factors such as fatigue, motivation, depression, or colleague stimulation. While one can imagine that differences among individuals in their creative ability might be related to early learning experiences and/or physiological factors, these are not topics for this investigation. From the standpoint of the creator, or of an administrator of an organization responsible for producing innovations, a person's creative ability represents a resource which may or may not be well used. Essentially, creative ability is an *input* to the creative process.

Outputs of the creative process, on the other hand, are products—scientific papers, artistic drawings, musical compositions, reports, devices, processes, substances. Such products vary in their "innovativeness" and "productiveness." Highly innovative outputs open *new* possibilities for further research, appreciation, development, or utilization; *productive* outputs, on the other hand, permit significant advances along *established* lines (Ben David, 1960). On the other hand, some outputs of the creative process may be low in innovativeness, productiveness, or both. Creative ability, we

117

expect, should be relevant for understanding the innovativeness of a person's output, though not for understanding its productiveness.

The formation of new, useful combinations of ideas—creative acts—does not happen in a vacuum. The person must be aware of a specific problem, task, or technological "gap," and he must be motivated to work on it. Furthermore, he must have at his command the discrete bits of knowledge and skills which, in combination, can contribute to its solution.

But a new idea, if it occurs, is only the first step in the creative process. The resulting association must be evaluated, communicated, and developed before it can contribute to an innovative product.

Let us sketch some of the stages a creative idea might go through in becoming an innovative product. One can imagine that the person who achieves a remote association must first evaluate that "new idea." Does it seem likely that this idea can contribute to solving some particular problem about which the person has been thinking? Implicit in the evaluation is the notion that there exists a set of criteria against which the person can assess his idea. This evaluation probably occurs both consciously and subconsciously. It may require anywhere from a fraction of a second to months or even years. While some ideas may be evaluated solely by thinking about them, others may be the objects of extended efforts at "private" investigation.

Once a technical idea has been judged appropriate or useful, or at least "worth trying," it will usually need to be communicated to others. Several factors suggest the need for such communication. Often additional resources will be needed for the further evaluation and developmenet of new ideas—additional information, computers, new tools, working space, time, and the like. Furthermore, often one "new idea" is not sufficient, and can result in an innovative product only if combined with several other new ideas.

Crucial issues, then, are whether the person is willing to communicate a new idea and whether he is able to. Relevant factors include his willingness to take the risks inherent in possible failure; his need for, and sense of, security in his job, family, and community; his perception of his own role and the appropriateness of his suggesting something different; the ease with which he feels he can approach other people—friends, colleagues, supervisors; his skills at making himself understood; and the willingness of others to listen to this man make new proposals.

Once an idea has been successfully "sent" by its originator, and "received" by other people, further action will often need to occur for the idea to be fully implemented. Whether this will occur will depend in part on the nature of the other activities already underway in the external environment into which the idea is sent, and the ease of accumulating or shifting the resources needed for a new effort.

Thus the creative process can be conceived as an input of new, potentially useful ideas, a series of developmental stages or hurdles which those ideas must pass, and an output of innovative products. The present research focuses on factors which affect the likelihood of a new idea crossing the hurdle-filled gap and being developed into an innovative output.

Design of the Study

GENERAL PROCEDURES

To test these ideas about social and psychological factors which may affect the creative process, data were obtained from 115 scientists, each of whom had been the director of a research project. It was reasoned that the conduct of scientific research provides a setting of some social significance where the creative process occurs, and where outputs can be evaluated for innovativeness and productiveness using criteria about which there is reasonable consensus.

As is described in more detail below, the scientists completed one questionnaire several years after the initiation of their projects to provide information about social and psychological conditions present during the course of the research. After termination of their projects, they were asked to identify the principal report of the research, a copy of which was subsequently obtained, abstracted, and rated for several scientific qualities by expert judges. Five years after the initial contact, the scientists were contacted again for administration of psychological tests of creative ability and intelligence and a follow-up questionnaire.

RESPONDENTS AND THEIR RESEARCH PROJECTS

The respondents were all medical sociologists who had directed a project dealing with social psychological aspects of disease. The 115 scientists on whom full data were available constitute about half (47 percent) of all directors of such projects which were listed in the *1953–60 Inventory of Social and Economic Research in Health.* A careful check showed no evidence of marked differences between these 115 respondents and the entire set of all listed directors with respect to 11 variables describing demographic characteristics, research role, and qualities of scientific performance.[2] Thus the project directors analyzed here can be assumed to be reasonably representative of all directors of such projects active during the period.

The median age of the respondents was 38 at the time they began the specified projects; 86 percent were male; and two-thirds had a doctoral degree (nearly all the rest had master's degrees). The most common professional fields were sociology, psychology, and medicine. The typical project director had had his degree for about 7 years at the time the project was undertaken and had directed 2 or 3 previous projects. Fifty-eight percent claimed their primary activity was as a researcher; others mentioned teaching or administration in about equal proportions. Just over three-quarters, however, said their *preferred* activity was research. Typically, they spent half to two-thirds of their working time directly on research, and roughly half of the research time was devoted to work on the specified project.

Nearly all respondents (94 percent) felt they had "considerable" or more influence over the people who made decisions about their work goals; 87 percent felt their colleagues and superiors had "considerable" or "complete" confidence in their abilities; and 70 percent claimed their sense of involvement with the specified project had been "strong" or "very strong." Four out of five said they had "much" or "very much" responsibility for initiating new activities.

As a group, the respondents scored very high on a measure of verbal intelligence. The mean score for respondents was: 41.2, standard deviation: 8.0; by comparison, the mean for all employed Americans is 21.5, standard deviation: 9.4 (U.S. Dept. of Labor, 1967). While no national norms exist for the Remote Associates Test (a measure of creative ability), these respondents scored slightly higher than a large group of undergraduates at the University of Michigan, in which the mean score for respondents was: 17.8, standard deviation: 5.4; mean for 2,786 undergraduates: 16.4 (Mednick and Mednick, 1966).

As for the research projects themselves, about two-thirds were "problem oriented" (the others were mainly "theoretically oriented"); the median length was 2–3 years; and they typically had a staff of one or two professional people in addition to the project director. Findings from most projects were published as an article in a professional journal or as a health agency report. The most frequently mentioned laboratory sites were health agencies, academic social science departments, and medical schools.

MEASURES EMPLOYED

The measures to be discussed in this chapter fall into three broad types: (1) two mental abilities—creative ability and verbal intelligence; (2) a large number of factors characterizing the social and psychological environment in which the research took place; and (3) two qualities of the project's output—innovativeness and productiveness.

Creative Ability. The measure of creative ability was the Mednicks' Remote Associates Test (RAT). This is a timed, 40-minute, paper-and-pencil test which closely operationalizes Mednick's associational theory of creativity (Mednick, 1962). The person taking the test is presented with a series of items each containing three words. He is asked to think of a fourth word which can be associatively linked with each of the three given words. The following is an example of the type of item used:

ITEM: rat blue cottage   ANSWER: cheese

Studies on architecture students, psychology graduate students, suggestion award winners in a large business firm, and children have shown that people scoring high on the RAT tended to receive higher ratings for the creativity of their products (architectural designs, research projects, suggestions, and drawings, respectively) than low scorers (Mednick and Mednick, 1966). Furthermore, on a sample of scientists Gordon and Charanian found that those who scored high on the RAT tended to write more research proposals, to win more research grants, and to win bigger grants than low scorers (Gordon and Charanian, 1964). A study by Andrews (1967), however, found scientists' RAT scores to be unrelated to their output of papers, patents, or reports, and unrelated to the judged quality of their technical contribution or organizational usefulness. This lack of overall relationship seemed attributable to two opposite effects which were self-canceling; scientists in flexible settings showed positive relationships between RAT scores and performance; those in inflexible settings, negative relationships.

Taking a somewhat different approach, which may also be relevant for scientific innovation, Mendelsohn and Griswold (1966) found that high scorers on the RAT were more likely than others to make effective use of information which at first seemed irrelevant, but which in fact could be helpful in solving the problems presented.

The RAT has been shown to have very satisfactory inter-item reliability. For several different groups, the reliability has been consistently above .9 (Mednick and Mednick, 1966).

Although the Remote Associates Test has high reliability and appeared promising in the validity studies cited above, there remain some doubts as to whether it "really" measures creative ability.[3] We make no claim that the RAT is a perfect measure of this ability, but in view of its close ties to an explicit theory of association and incorporation of a usefulness criterion it seemed an appropriate measure to use in this situation.

Since the Remote Associates Test requires a close familiarity with colloquial American English, it does not yield valid scores for people who grew up learning a different language. As part of the data collection procedures, respondents were asked to indicate their childhood language. Those who did not check "American English" were excluded.[4]

Intelligence. The psychological test used to measure intelligence was the V scale of the General Aptitude Test Battery, Form B-1001, Part J, (GATB) (United States Department of Labor, 1967).[5] This test consists of 60 items, each containing four words. The test taker is asked to identify that pair of words which have similar *or* opposite meanings. One sample item is:

ITEM: big large dry slow   ANSWER: big and large

The test has a five-minute time limit.

The test is a widely used measure of verbal intelligence, is appropriate for adults, and is sufficiently difficult that very few of these scientists—a very bright group compared with the general population—hit its maximum score.[6]

The Laboratory Environment. Data about the social and psychological setting in which the specified project was conducted are based on respondents' answers to two questionnaires. They included items assessing decision-making power, independence from colleagues and supervisors, the quality of communication channels available, sense of professional security and environmental support, level of motivation, opportunities for initiating new activities, research roles, the size and duration of the project, and the adequacy of facilities and resources.

Since some (but not all) projects had been completed several years prior to the time respondents were asked to answer the first questionnaire, and since five additional years elapsed before the administration of the second questionnaire, opportunities for errors in recall were substantial. To check the extent of such errors, ten ordinally scored items which had been part of the first questionnaire were repeated in the second. The reliabilities of these ten items ranged from $\gamma = .81$ to $\gamma = .37$, with a median gamma of .55.

Although reliabilities in this range are far from perfect, they do serve to show that memory errors did not grossly distort the data in the five-year interval between the administration of the two questionnaires.[7] It seems reasonable to infer that memory errors similarly did not markedly obscure the data during the interval between the time the project was underway and the time it was described by the respondent on one of the questionnaires.[8]

Quality of Output. Each respondent was asked to indicate what was the principal report or major publication of a designated project he had directed. Copies of these reports were obtained and abstracted, and the abstracts were then rated on the following two qualities within the context of disease control and treatment.[9]

Innovativeness: The degree to which the research represents additions to knowledge through new lines of research or the development of new theoretical statements of findings which were not explicit in previous theory.

Productivity: The extent to which the research represents an addition to knowledge along established lines of research or as extensions of previous theory.

The judges who performed the ratings were persons chosen as leaders in medical sociology by members of the Section on Medical Sociology of the American Sociological Association. The number of judges independently rating each project ranged from one to seven with a median of 4.5 per project. The scores of the different judges evaluating a project were averaged to determine a final score for that project on each of the two qualities.

Although a measure of agreement among these judges has not been computed, their ratings were compared with ratings of the same reports obtained by similar methods from two other groups of judges, medical doctors, and administrators of medical sociology research. Agreement coefficients (Pearson r's) for innovation and productivity ranged from .42 to .53. Since the medical sociologists probably agreed more among themselves than they did with other groups of judges, it seems probable that the inter-judge agreement among the medical sociologists was at least .5. Application of the Spearman-Brown Formula would thus suggest these quality ratings have a reliability of at least .8.

Derivation of Adjusted Innovation Scores. A preliminary examination of the innovativeness and productivity ratings showed a possible "halo" effect: projects that received a high rating on one quality rating tended to also receive a high rating on the other ($r = .76$).

Since our interest focused on the extent a project was innovative, we sought a way of removing the effects of extraneous qualities from the innovation scores. This was achieved by computing a residual innovation score (hereafter called the "adjusted" innovation score) which consisted of the deviation of the project's actual innovation score from that score which would have been predicted solely on the basis of the productiveness of the project.[10] Thus, the adjusted innovation scores indicate the innovativeness of the project *after* "allowing for" or "holding constant" the productiveness of that project.

Parallel analyses were subsequently carried out for both the raw and adjusted innovation scores. In general the same conclusions emerged from each, though the adjusted scores tended to show sharper effects.

Findings I: Relationships among Creative Ability, Intelligence, and Qualities of Creative Output

CREATIVE ABILITY AND QUALITY OF SCIENTIFIC OUTPUT

As is shown in the top row of Table 5.1, creative ability, as measured by the Remote Associates Test, was virtually unrelated to either the innovativeness or the productiveness of the scientists' output.

This is in direct conformity with previous findings which showed RAT scores to be unrelated to several qualities of scientific output (Andrews, 1967). Nevertheless, the present finding came as a surprise because in the writer's previous study innovation had not been one of the qualities of scientific performance specifically examined. Here it was, and although numerous factors were expected to intervene between a scientist's creative ability and his producing innovative output, a stronger relationship was

TABLE 5.1.   *Relationships among Creative Ability, Intelligence, and Two Qualities of Scientific Output.*

	Intelligence	Innovativeness (adjusted)	Innovativeness (raw)	Productiveness
Creative ability	.41	.05	.07	.05
Intelligence		−.11	−.09	−.01
Innovativeness (adjusted)			.65	.00
Innovativeness (raw)				.76
Productiveness				

NOTE: Each correlation is based on about 100 cases.
　　　Coefficients are Pearson *r*'s.

expected than the .05 or .07 shown in Table 5.1. (The low relationship between creative ability and productivity was predicted: productivity had been defined as progress along *established* lines, and was not expected to require creative ability.)

The lack of even a modest relationship between creative ability and innovation might be explained in at least two ways. One is that creative ability or innovation (or both) may have been inadequately measured. However, other relationships in Table 5.1 indicate that these variables clearly consisted of more than just "random noise." The correlation between creative ability and verbal intelligence (.41) was similar to results obtained from other groups which have taken both the Remote Associates Test and a verbal intelligence test (Mednick and Mednick, 1966). Similarly, the fact that the raw innovation scores correlated substantially with the productivity scores further suggests that the innovation scores were not merely "noise." The validity studies cited previously for the RAT, and the fact that different judges showed moderate agreement on innovation, suggest that these scores should at least be related to the concepts they were intended to measure.

The other explanation—which we tend to favor—is that social and psychological factors may so affect the translation of creative ability into innovative performance that there is no general effect which one can describe or identify. This is what seemed to account for the lack of an overall relationship observed previously by Andrews, and, as will be shown below, can also explain the phenomenon here.

Before turning to the examination of the social and psychological factors, however, several other comments may be made about results shown in Table 5.1.

INTELLIGENCE AND QUALITY OF SCIENTIFIC OUTPUT

The second row in Table 5.1 shows relationships between verbal intelligence and the several qualities of scientific output. One can see that verbal intelligence was virtually unrelated to these qualities.

Verbal intelligence was included in this study because it might have confounded relationships between the Remote Associates Test (with which it was known to be correlated) and the quality measures. Finding intelligence unrelated to the quality measures removed our initial concern, but was contrary to the folklore which says that the research output from the brightest scientists will be seen as the best.[11] After an extended and unsuccessful search for possible contingency effects, our data suggest this bit of folklore is simply wrong. Among successful researchers (all of the respondents were project directors), verbal intelligence was not a useful predictor of these qualities of output.

RELATIONSHIPS AMONG OUTPUT CHARACTERISTICS

Also included in Table 5.1 are the interrelationships among the several qualities of the project reports. The substantial relationship shown at the bottom of the table, the .76 correlation between raw innovation and productivity, was what suggested the advisability of computing an adjusted version of the innovation score.

Correlations of these adjusted innovation scores with the other quality measures appear in the third row of the table. One can note that the adjusted scores correlated substantially (.65) with the original raw scores and were completely independent ($r = .00$)—as intended—from the productivity scores.

DISCUSSION

This first set of findings contains two key results: (1) the lack of relationship between creative ability and innovativeness, and (2) the lack of relationship between verbal intelligence and either innovativeness or productiveness. Given that at least moderate relationships might have been expected, that the measures themselves seemed to show convergent and discriminant validity, and that there was adequate variability among the respondents for some relationships to emerge if they were present, these nonrelationships called for further exploration.

For both creative ability and intelligence it was suspected that the apparent lack of relationship with certain output qualities might be the result of opposite, self-canceling effects.[12] An extensive analysis of possible social and psychological factors was undertaken and it was concluded that these did in fact have an important influence on the process by which creative ability was translated into innovative outputs. These results are detailed in the following section.

On the other hand, a similar analysis conducted with respect to intelligence showed that such factors could not explain the observed lack of relationship between verbal ability and output qualities. Convinced that differences between respondents in intelligence would not confound other analyses, we made no further use of the intelligence measure.

Findings II: Social and Psychological Effects on the Relationship Between Creative Ability and Innovation

OVERVIEW OF RESULTS

Prior to examining the specific analyses which lead to the conclusions of this section, it will be helpful to sketch these conclusions very briefly.

Although the magnitude of any social-psychological effect on the creative process was not very great, it was observed with reasonable consistency that creative ability tended to pay off more (in the sense of being more positively related to innovativeness of output) in the following kinds of settings: (1) when the scientist perceived himself as responsible for initiating new activities; (2) when the scientist had substantial power and influence in decision-making; (3) when the scientist felt rather secure and comfortable in his professional role; (4) when his administrative superior "stayed out of the way"; (5) when the project was relatively small with respect to number of professionals involved, budget, and duration; (6) when the scientist engaged in other activities (teaching, administration, and/or other research) in addition to his work on the specified project; and (7) when the scientist's motivation level was relatively high. These findings were in line with our expectations. We were surprised, however, to find that various communication factors and several indications of environmental constraints showed no consistent effect on the payoff from creative ability.

When several of these factors were considered simultaneously, very substantial and statistically significant effects emerged, though the number of scientists in the specified environments was sometimes extremely small.

SPECIFIC SOCIAL AND PSYCHOLOGICAL EFFECTS

Responsibility for Initiating New Activities. One of the psychological factors which was expected to influence the payoff from creative ability was the extent the person saw himself as having opportunities and responsibilities for innovating.

Three items in the questionnaire were relevant here. One asked directly "In the setting in which you did this project, to what extent were the following present . . . responsibility for initiating new activities?" The respondent checked a five-point scale ranging from "none" to "very much." The second question posed the matter oppositely and asked to what extent the resepondent saw himself as "effective as a 'right-hand man' carrying the ball for a more experienced advisor." The third item concerned the extent the project director had been involved in determining the focus of his project.

Table 5.2 shows that all of these items affected the relationship between creative ability and innovativeness in the expected direction. Scientists who saw themselves as having relatively high responsibility for initiating new activities, those who placed themselves relatively low with respect to acting as a "man Friday," and those who had been partially or wholly responsible for determining the research problem were the ones for whom mild positive correlations between RAT scores and innovativeness emerged. For other scientists, the correlations were consistently negative.[13]

TABLE 5.2. *Correlations between Creative Ability and Innovativeness (adjusted) According to Scientist's Role in Initiating New Activities.*

	*RAT scores and Innovativeness**	
	r	*difference*
Responsibility for initiating new activities:		
"much" or "very much" (N = 84)	.10	.32
"none" to "some" (N = 22)	−.22	
Effectiveness as a "right-hand man" for more experienced advisor:		
relatively low (N = 70)	.11	.35
relatively high (N = 34)	−.24	
Determination of research problem:		
determined by R himself (N = 57)	.12	.23
partially determined by R (N = 19)	.22	
determined before R became involved (N = 19)	−.11	

* Adjusted for productivity level

Thus the opportunity or responsibility for innovation was one factor which influenced the creative process. Without this, creative ability did not "pay off" in innovative output.

Influence Over Decision Making. Another effect which emerged with substantial consistency was related to the creator's role in decision making. Since a creative idea often requires development before it can result in an innovation, it was expected that people who were in positions to promote such development would be more likely than others to see their creative ideas carried through to innovative outputs.

As shown in Table 5.3, scientists who said they exercised relatively large amounts of influence in decisions about project-relevant matters tended to show stronger positive correlations between creative ability and innovativeness than less influential scientists. Out of eight items dealing with influence in decision making, seven generated differences in the expected direction.

As with the data shown in Table 5.2, this one effect was not very strong, but occurred with fair consistency.[14] It looked as if an ability to influence

TABLE 5.3. *Correlations between Creative Ability and Innovativeness (adjusted) According to the Scientist's Influence over Designated Decisions.*

	RAT scores and Innovativeness*	
	r	difference
R's influence in hiring personnel:		
relatively high (N = 56)	.12	
relatively low (N ≐ 42)	−.06	.18
Who had power to hire a research assistant?		
R alone (N = 68)	.12	
others above R (N = 22)	−.13	.25
R's influence over allocation of research funds:		
relatively high (N =48)	.11	
relatively low (N = 54)	.04	.07
Who had power to purchase a $500 machine?		
R alone (N = 45)	.14	
others above R (N = 53)	−.03	.17
Who had power to requisition under $50 of supplies?		
R's subordinates (N = 29)	.26	
R alone (N = 52)	.12 ⎫	.61
others above R (N = 20)	−.49 ⎬	
Who had power to publish a controversial finding?		
R alone (N = 66)	.11	
others above R (N = 26)	−.10	.21
Ability of R to influence decisions about his technical goals:		
"great" or more (N = 66)	.06	
"no influence" to "considerable" (N = 43)	.03	.03
Exception		
R's influence in formulation of research design:		
relatively high (N = 54)	−.09	
relatively low (N = 55)	.18	−.27

* Adjusted for productivity level

decisions was a social factor which could reduce the "gap" between creative inputs and innovative outputs. Interestingly, this finding replicates a result obtained in a previous study (Andrews, 1967).

Of course, faced with the data in Table 5.3 one wonders whether it might simply be a seniority effect. Table 5.4 brings together data relevant to this issue and shows that older, more experienced or more educated scientists did *not* consistently get higher payoff from their creative ability. (Note the lack of consistent direction and low values shown in the "difference" column.) Thus it appeared that what was important was ability to influence research decisions, not just age or experience or formal education.[15]

TABLE 5.4. *Correlations between Creative Ability and Innovativeness (adjusted) According to Level of Seniority and Experience.*

| | RAT scores and Innovativeness* | |
	r	difference
Years of prior research experience:		
0–3.0 years (N = 36)	.15	
3.1–5.0 years (N = 21)	−.02	.10
More than 5 years (N = 40)	.05	
Numbers of projects previously directed:		
0–2 projects (N = 47)	.03	
3 or more projects (N = 49)	.10	−.07
Highest degree:		
Ph.D., M.D., or other doctoral degree (N = 64)	.09	
nondoctoral degree (N = 31)	.04	.05
Years since receiving highest degree:		
0–5.0 years (N = 42)	.11	
5.1–10.0 years (N = 22)	−.35	−.09
More than 10 years (N = 32)	.20	
Age at time study began:		
35 years or less (N = 37)	−.01	
36–40 years (N = 21)	.34	.07
41 years or more (N = 38)	−.08	

* Adjusted for productivity level

Security. The creative process may be a risky operation for the would-be creator. Hence his sense of security would be expected to influence his willingness to discuss and act upon new ideas.

Table 5.5 brings together 14 items relevant to the scientist's sense of

TABLE 5.5. *Correlations between Creative Ability and Innovativeness (adjusted) According to the Scientist's Sense of Professional Security.*

| | RAT scores and Innovativeness* | |
	r	difference
Confidence of colleagues and superiors in R's abilities:		
"complete confidence" (N = 40)	.18	
"considerable confidence" or less (N = 67)	−.05	.23
Stability of employment:		
"very much" (N = 53)	.22	
"much" (N = 30)	−.03	.57
"none" to "some" (N = 22)	−.35	
Basis on which R worked on project:		
"permanent member of organization" (N = 64)	.16	
not a permanent member of organization (N = 28)	−.26	.42

TABLE 5.5 *(continued)*

	RAT scores and Innovativeness*	
	r	*difference*
Ease of moving to a comparable position elsewhere:		
"rather easy," "no trouble at all" ($N = 69$)	.16	
"impossible" to "so-so" ($N = 38$)	−.13	.29
Extent roles were defined for professionals on project:		
relatively well defined ($N = 47$)	.27	
relatively undefined ($N = 45$)	−.14	.41
Extent administrative superior got along with R personally:		
relatively well ($N = 39$)	.22	
relatively poorly ($N = 35$)	−.09	.31
Extent of disagreement with administrative superior on methods used:		
none or not discussed ($N = 62$)	.21	
some ($N = 13$)	−.67	.88
Extent of disagreement with administrative superior on study's purpose:		
none or not discussed ($N = 64$)	.17	
some ($N = 11$)	−.44	.61
Extent of disagreement with administrative superior on definition of problem:		
none or not discussed ($N = 63$)	.23	
some ($N = 12$)	−.32	.55
Extent of disagreement with administrative superior on interpretation of findings:		
none or not discussed ($N = 52$)	.27	
some ($N = 15$)	−.45	.72
Extent first-named colleague understood R's role on the project:		
relatively well ($N = 39$)	.16	
relatively poorly ($N = 41$)	.04	.12
Exceptions:		
Quality of professional relationship with first-named colleague:		
relatively good ($N = 53$)	−.02	
relatively poor ($N = 28$)	.20	−.22
Extent of disagreements about work activities with first-named colleague:		
little disagreement ($N = 46$)	−.06	
relatively much disagreement ($N = 36$)	.20	−.26
Risk-taking—what would happen if a year's activity led nowhere?		
"nothing, told to continue" ($N = 61$)	−.08	
"severe criticism" to "mild" ($N = 44$)	.17	−.25

* Adjusted for productivity level

professional security and shows their effect on the relationship between creative ability and innovativeness of output. Considered here are the scientist's relationship with his colleagues and administrative superior, the stability of his employment, the ease with which he could find a comparable position elsewhere, and the consequences of taking a risk that failed. Out of these 14 items, 11 showed effects in the expected direction: higher payoff from creative ability tended to occur among scientists in the more secure settings.[16]

It has already been shown that several seniority factors did not consistently or markedly affect the relationship between creative ability and innovativeness (Table 5.4). Thus it follows that the "security effect," present in Table 5.5, was not attributable simply to seniority.

From the magnitudes of the effects, it appeared that disagreement with the administrative superior on such fundamental aspects as a study's goals, methods, or interpretation of results was particularly debilitating. Conversely, there was inconsistent evidence about how the relationship with the first-named colleague (usually, the man's most important colleague) affected payoff from creative ability. Two of the three items which specifically mentioned this person suggested that a less than maximally comfortable relationship enhanced payoff from creative ability. (The third item was mildly opposite and favored the security notion.)[17]

Table 5.5 suggests that, with the possible exception of relationships with the first-named colleague, a sense of security in a scientist's professional life seemed to promote effective utilization of creative ability.

Role of the Administrative Superior. Our orientation to the creative process emphasizes the existence of various "hurdles" which a creative idea must pass in the course of its development into an innovative output. One such hurdle may be an administrative superior—a person who, in some instances, has much to say about the goals and methods of the creator's work, and the resources available to him.

As shown in Table 5.6, project directors whose administrative superiors "stayed out of the way"—at least with respect to the actual conduct of the research—were the scientists who tended to obtain higher payoff from their creative abilities. The first three items shown in Table 5.6 were different ways of tapping general involvement by the administrative superior. Thereafter, the items refer to his influence over funds, hiring, research design, and decisions about goals and objectives. Consistently, the higher payoff occurred when the superior was less involved or exercised less influence.[18] It seemed as if creatively able people needed to run their own show if their efforts were to result in innovative outputs.

Several cautions need to be added lest the results of Table 5.6 be interpreted to mean that the superior has *no* role to play. Recall, first, that all the respondents were directors of their own projects. Presumably they were reasonably competent scientists with at least some administrative

TABLE 5.6. *Correlations between Creative Ability and Innovativeness (adjusted) by Role of the Scientist's Administrative Superior.*

	RAT scores and Innovativeness*	
	r	difference
Extent administrative superior involved himself in the research:		
relatively little (N = 29)	.32	
relatively much (N = 45)	−.15	.47
Extent administrative superior interfered in the research:		
relatively little (N = 54)	.15	
relatively much (N = 20)	−.17	.32
Extent administrative superior limited R's research activities:		
relatively little (N = 37)	.23	
relatively much (N = 37)	−.12	.35
Influence of administrative superior over all allocation of funds:		
relatively little (N = 33)	.32	
relatively much (N = 35)	−.23	.55
Influence of administrative superior over hiring of personnel:		
relatively little (N = 31)	.21	
relatively much (N = 34)	−.10	.31
Influence of administrative superior over research design:		
relatively little (N = 31)	.25	
relatively much (N = 42)	−.09	.34
Influence of administrative superior on deciding goals and objectives:		
relatively little (N = 63)	.13	
relatively much (N = 46)	−.06	.19
Scientist has no administrative superior (N = 23)	.15	

* Adjusted for productivity level

experience. The appropriate role for the administrative superior of a person at this level may involve encouragement, facilitation, friendly criticism, and administration of the laboratory, rather than close involvement with the details of others' research. By hindsight, we regret not having included questionnaire items to measure these aspects of an administrative superior's role.[19]

Size and Time Factors. In line with the reasoning that high creative ability will be more likely to be translated into innovative outputs if the creative process occurs in a flexible setting, one would expect that short, small projects would provide better settings for innovation than massive projects involving many professionals and/or lasting many years.

TABLE 5.7.   *Correlations between Creative Ability and Innovativeness (adjusted) by Size and Duration of Project.*

	RAT scores and Innovativeness*	
	r	*difference*
Number of professionals on project staff:		
R worked alone ($N = 14$)	.13	
R worked with one other ($N = 17$)	.36	
R worked with 2–3 others ($N = 35$)	.07	
R worked with 4+ others ($N = 28$)	−.07	
R's preference for individual or team research:		
R prefers to work alone ($N = 33$)	.28	
R prefers to work as part of a team ($N = 53$)	−.01	.29
Size of project budget:		
Median size or below	.15	
Above median size	−.04	.19
Duration of project:		
Under 1 year ($N = 18$)	.44	
1–2 years ($N = 32$)	.20	
2.1–3 years ($N = 20$)	−.09	
3.1 years or more ($N = 17$)	−.16	
Did the costs of the study exceed initial estimates?		
no ($N = 51$)	.16	
yes ($N = 23$)	−.37	.53
Did project exceed original time limit?		
no ($N = 31$)	.24	
yes ($N = 41$)	.00	.24

* Adjusted for productivity level

The results in Table 5.7 are in line with these expectations and replicate earlier findings (Andrews, 1967) with respect to the advantage of flexible situations for effective utilization of creative ability. Note that projects in which the scientist worked either alone or with one other professional showed the most positive correlations. As the number of professionals became larger than this, the correlations receded toward zero and then turned mildly negative.[20] Similarly, respondents who preferred to work alone showed more positive correlations than those who preferred to be part of a team. Unfortunately, no item had been included to distinguish between preferences for small teams versus large teams.

Table 5.7 also shows that projects with relatively small budgets and short durations were the ones where the director's creative ability showed the highest correlations with innovativeness of output. Finally, it was important that the project stay within its initial time and money estimates.[21]

Allocation of Effort. Turning next to the range of activities involved in the scientist's job, Table 5.8 shows that project directors who had considerable diversity in their work tended to have the more positive correlations between creative ability and innovativeness. Based on these data, it would appear that for optimizing payoff from creative ability a project director should spend up to three-quarters of his time on research (but not all of it devoted to a single project), some time on teaching, and/or some time on administrative duties not directly related to his own research.

TABLE 5.8. *Correlations between Creative Ability and Innovativeness (adjusted) by the Scientist's Allocation of Effort.*

	RAT scores and Innovativeness*	
	r	difference
Time allocation to all research activities:		
1–50% (N = 45)	.19	
51–75% (N = 29)	.13	.37
76–100% (N = 34)	−.18	
Time allocation to this project:		
1–25% (N = 57)	.19	
26–100% (N = 40)	−.14	.33
Time allocation to teaching:		
some (N = 64)	.20	
none (N = 32)	−.08	.28
Time allocation to unrelated administrative duties:		
some (N = 46)	.27	
none (N = 51)	−.09	.36

* Adjusted for productivity level

Although our theoretical orientation had not specifically predicted the diversity effect which is consistently present in Table 5.8, one can well imagine that some diversity in work roles may be another aspect of the overall flexibility phenomenon discussed previously. Through such diversity, a person may receive useful stimulation, increased knowledge, and may also see opportunities for ways of translating creative ideas into innovative outputs. Furthermore, diversity may facilitate a work schedule which includes legitimated "incubation periods" for creative ideas. The notion that having time away from the task is a requisite part of the creative process has been mentioned by various eminently creative people.[22]

Motivation. It was expected that people who were more motivated by their projects would be more likely to develop their creative ideas to the point where they could result in innovative outputs.

Two attempts were made to tap the scientist's level of motivation. One item asked about his sense of involvement with the project, the other asked how important he felt the project was when the study began. As shown in the upper portion of Table 5.9, both items produced mild effects in the expected direction.

TABLE 5.9. *Correlations between Creative Ability and Innovativeness (adjusted) According to the Scientist's Level of Motivation.*

	RAT scores and Innovativeness*	
	r	*difference*
Sense of involvement with project:		
relatively high (*N* = 45)	.13	
relatively low (*N* = 64)	− .02	.15
Sense of study's importance when study began:		
relatively high (*N* = 36)	.10	
relatively low (*N* = 56)	.01	.09
Sense of involvement with project:		
Doctoral scientists:		
relatively high (*N* = 27)	.27	
relatively low (*N* = 37)	− .12	.39
Nondoctoral scientists:		
relatively high (*N* = 13)	− .02	
relatively low (*N* = 20)	.04	− .06

* Adjusted for productivity level

An earlier analysis by the writer on how motivation level affected the payoff from creative ability had suggested that high motivation enhanced payoff only among doctoral scientists who worked in "research" labs (as distinguished from "development" labs) and that among nondoctoral scientists the effect was opposite (Pelz and Andrews, 1966). Would the same results occur in the present body of data? As is shown in the lower portion of Table 5.9, the answer is "yes." Clearly, the effect for these doctoral scientists (all of whom worked in research labs) was stronger than for nondoctorals, and among the nondoctorals the effect was virtually nonexistent and slightly negative.

While it is not clear why motivation level should have a greater influence over the creative behavior of doctoral scientists than nondoctorals, the explanation may lie in the greater independence that doctoral scientists customarily enjoy. Perhaps the work of nondoctorals is more affected by external stimuli in their laboratory, whereas that of doctorals is influenced to a greater degree by their own involvement and interest in a project.

Constraints. It seemed reasonable to expect that the scientists who perceived fewest organizational constraints in their laboratory would be most likely to succeed in translating creative ideas into innovative outputs.

Seven items from the questionnaire were relevant here; however, no consistent set of results emerged from their analysis. (No table shown.) The most direct item, "How adequate were the facilities and resources?" produced a moderate effect in line with expectations. However, three other items which asked in a general way about the role of the scientist's institution and discipline produced virtually no effects, and the three remaining items, which dealt with adequacy of time, money, and office space, produced moderate effects contrary to expectation. Thus the present data provide no consistent indication about how the creative process is affected by environmental constraints.

Communication. Ease of communication was another organizational factor which had been expected to facilitate the translation of creative ability into innovative outputs. Of six items relevant to this area, however, four showed little or no effects, and the other two showed inconsistent effects.[23] A previous study also examined several communication factors, but, as here, only weak and inconsistent interaction effects emerged (Andrews, 1967). Thus the two studies agree in suggesting that there is no massive, general effect of communication on the creative process—at least within the range of communicative phenomena measured in these laboratories.

SIMULTANEOUS PRESENCE OF SEVERAL ENVIRONMENTAL FACTORS

Up to this point social and psychological factors have been examined one at a time. Our orientation, however, suggests that one should consider the total impact of the environment on the creative process.

With only 115 cases there were insufficient data to examine in great detail the simultaneous presence or absence of numerous factors. As a step in this direction, however, and to see whether the several effects identified above would be cumulative in their influence—as our orientation suggested they should be—the analysis shown in Table 5.10 was carried out.

One "indicator item" was chosen from each of the following four areas: opportunity/responsibility for innovation, influence over decision making, noninterference by supervisor, and security. The specific items were chosen on the basis that they produced at least a moderate interaction effect when investigated separately, and that there existed an adequate number of cases in each of the split categories.

As can be seen in the table, the correlations between creative ability

TABLE 5.10.   *Correlations between Creative Ability and Innovativeness (adjusted) by Number of Factors Present in Research Setting.**

	RAT scores and Innovativeness**
4 factors present (0 absent) ($N = 26$)	+.55
3 factors present (1 absent) ($N = 32$)	−.07
2 factors present (2 absent) ($N = 21$)	−.19
1 factor present (3 absent) ($N = 8$)	−.40
0 factors present (4 absent) ($N = 4$)	−.97

* The four factors considered in this analysis and their indicator items were:

> Initiation: Responsibility for initiating new activities—high.
> Influence: Power to hire research assistant—respondent alone.
> Role of superior: Interference from administrative superior—none.
> Security: Stability of employment—high.

** Adjusted for productivity level

NOTE ON STATISTICAL SIGNIFICANCE: Given the numbers of cases in the subgroups, the −.97 and +.55 correlations are statistically significant beyond the .05 level. Consistent progression among five correlation coefficients in the predicted direction (high to low) would occur with probability = .06 under random conditions.

and innovativeness of output ranged from +.55 (where all four factors were present) to −.97 (in settings where none of the four factors was present). Furthermore, despite the small number of cases in some categories, the progression of the correlations was perfectly consistent with the decrease in the number of factors present.

Of course we have "stacked the cards in our favor" by selecting items which we knew had individual effects. Table 5.10 demonstrates, however, that the several individual effects were *cumulative,* and that the cumulated effect was of substantial size.

It is worth noting that the results shown in Table 5.10 were closely parallel to results obtained previously in an analysis of a different body of data. Among scientists who were involved in initiating new activities, and who were simultaneously high in influence, self-confidence, status, and motivation, there emerged a +.37 correlation between creative ability and "technical contribution." Among other groups of scientists correlations were close to zero or negative (Andrews, 1965).

Three of the four factors included in Table 5.10—responsibility for initiation, influence, and security—closely match factors in this previous analysis, and a marked similarity in overall trends emerged. On at least two occasions, therefore, a cumulative impact of several social and psychological factors on the creative process has been demonstrated.

It is interesting that a positive correlation occurred in Table 5.10 only when all four factors were present. This suggests the possibility that the identified factors were "prerequisites" to achieving payoff from creative ability. If even one of these factors was absent, high creative ability apparently failed to get translated into innovative output.

With several factors absent, creatively able project directors actually produced *less* innovative outputs than other directors. Why might this be so? If a scientist has potentially creative ideas which repeatedly fail to get translated into innovative outputs because of the nature of his laboratory setting, one can imagine this man losing self-confidence, becoming dejected with his work, experiencing an intense sense of frustration, and eventually performing in maverick ways or perhaps hardly performing at all. While the idea that creative ability could be negatively related to innovation seemed surprising, this clearly occurred under certain circumstances. The oft-cited need to consider the "fit" between a scientist's abilities and the setting in which he works receives must support from this analysis.

DISCUSSION

This section has provided an explanation for the surprising finding of the preceding section that creative ability was apparently unrelated to innovativeness of output. The answer, it seems, lies in the social and psychological characteristics of the environment in which the creative process occurs. Under "favorable" conditions the higher one's creative ability the more innovative one's output. Under unfavorable conditions, however, the reverse was the case, and creative ability was negatively related to innovation. This is strong evidence for the proposition that it is important to consider the social and psychological setting in which the creative process occurs if one wants to understand the dynamics of that process.

Results presented here provide indications about the Specific social and psychological factors which have an influence on the creative process. These have been summarized in the "Overview of Results" which opens this section and need not be repeated here. It is worth noting, however, that while the impact of any one factor considered alone was often not very large, the impacts seemed to be cumulative, so when several factors were considered together they produced a very substantial influence on the process by which creative ability became manifested as innovative outputs. Only when each of the several factors being analyzed were simultaneously "favorable" did a strong positive relationship emerge between creative ability and innovation.

Findings III: Relationships of Social and Psychological Factors to Creative Ability and Innovation

Although the main thrust of this chapter has been to examine the effects of social and psychological factors on the relationship between creative ability and innovation, the data also permit examination of two other interesting questions: 1) How did social and psychological conditions (as perceived) differ between scientists high and low in creative ability? and 2) How did these factors relate to innovativeness of output?

Either of these question could appropriately be the topic of a major analysis, and our discussion will only highlight some of the stronger relationships. Even these, however, provide interesting insights into the creative process.

CREATIVE ABILITY AND SOCIAL AND PSYCHOLOGICAL FACTORS

In general, scores on the Remote Associates Test were not strongly related to the kinds of social and psychological conditions tapped by the questionnaires. Among the stronger trends, however, were indications that scientists high in creative ability tended to describe themselves as "loners": they preferred to work alone, saw themselves as relatively isolated from their discipline, had less contact with colleagues and other professionals, and received less aid from their institutions. They also tended to feel relativey insecure and uncomfortable in their organizational settings. Specifically, they were less likely to be permanent members of their organizations, they believed the consequences of taking a risk that failed would be more dire, and they got along less well with their supervisors. These scientists also tended to spend more time on research and were more likely to have their primary role in research rather than in education or administration. To summarize: high creative ability tended to be accompanied by aloneness, insecurity, and greater focus on research.

These relationships agreed surprisingly well with the folklore which describes the creatively able person as a rather lonely, isolated, and often frustrated worker. Of particular interest was the relationship between creative ability and insecurity, for security was one of the environmental factors which affected the payoff from creative ability. This may pose one of the true dilemmas of managing an organization which includes creative individuals—the flow of risky new ideas, which may be unsettling to organizational stability, may elicit responses from the organization which erode the creator's sense of security. But that sense of security needs to be high if there is to be an effective utilization of those ideas. The contradiction between the kinds of environments which seem to promote payoff from creative ability and the kinds of environments in which creatively able people find themselves might be called the "security dilemma."

INNOVATION AND SOCIAL AND PSYCHOLOGICAL FACTORS

Among the more interesting relationships between innovation and the social and psychological factors was the tendency for people who had relatively *poor* relationships with their administrative superiors to produce somewhat more innovative outputs. These were scientists who said they got along poorly with their administrative superior, had difficulty communicating with their superior, had disagreements with their superior on the study's methodology and purpose, believed their superior held their work in relatively low esteem, and felt their superior had a poor understanding of their work.

DISCUSSION: THE "SECURITY DILEMMA"

It cannot be determined, from the present data, whether scientists had poor relationships with their superiors and felt insecure *because* of their creative abilities and innovative output, or whether the direction of causality was just the opposite. (Our theoretical orientation suggests the former.) One can, however, imagine a kind of homeostatic model which would parsimoniously encompass the several relationships which have been identified.

One could speculate that as a creatively able person puts forth numerous new, untried, perhaps risky ideas, he tends to "make problems" for his administrative superior; as a consequence, his superior may reduce (or fail to increase) the security aspects of the person's job; whereupon negative feedback occurs, and the person becomes less willing to propose risky new solutions in the future, and his rate of innovation falls until it is "in balance" with the level of security he encounters in his professional environment. The model might look something like this:

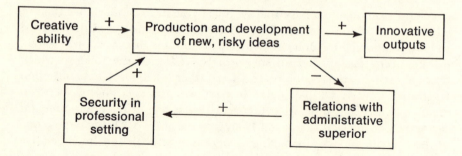

If the administrative superior could reduce the impact of the cycle, by providing relatively high independence for the person and/or by ensuring his security, the payoff from high creative ability might be enhanced.

Summary and Implications

One can conceive of the creative process as consisting of an input of new, potentially useful ideas, a series of developmental hurdles over which those ideas must pass, and an output of innovative products. The present research focuses primarily upon social and psychological factors which affect the likelihood of a new idea successfully becoming developed into an innovation.

The setting is the scientific laboratory. Creative ability (measured by

Mednick's Remote Associates Test) is taken as the input variable. The innovativeness of scientific reports (assessed by panels of expert judges) is the output variable. And the scientist's report about conditions in the laboratory where he conducted a specified research study provides information about the developmental "hurdles" and the process by which they were overcome.

The data about creative ability and organizational setting were obtained from slightly over 100 directors of research projects which investigated social psychological factors and disease. An abstract of the principal report of each project was independently assessed by 4.5 judges (on the average) for its innovativeness and productiveness. (The innovativeness judgments were subsequently adjusted to remove variance attributable to productiveness.) The adjusted innovativeness scores form the primary dependent variable.

Creative ability was found to be virtually unrelated to the measured qualities of scientific outputs when all project directors were considered together. (A measure of the project director's verbal intelligence was also unrelated to these.) However, mild positive relationships emerged for directors who: (1) had responsibilities or opportunities for innovation; (2) exercised considerable influence over decisions affecting the research; (3) felt a sense of professional security; (4) were allowed considerable independence by their administrative superior; (5) were strongly motivated toward the project; (6) worked on small, short projects; and (7) had diverse activities included as part of their work role. (Two other sets of factors—the presence of institutional constraints, and the ease of communication—were also examined, but produced inconsistent results.)

When the first four factors listed here were considered simultaneously, the correlation between creative ability and innovativeness of output varied from +.55 (all four factors present) to −.97 (all factors absent), showing that the different social and psychological factors could, cumulatively, exert a very substantial influence on the creative process. The nature of this multiple relationship suggested that these various factors might be acting as "prerequisites" for obtaining innovative payoff from creative ability.

Finally, a brief examination was made of the direct relationships between the various aspects of the research setting and creative ability and innovativeness. It was found that scientists with higher creative abilities tended to be relatively isolated from their colleagues and institutions, relatively low in their sense of professional security, and more exclusively research oriented. Those who produced more innovative outputs seemed to have more trouble than others in relating to their administrative superior. These results suggested that organizations seeking innovation may face a fundamental "security dilemma." Creative activities may be incompatible with organizational stability; as a consequence the creator's professional security erodes; but without that security he is unlikely to be able to effectively utilize his creative ability.

This research has both theoretical and practical implications. On the theoretical side, it shows the need to include social and psychological factors in theories about the dynamics of the causal process. Apparently it is not safe to assume that people with high creative abilities will generally produce highly innovative products. Some of the specific conditions which may enhance or block such a translation of input into output have just been described. Further investigation of the impact of these factors on the creative process in settings other than research labs would be in order, as would be attempts to identify additional factors which may also influence the creative process.

If it is determined by subsequent research that social and psychological factors have widespread influences on the creative process similar to those indicated here, this will have important implications for the validation of proposed measures of creative ability. Given a trait which may have either "positive" or "negative" effects, depending on the situation, and where the average effect may be close to zero, it would be inappropriate to assess validity by simply relating a measure of this trait (e.g., creative ability) to some criterion measure (e.g., innovativeness).[24] In assessing the validity of such a trait, appropriate social and psychological factors would have to be taken into account.

One of the central difficulties with the field of "creativity research" has been its failure to develop a set of unequivocal measures of creative ability which show high convergent validity among themselves. It is possible that this difficulty stems from the general neglect of social and psychological factors which may critically influence the creative process. Paying increased attention to such factors might result in both improved understanding of the creative process, and also a clearer conceptualization and measurement of the fundamental concept in the field—creative ability.

The present findings also have practical implications. They show that individuals concerned with promoting innovation within organizational settings (administrators of research and development, scientists, and certain members of many organizations devoted to activities other than research and development) need to ensure that the organizational climate facilitates the translation of new, potentially useful, ideas into innovative outcomes. The first part of this section summarizes some of the specific social and psychological factors which merit attention.

Notes

1. This research makes use of data collected previously by Dr. Gerald Gordon, my collaborator in a more general project of which just one part is reported here. His stimulation and support are gratefully acknowledged, as is the assistance received from Dr. Don-

ald Pelz, Frances Eliot, Ann Smith, and Lia Kapelis, who overcame many difficult problems in collecting new data for this study. The National Institute of Health, through grant GM-13507-01, provided financial support. Statements made herein are the responsibility of the author and not of the Public Health Service. This chapter is based on an unpublished paper titled "Social and organizational factors affecting innovation in research," presented at the 1970 Annual Convention of the American Psychological Association.

2. The following variables were examined: age, education, professional experience, principal professional activities, time allocation to project, role on project, size of project staff, project duration, involvement of administrative superior on project, and two qualities of performance: innovativeness and productiveness.

3. Goodman, et al. (1969), for example, found RAT scores did not correlate substantially with several other attempts to measure creative ability.

4. There were 13 people in this group. A check showed that the average score they obtained on the RAT was a full standard deviation lower than the mean for those who learned American English in childhood. (The mean for this latter group was 17.8; the standard deviation, 5.4.)

5. Used with permission from the Michigan Employment Security Commission.

6. To assess scoring reliability a 25 percent sample of the completed RAT's and GATB's were rescored by a second test scorer. The percentage of items where the two scorers agreed exceeded 99 percent, a highly satisfactory level.

7. Somewhat comparable retest reliabilities of questionnaire items answered by scientists have been reported by Pelz and Andrews (1966, p. 292). For 89 items over a two-month interval, they report a median correlation coefficient of .62.

8. As a further precaution against unreliability in data about the laboratory environment, separate parallel analyses have been conducted for each questionnaire item relevant to a given concept. Conclusions have been drawn only when nearly all such analyses point to the same finding.

9. Gordon (1963) compares ratings based on abstracts of project reports with ratings based on the full report of some of the projects included in the present study. From data he presents one can determine that the magnitude of agreement between the two ratings was $\gamma = .50$ for innovativeness and $\gamma = .67$ for productivity.

10. This prediction was achieved by the simple regression equation: $X = 11.88 + 0.77Y$, where X was predicted innovation and Y was observed productiveness (scaled to have a mean of 50 and a standard deviation of 10).

11. For other instances in which intelligence was found to be unrelated to occupational performance, see Super and Crites (1962) and Kraut (1969).

12. In statistical terminology these would be known as an "interaction." Other terms sometimes used for these phenomena are "moderator effects," "contingency effects," or "conditioning effects."

13. The fact that these three environmental factors were only modestly related to one another (gammas ranged from .11 to .31) made the finding of a consistent effect particularly interesting.

14. As before, the demonstration of a consistent effect becomes more meaningful if the items that produced that effect represent somewhat different ways of tapping an underlying concept. The gammas across the 28 possible pairs of these 8 items had a median value of .43 and ranged from .07 to .83.

15. Lest the reader be tempted to conclude, on the basis of data shown for age in Table 5.4, that the late 30s were an especially propitious time for translating creative ability into innovative output ($r = .34$), note that the data for years since receiving highest degree—most often a doctoral degree among these scientists—were directly contrary. People with 5–10 years research experience, most of whom would be in their 30s, showed a *negative* correlation ($r = -.35$). The lack of consistency suggests we have not identified any real effect.

16. Omitting the three items referring to the scientist's first-named colleague, the median gamma among the 55 pairs of remaining items was .27 (range: $-.20$ to .91). Thus the generally consistent interaction effect was not attributable to a uniformly high relationship among these items.

17. Pelz and Andrews (1966) have described a possible "dither" effect: that some mental

"shaking" may be required to keep innovating scientists keen and fresh. The finding that creative ability related more positively to innovativeness when a scientist tended to disagree with his main colleague and felt their professional relationship was relatively poor could be attributed to such a dither effect.

18. Once again the reader is reminded that the effect apparent in Table 5.6 was not simply a matter of seniority or prior experience (see Table 5.8). Nor was the consistent effect attributable to very high relationships among the items—median gamma was .34 (range: .16 to .87).

19. In a different study involving some of the same concepts, Andrews and Farris (1967) found that innovativeness in scientific teams tended to be higher when the team supervisor was seen as effective in such "task" functions as exercising technical skill, critical evaluation, and influence on goals. Two important distinctions are to be noted between the present study and the Andrews and Farris study: first, the present study focuses on the relationship between creative ability and innovativeness, not the absolute level of innovativeness; second, the superior-subordinate relationship investigated in the present study exists between people relatively high in a laboratory hierarchy, whereas the Andrews and Farris study examined the superior-subordinate relationship among people relatively low in the hierarchy.

20. This is one of the few places where the unadjusted innovation scores were more affected by one of the control factors than the adjusted scores. The basic trend, however, was similar to that described here.

21. A subsequent section on "constraints" discusses the effects of insufficient time or money.

22. A discussion of diversity and its *direct* relationship to scientific productivity appears in Pelz and Andrews (1966, chapter 4).

23. The six items tapped the following areas: sense of isolation from parent discipline, frequency of contact with colleagues, ease of getting across new ideas, problems in communicating with administrative superior, extent that work got discussed with people on other related projects, and whether the scientist maintained contact with other studies.

24. As an example, see Baird's (1972) review of the Remote Associates Test. As evidence questioning the RAT's validity, he cites previous research of the present writer showing that the RAT did not generally relate to several qualities of scientific performance. However, Baird does not go on to add that the relationships were affected by environmental conditions and that positive relationships emerged under certain conditions.

References

Andrews, F. M. Factors affecting the manifestation of creative ability by scientists. *Journal of Personality*, 1965, *33*, 140–152.

Andrews, F. M. Creative ability, the laboratory environment, and scientific performance. *IEEE Transactions on Engineering Management*, 1967, *14*, 76–83. (Note: same material also appears in Pelz and Andrews, 1966, chapter 9.)

Andrews, F. M., and Farris, G. F. Supervisory practices and innovation in scientific teams. *Personnel Psychology*, 1967, *20*, 497–515.

Baird, L. L. Review of Remote Associates Test. In O. K. Buros (Ed.), *The seventh mental measurements yearbook*. Vol. 1. Highland Park, N.J.: Gryphon Press, 1972.

Ben David, J. Scientific organization and academic organization in nineteenth century medicine. *American Sociological Review*, 1960, *25*, 828–843.

Goodman, P., Furcon, J., and Rose, J. Examination of some measures of creative ability by the multitrait-multimethod matrix. *Journal of Applied Psychology*, 1969, *53*, 240–243.

Gordon, G. The problem of assessing scientific accomplishment: a potential solution. *IEEE Transactions on Engineering Management*, 1963, *EM-10*, 192–196.

Gordon, G., and Charanian, T. Measuring the creativity of research scientists and engineers. Working paper, Project on Research Administration, University of Chicago, 1964.

Kraut, A. I. Intellectual success and promotional success among high-level managers. *Personnel Psychology*, 1969, *22*, 281–290.

Mednick, S. A. The associative basis of the creative process. *Psychological Review*, 1962, *69*, 220–232.

Mednick, S. A., and Mednick, M. T. *Manual: Remote Associates Test.* Form I. Boston: Houghton-Mifflin, 1966.

Mendelsohn, G. A., and Griswold, B. B. Assessed creative potential, vocabulary level, and sex as predictors of the use of incidental cues in verbal problem solving. *Journal of Personality and Social Psychology*, 1966, *4*, 423–432.

Pelz, D. C., and Andrews, F. M. *Scientists in organizations: Productive climates for research and development.* New York: Wiley, 1966.

Super, D. C., and Crites, J. O. *Appraising vocational fitness.* New York: Harper & Row, 1966.

U.S. Department of Labor. *Manual for General Aptitude Test Battery.* Washington, D.C., October 1967.

6. *The Solitariness of Self and Its Mitigation Through Creative Imagination*

Frank Barron

THE VERY CONSIDERABLE increase in research on creativity during the past two and a half decades is due in large part, I think, to massive social forces quite outside psychology as a professional and scientific discipline. These are too familiar to anyone who keeps up with the newspapers to warrant repeating here: in brief, they are the forces of radical change in social mores, in basic interpretations of the nature of reality, in technology, in relationships between nations, and in the opportunities in prospect for great masses of individuals to develop their own personal potentials to the fullest.

But the eagerness wih which psychologists have turned to research on creativity has another, possibly related but largely independent cause, I believe. The manifold of problems now being tackled under the rubric of "creativity" are largely the problems of general psychology and philosophy, especially as those problems were conceived and stated in the period from 1880 to 1910. What creativity research has done is to reopen some of the doors that were closed to psychology when it self-consciously separated itself from philosophy.

My own view has long been that psychology gains great strength from its origins in philosophy, and now that it has weaned itself and, indeed, come of age as a science, it can well afford not just an attitude of compassion but perhaps even a new relationship of mutuality with the mother of the sciences.

The psychology of creativity is related quite fundamentally to several of the enduring problems of classical philosopsy. I shall address myself primarily to only one of these in this chapter, but one could approach other philosophical problems with the same method of psychological analysis. I myself have attempted such an analysis of the freedom-determinism question (Barron, 1968), and as I have argued elsewhere, the psychology of symbolism provides a link between the optimism-pessimism dimension and the problem of induction. And certainly Norman Brown's important treatise on the eschatological implications of Freud's theories (*Life Against Death,* 1959) brings the philosophy of history into intimate relationship with psychological analysis.

The Solitariness of Self

Singularity from the cradle to the grave is the fate of man. Alone he comes into the world, and alone he leaves it. Mothered though he is and welcomed on arrival though he may be, he is separate, distinct, individual; and however companioned at his going, however surrounded by loved ones, plagued still by problems or beguiled by dreams, however unfinished his projects and incomplete his plans, his vessel is emptied willy-nilly and alone he goes again into the darkness.

"Lo, I am alive; but alas, I am alone!" So might run the message on the crib. "Cast a cold eye/On life, on death/Horseman, pass by." So stands the inscription on the grave of the poet.

In the meantime, of course, things are not all that bad. Not only are there pleasures and even a source of pride in solitariness, but there are ways to relieve it, and help available to do so. Myth, songs, art, family, community, nation, world, religion, the company of the great remembered dead, the sense of participation in the future through oneself as vehicle for the transmission of life and culture—these are some of the ways in which solitary selves form bridges to one another and perhaps, some would say, to the Great Self unbegotten and without a name.

As a problem for philosophers, the condition of human solitariness is considered as an assumption and given a name: the problem of solipsism. Solipsism, from *solus, alone* and *ipse, self* is the assumption that the self knows and can know nothing but its own modifications and states. In a stronger form of statement, it is the hypothesis that the self is the only existent thing.

William James (1890), in *The Principles of Psychology,* puts the matter thus:

> The only states of consciousness that we naturally deal with are found in personal consciousness, minds, selves, concrete particular I's and you's. Each of these minds keeps its own thoughts to itself. There is no giving or bartering between them. No thought ever come into direct *sight* of a thought in another personal consciousness than its own. Absolute insulation, irreducible pluralism is the law. It seems as if the elementary psychic fact were not *thought,* or *this thought* or *that thought,* but *my thought,* every thought being *owned.* Neither contemporaneity, nor proximity in space, nor similarity of quality and content are able to fuse thoughts together which are sundered by this barrier of belonging

to different personal minds. The breaches between such thoughts are the most absolute breaches in nature.

The existentialist theologian of the Russian Orthodox Church, Nicolas Berdyaev, attempts to salvage a form of mental community for men by distinguishing between man as individual and man as personality. He puts the matter as follows:

> Man, as an individual, endures the experience of isolation, egocentrically engulfed in himself, and called upon to wage a tormenting struggle for life, as he defends himself against the dangers that lie in wait for him. He finds his way out of the difficulties through conformism, through adaptation. But man as a person, the same man, gains mastery over egocentric self-confinement by disclosing a universe in himself. . . . Personality is a universe, it is filled with universal content. Personality is not born of the family and cosmic process, not born of a father and mother, it emanates from God, it makes its appearance from another world. It bears witness to the fact that man is the point of intersection of two worlds, that in him there takes place the conflict between spirit and nature, freedom and necessity, independence and dependence.

Leaving aside the theological content, though to do so perhaps weakens the argument, what Berdyaev is saying here is that by identifying himself with what is universal in himself and understanding himself as a universe, the individual man may break out of solipsistic confinement and participate in a human community in which spiritual evolution is being worked out, or, better, in which spiritual evolution of the species is recognized as the main task.

C. S. Peirce (1955), in his fundamentally important paper, "The Law of Mind," carries the analysis a step further, to the question of how intercommunication between forever separate minds and singular experiences is possible. The following passage occurs in the context of his discussion of the continuity of ideas and of the continuity between sensations and the stimuli which excite them:

> Even the least psychical of peripheral sensations, that of pressure, has in its excitation conditions which, though apparently simple, are seen to be complicated enough when we consider the molecules and their attractions. The principle with which I set out requires me to maintain that these feelings are communicated to the nerves by continuity, so that there must be something like them in the excitants themselves. If this seems extravagant, it is to be remembered that it is the sole possible way of reaching any explanation of sensation, which otherwise must be pronounced a general fact, absolutely inexplicable and ultimate. . . .
>
> The recognition by one person of another's personality takes place by means to some extent identical with the means by which he is conscious of his own personality. The idea of the second personality, which is as much as to say *that second personality itself*, enters within the field of direct consciousness of the first person, and is as immediately perceived as his ego, though less strongly. At the

same time, the opposition between the two persons is perceived, so that the externality of the second is recognized.

The psychological phenomena of intercommunication between two minds have been unfortunately little studied. . . . But the very extraordinary insight which some persons are able to gain of others from indications so slight that it is difficult to ascertain what they are is certainly rendered more comprehensible by the view here taken.

Let me conclude this collection of quotations with excerpts from one of the great English poets of the modern age, or perhaps I should say the age now ending, William Butler Yeats. Then I shall try to apply these observations to the psychological problem of intercommunication between persons, which in spite of its great practical importance still awaits comprehensive study.

First, the quotation from Yeats, from one of his last poems, "The Man and the Echo," in which Yeats addresses himself to his own Mask, which he calls Rocky Face. The echo, from the cavern of the self, tells him to "lie down and die" when he asks whether the struggle for meaning in life is worth continuing. Then the poet, wondering what is to be gained by that, asks:

O Rocky Voice,

Shall we in that great night rejoice?
What do we know but that we face
One another in this place?
But hush, for I have lost the theme
Its joy or night seem but a dream;
Up there some hawk or owl has struck,
Dropping out of sky or rock,
A stricken rabbit is crying out,
And its cry distracts my thought.[1]

[pp. 338–339]

Yeats again, this time in a prose passage from one of his journals:

I believe . . .

1. That the borders of our minds are ever shifting, and that many minds can flow into one another, as it were, and create or reveal a single mind, a single energy.

2. That the borders of our memories are as shifting, and that our memories are a part of one great memory, the memory of Nature herself.

3. That this great mind and great memory can be evoked by symbols.[2] [p. 28]

And again, in a poem:

Mirror on mirror mirrored is all the show. . . .[3]

[p. 323]

As I did in my earlier analysis of the freedom-determinism paradox, let me begin by distinguishing two aspects of the problem: solipsism as a theory about the nature of reality, and *solitariness as a feeling* which individual men *experience in varying degrees,* and which may be relieved in a variety of ways. This latter aspect in turn may fruitfully be approached: (1) in terms of psychodynamics, conceiving the feeling of solitariness as akin to other feelings in its relationship to instinctual strivings and ego-defenses: in brief, feeling like other feelings, and subject to the usual vicissitudes of feelings in the psychic economy; and (2) in terms of aptitudes and abilities of the sort we refer to when we speak of intuition, empathy, symbolic scope, social intelligence, and sociability, traits which may have mixed determination by heredity and by environment, and which may be improved by training and cultivation.

For James, Peirce, Berdyaev, and Yeats in the quotations I have given, solipsism as a theory about the nature of reality is the central concern, although in the latter three there are specific suggestions of the link to the qualities of mind in general: Peirce through the idea of formal continuity between the exciting stimulus and the state of excitation in the responding organism, a radical Gestaltist position; Berdyaev through the idea of universal spiritual process in which the individual who is free of ego concerns has immediate knowledge of his divine sources and nature, a radical neoplatonic position; and Yeats through the idea of a heightened sensibility which pierces, as the stricken rabbit's cry does in his poem, the enclosed cavern of the self in which only one's own echo may be heard (which I dare to hope is a pre-twenty-first century psychological position).

As for James himself, we know of his unceasing search for relief from the desperation of his feeling that no one could ever really know anyone else, expressed most poignantly perhaps in the final chapter of the *Principles,* which virtually undoes all that has gone before. In the writings both of Henry and of Alice James the same sense of desperate loneliness is the most constant theme. In such persons "the intersection of two worlds," as Berdyaev put it, is raised to the utmost intensity, and in them we can perhaps come to see better the relationship of the existential philosophic problem to the psychological problem posed by the fact that *one's self is one's situation.* An extremely sensitive self may be intrinsically a lonely one. Yeats wrote in *Reveries,* "I remember little of childhood but its pain. I have grown happier with every year of life as though gradually conquering something in myself, for certainly my miseries were not made by others but were a part of my own mind."[4] But we must look closely at this proposition, and it is here that psychological biography may be of immense help in elucidating the conditions in the childhood interpersonal environment that go along with strong feelings of solitariness.

This latter enterprise is at the heart of my own current research at the

Laboratory for the Psychological Study of Lives. I have returned to the interview data gathered in our study of writers, concentrating on their reports of their memories of childhood. There is a strong trend in the data to support the notion that as children these writers felt isolated, intensely sensitive, often unhappy. A similar finding has been reported by Ravenna Helson in her study of creative women, and Helson adds the observation that relief was found by having recourse to "complex, unstereotyped symbolic activity." In Helson's (1965) research, the design called for a comparison of college women nominated as having high creative potential with a group matched in terms of grade-point average and S.A.T. scores but not considered especially creative. The assessment staff was kept in ignorance of these ratings. As an interviewer in that research, however, I soon found myself being quite sure of who was who. The key interview question which invariably tipped me off was "How often do you cry?" The creative young women had quite commonly cried that very day, or the day before, or even, in one case, while waiting outside my door for the interview to begin! One might dismiss this as related to the problems creative women in particular must feel in our society, but in fact the question was put into the interview schedule because the most powerful single item in my Independence of Judgment scale, developed and cross-validated on male samples, is "I have seen some things so sad that I almost felt like crying." Answered *true* by independents, of course. The Independence of Judgment scale, in turn, has proved one of the most consistent predictors of creativity in our studies.

In terms of psychodynamics, I believe that the common and indeed adaptive "normal," "healthy-minded" defense against the feeling of solitariness is repression. The creative response to this and other painful aspects of fate is not repression, however, but openness and depth of feeling. I have expressed this elsewhere (Barron, 1969) as betokening "innocence in the face of fate." Such unrepressed intense sensibility often leads to trouble, of course, but at least it is *expressive* trouble and keeps open the possibility of *recognition of the self by another who is in the same boat*. The creative act is courage in realizing one's situation, and the reward for it, when there is a reward, is *company*.

While I believe the process I have been describing is basic and is usually initiated in early childhood by brave selves with little help, I also think it can be aided through creative education. I shall therefore turn now to the second aspect of the psychological problem of solipsism and its mitigation.

Before doing so, however, let me add that I conceive psychodynamics, including choice of characteristic defenses, to include individual differences of a biological and hereditary sort. "Intense sensibility," for example, may be the product not only of inherited dispositional tendencies in the realm of feeling, but of cognition as well, including inherited factors in intelligence. A student of mine at Santa Cruz recently showed (Michaels, 1973) that kinesthetic figural after-effect (using the method which A. N. Petrie (1967) introduced and made the focus of her research in *Individuality in Pain and Suffering*) is consistently related to measures we have found important in predicting creativity. Both the Barron-Welsh Art Scale and the Aesthetic Values scale of the Allport-Vernon-Lindzey scale of values are correlated positively with the tendency to *amplify* experience, in the sense in which Petrie uses the term. I would suggest that children of high creative potential are amplifiers rather than reducers of their own experience, including the experience of loneliness or solitariness in childhood.

Techniques to Stimulate Imagination and Creativity

Let me turn now to a description of some methods for enhancing creativity. These were employed in a year-long program in the Goleta, California School District by George Brown and myself. Brown has since gone on to develop a great many more exercises for use in his program of "confluent education" for teacher trainees in the College of Education, University of California at Santa Barbara.

The first set of techniques I shall describe were developed for use in a program designed to increase creativity in an ordinary school room situation. The premise was that classroom climates favorable or unfavorable to creativity were produced primarily by the teacher, and so we began by working with teachers themselves, leaving it up to the teachers to carry through into the actual classroom work. The procedures we developed had two basic aims: (1) to increase emotional understanding and empathy, which would include reciprocal action or appropriate communication of feelings; and (2) to free the imagination through apt metaphorical thinking and feeling.

The "empathy" exercises were similar in some ways to the Stanislavski method in teaching actors. An effort was made to suspend ego-feelings and to feel exactly as some other person, or animal, or even inanimate object might feel in its essential being. A state of quiet meditation was thus the precursor of the effort at empathy. Sometimes particular persons were chosen for the imaginative act of empathy. For example, instructions were given to think of a person with whom one was at odds, or perhaps whom one hated or despised. The task now was to feel just as that person felt about himself and others. Impersonal, inanimate objects were also made the object of the empathy exercises: for example, a seashell, or a pebble, or a microphone. One exercise that proved especially popular with both teachers and pupils was to imagine what it would feel like to be "a misspelled word."

By way of introduction to the "biological analogies" feature of the

Synectics method we developed an exercise in which step 1 of the instructions asked the participants to "think of all the gadgets and machines you can that are like parts or functions of the human body." Children are especially responsive to this exercise and manifest delight at realizing that so many mechanical things in their world are modeled on the human form. Then in step 2 the task is reversed, and they are asked to think of things about people for which there is no mechanical equivalent. This is incidentally an intriguing way of inducing the fundamental questions in the mechanism-vitalism problem, and one soon realizes that children at age five or six have available to them all the necessary concepts for stating the classical problems of systematic philosophy.

Another way of expressing our goals in this program would be to say that we were attempting to raise to a higher level of consciousness the idea that man is like a machine, albeit a soft and porous machine, but *a machine with feeling*. To seek a way of thinking about the nature of man is a good beginning in the process of opening the mind to the mystery of self and universe. It is interesting in this connection that psychoanalysis, in spite of its ostensible goal of "making the unconscious conscious," adopts a strategy whose hidden premise is that the person is a machine, and that the person as patient is a machine in need of repair or overhauling or tuning up. Moreover, by making its central technique the encouragement of transference for the sake of analyzing it, psychoanalysis as a therapy may actually reinforce the sense of solitariness, thereby indeed assuring that the process will prove interminable. The real aim of analysis, of course, is to break through the walls in which the ego has imprisoned the self, so that *genuine encounter* with another person, the analyst, may occur. Thus, when it is successful, psychoanalysis too is a method for establishing communication with another person.

Another technique that I have used in a variety of other studies employs standardized psychological tests as measures of how well one understands a given other person. In my first use of it, I asked several children to fill out an adjective checklist as *me*. I confess to being rather taken aback by the results, but at least it was instructive. This first bad news about the generation gap reached me some ten years ago, and it was with some feeling of satisfaction that I learned of the results of my own study (Barron, 1968) of generational differences in philosophy, and misperceptions of same by offspring as well as parents.

In this latter study, I asked a group of students who were representative of the recent graduating class of the University of California at Berkeley to respond to the 150 questions of my Inventory of Personal Philosophy, first as themselves and then in turn as their father would and as their mother would. Then I asked them to mail the questionnaire to their parents and ask the parents to take the test, first as themselves and then as their offspring, the student. Thus I was able to study genuine generational differences in philosophy of life, as well as misperceptions of parents by young people and of young people by their parents.

The result most interesting in the present context is the very large amount of misunderstanding of parents by their children. I have a feeling that teachers are just as often misunderstood by their students. Who is to blame is perhaps another matter. Regardless of these details, the main point I am making is that standardized psychological tests may be useful in measuring empathy or understanding of another person by the test respondent who takes the tests as the other.

I have used this technique both in other research and in my classes at University of California, Santa Cruz. In a study of role conceptualization in actors, I asked the cast of a student production of "King Lear" to take tests, such as the California Psychological Inventory and the Gough Adjective Check List, first as themselves and then as the character they were to play. Then on the basis of actual performances I had skilled clinical psychologists take the same tests as they perceived the enacted character. I have used the same method in graduate seminars, asking students to take such tests as a person whom they had just interviewed (and who had taken the tests previously) would.

The basic exercise, in brief, calls upon the subject to imagine another person and then to behave like that other person in response to a standard set of stimuli. With this sort of operational definition of empathy, and with this sort of measure of it available, one is in a position to develop means for increasing it.

I have also used Gestalt art techniques of the sort described by Rudolf Arnheim (1969) in *Visual Thinking* (notably his methods for eliciting self-perception through symbolic self-portraits at different temporal points in the life process) in conjunction with the standardized questionnaire method described above. Mad though the coupling might seem, graduate students in my psychobiography seminar report from their own experience that their clinical-intuitive-empathic senses are sharpened as a result. Because these developments in my teaching are very recent, I have not yet attempted to obtain quantitative evidence of such enhancement of empathy or symbolic scope, but it is quite apparent that the methods themselves could be made to yield an index of change. It is interesting that so many assessment measures developed for quantitative research on creativity have proved to be useful as exercises to increase creativity! And others might be added, from role playing to self-hypnosis.

Even the psychedelic drugs may yet find controlled use in increasing intuition, though at the moment their uncontrolled use or abuse seems to have eclipsed all the worthy potentialities they in fact possess. An induced experience which can increase in the beholder an appreciation of great works of art—and this I consider a confirmed effect of some of the psychedelics—must not be discarded prematurely. Such an effect confers significance of a high order on these controversial substances. What is empathy but imagination in the realm of feeling, and of what more sublime form of empathy are we capable than to assume in imagination the perspective of the creator?

Taken as a class, these means for the mitigation of solitariness may be understood in terms of the expansion of awareness of self in relationship to other selves or to clusters of selves, and their collective products—to lover, friend, religion, family, town, country, race; to tradition, myth, customs, social forms, a way of living and thinking in common; to the arts, singing, dancing, painting, sculpting, playing, the grace of the Muses; to religion, the fundamental experience of the *tremendum* and the forms in which creed and cult become institutionalized.

Madness too may be a sort of relief, to which the solitary self has recourse when it can no longer contain the scream within. Screaming madness is like the suicide of the proud, a cry to the Great Self to confer meaning if there is any.

Whim and irony must be numbered among the ways to dignity in the face of an intense consciousness of solitariness and injustice at the arbitrary sentence of death imposed on each of us and from which there is no appeal or reprieve. We might just as well add Brendan Behan and Red Skelton to our faculty of philosophers and poets. Someone once asked Brendan whether he ever thought of death, to which he replied vehemently and aghast, "Bejesus, I'd rather be dead"; and Red Skelton remarked under similar provocation, "If I wasn't insane I'd go crazy."

For it must be added that the problem of solipsism is linked logically to the general question of the meaning of life. Yeats' poetry abounds in evocations of the irony of man's situation—"consciousness harnessed to a dying animal." Single, solitary, never-to-be-again consciousness. What meaning can its development have? Can something foredoomed to end in death be worth all the trouble?

My general thesis has been that creative imagination may reduce meaninglessness and mitigate the situation of "the self alone." It does so through the great forms in which consciousness shows itself evolving: art, science, religion, community.

As a philosophical position, solipsism may be seen simply as a radical form of subjective idealism; but as a fact of human existence, solitariness and the need to establish meaning and community are primary motives in creativity.

Notes

1. Reprinted with permission of Macmillan Publishing Co., Inc., from *The Collected Poems of W. B. Yeats,* by W. B. Yeats. Copyright 1940 by Georgie Yeats, renewed 1968 by Bertha Georgie Yeats, Michael Butler Yeats, and Anne Yeats. pp. 338–339.

2. Reprinted with permission of Macmillan Publishing Co., Inc., from *Essays and*

Introductions by W. B. Yeats. © Mrs. William Butler Yeats, 1961. p. 28.

3. Reprinted with permission of Macmillan Publishing Co., Inc., from *The Collected Poems of W. B. Yeats* by W. B. Yeats. Copyright 1940 by Georgie Yeats, renewed 1968 by Georgie Yeats, Michael Butler Yeats, and Anne Yeats. p. 323.

4. Reprinted with permission of Macmillan Publishing Co., Inc., from *Autobiography of William Butler Yeats*. New York: Macmillan, 1916.

References

Arnheim, R. *Visual Thinking*. Berkeley: University of California Press, 1969.

Barron, F. *Creativity and personal freedom*. New York: D. Van Nostrand Co., 1968.

Barron, F. *Creative person and creative process*. New York: Holt, Rinehart & Winston, 1969.

Brown, N. O. *Life against Death*. Middletown, Conn.: Wesleyan University Press, 1959.

Helson, R. Childhood interest clusters related to creativity in women. *Journal of Creative Psychology*, 1965, *29*, 352–361.

James, W. *The Principles of Psychology*. New York: Holt, 1890.

Michaels, G. *Perceptual reactance and cognitive organization: A biological basis for creativity*. Senior thesis (unpublished), Board of Studies in Psychology, University of California, Santa Cruz, 1973.

Peirce, C. S. The law of mind. In J. Buchler (Ed.) *Philosophical writings of Peirce*. New York: Dover, 1955.

Petrie, A. *Individuality in pain and suffering*. Chicago: University of Chicago Press, 1967.

7. Painters and Painting

Anne Roe

MY FIRST STUDY of creative people was not primarily a study of the people as such, or even of the creative process, but rather a study of the effect of the use of alcohol upon artistic creation, in that case painting. I was then on the staff of the Yale School of Alcohol Studies, and this was an assignment thought up by the director of the school. I was completely uninterested in his suggestion that it be a library study of painters of the past through their biographers, but made the counterproposal that I get in touch with some modern painters and ask them. Although neither he nor some of the first persons I consulted thought that I would be able to get such information in so simple a way, he consented to my trying it. To be frank about it, I really was not interested in the alcohol angle, but I was interested in painting and painters, although my ignorance of modern painting was abysmal. I thought, too, that if I could actually get to interview such men, it would be foolish not to do more than just ask them about alcohol and its effect, if any, on their painting. I wanted to do a fairly comprehensive clinical study—what kind of people they were, why they chose painting as a profession, why they painted what and how they did, and all the rest of it. This proposal, too, was agreed to.

My first problem, of course, was the sample. I decided early on that I would confine myself to accomplished and recognized painters, and to discover who these might be I spent a great deal of time in an art library after all, but checking up on who was invited to major shows, and reading reams of art criticism (which I do not recommend as a pastime!). I also had the good fortune to be helped by Lloyd Goodrich, then at the Whitney Museum, who was sympathetic and encouraging from the start. The art critic of the *New York Times*, Howard Devree, was also helpful, although less concerned.

157

The problem of selection of the sample was complicated by the fact that I wanted representatives of a range of types of painting, from fully abstract to fully representational, and I also wanted a group whose drinking habits ranged from the teetotal to the alcoholic, an item not ascertainable from art criticisms. In this I was helped, not only by Goodrich but by two painters to whom he referred me, saying that if I could get their support they would influence many others, and also be able to give me even more personal information than he could about some of the men. This worked out remarkably well. I selected a sample of 23 men, and 20 of them agreed to participate. I never did find a teetotaler, but I did find one who drank very rarely, and then only on special occasions and to avoid social criticism.

The results, so far as alcohol was concerned, are easily summarized. For only one man was it of any significance with respect to his painting. He was one of the alcoholics, on the wagon when I saw him, who had in the past relied on alcohol to get him through the great difficulty he experienced in getting started on a new painting. For the others—moderate, steady, or heavy drinkers—there was no connection, except that a few reported that after a long day's work alcohol in moderation could be relaxing, and perhaps over-all that was a general aid. Technical reports of the study are listed in the references. The whole think was beautifully summed up in a short verse which was published in the *New Yorker,* after an article about the study had appeared in the *New York Times*. I think it will amuse you.

Homily for Art Students*

Study of Painters Shows Drink Does Not
Help Creative Work. The Times.

Turners, Dürers, or Bellinis
Do not spring from dry Martinis.
Goya's genius, Rubens' powers
Did not stem from whiskey sours.
Fumy brandies, potent ciders
Make no Holbeins, make no Ryders.
Alcohol's ingurgitation
Is, in short, no substitution
For creative inspiration
Or artistic execution.
   Guzzle vino
       Till you're blotto
Splotches will remain but splotches.
   Perugino,
       Ingres, Giotto
Were not born of double Scotches.
Nor, alas, will full sobriety

Whisk you into their society.
—Arthur Kramer

But it was other aspects of this experience which started me on the lines of research which I have pursued ever since. In addition to getting some personal history from each man, I administered a Rorschach to all of them, and a TAT to most of them. I selected the Rorschach in part because it had been supposed to carry indications of creative potential,[1] and the TAT for what further light it might throw on personality dynamics.[2] The Rorschach was easily administered; most of them thoroughly enjoyed it, and many of the records were very rich. On the other hand, administration of the TAT was often extremely difficult because they were all so incensed by the artistically objectionable quality of most of the pictures that it was often difficult, and in one instance impossible, to keep them to the task. Nevertheless, I found both techniques of considerable help, when one used them to interplay with the historical record, and the type and content of painting. When, as usually was the case, my interpretations were discussed (discreetly) with the subjects, this often brought out further important information and aided greatly in my understanding of the men and their work.

I also took down verbatim their statements of how they went about developing a painting. These were typed separately, headed "Creative Process," and then largely ignored except as they fed into aspects of the personality in relation to the type of painting. It is only now, almost thirty years later, that I have pulled these out and have attempted some analysis of them. Most of the rest of this report will be devoted to these materials (although I want also to note comparisons with scientists) since I think they are probably unique in the way in which they were collected. The reason for my neglect of them is that other things were taking my attention (and perhaps the fact that "creativity" was not then an object of study in itself). Those other things had to do primarily with what seemed to me the extraordinarily apparent relations among the personal histories of the men, their choice of a profession, their manner of pursuing it, and their personal characteristics. I am quite sure that in no other group, even in writers, could this become so beautifully clear. Some of this has been reported previously, of course, but I know more now than I did then, and the passage of time also makes it possible to carry some of these analyses further than I could then, since many of the men can be identified from them. Few of them are still living. None, so far as I am aware, is now in the center of things artistic as they were then.

Let me first give you very briefly some demographic data. They were then 38 to 68 years old, average 51. Four of them were born abroad, three in Russia and one in Japan, one coming to this country with the family at age 5, and two at 14, the other alone at 13. Their fathers' occupations included at one extreme a farmer and an usher and at the other a well-to-do businessman and a brigadier general. I would rate socioeconomic status of the families as lower or lower middle for seven of them, middle at seven, and upper middle or upper for six. The fathers of three were themselves professional painters, one was an art editor, one an amateur artist, and one a jewelry designer, but others were unconnected with the artistic world in any way, usually not even in interest. These data alone show marked differences from the usual findings with eminent scientists, very few of whom come from families in the lower economic groups. All of the artists were or had been married at least once (but two not until their 40s), and one four times. Seven of their wives were themselves artists, two were daughters of an artist, one an actress, and one a dancer, but I do not know about the others. As I observed them, I thought three of the enduring marriages were of major importance in the lives of these men.

They differ from scientists markedly also in the age at which they enter upon their chosen professions, most of them going to art school in their teens, sometimes without finishing high school. Only three were college graduates, and two more had a year or two of college. Most of them had to put themselves through art school, working at anything they could get and living on very little.

I have no measures of intelligence for the painters, but would judge from conversations and personality test data that they range from little above average to superior, although not many of them would be classified as the latter. But cognitive skills are of little importance in their work.

Most of the fathers, including all of the artists, disapproved of the choice of profession, usually on the ground that it was economically risky, to say the least, but in at least one instance because "artists are queer people" (not in the current meaning of "queer"). The mothers who were wives of artists usually also disapproved, but most of the mothers either approved definitely or, more commonly, thought that their sons should do as they wished.

I think the matter of parent-child relations is also a differentiating factor between scientists and artists. In general I found that relations between natural scientists and their parents were likely to be good, although a few of the physicists had rather derogatory attitudes toward their mothers. Social scientists frequently still had unresolved conflicts with their parents. With the artists, there were quite often indications of unresolved oedipal problems, and one wonders to what extent the entering a profession in the teens is related to these.

Six of the artists suffered fairly extreme social isolation or rejection, three had serious illnesses when children, and six of them lost a parent or younger brother in their teens. Early acquaintance with death happened to a number of the scientists, and in some instances it colored their later work. In the case of four of the artists, the results of this experience were still apparent in their personality dynamics and their paintings.

The Creative Process

"Painting," says one of them (no. 12),[3] "is an absolutely autobiographical thing. You put down what you are, you can't put down more than you are." This is explicitly stated by a few of the others, and it is probably true that all of them feel this way, although it is not always at a fully conscious level. "Whether you know it or not, your subconscious is putting your personality into the thing (no. 15)." This painter has the greatest difficulty of any of them in finding a subject for a painting, and I think there is no question but that a great fear of self-revelation is at the root of his trouble. This comes out quite strongly in the clinical material, and is suggested in his painting, of which one critic says, "He is always on the outside looking in." This is primarily a fear of being found ridiculous, going back to early childhood experiences.

In this respect, science serves a very different function. To a very considerable extent, the productions of scientists, their reports, are so formalized that, except for a few cognitive characteristics, the man is well hidden in the report. There are, of course, some suggestions of the kind of person he is in what he does and how he approaches it, but these are negligible compared to the way in which the painter exposes himself. This is not to suggest that science is chosen as a protective device, but it may well be that any form of art is chosen as an expressive device, although the need for expression may have to overcome a fear of self-revelation. When this happens, as in the case of no. 15, I suspect that it is not so much the need to express oneself to others, but to find out what one really is.

These men differ in the ease with which they start on a new painting after finishing one or putting it aside for some reason. Half of these men say that they never have nonproductive periods, but give different explanations for this. (A brief relaxation now and then, which is also typical of many scientists, does not count as a nonproductive period.) Two of them keep books of notes, sketches, from which they can always draw a subject if no more immediate one is available. For several it is just a matter of having a model regularly available. Others seem to have more ideas than they can keep up with. Descriptions of the way in which these men start and develop a new painting fall into four general groups. In the first, the stimulus comes from within, from an idea or emotion. The precipitating stimulus for the second group comes from without, although in this group there are marked variations in the extent to which mood enters into what is reacted to at the time. For the third group, external and internal are closely interwoven. Finally, two painters may work sometimes from internal and sometimes from external stimuli. I will give here a few examples, but I have also put in the appendix selections from the reports of all of the others, because there is considerable individual variation.

STIMULUS INTERNAL

There are only five painters in this group, and none of them is a representational painter. Only one is completely abstract, but the others, although not completely abstract, are quite highly stylized.

The painter whose work is now completely abstract (no. 5) says, "I start on a picture with a feeling of little forces. I make a sketch, I feel a force going this way and then there must be others. I construct a balance of equilibrium using lots of different pieces of paper so I can copy and take it one step further. I have when I start no idea of a finished picture." He had some ten years earlier still been using elements of forms; somewhat later he was "still holding on to reality by the eyelash. . . . I hated to but I had to leave representational painting completely. You just fight to hold on to reality. Now I feel free. Now I am so free I can put reality in again." (Reality is not evident to the casual observer.)

Another in this group is the youngest man (no. 17). His important paintings are all large canvases, over each of which he may have spent some years. Work on such as these is sometimes interrupted when he dashes off a few small ones to be sold, which they are immediately. "It is important to start off with an idea of what you want to say and that is the things you have felt over a period of time, not a reaction to any one particular experience, but an accumulation of a lot of things. All these things come together in some kind of form and that becomes the idea of a picture and the dominant factor becomes jelled and you see them in their relationships and then you can go ahead and paint it. . . . If you have any idea about painting at all that idea is sort of born in its entirety, it isn't an idea in line or color or in terms of an anecdote but a completely organized thing almost from the start, and it has to be born from material which you can express. The ease with which you can realize it develops in proportion to how close it can be assimilated in terms of your original idea."

STIMULUS EXTERNAL

For this group, the stimulus may be simply something seen casually in passing which pleases or interests the artist. They make rapid sketches on the spot, and are more likely to do this and paint in the studio than to paint from the scene itself, landscape, street scene, people, or objects. The degree to which mood or feeling is involved varies considerably both from time to time for any one of these, and from painter to painter as the examples will show. Only one of these men is now almost entirely an abstract painter, but the paintings of several others, although not entirely non-representational, are highly stylized.

For no. 12, different types of subject matter are handled somewhat differently. For portraits, "the person animates me to paint the picture. For instance I met this girl, and had a feeling about her sprightliness. . . . I can't paint any more unless I see it finished before I start it." The others who do landscapes almost never now do them on the spot, but he does. "I go around a lot, until I find a time of day and light, etc., that I like and then set up an easel and paint. I seldom paint landscapes in the studio. In the country I see it fresh after a winter in the studio. Landscape is very chaotic. The business of the artist is to make some kind of symbol with a sense of order in it. . . . Unity is the distinctive quality of any work of art." For still life: "I try to get three or four major differences and select objects, differences in color and shape and area. The still life I start is a very living thing, and then the canvas becomes the living thing and I use the still life as a sort of reference. . . . It sometimes is more alive than the thing itself because the canvas is ordered." (That the painting may take on its own reality apart from the painter is quite often noted.)

Painter no. 7[4] says he is never at a loss as he has sketch books full of subjects he has never developed. It is his practice, wherever he is, particularly in the country in the summer, or at parties where there is music (the musicians interest him particularly), or backstage at the ballet, to sketch with pen whatever he sees that particularly attracts him. This is usually a group of people doing something. Later he goes over these pen sketches with water color, pastes them neatly in books, and refers to them when he wishes a subject. The pen sketches are the most difficult part, and hard work; the actual painting is just a technical matter which he finds easy. His choice of subjects is characteristic and limited. When he is ready to start a new painting, if nothing in the immediate environment strikes him, he looks through these notebooks until something does.

Number 14 describes the inception of a particular painting this way: "A friend of mine has a penthouse across the street. One day last summer I looked at it and it hit me, that's my stuff, it's something I'd like to do, so I made a pencil drawing and then went up and made a bad color drawing. (It was later finished and bought by a museum.) What might at one time be banal, suddenly all the circumstances hit you and then you may never get it again, you lose it. I felt I had to grind that out somehow. I simply started something. It's unlike but in many ways it's like, then it became something in itself. . . . I may see something in which the whole thing is objective; I may try to make a definite study and other times it just starts me going on what has accumulated through years of study. . . . There is great variation in how long it takes me to paint and how long it takes a picture to mature. It might come in a couple of weeks or it might be a year.

A sketch may kick around, but there may be more emotional satisfaction for those you do quickly. There's a question of sustaining the emotional tone. If a picture goes wrong you have somehow lost the emotional feeling. With many I've reduced the technique to simply putting paint on canvas and while it can go wrong technically that's not the problem. So if I do get stuck it's usually a question of losing the emotion with which you started. . . . When you get things that click you feel as though you want to turn around and fight for something."

Number 3 reports: "I used to wander around looking for interesting things to paint. Then the Armory Show [this was mentioned by a number of the men as a turning point for them]. I changed from painting a scene as it was and began incorporating other things simultaneously. That went on for a number of years and then I had noticed while tramping around that some days there wasn't anything interesting to paint and other days there would be. At first I thought this was subjective, then I discovered it was the light, for example, on a brilliant day the pattern of the shadows wasn't interesting. Then I began to paint what was interesting about it and not how it looked. Now I go out and look and make drawings and do the painting in the studio." Then he spoke more about his shift to abstract painting. "In the meantime all this was taken from some special subject of nature, but from the process of painting indoors which required more analysis I became more aware of what was on the canvas without relation to what it was like. If a picture looked bad it was not because it lacked identity with an object in nature but because it wasn't balanced within, the forms or the color was wrong. Now I have learned the technique of taking what is dimensionally interesting in a subject and letting the rest come. Abstract painting has the same subject matter that all painting has, the available subject matter of life and cannot be anything else. . . . Now instead of going out and looking at something whenever I see anything that is interesting (and does not disturb him) I make a note of it and when I get a store of that stuff which seems to go together it is synthesized, there is a desire to put it together."

COMBINATION OF IDEA OR MOOD AND VISUAL EXPERIENCE

Although mood is mentioned by some of the previous group, an idea or sentiment plays a greater role in this one. Here it would seem that the idea, which may indeed have a powerful emotional component, tends to govern the use of a visual experience, whether fortuitous or sought out. However, distinction between this group and the preceding one is not very great, and is based in part on my memory of their paintings, as well as on the record of what they said about them.

Number 4 says, "I always paint from a model but I get the composition clearly in mind first. This is how I painted one canvas, for example. At the Met there is a beautiful painting by Corot. I thought of that picture except that I wanted to make a classic, modern American landscape, and I wanted to use the idea of gesture which the modern artists have practically forgotten. Then I noticed people going to church on D-Day and I thought about that and then I remembered the Corot in the Met. I wanted to paint a valley which would give the feeling of a classic American landscape, so I hunted and found one, and painted the picture on the spot. I got my wife to pose for the figure in the foreground. The idea for the painting came from the junction in my mind of the Corot and the people praying. . . . For large or important pictures I make sketches. Sometimes the name comes first, and then I find models for it. . . . There are no times when I can't paint because if I have no particular subject in mind I can always take any person, any girl, and paint head or shoulders, I don't have to look for subjects."

Number 16 says, "I think I was rather older than most students before I realized that there was something more to it than I'd been shooting for. It was a question of basic reality. . . . It began to dawn on me that you have got to scoop something out of your self. Things of horror and feeling and all of those things, things that you seem to try to experience within yourself and project onto the canvas rather than looking at the aspect. Technique has always been a very difficult thing for me and I have never had enough so I just have to trust to luck on its doing the job. . . . I never have been able to stay within my ability to perform." A description of the development of one painting begins with a somewhat startling incident involving the sudden announcement of the death of a relative while he was on the way to a party. The painting was stimulated by the whole situation and feeling about it. "I usually think of a picture as a whole, I think of a movement maybe, and I'll locate that on canvas; nearly always there is some little part that hasn't been completely solved and will give trouble because you haven't known before you started what it would be and trust to luck an idea will turn up." Many of his paintings have a symbolic death-in-life atmosphere.

EXTERNAL AND INTERNAL STIMULI BOTH EFFECTIVE

There are only two men in this group, and the painting of each is unusually distinctive, even for this sample.

Number 19: "My approach to landscapes and to figures is different. For landscapes I go out and draw, just quick sketches, sometimes I write in color notes, but I never paint outdoors. I have a very natural feeling about the outdoors and I like to tell about it. The memory plus the sketch is enough and then I can let my imagination play and I'm not disturbed by the endless beauty of the details, there is simplification. You can change the mood, too. My approach to landscape is very simple and direct, but may be considered lyrical and romantic. But when I do people a strange thing happens. I never have a model, although I may make quick sketches of people wherever I am and then use them in any kind of composition. With figures I may start with an idea and work out a way to tell the story. They are often satirical and unpleasant and mean. . . . I'm never at a loss because I have these books and books of notes, and I can leaf through them and maybe find something that at the time, just after I took it, I didn't want to use and now it comes to me, and I do that."

Number 9: "I work almost any way that any artist ever devised. From the quick impulse with extremely rapid execution to the design beforehand, work up the material, get models to study parts. I think I excel on the quick stuff. I both get an idea and hunt for subjects for it and vice versa. I run very few subjects and keep the same ones running and sort of work ahead all the time. I never had a nonproductive period." From a written statement: "I have turned from the industrial scenes, railroads, harbors, etc., to an almost exclusive interest in men and women on the streets in New York, with almost always a man-made building in the background— except for some beach scenes. The men are of two kinds: (a) naked as on the beach, young with fine body, the kind that filled me with so much admiration in youth, and (b) clothed, old, generally featured like an old Shakespearean actor (resembling my father) and on the bum—depicting a blissful descent, antisocial, decayed and disinterested in sex—myself as I would like but not hope to be. The women are of one kind, young, buxom, wonderful to see, feel, handle, smell, taste (caress) (blond for the sake of picture visibility only), strong, energetic, disdainful of the glances of men —this denotes my strong appetite."

What can be said about the creative process in artists in general? And how is it the same or different from that in science or other fields?

Ghiselin (in Taylor and Barron, eds., 1963) remarks that "a creative product is distinguished from all others by the presence in it of a configuration which is intrinsically new. . . . The escape from the closed world of configurations is accomplished neither by drifting nor by willful propulsion. The creative mind is drawn out of it by desire for an order that does not exist, for some distribution of its energies which no configuration is available to determine. . . . An idea of creation is the single action of the whole mind in production of some new configuration, the primary evidence of creative ability must be freedom and power in configurative action" (pp. 306–364).

These statements seem to me to apply equally to the creative process in art and in science. As many of the artists have emphasized, it is the ordering, the arrangement, the configuration that is the crucial aspect of the composition of a painting. That their concerns are primarily in terms of the ordering of visual elements, rather than of cognitive ones, changes only the mode of expression.

The visual mode of thought is predominant in all painters, even in those for whom the major stimulus for a painting comes from within. For most of them, furthermore, visual stimulation, reaction to things seen, is intense, sometimes almost painfully so. Even .the most representational of them is concerned with bringing these stimuli under control, by ordering their presentation, emphasizing some details, eliminating others, making sometimes subtle changes here and there, and infusing the presentation with whatever emotional reaction they feel. Most of them have a quite clear picture in mind of what they want to produce before they start, but this is sometimes only a rather vague whole, and the details remain to be worked out. Some work out details, or even the major part of the picture directly from models, some from sketches. For most, too, the preliminary work, the arrangement either in fact, as for still life, or in the mind, is the most important part of the process. Although a few cite technical difficulties, this is rather rare; for the most part they feel fully competent to "say" what they want to say, once they have decided what that is. What that is may result from a long process of mulling over an idea, but then may suddenly come to fruition when something "clicks," or it may come suddenly and without warning, when the artist, in a receptive state of mind, sees something that stimulates him, or that matches his mood of the moment.

Except for the few men in the first group, whose painting is primarily to express an idea or a sentiment, the creative process in artists lacks the directedness of the process in science, and this is a major difference. The "groping in the dark," the sudden insights happen in both. Technical mastery for painters is essentially the equivalent of the scientist's mastery of his field of knowledge.

For both artists and scientists, emotion is involved in the creative act itself, although they express it differently, if scientists express it at all. Some painters may use a sexual analogy directly, although this is far from universal among them, but I have never heard it even remotely suggested by a scientist. For both, too, the whole person is intimately involved in the production.

For both artists and scientists, life experiences and personality characteristics are intricately related with their work, but the relations are much more obvious in artists. I have discussed these in quite full detail for ten of the painters in an earlier publication (1946*a*) and will not repeat examples here.

Many of the characteristics of scientists as listed by Taylor and Barron (1963) are not found in most painters, largely because of the cognitive aspect. Artists do need a high degree of autonomy, self-sufficiency, and self-direction. To an extent even greater than among scientists they are fully on their own, and a great deal of self-discipline is required. They only teach, or accept commercial commissions when they must, but this is a minor aspect of their work. They are more likely to be impulsive than over-controlled. The scientist's "drive toward comprehensiveness and elegance in explanation" is paralleled by the artist's desire for beauty in his paintings.

What can be said further is that the general pattern of personality structure is rather different in the two groups. A particularly frequent pattern among painters is one of basic passivity and almost feminine submissiveness, which relates in part to a rich responsiveness to external stimuli, especially sensually toned ones. This seems in this group at least rarely to have been accompanied by overt homosexual expression, although in a few there are suggestions of such an underlying trend. In the few artists who show aggressive traits to any marked degree, these can usually be seen as defensive, and they may involve considerable conflict over aggressive expression. This sort of basic passivity is lacking among scientists, and while as a rule they are nonaggressive, they also tend to a sort of stubbornness which is not unrelated.

For both groups their products may take on a life of their own, apart from them. This does not prevent either from being extremely sensitive to criticism of what was once at least an intimate part of them. Creativity, as seen in both artists and scientists, does not come from any sudden inspiration invading an idle mind and idle hands, but from the labor of a driven person.

Appendix
Genesis and Development of a Painting

STIMULUS INTERNAL

For No. 18 reality has never been a bother. "I'm affected by environment and society and the life around me, they influence me in subject matter and point of view. I don't use models, it's all imagination and interpretive. I'm not affected by the image in front of me, it's pure expression so I'm free in that sense. The same applies to color and design."

For No. 2, although he does make use of things seen in passing, to which he gets an emotional reaction, as in an occasional still life, his more usual, and he thinks his best painting, comes about from trying to find a way to express some idea about which he feels strongly. For example, one picture came from a basic idea, that he wanted to show the suffering of the people in Europe, the bravery of children, the courage of mothers. "I wanted to make a statement about these people. I started to fumble with the woman, and I felt, 'How can I express that sorrow?' . . . until I had made a composition in which the lines also express suffering, but I don't know how they do. Or I might paint something to express how we felt about the end of the war, with the men coming back and rejoicing with people, but I didn't do it in a realistic way, I wouldn't have all the uniforms and firearms accurately copied from exact detail. . . . I believe in going to the fundamentals. It's a question of what is fundamental. If I sat down in front of a thing and made a minute drawing of it, it would bore me stiff. ... The more I paint the less near to things I seem to get."

Number 7 says: "There begins a peculiar kind of groping within, an appetite back of the groping, the search for the thing, like searching for the dark in a bureau drawer, for a solid, a concrete, definite thing ... then I seem to find a clue—it's a form, an object, and then the problem is one of trying to get unity with pressures. The background and the form are potentially equal." In a landscape by the sea, for example, the clue was a particular shape of a headland, and from this the whole picture was built up. The lighting coming from behind forced certain modifications, and the shape of the headland was deliberately repeated here and there (in clouds, for example). He describes his aim: "My appetite in my own work and what I tell and have kind of reverence for is the body. Even in my landscapes it's still the body that is the subject; that is the ultimate object as I see it." (One critic remarked that there is more genuine feminine presence in the cloudlands and the hills than there is in the figures.)

STIMULUS EXTERNAL

For No. 13 "Everything is paintable. In painting a landscape, still life, or an interior that I like, I feel much as I do in painting a portrait—if the subject is good to start with, I don't see any reason to do much altering. I am awfully interested in what I see. I place nature in the forefront always, if there is any art in my painting it exists in how I execute what I see. ... Although I have very little sense of organization in my life, I hate to plan stuff, but when it comes to my painting it's pretty well planned out. The more you plan ahead the easier it is to do. I make very careful drawings without thinking much of the composition, I'm pretty literal. Then on a fresh piece of paper I try to compose it, spot it. Then with that plus careful study I come back here and do the painting. I paint sort of as a souvenir."

Another, No. 7, says: "What I use as a painter I get mostly from observation, from senses, hardly at all from memory. My work is purely representational and always was. When I want to make a scene I make some sketches on the spot and then get models to take the positions I had observed, here in the studio. I usually carry a picture in my mind for a long time before I start to paint it, maybe for a year. I paint in a limited group of subjects, I'll start one group and keep working on it for some time."

Number 11 says "The thing itself is what supplies me with my imagination. My imagination doesn't produce the thing. You may see a landscape a dozen times but just a sudden moment it strikes you, maybe the light or the time of day, and then I see it as *my* picture. Similarly with a still life. For example, one with vases. They had been on the mantle for a long time, but once they were removed and then I was struck by the dignity.

First I thought how to place them, then searched for the props and situation which needed to be related only as they would convey the same feeling. In the case of figures you are struck by a model who seems to fit into your scheme of things. It's almost impossible if you see a person at a restaurant or home, to reproduce in a studio. The position is changed completely so I never attempt to reconstruct what I saw but I try to get the feeling that the person gave me."

For No. 15 "The difficulty is to get started. I go so long between pictures. I usually stalk around the city. That's the great puzzle to me, I don't know what starts me. I keep looking and I go to the places that have interested me before, hoping to find the same interest or something new. It's the glamor of the city, the kind it has for me that I am looking for. It just seems to me as if I have so many pictures a year in me and I can't force it. I have always been interested in that sort of headland structure of a building, where the streets come together at an acute angle, and in lighted interiors. The initial thing goes into it from your subconscious. I think my conception is in my mind, vague and fluid, but everything I put on that canvas is destroying my original vision. I am never completely satisfied. I think if I am not enthusiastic I am more likely to get stuck, but it's technical matters that stick me. If an artist says he is not stopped by these (as a number of them do) he's just not a good enough artist for it to matter. If I forget the mood and get involved in technical difficulties I have to check myself and try to get back to it."

For No. 20, whose painting is highly stylized, "The impulse always comes from nature. I had a period where I was totally abstract but even then it had its initiation in nature but so far removed no trace was recognizable. In this later period the nature still remains very evidently there but it's very arbitrary sometimes. . . . Things seen are sure to arouse an emotion of some kind or they don't have any value. It's hard to define because there is a long gamut covered by emotional reaction. Mine is a reaction to forms seen and their relations. Sometimes a picture, material for a painting may lie dormant for several years and then be picked up. It's usually material that lends itself to the concept of that time of what represents desirable combinations of forms and shapes. I usually go through a series of diagrams to establish the content of a picture. Then usually go through a full size drawing. The picture really exists in my mind complete before I start painting."

COMBINATION OF IDEA OR MOOD AND VISUAL EXPERIENCE

Number 8: "I develop ideas, very vague ones. Maybe I feel very happy and want to paint a gay picture, and that will suggest to me a woman with a certain kind of material and gesture. . . . My experiences all come from my emotional reactions so if sometimes I don't feel the same way I put that picture aside and work on some other. I sometimes get ideas through different things but most ideas I have exercised before, they come from a long process of thinking about it and rehashing it in my mind, before I finally come to do it. E.g., I do paint still life. Every day when I walk around the streets, even if I see a little stone, and the shape and color is interesting to me, I carry it back to my studio or if I see in antique stores, or window shopping. . . . I gather those things together and leave them kicking around the studio so I get used to them, so when I put these things together into a composition, colors, textures, shapes, I know thoroughly well what is this all about."

For No. 10, "All the works of art which have lasted through the centuries, no matter what their message was, have remained works of art because they were great designs in form and color. . . . It's easy to make an abstraction but when you have to organize, that's something. You carry motives in your mind for a long time before you make a picture. Here is one—I painted this in the summer on the Cape, the barn, rocks, trees, and so on, all part of the life of the Cape and I just had them all. Then in New York I said to myself I'd love to paint a picture of the fertility of this, so I designed this in New York, then went to the Cape and painted it all from nature. You carry all these things in your mind and think of them in juxtaposition and things gradually reveal themselves to you. Then you go to nature. It's a wonderful feeling, but you aren't copying nature ever. You feel happiest when it's going, it's almost like a perfect love match. . . . You almost hold your breath it's so wonderful and you have a sort of sensual pleasure in putting the picture on the canvas."

Notes

1. I was so surprised that very few of these records indicated that the subject was an acknowledged creative artist, that I sent them to Klopfer for blind analysis. He was told only the age of the man and that all were professionally successful. Although in two instances it was impossible to delete material which made it obvious that the subjects were artists, he felt that only one of these could possibly be a successful painter, and that it must be an avocation with the other. In the other 18, he noted "creative ability" as present in five, although probably not usable in two of these, and he remarked specifically upon its absence in five other subjects. Afterwards, he expressed considerable surprise when informed that all of the men were painters. Apart from this, we did not disagree seriously about the personality dynamics of most of the men, in spite of my own limited experience with this technique.

2. I had had equally little experience with the TAT, and we thought it would be interesting to send it to several persons for blind analysis with the same limited information. We had in mind a comparative study of the analyses. I regret to report that they were so divergent in coverage, tone, and inference that this seemed an impossible task, and was never carried out.

3. The painters are identified by numbers, which have no relation to any classification of them.

4. It was impossible to make a verbatim record of this painter's remarks, which poured out in a disconnected flood, interspersed with extensive invective against his ex-wives, the government, and so on.

References

Ghiselin, B. The creative process and its relation to the identification of creative talent. In C. W. Taylor and F. Barron (Eds.), *Scientific creativity: Its recognition and development*. New York: Wiley, 1963.

Roe, A. Alcohol and creative work: Painters. *Quarterly Journal of Studies on Alcohol*, 1946, *6*, 415–467. (*a*)

Roe, A. Artists and their work. *Journal of Personality*, 1946, *15*, 1–40. (*b*)

Roe, A. Painting and personality. *Rorschach Research Exchange*, 1946, *10*, 86–100. (*c*)

Roe, A. The personality of artists. *Educational and Psychological Measurement*, 1946, *6*, 401–408. (*d*)

Roe, A. Personality and vocation. *Transactions of the New York Academy of Sciences*, Series II, 1947, *9*, 257–267.

Taylor, C. W., and Barron, F., Eds. *Scientific creativity: Its recognition and development*. New York: John Wiley & Sons, 1963.

8.   The Strenuousness of the Creative Life

Salvatore R. Maddi

I AM NOT much of an historian. Nor does my personal involvement with the creativity area stretch back very many years. But it does seem to me that much creativity study has labored for some time under a serious limitation due to the failure to recognize fully the enormous strenuousness of the creative life. Perhaps we stand so much in awe of creativity that we cannot imagine pain, suffering, or loss associated with its pursuit. Nor have we always regarded creative endeavor as something to which persons are inexorably driven, regardless of the obstacles they may encounter. It may be that this difficulty can be traced to excessive emphasis in research on the characteristics of creative acts and the strictly cognitive processes involved in bringing them about, coupled with some neglect of the motivational factors in and sociopolitical implications of the life dedicated to creative endeavor.

The Situational View of Creativity

One expression of the view of creativity I am criticizing is the persistent theme in creativity study that situational structure, pressure, and constraint have an inhibiting effect upon innovative tendencies. This position has been taken by many investigators not only in psychology, but in education and industrial management as well (e.g., Bloom, 1958; Bradley, 1955; Dye, 1963; Fiedler, 1960; Hopkins, 1956; Kuhn and Kaplan, 1959; Melby, 1954; Oriel, 1959; Raudsepp, 1958; C. Taylor, 1963; Thorner, 1957; Weisberg and Springer, 1961). I am not disputing that some of these studies include data indicating that the average level of imaginativeness and flexibility in randomly selected samples of persons increases under unstructured, permissive, and nurturant environmental conditions. What is in question for me is the supposed importance of such findings for understanding creativity.

One problem is whether the behaviors involved are remarkable enough to be considered creative. A typical way of studying originality, for example, involves the subjects in imagining unusual uses for common objects, such as bricks and paper clips. When a subject suggests a use which occurs infrequently in the sample as a whole, he gains points for originality. It is assumed that the originality score thus derived expresses creativity. I have often wondered whether persons who have proven their creativity by producing things and ideas that have shaped the beliefs and meanings of others would do well on such laboratory tests of originality. These tests seem generally expressive of wit rather than any really ground-breaking insight. It is certainly not surprising that untaxing conditions bring out the best in ordinary persons. But there is an even more serious objection to generalizing from the findings mentioned above to creative endeavor. I am skeptical that the subjects who needed such a felicitous, warm, supporting environment to increase in imaginativeness would ever be able to manage creativity in the real world of varying and uncontrollable pressures and constraints. Quite possibly, naturally occurring creativity is enacted by far from ordinary persons.

Yet it has been common to assume that a good way to train persons for creativity is to put them in an unstructured, permissive environment for a time. For example, brainstorming sessions are supposed to increase creative potential by freeing participants to think and say anything, no matter how ridiculous it might seem in more conventional circumstances (e.g., Arnold, 1956; Bittel, 1956; Chapman, 1957; Clark, 1958; Fuller, 1958; Gould, 1957; Hix, 1956; Kneeland, 1958; McCloskey, 1957; Mason, 1962; Pleuther, 1958; Rapp, 1960; Upton, 1960). The various programs available for encouraging creativity in the schools generally regard as basic those provisions whereby students can be made to feel free to explore unusual approaches without fear of criticism (e.g., Anderson, 1961; Andrews, 1940; Barclay, 1958; Bryson, 1960; Burger, 1950; Derell, 1963; Durfee, 1961; Guilford, 1956; Hallman, 1964; Hasbrook, 1931; Henry, 1959; Hill, 1960; Houle, 1957; Jennette, 1963; Kaufman, 1957; Mearns, 1936; Melby, 1952; Parnes, 1963; Simberg, 1964; Suchman, 1971; Taylor, 1964). The common theme in all these training programs is that an important way to produce a stable increase in creativity is to have persons function for a time in an unstructured and permissive environment. While there is certainly evidence that the volume and diversity of ideas can be temporarily increased in this fashion, it has not been definitely demonstrated that this effect persists beyond the training sessions long enough to shift the whole course of a life toward creative endeavor. And, once again, I must ask whether the mild shift in ideas that takes place is remarkable enough to have significant implications for real creativity.

Although this approach to the understanding and fostering of creativity emphasizes environmental factors, it does make assumptions about human nature. After all, there is no way of trying to explain behavior without making such assumptions. A convenient way to find the view of human nature involved in the situational explanation of creativity is to consider what the human being must be like if it requires an unstructured, permissive surround in order to perform.

The impetus to produce novel and useful acts much be very frail indeed if it can be significantly curtailed by structured, evaluative environments. There must be considerable vulnerability and lack of self-confidence for opposition and criticism from the outside to make so much difference. Presumably, the person's own ideas and self-structure are not clear, important, or strong enough to withstand disapproval and compete with existing structure external to him. Whatever the protests of situationists that they are being misunderstood, the picture that emerges is of a human being who is basically dependent and weak, and too prone to crippling anxiety, therefore, to manage vigorous creativity when constrained or criticized.

Sometimes, the position that emphasizes the flowering of creativity in permissive, unstructured circumstances occurs without any position on how creativity can be trained. This is very understandable because of the situational emphasis in the creativity explanation. What is assumed here is that the human is by nature capable of creative acts, there being little if anything that can be taught which will influence this. Perhaps the development of certain skills and funds of information is useful, but these play a merely catalytic role to a creative capability rooted in the conditions of birth. The picture emerging here is that if the outside world would only desist from manipulating and exploiting the person, his frail though inherently patterned creative potential would find its greatest expression more or less spontaneously.

Sometimes those who consider creativity to be heavily influenced situationally do believe that training can affect creativity level. But the training advocated is rather restricted to cognitive exercises for growing in imaginativeness, by such means as restructuring problems, self-consciously thinking of low probability solutions, and operating through analogies and metaphors. There are virtually no exercises emphasized for developing other characteristics than imaginativeness, such as the values and habits of persistence, authenticity, and self-reliance. The implicit assumption being made here is virtually the same as if no training procedures were specified. The picture is still of creativity as an inherently patterned capability that can be sharpened by exercise, but cannot be radically altered by how one develops, by one's life style and personal commitments. This position is quite consistent with an emphasis on the unstructured and permissive environments as indispensable to vigorous expressions of creativity.

Self-Actualization as the Good Life

One reason why the view of creativity I have talked about thus far has been influential in research and conceptualization of late is that it corresponds with an over-all attitude toward the good life that is in the ascendancy. The good life, according to this attitude, is that in which one's inherent potentialities are actualized. As you will recognize, this view has been given influential expression by such psychologists as Rogers (e.g., 1961) and Maslow (e.g., 1955). Like acorns growing to oaks, human beings are construed as possessing a sort of genetic blueprint which is to be enacted in the process of living and developing. Although actualizing one's potentials is not exactly an automatic, nonintellective process, it is organismically patterned in a deep, evolutionary sense. Actualization will tend to take place without the aid of socialization. Indeed, society is usually regarded in this view as an obstruction because it forces individuals into molds, roles, conventions that have little to do with their own unique potentialities. The best thing society can do is impinge upon the individual as little as possible. No wonder that actualization theorists are natural social critics, typically finding existing societies overly structured and evaluative (see Maddi, 1972).

As societies tend to obstruct the actualization process, so too do attempts at special mental resolve or self-discipline, however worthy these attempts may appear. The trouble, according to actualization theorists, is that self-discipline and mental resolve to lead the good life are heavily expressive of the conventional values, taboos, and sanctions inculcated through socialization. The definite implication here is that true actualization is an organismic, mysterious process only to be misunderstood and distorted by attempts to plan, problem solve, work hard, and reflect upon experience. Just how extensive is the rejection of rationality is exemplified by Rogers (e.g., 1959), who decries "conditions of worth" (which are, after all, nothing really different from ideals applied to oneself) as inhibiting and therefore crippling expressions of mind. Instead, one should be "open to experience," "trust one's organism," and "live spontaneously." If this is accomplished, one's self-concept will change rapidly, and one will define himself as his activities. Self-reflection will be minimal. Mental life will be little more complex than a generalized sense of well-being. There will be little pain and suffering.

This approach has been popular in everyday life for a sufficient number of years to have found several expressions. The emphasis upon sensitivity-training groups is a clear example. Indeed, Maslow, and to some extent Rogers, have emerged as popular leaders of this movement. The emphasis of sensitivity-training groups is to help participants gain in social intimacy by losing their tensions and inhibitions. The assumption is not that one has to try hard for intimacy, but rather that one has only to give in to what comes naturally. It was predictable from this assumption that the early emphasis in such groups on uninhibited verbalizations would give ground to playing at touching and feeling perfect strangers, which would in turn lead to group sessions held in the nude. The attempt is to produce an idyllic scene incorporating visions of what it must be like to be somewhere between a child and an animal, all in the service of learning to be at ease with others and love them. But after an initial flurry of optimism concerning such techniques for encouraging intimacy, sober research (e.g., Lieberman, Yalom, and Miles, 1973) has begun to indicate that the sense of interpersonal ease and psychological growth claimed by actualization proponents of sensitivity-training groups is not what is materializing. Some participants are actually hurt by what transpires, and it is far from clear that this reflects their own limitations.

I do not regard it as farfetched to suggest that drug abuse is another phenomenon encouraged by the actualization view adopted popularly. After all, if you believe that life should be devoid of tension, pain, and suffering, and that what is of value is what comes naturally and easily, you have no basis for abstaining from anything that feels good and relaxes you. You will not be especially afraid of what produces the desired effect, even if it is a drug that could be addicting or in other fashion injurious, though painless. So entrenched is the assumption that what feels good is good, that drugs, with their rapid reaction requiring very little initiative on the user's part, seem a godsend.

Only now, after several years of widespread drug abuse, is the fallacy involved becoming apparent. I recently listened to Richard Alpert, a pioneer in the use of the "magic mushroom" and LSD, hold an audience spellbound for hours about the evils of drug use. According to him, the supposed insights surging to consciousness during the drugged state simply did not carry over to the nondrugged state for him and his friends. Soon they found themselves spending more and more time in the drugged state, however untenable this made their lives (fortunately, several of them were wealthy). Then Alpert met a guru, who seemed to have drug-like insights though he had never used any drugs in his life. To his credit, Alpert recognized the superiority of insight as the result of serious, persistent, self-reliant, strenuous effort to the pseudo-insight of the drugged state. Like so many alcoholics before him, he had a conversion experience, and began to preach a very different word than the popularized actualization position he had previously lived.

The situational view of creativity I discussed at the outset comes right out of the actualization view. Indeed, actualization theorists often refer to the life independent of social and mental constraint that they have described as creative (e.g., Maslow, 1955; Rogers, 1961). Charming though this view of creativity may be, I think it quite mistaken. Was it freedom from social constraint and an absence of mental discipline that sparked the creativity of Einstein, Michelangelo, Shakespeare, Plato, Christ, Freud, or anyone else history remembers (Maddi, 1965)? Were the creations of these persons emanations from some mysterious organismic pool of potentialities relatively uninfluenced by education and experience? Was their typical life experience one of simple well-being, devoid of suffering, conflict, alienation, self-consciousness, and the like? The answer to all these questions is: Of course not!

It is a trivial view of creativity that derives from the actualization position. It confuses garden-variety imaginativeness, day-to-day shifts in ordinary life experience, and an unreflective immersion in one's activities, with the stuff of greatness. Once the concept of creativity is democratized sufficiently to be an actuality for everyone, if he will only "stay loose" and avoid restriction, it has ceased to mean anything of importance.

Suggestions on Creativity Definition

I am aware of the danger, in defining creativity, of substituting my value judgment for another which I find unacceptable. A Chinese wise man is reputed to have said, "If you would know what a man holds dear, ask him to define intelligence." In our culture and era, this insight is even more true of the creativity concept. Nonetheless, each of us must push ahead with his definition of creativity, trying to make it as relevant as possible, and hoping through argument and experiment to convince the others that it is best.

Bruner's (1962) position seems cogent to me, because he defines a creative act as not only novel but also useful or valuable or effective. Acts can be useful in such ways as aiding in or constituting the solution of an existing problem, or by producing an aesthetically satisfying whole. In contrast, actualization positions tend to emphasize only the novelty component of creative acts. When focusing on the personal characteristics rendering novel acts likely, Bruner's position and actualization positions would both stress imaginativeness, in such forms as disjunctive thinking and spontaneous flexibility. But whereas actualization positions often stop there, Bruner would concern himself with the person's judgmental processes which could help him fashion acts that were useful rather than merely novel. Once you add judgment to imaginativeness as relevant abilities, you already have a view of the creative person emphasizing more discipline, planfulness, and self-criticality than would appear desirable in the actualization position (see Maddi, 1970).

I like the connotations of Bruner's approach which render creativity as hard work rather than "fun and games." Judging what would be useful and effective is certainly a difficult endeavor. Equally—if not more—difficult is the exercise of imagination in the direction of producing something not only useful but also new. We should not, in our admiration of creative acts, construe them as tumbling out of those fortunate persons who have been born right and are blessed by favorable environments. It is easy to function conventionally, producing nothing new, and availing oneself of the standards of usefulness provided by others. To function creatively is enormously taxing, I would contend, even for those giants who shape our lives by their efforts.

We should not let ourselves be confused about this by those descriptions by creative persons of how a great insight came to them when least expected or focused upon. The business end of their creativity was the long, grueling, intense period of hard mental work preceding the flash of insight. During this work period, the person is organizing his capabilities so as to optimize the emergence of a novel and useful product. En route, many possibilities are considered and discarded as ineffective, and hence the hard work may seem for naught. When the creative solution finally comes, it very likely is greeted with wonder. There, in pure, shimmering form is the long-sought solution! It is a romantic, though understandable reaction, to imagine the creative act to be unrelated to the exhausting, seemingly unsuccessful toil that preceded. In all probability, there would be no creative flash without the work leading up to it.

But the creative life is even more strenuous than that. To demonstrate, let me ask a naïve question: Why does anyone bother with creative endeavor, if it is so difficult by comparison with more ordinary pursuits? The actualization position would offer two related answers. One would contend that human beings are propelled into creative endeavor by their natural curiosity, exploratory tendencies, and interest in novelty. Offered as evidence would be such demonstrations as that of Butler and Alexander (1955) to the effect that monkeys will work harder for the privilege of observing a child's moving train than to observe food. Even more to the point is Harlow, Harlow, and Meyer's (1950) demonstration that primates will spend considerable time manipulating simple puzzles, such as hasps, as if they were interested in solving them. If even apes show exploratory behavior and curiosity, surely humans must be similarly inclined. Indeed, some of my work (Maddi, Propst, and Feldinger, 1965; Maddi and Andrews, 1966) and that of others (e.g., Berlyne, 1960) indicates the motivational status of curiosity, novelty-seeking, and boredom avoidance in humans.

I am no longer able to regard such motivational tendencies as convincing explanations of the push toward creativity despite its strenuousness. There is considerable question as to whether the studies on primates are even relevant to understanding creativity. Many years ago, Kohler (1925) did careful studies of the development of insights significant enough to be considered creative in chimpanzees who had been posed problems undoubtedly taxing their mentality. It was a rare ape indeed who, after weeks of fumbling and trial and error, happened upon the insight that two sticks could be put together to form a longer one for the purpose of pulling into the cage food that was otherwise out of reach. Most of the subjects never solved this puzzle. If the capability of primates for creative activity is so limited, how can we possibly assume that the expressions of curiosity and exploratory behavior they manifest are the motivational underpinnings of creativity?

Although humans are indisputably more capable of insight and problem solving than apes, it is far from clear that the studies of curiosity and novelty-seeking which have been done are relevant to creativity. My own work is typical of the difficulty. Actually, I have always had trouble thinking of it as relevant to creativity, though it does seem to demonstrate that humans possess a need for variety. One measure of this need is the passive expression of boredom and wish for change; another is the rather orderly penchant for asking questions; and the third is the tendency to produce one's own novelty in an active manner (Maddi, et al., 1965; Maddi and Andrews, 1966). However relevant to creativity some or all these measures may seem, I can assure you that when what the subject has to do in order to achieve high scores on them is scrutinized, the appearance of relevance falls away. Perhaps the most seemingly relevant of the three is the production of one's own novelty, which is scored from stories composed by the subject. But most subjects write such absolutely banal stories that one obtain a high novelty score by doing little more than naming the characters in the story, by giving them occupations just barely out of the ordinary, and by injecting a mild note of irony or humor. To my mind, such activities are too far removed from creativity to contribute to its understanding. Other studies (e.g., Berlyne, 1960) typically show that humans will look longer at complex or strange stimuli than ordinary ones. This too is hardly a convincing demonstration of the kind of burning motivation that would account for throwing oneself into such a difficult endeavor as creative activity. As White (1959, 1961) concludes, curiosity and interest in novelty are certainly present in many species, but are gentle motivations, easily submerged by other internal concerns and external pressures.

The other answer implicit in the actualization position as to why persons engage in something so difficult as creative endeavor is that it is genetically patterned in all human beings. Because the nature of organisms is to develop their potentialities, there is an inexorable push toward creativity. In contrast to the other answer, this one does not require that the person enjoy creative endeavor and therefore is more plausible on that ground as an explanation for engaging in taxing activity. But the position must contend with the obvious next question about how it can be that there are some persons who show little creativity. Once again, what will be deplored is the existence of inhibiting social structure and pressure. At this point, the position runs afoul of observations to the effect that virtually all those who we remember as having been creative were so despite enormous social forces arrayed against them. Galileo, Marx, Darwin, Freud, Dante, Byron, Yeats, Christ, Michelangelo, Zapata—the list is very long indeed of those whose creative endeavors involved sociopolitical risks and punishments. Once again, I must point out that garden-variety imaginativeness is not the same as creativity.

Creativity as a Sociopolitical Threat

I do not think it accidental that the list of persons who ran social, political, and economic risks in their creative endeavors is so long. It can be cogently argued that the function of social systems, institutions, and groups, is mainly that of maintaining the status quo (e.g., Durkheim, 1951; Merton, 1957). Thus, laws, conventions, values, traditions, folkways, and mores evolve whenever persons interact in order to preserve the common good. The common good usually amounts to the greatest service to an individual's or group's interests without thereby infringing on another individual's or group's interests sufficiently to cause conflict. The whole weight of this is in the direction of finding some workable balance and maintaining it.

But a common effect of creative endeavor is a disruption of the social status quo, regardless of the subject matter involved, or the insightfulness of the creative person into the implications of his actions. Perhaps the creative act could lead in the long run to a new and even more useful balance of sociopolitical interests, but in the short run the effect is disruption of the status quo. Nor is this true only in the case of those persons whose creativity has obvious social content; for example, Christ, Marx, and Freud. Even apparently value-free and scientific creations disrupt the status quo in the relevant professions (in such fashion as shifting the patterns of prestige and power, and requiring the reorganization of research and teaching efforts) and usually have social change side effects (as in the development of controlled nuclear energy leading to the atomic bomb). It is hardly a stretch of the imagination to contend that creative acts and persons are threats and are reacted to as dangerous in direct relationship to their effectiveness. Whatever else is involved, to create is to disrupt the status quo.

We should not be deluded by the alacrity with which modern, industrialized states mouth creativity as a value. By and large, the social structures and publics involved are not prepared to accept changes or disruptions affecting their own lives. Actually, in traditional, primitive, preindustrial societies there is little pretense that creativity is a virtue. What leads toward change is rather frankly regarded as dangerous in such contexts.

If this analysis is correct, then the true extent to which the actualization position is mistaken can be seen. To regard unstructured and permissive environments as prerequisites to creativity is to misunderstand the nature both of societies and of the creative endeavor. To train for creativity by carefully constructing mock environments that are unstructured and permissive is to fail in producing persons hardy enough to create under natural circumstances. If a person needs such unantagonistic environments in order to enter into creative endeavor, he has little or no chance of doing anything importantly new and useful.

We should take seriously the findings of MacKinnon (e.g., 1961) and others (e.g., Black and Peterson, 1955; Guilford, 1958; Torrance, 1963), available for some time now, to the effect that creative persons are very self-confident, self-reliant, even egotistical, and do not regard the approval or even respect of others to be very important. Socially, they can get by with a few trusted friends. Biographies of creative persons yield similar results. Freud (Jones, 1953), for example, believed from childhood that he would be a great man, and maintained himself quite well with his inner circle of friends and colleagues all the while his society rejected him as a pervert and a devil. Christ, Marx, and Galileo are similar examples. Others such as Nietzsche and Kierkegaard resisted the rejection of polite society without even the cushion of close friends. If we want to help persons be more creative, we should be toughening them up by encouraging self-confidence, a belief in their own greatness, and an imperviousness to social approval or rejection, rather than having them practice little exercises in novelty in the hothouse climate of a permissive and loving laboratory.

The Driven Quality of Creative Endeavor

If correct, my analysis only raises more insistently the question of why persons engage in creative endeavor at all. Given the enormous difficulty of being creative and the very real sociopolitical risks it entails, the answer must take the form that the person has, in some sense, no "choice" but to operate thusly. There are four general approaches that I can think of which have this form. One assumes that if you have the genetic endowment for creativity, it will express itself no matter what obstacles there are. This seems unlikely to me. First, it is rather intangible, leaving creativity a mystery. Second, we would, I think, have to make the improbable postulation that such things as imperviousness to social approval and interest in self-discipline and hard work are genetically patterned along with the talents obviously relevant. Third, we are accumulating evidence in our field that all sorts of capabilities thought genetically fixed, such as intelligence, may be greatly influenced by training and experience.

In contrast, the other three general approaches to why creative persons seem to have little alternative appear rather cogent to me at this point. Let me outline them and urge that they become the focus of future comparative study (see Maddi, 1972).

One promising approach considers the motivation for creativity to emanate from deep-seated, unconscious conflicts of great significance in the life of the individual. These conflicts would presumably be due to some less than developmentally ideal response to the child's instinctual expressions on the part of significant adults. In order to avoid the pain of punishment and guilt, the child adaptively forces the conflict out of consciousness. But this freezes the conflict in an unresolved state which continues as a source of mysterious tension and discomfort that expresses itself in the self-discipline and willingness to face risk that characterize creative endeavor. You will, of course, recognize this as a psychoanalytic formulation. What is needed in the approach is some definite position on the content or form of unconscious conflicts that leads specifically to creative endeavor and not to some other kind of activity. It is not really enough to consider creative endeavor "regression in the service of the ego," which means little more, as far as I can see, than becoming childlike without being sick. Why do some persons regress in service of their egos and others not? Is it oral, anal, or phallic conflicts, or some mixture of these, or something of the manner in which conflicts have been defended against, which pushes the person inexorably toward hard creative effort? Whatever the answer here, the general contention of the psychoanalytic approach is that creative acts certainly express, and may actually resolve, the underlying conflicts motivating them. Barron (1963) has made a start on relevant research here, but more effort is needed.

Another intriguing possibility why people engage in creative work builds on the observation that social systems and groups attempt to preserve, whereas creative acts disrupt, the status quo. Perhaps the creative person's early learning has eventuated in a self-image as a lonely searcher and crusader for fulfillment amidst a multitude of drones. Perhaps the ostracism and risk he runs is actually valuable, because it confirms his expectations concerning himself and others. Given this basis for thrusting himself into conflict with social forces, the creative person can thereby reap the benefit that comes through the antagonism. What I am suggesting is that the conflict between society's opposition to and one's own effort toward change can actually be stimulating, enlivening, and challenging. This effect is rendered likely if one not only expects the conflict, but almost looks forward to it as a kind of fulfillment of his self-definition and worldview.

I have formulated this possibility on the basis of the life experiences of great persons, as written about in autobiographies, biographies, and letters. It seems to me very common to find in such persons the self-definition of the lonely, misunderstood fighter for truth and beauty, and the worldview of society and others as obstacles due to conventionality. For example, while in Rome, Michelangelo wrote long, painful letters to his brother about how he had been robbed of his freedom by rich, church-related patrons, who forced projects on him unmercifully. Michelangelo had to take on these unwanted commissions, not only because he needed the money, but also because the patrons were very powerful and could have destroyed him if they wished. He saw most of them as conventional, unsophisticated persons who nonetheless had power over him. Needless to say, he was very depressed, and exhausted from the unwanted work. From reading the letters, one would never guess that major masterpieces of sculpture and painting were issuing from his hands at an incredible rate!

Picture a wealthy and powerful patron insisting that Michelangelo make a pieta (he sculpted four, all commissioned) when that was the furthest thing from his mind. Imagine what feats of imagination and judgment the artist must have been forced to do in order to fulfill the commission and still do justice, in some sense, to his talents and wishes. One pieta of his shows a madonna who is the same age as the Christ she mourns. Are they mother and son, or lovers? This sculpture started a great controversy, and was considered heretical by some. Another pieta includes a mourning figure in the background who looks suspiciously like Michelangelo himself. Does this scene depict a painful episode of history, or the universality of spiritual and physical death? Perhaps Michelangelo was spurred to this stretching of the traditional meaning of the pieta by being forced to take on projects he disliked.

A third possibility as to why some persons are driven to creative work concerns the attempt to avoid alienation (Maddi, 1971). Theorists from Hegel (1949) and Marx (1963) to Fromm (1955), Kierkegaard (1945), and Heidegger (1962) agree that the unique attribute of humans is the cognitive ability to reflect upon their experience. Animals can perceive, remember, and make simple judgments, but only the human can raise questions of value, necessity, and alternatives. Not to exercise and develop this self-reflective ability is to remain a conventional person, which is as close to the animals as humans can be. But once one engages vigorously in self-reflective thought, the result very rapidly becomes alienation, that feeling of separation from the world and even from oneself that is the especially human pain. Frankl (1955) puts it well when he asserts that only man can question the "whole dubiousness of being" and even commit suicide. For these theorists, the main purpose of life is to establish its meaning for oneself. Put in dramatic terms, this search for meaning is the human's way of avoiding suicide (Camus, 1955).

How can one find meaning in life? Some have done so by accepting traditional, familial, or religious values. While these may keep you going, they indicate conventionality, in the sense that the values are given to you from outside and do not emerge from your own reflection on your experience. If you accept tradition, you assert that the old ways are best. Familial values assume that family members, functions, and responsibilities come first, no matter what. And religious values incorporate the two in tying meaning to some supernatural (rather than internal) frame of reference. The locus of meaning is outside the person in each of these cases. Not only are these values not the highest form of human development, they may also expose the person to the debilitating effects of such stresses as social upheaval and threat of death (Maddi, 1972). Because external, socially imposed values are by their nature conventional, they are rather easily disconfirmed by the stresses I have mentioned. These stresses are quite common in modern industrialized states, and hence espousal of traditional, familial, and religious values may not even be very adaptive any more.

By far the best antidote to alienation is creative endeavor. Through producing new and useful acts, the person literally constructs a framework of meaning which is personal rather than imposed externally. Perhaps persons who dedicate themselves to creative endeavor have developed their human faculties of self-reflective thought to such a high degree that the enormous alienation which results can only be assuaged through producing their own meaning.[1] The kind of relationship I am suggesting between alienation and creativity is frequent in the lives of great persons. By way of barest example, recall William James, who was in the throes of a severe and agonizing sense of meaninglessness for several years preceding his appointment to teach at Harvard at the age of 32. At the point of accepting the job, he wrote to his brother Henry about how uplifted he felt at the prospect of using his energies and talents in the process of inquiry and discovery. At about the same age, Max Weber went into a serious existential tailspin that lasted nearly four years, during which time he did very little writing or teaching, being unable to manage more than cogitation and travel. After that period of time, however, he came back to his professional activities, with the whole character and impact of his research radically altered. His enormously significant works, that virtually formulated modern sociology and deeply infused modern culture in general, were largely written after his bout with meaninglessness. It goes without saying that the life styles of men such as these were at the same time enormously strenuous and a pinnacle of humanness.

The overall attitude toward the good life inherent in the formulation of creativity as an antidote to alienation is a far cry from the actualization position. Rather, it is an existential position (Maddi, 1970, 1972; May, 1958), in which life is conceptualized as a series of decisions, each of which can be made in a direction that propels the person into future-oriented growth through new experience, or pulls him back into the stagnation of a familiar past. The position assumes that it is the nature of human beings to grow and develop. This does not mean, however, that choosing the future, is an easy decision. The future is unpredictable, and hence its choice is fraught with anxiety. But to choose the past only brings the guilt of missed opportunity, because stagnation is a violation of human nature. In choosing the future, the person can be aided to persist in the face of anxiety by the courage (Tillich, 1952) based on an awareness of the true nature of life and the importance for achieving humanness of growing into distinct individuality (Maddi, 1970). To attempt this, the person must have all his mental capabilities about him. He must practice self-reflective thought, and become a disciplined person with clear views of what is important for purposes of development. I am describing a process of self-perfection that is wholly inconsistent with the mentally passive, emotionally hedonistic directives of the actualization position.

The existential position would not lead to emphasis on sensitivity-training groups. Intimacy would definitely be advocated in social relations (Maddi, 1970), but the difficulty of achieving this would also be recognized. Emphasized would be disciplined exercises in generosity, tolerance, and appreciation of individual differences (see Fromm, 1956), rather than touching games and nude bathing among persons who remain essentially strangers and have little reason aside from possessing human bodies for interacting. Nor would the existential position encourage drug abuse. Certainly, the raising or expanding of consciousness would be regarded as important, but the use of artificial, chemical means to achieve this end would not be acceptable. The use of artificial techniques is too passive to imply growth. According to the existentialist, the anxiety inherent in fully facing the unpredictable future cannot be circumvented because an important facet of development into individuality is assuming responsibility for one's own life in full recognition of the hazards of failure. Clearly, the existential position would not adopt a situational view of creativity emphasizing the importance of being approved of and nurtured by others. This would be quite inconsistent with the value of creating one's own meaning as an antidote to alienation.

Of the three contenders for explaining the seemingly driven quality of creative endeavor, I have clearly displayed a preference for the existential position. At the moment, however, there is no more evidence for it than for the other two. Nor is it clear that the three are mutually exclusive, though their implications differ. For example, the person who throws himself into creative endeavor believing that the clash between himself and others more complacent than he is inevitable, could very well, at another level of analysis, possess an unconscious, unresolved conflict consistent with his belief. This kind of belief could be harbored by someone feeling quite alienated and attempting to overcome meaninglessness through creative endeavor. It is even possible, I suppose, that someone could find great similarity between the existential and psychoanalytic views (though the differences seem enormous to me).

What I would do is take seriously the differences among the three possible explanations as stated. Then I would build research around these apparent differences in such fashion that the power of each view in the understanding of naturally occurring (not laboratory-inspired) creative endeavor could be compared with the other views. If all or some combination of views boil down to the same concept, that result would become apparent before long.

The Future

It is my impression that in the last 25 years we have done quite enough research on the characteristics of creative acts and the environmental conditions that facilitate their emergence. In the future, our efforts should focus upon the personality and motivational factors which, when present, literally force the person into creative endeavor, no matter what the cost in strenuousness and risk. Only when we have done this will our conceptualization of creativity be such that we can convincingly understand the lonely, driven giants whose efforts shape their own and our worlds.

Note

1. I have Irving Taylor to thank for his suggestions along these lines.

References

Anderson, H. H. Creativity and education. *College and University Bulletin*, 1961, *13, 14*.

Andrews, E. G. The development of imagination in the pre-school child. *University of Iowa Studies of Character*, 1940, *3*, (4), 1–64.

Arnold, J. E. Brainstorming: Personal development—an individual approach. *Machine Design*, 1956, *28*, 95–96.

Barclay, P. M. Take the lid off creativity. *School Arts Magazine*, 1958, *57*, 5–8.

Barron, F. *Creativity and psychological health*. Princeton, N.J.: Van Nostrand, 1963.

Berlyne, D. E. *Conflict, arousal, & curiosity*. New York: McGraw-Hill, 1960.

Bittel, L. R. Brainstorming: Better way to solve plant problems. *Factory Management*, 1956, *114* (5), 98–107.

Block, J., and Peterson, P. Some personality correlates of confidence, caution, and speed in a decision situation. *Journal of Abnormal and Social Psychology*, 1955, *51*, 34–41.

Bloom, B. S. Some effects of cultural, social, and educational conditions on creativity. In C. W. Taylor (Ed.), *The second (1957) University of Utah research conference on the identification of creative scientific talent*, pp. 55–56. Salt Lake City: University of Utah Press, 1958. (Out of print)

Bradley, P. *Happiness through creative living*. Garden City: Hanover House, 1955.

Bruner, J. S. The creative surprise. In H. E. Gruber, G. Terrell, and M. Wertheimer (Eds.), *Contemporary approaches to creative thinking*. New York: Atherton, 1962.

Bryson, L. Training for creativity. *School Arts Magazine*, 1960, *60*, 5–8.

Burger, I. *Creative play activity*. New York: A. S. Barnes, 1950.

Butler, R. A., and Alexander, H. M. Daily patterns of visual exploratory behavior in the monkey. *Journal of Comparative and Physiological Psychology,* 1955, *48,* 247–249.

Camus, A. *The myth of Sisyphus and other essays.* Trans. by J. O'Brien. New York: Knopf, 1955.

Chapman, J. L. Introduction to brainstorming. Paper presented at *The Edison Electric Institute Housepower Workshop,* October, 1957.

Clark, C. H. *Brainstorming.* Garden City, N.Y.: Doubleday, 1958.

Derell, G. R. Creativity in education. *The Clearing House,* 1963, *38,* 67–69.

Durfee, R. A. How to stifle creativity. *Personnel,* 1961, *38,* 63–66.

Durkheim, E. *Suicide.* New York: New York Free Press, 1951.

Dye, Sister M. An inquiry into creativity and its nurturing climate: An exploratory study. Doctoral dissertation, St. Louis University, 1963.

Fiedler, F. Leadership, group composition and group creativity. *American Psychologist,* 1960, *15* (7), 390.

Frankl, V. *The doctor and the soul.* Trans. by R. Winston and C. Winston. New York: Knopf, 1955.

Freud, S. The relation of the poet to daydreaming. (1908) In *Collected papers.* Vol. 4, pp. 173–183. Trans. by Joan Riviere. London: Hogarth Press, 1948.

Fromm, E. *The sane society.* New York: Fawcett Premier Books, 1955.

Fromm, E. *The art of loving.* New York: Harper, 1956.

Fuller, H. E. *Uses of brainstorming in veterans administration.* Buffalo: Creative Education Foundation, 1958.

Gould, R. E. Brainstorming at work. *Ceramic Industry,* 1957, *68,* Part I. 131–133, 135; Part II. 92–93.

Guilford, J. P. Can creativity be developed? *Art Education,* 1956, *11,* 14–18.

Guilford, J. P. Traits of creativity. In *Creativity and its cultivation. Addresses presented at the interdisciplinary symposia on creativity, Michigan State University, 1957–1958,* pp. 142–161. New York: Harper, 1959.

Hallman, R. J. Can creativity be taught? *Educational Theory,* 1964, *14,* 15–23.

Harlow, H. F., Harlow, M. K., and Meyer, D. R. Learning motivated by a manipulation drive. *Journal of Experimental Psychology,* 1950, *40,* 228–234.

Hasbrook, E. The conditions of creative work. *Progressive Education,* 1931, *8,* 648–655.

Hegel, G. W. F. *Phenomenology of mind.* Trans. by J. B. Baillie. Rev. 2nd ed. New York: Macmillan, 1949.

Heidegger, M. *Being and time.* Trans. by J. Macquarrie and E. Robinson. New York: Harper, 1962.

Henry, J. The problem of spontaneity, initiative and creativity in suburban classrooms. *American Journal of Orthopsychiatry,* 1959, *29,* 266–279.

Hill, J. Fostering creativity. *Elementary English,* 1960, *37,* 23–46.

Hix, C. F., Jr. Brainstorming: Planned training. A composite method. *Machine Design,* 1956, *28,* 96–98.

Hopkins, L. T. Classroom climate can promote creativeness. *Educational Leadership,* 1956, *13,* 279–282.

Houle, J. A. How to produce more ideas. *Tool Engineering,* 1957, *38,* 71–74.

Jeanette, R. C. Have a creative corner in your room. *School Arts Magazine,* 1963, *62,* 33–35.

Jones, E. *The life and work of Sigmund Freud.* Vol. 1. New York: Basic Books, Inc., 1953.

Kaufman, I. Education and the imagination, *School Arts,* 1957, *56,* 5–8.

Kierkegaard, S. *The sickness unto death*. Trans. by W. Lourie. New York: Doubleday, 1954.

Kneeland, N. Brainstorming. *American Vocational Journal*, 1958, *33*, 29–30.

Kohler, W. *The mentality of apes*. Trans. by E. Winter. New York: Harcourt, Brace, 1925.

Kuhn, T. S., and Kaplan, N. Environmental conditions affecting creativity. In C. W. Taylor (Ed.), *The third (1959) University of Utah research conference on the identification of creative scientific talent*, pp. 313–316. Salt Lake City: University of Utah Press, 1959. (Out of print)

Lieberman, M. A., Yalom, I. D., and Miles, M. B. *Encounter Groups: First facts*. New York: Basic Books, 1973.

McCloskey, W. R. Brainstorming. *Journal of Home Economics*, 1957, *49*, 705–706.

MacKinnon, D. W. Characteristics and backgrounds of superior science students. *School Review*, 1956, *15*, 67–71.

MacKinnon, D. W. Characteristics of the creative person: Implications for the teaching-learning process. In *Current Issues in Higher Education*, pp. 89–92. Washington, D.C.: National Education Association, 1961.

Maddi, S. R. Motivational aspects of creativity. *Journal of Personality*, 1965, *33*, 330–347.

Maddi, S. R. The search for meaning. In M. Page (Ed.), *Nebraska symposium on motivation*. Lincoln, Neb.: University of Nebraska Press, 1970.

Maddi, S. R. *Personality theories; A comparative analysis*. 2nd ed. Homewood, Ill.: Dorsey, 1972.

Maddi, S. R., and Andrews, S. The need for variety in fantasy and self-description. *Journal of Personality*, 1966, *34*, 610–625.

Maddi, S. R., Propst, B., and Feldinger, I. Three expressions of the need for variety. *Journal of Personality*, 1965, *33*, 82–98.

Marx, K. *Early writings*. Trans. and ed. by T. B. Battomore. New York: McGraw-Hill, 1963.

Maslow, A. H. Deficiency motivation and growth motivation. In M. R. Jones (Ed.), *Nebraska symposium on motivation*. Lincoln, Neb.: University of Nebraska Press, 1955.

Mason, J. G. Suggestions for brainstorming technical and research problems. In S. J. Parnes and H. F. Harding (Eds.), *A source book for creative thinking*, pp. 291–296. New York: Scribner's, 1962.

May, R. Contributions of existential psychotherapy. In R. May, E. Angel, and F. E. Clenbogen (Eds.), *Existence*. New York: Basic Books, 1958.

Mearns, H. Providing for creative self-expression. *New York State Education*, 1936, *24*, 201–203.

Melby, E. O. Education: Freedom and creativity. *Music Educators Journal*, 1952, *38*, 14–17.

Melby, E. O. Cultural freedom and release of creativity. *Education Digest*, 1954, *19*, 14–16.

Merton, R. K. *Social theory and social structure*. Glencoe, Ill.: Free Press, 1957.

Oriel, A. E. Environmental factors and research creativity. *National Electronics Conference Proceedings*, Chicago, 1959, *14*, 928–935.

Parnes, S. J. How to nurture creativity. *Chemical Engineering Progress*, 1963, *59* (12), 37.

Pleuthner, W. A. *A summary of brainstorming results*. Buffalo: Creative Education Foundation, 1958.

Rapp, M. A. Brainstorming attitude. *School Arts Magazine*, 1960, *59*, 5–8.

Raudsepp, E. The industrial climate for creativity. *Management Review*, 1958, *47* (9), 4–8, 70–75.

Rogers, C. R. A theory of therapy, personality, and interpersonal relationships, as developed in the client-centered framework. In S. Koch (Ed.), *Psychology: A study of a science*. Vol. 3. New York: McGraw-Hill, 1959.

Rogers, C. R. *On becoming a person*. Boston: Houghton-Mifflin, 1961.

Simberg, A. L. How to understand, support, and encourage creativity. *Product Engineering*, 1964, *35*, 110–113.

Suchman, J. R. Motivation inherent in the pursuit of meaning: Or the desire to inquire. In H. I. Day, D. E. Berlyne, and D. E. Hunt (Eds.), *Intrinsic motivation: A new direction in motivation*. Toronto: Holt, Rinehart and Winston, Ltd., 1971.

Taylor, C. W. A search for a creative climate. Presented at fourth session, 17th National Conference on the Administration of Research, Estes Park, Colo., September 1963.

Taylor, C. W. Evoking creativity (in Clues to Creative Teaching series). *The Instructor*, 1964, *73* (9), 5.

Thorner, M. W. Creativity and the environment of industrial research. In *Columbia University Department of Industrial and Management Engineering, Human relations in industrial management, including papers from the sixth and seventh Annual Conferences on Industrial Research, Columbia University, 1955 and 1956*, pp. 301–308. New York: Columbia University Press, 1957.

Tillich, P. *The courage to be*. New Haven, Conn.: Yale University Press, 1952.

Torrance, E. P. The creative personality and the ideal pupil. *Teachers College Record*, 1963, *65*, 220–226.

Upton, A. *Systematized brainstorming*. Whittier, Calif.: Whittier College, 1960.

Weisberg, P. S. and Springer, K. J. Environmental factors in creative function. *Archives of General Psychiatry*, 1961, *5*, 554–564.

White, R. W. Motivation reconsidered: The concept of competence. *Psychological Review*, 1959, *66*, 297–333.

White, R. W. Competence and the psychosexual stages of development. In M. R. Jones (Ed.), *The Nebraska symposium on motivation*. Lincoln, Neb.: University of Nebraska Press, 1960.

9.   Moving Toward Working Models in Creativity: Utah Creativity Experiences and Insights

Calvin W. Taylor and Robert L. Ellison

A Preview of Emerging Approaches

WORKING WITH CREATIVITY resembles working with electricity. In neither case do we understand very fully what "it" is, but we may gradually learn how to partially uncover "its" potentials and set the stage so "it" turns on a little, and otherwise learn to work with "it."

We have been strongly empirically based, using a "business and industry" approach of being highly criterion-oriented—focusing on the target of career creative performance with any groups feasible. More efforts have frequently been given to the criterion problem than to predictors. In fact, our research style has been to obtain multiple criterion measures from multiple sources. We use existing criterion scores but we mainly build many new criterion instruments in teamwork with the professions and organizations involved.

This criterion approach ensures a continual aiming at the essence of creativity. That is, our focus is a continually vigilant criterion one so we will *not* miss the big fish and get only some little minnows.

Mooney (1963) reported at our second (1957) creativity research conference that the four main categories of research focus are the product, the process, the person (including his characteristics), and the environment (or the place). Across these four categories we have published nine volumes (with two more in a mimeographed manuscript stage) and have done 25 research studies plus supervising a dozen or more relevant theses and dissertations. Several studies measured the products of creative persons. We have had one direct and other indirect ventures into scientifically studying the inner creative processes; several ventures into measuring the person and his characteristics, both as criteria and predictors; and nine studies on the environment or climate for creativity.

In some areas we have worked with a very "detailed brush" while in other areas we have swept with a very "broad brush." Our approaches have diversified as we have continued our work. Our challenge is not so much to sense problems but primarily *to sense opportunities* or to discover and generate opportunities for further efforts in creativity. We appreciate and have the greatest respect for all those who have sensed opportunities with us and have jointly helped cultivate such opportunities.

Measurement has often been the strongest feature in our approach, with growing evidence of the merit of constructing new measures that are carefully and thoroughly built and tailor-made for our particular purposes. The new measures have involved a great variety of types of techniques designed to be used as criterion measures, predictor measures, climate measures, and so on.

Existing measures, sometimes revised to make them more appropriate, have also been used. We repeatedly check our measures empirically, and continually try to find livewood replacements for deadwood items. Consequently, we seek for "working validities," adding more meaning and deeper insights as we move along.

Our newly constructed measures have a very high batting average in beating presumably the most relevant existing measures. Often the more fancy the theory underlying existing tests, the flatter these tests have fallen toward zero validity under a severe empirical validation check-up. We have therefore become cautious about prematurely fancy theories.

Considerable attention has been given to measuring world-of-work activities and career performances, particularly in several professional career fields, such as scientists, engineers, physicians, nurses, and teachers. For example, from over two decades of research we have found that performance as a medical student is almost unrelated to performance as a physician (i.e., there are two different worlds, the academic world and the professional career world). Also the typical psychological achievement and aptitude tests have little or no validity in predicting performances in several careers. With education being a test often of 12–16–20 or more years in length, it is sad to know that grade point averages (the scores on this lengthy and expensive test) have preciously little or no validity in predicting professional career and other adult performances (for example, see Price et al., 1973, and Hoyt, 1965).

Our Early Beginnings in Creativity

Initially, our interest in creativity was stimulated early in 1940 by L. L. Thurstone, who worked in Edison's laboratory for a period as mechanical engineer and later became a psychologist. Eventually Thurstone was able to partly fulfill a lifetime interest before he died in the 1950s by doing a creativity study at AC Spark Plug, which never became widely known, though we once wanted to publish it.

Thurstone analyzed intellectual and personality characteristics as well as worked on psychometric and factor analysis techniques during his last two decades. The first author was one of the first in his lab whose dissertation used open-ended responses at a time when his laboratory had extended the number of intellectual talents (factors) beyond 20 in number. That dissertation (Taylor, 1947) isolated two new factors which could be called *fluency of ideas* and *fluency of expressions,* both with some relevance to creativity.

At the first of three factor analysis conferences organized by John French at ETS which involved stocktailing of intellectual and personality factors, I met Dr. Guilford for the first time. I later made a full presentation of Dr. Guilford's 1950 APA presidential speech on creativity to my large psychology class the day after I received a copy.

Through Dael Wolfle, another of my former professors, I was invited to work from 1952–54 for the National Academy of Sciences—National Research Council to help the National Science Foundation get started in their first program, the NSF graduate (and post-doctoral) fellowship program. We were seeking future scientists who might make a major difference in the nation's scientific progress. Consequently we constructed lengthy new sets of application materials and included ratings from recommenders on three "new idea abilities" as well as several other ratings important to career productivity. We also started a long range follow-up research program on the awardees and nonawardees.

One result upon return to Utah from that project was a series, beginning in 1955 (with NSF support), of eight international creativity research conferences to date (Taylor, 1956, 1958, 1959, 1964a, 1964b, 1972; Taylor and Barron, 1963; Taylor and Williams, 1966). As the rarest bird of all, Dr. Guilford has been selected and has participated in every one of them.

The main emphasis has changed at each research conference, from scientific creativity through widening horizons to instructional media and creativity and educational challenges as well as climate for creativity. The fourth conference was a stocktaking one which summarized the past progress and looked at the future potentials in the total creativity field. In each case we have not only experienced the entire conference first-hand but have also recorded and transcribed, completely verbatim, every conference report and the discussions.

Then we prooflistened to the entire recording against the drafted transcript, and proofread, revised, and edited again, and then prepared each manuscript for publication in book form. In this manner we have relived the conferences three or more times through multiple sensory and inner processes so that we have become fully absorbed in what happened. Consequently, our own work has been greatly affected and diversified by these reported research ventures and findings of others.

The evidence in files indicates that these research conferences and their published volumes have contributed the creativity awakening and awareness that now exists almost everywhere in our nation as well as in many other parts of the world. Our incoming letters from near and far could be classified into many types. Only last week I received another one of those beautiful letters telling of the person's discovery of the importance of creativity, a letter which ended by asking me to suggest the problem in creativity on which he should work for his dissertation.

Business and industry have shown at least a superficial interest by having sought out these creativity reports from the moment the first one was published with almost no advertising in 1956 through our University Press. In contrast, education appeared to be disinterested, with almost no requests for these volumes until after the Sputniks went up. Creativity has now become a common part of the language in educational discussion circles, though there are still preciously few places that have yet taken many official positive steps toward putting their own money behind creativity in classrooms.

Quantity versus Quality versus Creative Quality

Upon isolating the ideational fluency factor in 1946, we were aware that it involved the quantity of ideas produced, regardless of quality. In an oral rather than a written version of the tests, manics would score highest because of their continuous flow and output of ideas and the uninhibited tangentiality (divergency) in their associational stream. Since then, the issue of quantity versus quality of ideas has periodically reoccurred to us.

Our experiences have strengthened the view first to get both the ideas and their output flowing in sheer quantity; then students can select among and rework these expressed ideas for quality. A later approach still has them thinking up a stream of ideas in their own minds, but learning to express only the higher quality ones. Thus we expect to find the creatively productive among all those who are productive. Eyring (1958) said the same thing in our 1957 creativity research conference: that we should turn as many of our students as possible into "hacks" and then go from there with them.

This "quality-within-quantity" also worked for the Russians. From the early 1950s, Russia was outproducing our nation each year in the *number* of new scientists and engineers at a rate that would soon surpass us in their total scientific manpower pool. Our nation generally debunked this as a quantity, not quality production, but history soon showed that quality emerged from the quantity of manpower produced.

Our criterion research showed at least two different types of quality that are measurable. One is a *sanitary* type of quality, factorially independent from the other *originality* type (a "nonsterile" type of quality). For a scientist to have made a significant contribution, he had to produce something (a quantity factor); the significance of his product is a function of both types of qualities, with the originality type of quality being about three times as important a component as the purely sanitary quality (Taylor, Smith, and Ghiselin, 1963).

When truly cornered, we readily admit that we are initially working with quantity-of-thinking—a productive thinking talent rather than creative talent. If enough teachers are functioning so that students become "thinkers, rather than merely learners" (Hutchinson, 1963), then some teachers and students will learn how to move toward quality in productive thinking and then into more truly creative thinking processes. If enough of their students become sufficiently effective and powerful in using their creative processes, they may, as a quantitative mass-in-action, provide a strong press toward change upon the educational system, toward having the school fit them as they move onward in it.

We also believe that the greatest single help we can give students is to unearth any particular talent, such as creativity, that is still dormant within them and to get it functioning for the first time. Next we can help that talent to function more fully, more effectively, and in combinations with other functioning talents. Then even though that talent is again neglected for some time, it can be more readily unearthed and recalled into action than was possible the first time around.

Two Exploratory Air Force Projects Widen the Creativity Horizons and Opportunities

Our first major financed project occurred after we submitted an idea in 1954 to the Air Force about the potentially rich promise of exploring the verbal communication domain by broadening in several directions my dissertation on verbal fluency in writing. This new coverage included some reception and expression talents that might be a part of the complex creativity talent domain. Having had similar thoughts of his own, Robert M. W. Travers encouraged the idea, so that eventually a two-year project was funded with him as the monitor. Fortunately we were able to recruit Brewster Ghiselin (an English professor and poet and author of the best seller, *The Creative Process*, 1955), Boyd Sheets (nationally known professor of speech with a strong psychological background), and two enterprising graduate students, William R. Smith in psychology and John R. Cochran in speech, as the nucleus of our first Utah creativity research team. Initially the project was justified as a new approach for identifying and selecting instructors and afterwards as a new way for discovering good supervisors.

Our team generated ideas for several hundred test scores of verbal talents that might be important in any large organization. By using a great variety of testing and multiple scoring approaches, we created and constructed three large batteries of communication and creative talent test scores (totaling at least 200), the small minority of which were existing (land-mark) tests and test scores.

In the third (Heinz) battery with a deliberately wide variety of 57 pre-dictor scores, we constructed and added 19 live organizational tests yield-ing 27 talking, writing, listening, and reading criterion situational scores. Across the factor analysis results from the three batteries, we uncovered great complexity of more than 30 verbal communication and creative talents even though we barely sampled the listening and reading domains and had many, many ideas for other tests that we were unable to produce for use and include in the short two-year funded project (Taylor, Smith, Ghiselin, Sheets, and Cochran, 1958). Admittedly we could *not* also ex-plore nonverbal communication talents within the financial and time limi-tations of this project.

A sizeable number of these 30 factors were creative in nature or had strong creative components in them. To us, this approach of creative recep-tion, creative central processing, and creative expression in communicating is still one of the most promising routes into the heartland of creativity.

Although college freshmen are in their thirteenth year of language arts courses, our experiences indicate that they have experienced probably less than a third of the communication talents uncovered in this project. In other words, they have been deprived of activating the large majority of the potential communication talents so relevant to their total careers and life. Later, the Air Force Office of Scientific Research granted additional financial support under Rowena Swanson's monitorship to move this research program further, after which we published a full USGPO volume of our total effort and results (Taylor, Ghiselin, and Yagi, 1967).

Several years later a small sample of our battery of tests were converted into a teacher's manual of classroom exercises. The idea of converting talent tests (and also personality and biographical tests) into classroom exercises is one of the easiest examples to describe and possibly the most straightforward way to implement research findings into classroom prac-tices. The manual entitled "Opportunities for Creativity and Communi-cations" (IBRIC, 1966) has many times proved to be our best initial device in workshops for helping teachers to "break the ice" and start to change toward a student-focused, teaching-for-talent approach. This man-ual was first used in a most successful Title I project in Granite School District (James, 1967), where all the results were in the expected direction, with most of them being statistically significant.

Next, with Robert Travers again as the monitor, we undertook an ex-ploratory study at the Cambridge Air Force Research Center to measure and predict the productivity and creativity of scientists. The scientists immediately told us that they would cooperate if we were first willing to listen to all the things that they felt were important in measuring their career accomplishments to date. They would *not* allow us to take a narrow or superficial approach to measuring their scientific accomplishments and contributions, but insisted, for example, that we must *not just* measure publications and patents. Eventually we ended up with nearly 50 measures of their career accomplishments and performances, using a variety of measurement techniques and sources for observation and data collection in measuring their performances and attainments. William R. Smith was vital in the measurement, development, and field work on this project. This project exemplifies our multisource, multitechnique, multicriterion approach (Taylor, Smith, Ghiselin, Sheets, and Cochran, 1958).

We used a variety of predictor tests, finding that the biographical inventory, especially empirically keyed and also a priori keyed, was by far the best all-round predictor of all criteria used for validation purposes. It was also best for predicting the five most creative criteria. Other newly constructed ratings on self and on motivation were among the next best predictors. Some of the poorest predictors were typical existing personality and motivation test scores.

Intensive Biographical Efforts to Measure Creative Potentials

In early 1957 we met with top persons in the NASA personnel program. Independently we agreed from our separate experiences that the best single predictor device in which to put our efforts was a well constructed, item-alternative analyzed, and empirically keyed biographical inventory. The inventory should be designed for the particular criteria in the organization and for the given organizational setting.

Our biographical studies represent our largest single collective empirical effort in one approach to creativity. To us they display the value of a sustained large effort for a decade or two into a complex and important scientific area.

In about 1959 Robert Ellison came into the Utah research laboratory. After a brief exposure to the Air Force scientist project he focused upon the development and validation of biographical information items against creative and other productive criteria for scientists. Ellison finished both a master's thesis and a doctoral dissertation (Ellison, 1959, 1964) on biographical information. Fortunately, the opportunity arose for us to do criterion and biographical prediction studies of NASA scientists.

We started the NASA study in 1959. The NASA research was conducted over a five year period and involved more than 2,000 scientists and engineers in a number of geographical locations. Separate scoring procedures for biographical data were constructed within a number of NASA research centers which showed repeatedly high validities and thus generality across centers. Since then biographical data have generalized across a variety of fields of endeavor, as confirmed in a number of studies. In fact, the creativity scoring key developed from the NASA studies has since shown construct and empirical validity across a wide variety of large samples including industrial scientists and engineers, nurses, art students, and others. (IBRIC, 1973).

After completing the large NASA-wide study where validities held up well across different NASA centers, an article was published in *Science* (Taylor and Ellison, 1967) on our biographical studies. In it a graduate fellowship research project (Bunderson, Rigby, and Taylor, 1963) was reported on the selection of students for the graduate fellowship program on our campus. In the latter case the biographical scores predicted graduate performance more successfully than all the data in the application folder in combination with the wisdom of the total application committee—a result which certainly has implications for graduate selection programs.

Since these early beginnings, our biographical studies have been described as involving a dynamic biographical instrument rather than a standard, rigid one. Over 20 experimental forms of biographical inventories have been built to date. Each one generally has been item-alternative analyzed and validated against 10 or more criterion measures that already officially exist or that have been specially constructed for the purposes in that setting. Double cross validation techniques are always used, with cross validities (not initial validities) being reported.

Both validity and meaningfulness are sought in the biographical scores. Our second successful biographical attempt to measure motivation is illustrative. In spite of the most slim criterion targets that were available, the biographical scores worked, while an existing activities index with appropriately titled subscores for the purposes at hand yielded essentially no significant validities. This led Murray (1972) to show not only that a biographical inventory yielded valid motivation scores but that it could also be keyed to pick up the meaningful subscores titles from the activities index. In the end the biographical scores had both empirical validity and meaning.

Further Experiences with Biographical Inventories

After Ellison worked for a year at the Ford Motor Corporation, he returned to Utah to become the full-time research director at the newly formed Institute for Behavioral Research In Creativity (IBRIC)[1] which was founded in North Carolina and received its initial grant from the Smith Richardson Foundation in January, 1966.

Our first major projects at the Institute were primarily biographical studies, extending our NASA efforts into three industrial organizations. These studies were conducted during approximately the same years using similar approaches, to predict high level scientific performance within an industrial setting using biographical information. The studies involved

203 scientists and engineers in a large petroleum corporation (Ellison, James, and Carron, 1968), 294 in a large aerospace research company (Ellison, James, McDonald, and Taylor, 1968), and 296 in a large chemical corporation (Ellison, James, Fox, and Taylor, 1968).

In all three cases, the biographical inventory originally constructed for use on the NASA samples was modified and a new version used as the predictive instrument in each study. The number of criterion measures ranged from 14 to 60. The IBRIC Creativity Key and the empirical keys developed in each study had a consistent pattern of significant cross validities in predicting creativity criteria, with the majority of correlations in the .40s ranging up to the mid .50s.

The study at a chemical corporation not only entailed a greater number of criterion measures than the other two industrial studies but also involved 152 predictor measures (including scores from the Miller Analogies, the MMPI, the Strong Vocational Interest Inventory, and others) in addition to the Biographical Inventory (Form O) scores. When 20 of the most relevant criteria were selected for a separate analysis, all BI key scores had statistically significant relationships with all 20 of these criteria, while the next most valid scores was the Kuder Literary score which had a significant relationship with 10 of the 20 selected criteria.

Of particular interest was the comparative lack of validity of intelligence tests, college grade point average, and traditionally used personality tests for the majority of criteria on this sample of industrial scientists and engineers. The only criteria for which the intelligence tests were valid (validating generally only in the .20s) were those which were school-like in nature, such as written communication. In other words, a variety of talents were important for high level career performances, talents which were not adequately measured by intelligence tests, college performances, or personality tests.

In addition to the studies of scientists and engineers, the identification of high level talent with biographical data also has been examined in fields of nursing (Ellison, James, Fox, and Taylor, 1969) and in art students (Ellison, James, Fox, and Taylor, 1971). Both studies involved multiple analyses on a variety of criterion measures utilizing different sources of information and methods of measurement. On nurses the results from the IBRIC Creativity Key and the empirical keys constructed for this study revealed a varied but generally highly successful pattern of cross validities for the different types of nurses, with the validities ranging up to .64 for a creativity composite on fellowship recipients.

In the art study the cross validities with the biographical inventory keys were in the .40s for teacher ratings, as high as the .50s for some checklist items, and generally in the .50s for criterion composites based on combinations of the ratings and number of awards received (standardized by art area). Traditional academic achievement tests were generally not very predictive of performance in the arts. Finally, biographical data differentiated art students from nonart students very effectively (average cross validities of .67).

Other studies in addition to the above have utilized biographical data in academic settings. A number of analyses have been carried out on a sample of over 11,000 high school students in North Carolina. The first of these studies involved the development of the Alpha Biographical Inventory. The results indicated that the Alpha academic performance score was consistently more valid in predicting academic performance criteria —grades and teacher evaluation—than any of the other 24 scores from intelligence and achievement measures included in the study, since cross validities as high as .74 on whites and .65 on blacks were obtained.

The Alpha Creativity Score based on the responses of about 2,800 scientists and engineers from government and industrial research laboratories had a pattern of low to moderate relationships with conventional measures of talent and with criteria of academic achievement (IBRIC, 1968).

In examining these data, we found 54 students with the most extreme upward sloping profiles across the pair of predicted percentile ranks. Only students at the top on the creativity score (99, 98, and 97 percentile ranks) were considered. Among them, only those with academic percentile ranks below 67 were examined closely—that is, those with the most sloping profiles. The list found would be over eight times longer if we went below the top 3 percent and consider all those who were in the top 25 percent on creativity—but still not very promising academically.

Based upon the above lists it is estimated nationally that about 100,000 of our students leaving high school each year will *not* be seen by schools as promising persons and will find it difficult, if not impossible to get into and through college, even though they are highly talented (in the top 25 percent) in creative potential. No wonder we need new educational programs and new institutions for those students who are so promising in these heretofore neglected talents.

An unexpected though most heartening result on the above types of scores on the Alpha Biographical Inventory is that they are both unbiased scores as far as black versus white races are concerned. In other words, being independent of race, these scores provide equal opportunity for black students—a timely finding, indeed (Ellison, James, and Fox, 1970).

Other studies have since been carried out to further examine the lack of racial discrimination in the Alpha biographical scores. One involved the administration of a Biographical Inventory to a sample of Chinese college students in five Taiwan universities. Cross validities in the .50s were found for the Alpha academic performance key which indicates that scores from the Biographical Inventory (after translated into Chinese) could generalize cross culturally as a predictive instrument (Tseng, 1974).

Other studies have indicated that predicting either college attendance or whether a student will drop out or successfully complete high school can be more effectively predicted with biographical keys than with other available measures (high school grades, intelligence and achievement measures, etc.). In addition, the biographical correlates of family income have indicated that a broad pattern of deprivation exists in lower income families including lower self-concepts, lower academic achievement, and deprived patterns of activities and interests (Ellison, James, and Fox, 1970).

Two state-wide studies are currently underway, in North Carolina and in Pennsylvania, to identify different kinds of talent for special educational programs.

Creative Process Studies

We are interested not only in the external climate for creativity which surrounds a person as he functions, but also in what might be called his internal climate and the extremely important creative processes that might be unlocked and become functional, potentially to yield a very high level of creative experiences and products.

In our initial study of Air Force scientists, we developed two approaches to find, at least crudely, the degree to which a person was using creative versus noncreative processes in doing his scientific work. As a first attempt this measure showed some promise, though it was not an immediate glowing success (Ghiselin, Rompel, and Taylor, 1964).

The creative talent processes can provide enriching and rewarding experiences for people, some of whom will seek to have their creative processes function again and again just for their own intrinsic rewards from the experiences and expressions therefrom. Furthermore, our extensive experience with biographical data repeatedly shows that past performance is the best single basis of predicting future performance. From this we feel that the longer a person has lived, through school and otherwise, without really discovering and turning on his inner creative processes, the stronger the prediction will be that he will continue to use only noncreative processes in his functioning, while his creative potentials remain dormant. Contrarily, the earlier and more frequently a person has used creative processes in his activities, the more likely he will continue to be creative to some degree in the future and the more likely it will become a permanent part of his life style and pattern. Anne Roe (1972) has reported that the eminent scientists she studied longitudinally have generally continued to be highly productive throughout their careers, as Picasso and our Institute trustee, Leroy Robertson, did throughout their entire life.

The use of creative processes may be so rewarding to some persons that more and more they seek to use these rather than other processes. To them, creativity may not only be a way of life, but more and more could almost become their full life. Among other things, the biographical inventories built especially for creativity attempt to get indicators as to whether a person is moving more in the direction of fuller use of his creative processes.

Studies of Organizational Climate

Almost from the beginning we have been interested in problems concerning environments for creativity. This topic came out fully in our seventh National Creativity Conference (supported by the Smith Richardson Foundation and the National Science Foundation) which focused upon *Climate for Creativity* (Taylor, 1972). In addition to this published book we have done seven studies on climate and environment for creativity and have two other large studies now in process.

In the Air Force project on criteria and predictors of scientific performance, we also produced three by-product reports which emerged from listening to the scientists and studying their problems (Taylor, Smith, and Ghiselin, 1963, pp. 67–70). These three reports, indicating that the scientists were *not* working under the most favorable organizational climate conditions to be productive and creative, caught more attention at the top of the Air Force and had a bigger impact with them than did our regular criterion and predictor research report. These by-product reports also readied us to investigate climates for creativity as soon as opportunities could be cultivated. Every Air Force scientist studied and every scientist contacted elsewhere has shown considerable interest in the problems of hindrances and deterrents to good scientific work.

A small unfunded opportunity arose in 1965 to do a brief exploratory study on the organizational climate at a medium-sized government research lab. This venture further awakened the interest of top management and of the scientific staff so that they did not want to settle for a quick, superficial look but desired more solid evidence and insight into this potentially vital area.

Our first large scale study on organizational climate then emerged from the above preliminary work and used a climate measurement approach, together with an extensive analysis of various criterion measures of performance in that research laboratory. The criterion measures included such things as supervisory and peer evaluations, quantity and quality of publications, awards won, and salary advancement measures (Ellison, McDonald, James, Fox, and Taylor, 1969). An extensive multiple choice climate questionnaire was also developed which included measurement of style of supervision, compatibility of individual and organizational objectives, group interrelationships, self-descriptions, and so on. The relationships of these climate questions to the performance criterion measures were analyzed to determine the climate factors which are associated with different kinds of contributions made in a research laboratory—as facilitators or inhibitors.

Unusually high relationships for the climate scores (a number of cross validities in the .60s against creative and productive criteria) were found. This climate questionnaire approach therefore offers an extremely promising area for further research and eventual implementation.

This study stimulated the opportunity to undertake a current study of organizational climate with Department of Labor personnel. A multiple purpose system has been developed to analyze management operations as seen by employees, and to provide the results of the analysis to each supervisor at each level of the organization. Each supervisor receives a computer analysis output showing the strengths and weaknesses of his unit on 19 scores compared to all of the units studied. This system entitled Management Audit Survey (MAS) yields 19 climate areas, one of which is climate for creativity and innovation (IBRIC, 1973).

The MAS capitalizes on the individual employees as the best sources of information for reviewing personnel management operations. Initial studies on over 1,800 employees have demonstrated that large differences do exist in organizational climates, even within the same organization. The MAS describes these differences and provides a new channel of communication between employees and supervisors so that better efforts can be directed toward the attainment of mutually beneficial objectives.

Another climate questionnaire which shows much promise was developed for quite a different setting. The Student Activities Questionnaire (SAQ), developed by IBRIC for fifth and sixth grade students, is a multiple choice instrument which can be completed in approximately 30 minutes. It currently yields the following eight activity-supporting climate measures as viewed by the students:

Enjoyment of School	Independence Development
Classroom Participation	Democratic Classroom Control (Self Management)
Individualized Instruction	Self-Concept
Career Development	Multiple Talent Experiences (including Creativity)

We have considered developing other categories to add to the SAQ, such as Humanizing, Enlivening of Students and Teachers, Involving and Motivating, Groupizing (learning to work with and value others), and Total Strengthening of the Person. The results so far obtained indicate that the instrument is very sensitive to differences in academic climate and can be validly applied in educational settings.

In both of the above cases, creativity is being accepted as an integral part of an expanding official system, instead of vulnerably being added all alone. In the MAS case, creativity is being added along with other factors and in the classroom case, creativity is opening the way and adding other factors in with it.

Parents have requested that they be given instructions on how to establish a climate at home consistent with what the students were obtaining in our most advanced experimental school program as the Bella Vista elementary school in Utah's Jordan District. Consequently the Bella Vista staff has written a manual for parents to consider as they cultivate home environments for their children.

For more than a dozen years we have been working in architectural psychology, that is, whether buildings are well designed for people. In this program we have described our steps as being pathcreating rather than pathfinding. Most recently, we have been working on the problem of creativity and housing, or more broadly on creativity in the home. A dissertation by Gene Secrist (1974) tackles the total environment in relation to multiple criteria of the creativity and productivity of about 1,000 applied scientists and engineers in west coast Air Force installations. In his study he has measures of the physical environment, organizational climate, social climate, and personal characteristics in relation to these multiple criteria. Estimates of the relative importance of each of the environmental and personal factors in relation to a person's on-the-job performance and satisfaction emerged in the dissertation.

Creative Leadership and Creative Teaching

Many times in our 1964 research conference on "Instructional Media and Creativity" the point was stressed that teachers generally are the most potent of the instructional media in the classroom. Teachers can make other instructional media function well or they can readily override any other instructional media and make such media ineffective or even negatively effective.

Those in leadership positions generally tend to be the most powerful force or influence in determining the organizational climate under which their workers function. Even if the top levels were deliberately doing their best to produce an organization-wide climate for creativity, a lower level supervisor could counteract and almost reverse the atmosphere by generating anticreativity conditions for his own set of workers. Contrarily, any leader can "pitch an umbrella" over his portion of the organization and construct a positive climate for creativity for his workers, regardless of the climate above him. Of course, it is best for the total organization to have a healthful environment throughout all its subdivisions. From the reactions of many audiences who all show signs of yearning for better organization climates, it seems apparent that there is a widespread need for leaders who facilitate creativity.

We have asked hundreds of audiences whether they want creative teachers, or teachers who teach creatively, or teachers who teach for creativity. They have almost universally responded that they would like "all three of the above," but that these three are definitely not synonymous. Consequently, they almost invariably state that they primarily want the third type, namely those who teach for creativity and somehow ignite creativity in their students.

A parallel situation concerning creative leadership[2] occurs in organizations. One type of person can have a strong set of creative characteristics, so he creates new ideas and products largely on his own which the world may or may not be ready to accept. The more highly creative his outputs, the more likely they will *not* be immediately accepted. He may have few (if any) followers at that moment, though his creative leadership can become evident years or even centuries later, when much of the world may have eventually become his followers.

A second type is a leader who functions very creatively himself and blazes new trails into fertile fields, opening the way in such a manner that many people can start to follow him to cultivate and harvest these new fields—he is really an effective pioneer in his own day.

The third type is a leader for creativity in others around him. He may function as a subtle catalyst or he may enter in more directly to structure the situation, to set the stage, and to provoke and evoke creativity in others.

The fourth type we have described as "none of the above." We suspect that the largest single group of persons in leadership positions would be categorized here as being noncreative leaders in terms of both their own outputs and the outputs that their "psyche" can allow from their own subordinates.

Our challenging Peace Corps project was designed to help their selection program through using situational testing to identify those applicants with creative and other characteristics needed in the activities of volunteers overseas. Midstream we changed our thinking to seek volunteers who could catalyze and stimulate into action the problem-sensing, the innovative, and other talents of the local host country people. We wanted volunteers to catalyze others to become more creative and do the job instead of doing it for them. Eventually the Peace Corps had us modify our situational tests into situational training exercises for their training directors, who reported that this was the first Peace Corps research project to have any impact on their training programs (Taylor et al., 1967).

Development of a Theory of Education

At the beginning of the 1960s we were asked by Roy Hall, Assistant Commissioner for Research in the U.S. Office of Education, to review the 17 gifted and talented projects they were then supporting. After we rapidly accomplished our review which he liked, he next challenged us to take a look at education from outside, especially from the "basic educational sciences."

While engaged in that educational theory project we saw the potency of and the need for research and development in education, which led to our article on "Bridging the Gap between Basic Research and Educational Practice" (Taylor, Ghiselin, and Wolfer, 1962). The editor has us define research and development (R&D) in it because so few in education at that time would know its meaning.

Realizing its potential importance, we ordered reprints from the NEA Journal for distribution to all members of the Congress in April 1962. The article was also read into the Congressional Record. This article helped to set the stage for more attention to R&D in education. Yet many R&D programs that eventually emerged never flourished. We suspect that they did not give enough priority and effort to work across the vacuum area to do the vital "D" and implementation-into-classroom tasks. Instead too often they may have stayed in ivory tower labs (instead of working in the ongoing educational streams), trying to prove to academia that they were good "R" people and deserved better status as such.

In our final educational theory report (Taylor, Ghiselin, Wolfer, Loy, and Bourne, 1963) four different perspectives (or frameworks) described below within which any educational program could be viewed to show the features emphasized, deemphasized, or ignored.

A first perspective concerns itself with the identification and cultivation of all the nation's known human resources (with creative potentials as a prime example).

The second perspective is indicated in asking to what degree our educational programs utilize scientific research fully in this important scientific age. We recognize two different aspects of this problem, namely R and D. First, more basic research (R), is needed, in sciences basic to education as well as in education itself. Secondly, a much greater amount of developmental activity (D) is needed in conjunction with the research activity to ensure that the relevant research could promptly be implemented into educational practices. For example, considerable developmental work is sorely needed on the fruits of creativity research, else creativity may prove to be just another passing fancy in education.

Thirdly, education is viewed in relation to the requirements of world-of-work and other life activities. For example, scientists state their highest degree is the "on-the-job Ph.D." and that it takes several years for those who attain this degree after the academic doctorate, because some bad effects of our educational system have to be worn off and because additional high level characteristics, needed on the job but largely ignored in the usual education program, must be developed.

A fourth perspective is indicated in asking to what degree educational programs are giving persons greater self-understanding and self-awareness including greater insight into their own potentialities. This could lead to higher self-concepts.

We finally incorporated features of all four perspectives into an "educational theory" model, described briefly in a later section as our Multiple Talent Teaching Approach. By the time we delivered that final report, the Assistant Commissioner who requested it had left to become a Dean of Education. To our best knowledge the U.S. Office of Education has had no systematic follow up to that report or to a later report to them on *Instructional Media and Creativity* (Taylor and Williams, 1966), a research conference volume of ideas that are still largely uncultivated. Yet, after finding and reading this book on *Instructional Media and Creativity*, Rowena Swanson, the Air Force information processing specialist, told us that at least half of the U.S. Office of Education's efforts could be profitably spent in turning that volume into action.

Dissemination of Creativity Information

It soon became obvious that educators' initial interest in creativity was often as a stimulant to their discussion circles. However, decisions and changes in educational programs have traditionally been made almost entirely without help from researchers from the behavioral sciences. As a sharp contrast, Ralph Norris, a superintendent in Iowa, dedicated himself through the last decade in his position to implement the creativity research findings gradually and surely into his educational system.

A graduate creativity seminar was started in the late 1950s and repeated at least annually to stimulate graduate students in many fields (including educators) with the highly selected research efforts reported in our creativity research conference reports. A series of three of these courses in Jordan School District gradually led to our Bella Vista project.

In 1963 with help from Frank Williams (then a doctoral student) we also started an annual summer creativity workshop. Many creativity researchers and creativity implementers from across the nation have been guest speakers to stimulate the workshop participants who have come from all 50 states and from several other nations.

Hundreds, almost thousands, of speeches on creativity have been given to different professional and organization groups in nearly every state in the union, including Alaska and Hawaii. Our tendency has been to expose every audience to many different aspects of creativity. Invariably, our own insights have increased from informal discussions after speeches.

A request from Whitefish, Montana, led to our organizing a creativity traveling task force team to help them on their inservice summer workshop. Since then we have sent out over 50 different traveling task force teams of different sizes and personnel composition for different time periods to different parts of the nation.

We reviewed the state of knowledge and the themes and unsolved problems for the creativity symposium at the sixteenth International Congress of Applied Psychology in 1968 at Amsterdam. At the next (1971) meeting of that congress in Liege, Belgium we presented a paper on selecting creative scientists and another one entitled "All Students are now Educationally Deprived."

Request of all sorts for creativity information and articles have come from many different public and professional magazines, so much so that almost all of our writings have been published outside of the psychological journals. Some of the titles of articles written to educators have been "Clues to Creative Teaching," (Taylor, 1963–64), "The Creative Individual: A New Portrait in Giftedness" (Taylor, 1960), "Talent Awareness Training" (Taylor, Nielsen, and Clark, 1969), and "Good Scholars Not Always the Best" (Business Week, 1962). For the NEA Journal, *Today's Education,* we have produced two other articles "Multiple Talent Teaching" (Taylor, 1974) and "Be Talent Developers—as Well as Knowledge Dispensers" (Taylor, 1968), with over 30,000 reprints of the latter being jointly produced and distributed by us and Iowa Project Impact. In all speeches and correspondence we try to supply an abundant set of appropriate handouts and mailouts as dissemination and implementation stimulants.

Experiences in Implementing into Official Systems

Our viewpoint is that nothing is as practical as good insights and understanding. Conversely, any program instituted to be a practical one can prove to be most impractical and utterly wasteful if its people are lacking in any underlying understanding of or "feel for" its activities.

In any field it is ultimately to everyone's advantage—and especially to those doing basic and only basic "R" work—to have practical outlets and to have real effects eventually occur in official systems or establishments in society. Otherwise, the opportunities and support for those "R" efforts will tend to shrink.

If one wants to bring about change in any society concerning creativity, then not just "R" (research) work but "D" (development) work including implementation into the system must occur. Another important type of "R" effort is to study these bridging activities to learn what does lead to successful implementation.

Our recommendation, then, is that all creativity activities need to be adequately and properly manned and that by far the greatest current shortage of manpower is in the "D" efforts, including its final implementation stages. Then there will also be a manpower need in the subsequent new type of "R" efforts that can occur by studying the somewhat embryonic attempts to get creativity more fully functioning within official systems. Vast numbers of research problems will emerge from experiences in these daily operational areas as yet so untapped, with double payoff both for creativity's impact on society and for future creativity research. This viewpoint comes from our experience in dabbling at least a bit in these implementation frontiers of creativity.

In education we learned early that speeches set the stage but that "handles" on the approach were lacking and usually nothing in the system could take hold and implement the approach. We added live demonstrations as a further step which still fell far short of changing teachers who only sat and watched. Now we have teachers take turns in teaching for talents and in putting on the demonstrations themselves, using materials to be described later. For half a day, teachers in Polk County, Iowa, practice with summer school students what they learned in their training session the other half a day, thus readying themselves for talent teaching with their own students in September.

In each project we hope to find, as Toynbee has suggested, one or more sympathetic key persons within the establishment. Such persons must have enough breadth of perspective and interest and a willingness to be receptive and to team with research implementers on at least a trial basis of some kind. In the case of education we have become keenly aware that one should realistically expect only a small subsystem to be receptive initially and to gradually start working with us. To give any new things a full chance, a challenge for "D" persons and their organizational contacts is how to keep the rest of the system relaxed instead of threatened by the new things being tried in the subsystem.

Attempts to insert and impose new programs from higher organizational levels may end up without any permanent changes, followed by the explanation that "we tried it but it really didn't last." This has too often occurred to outside funded programs in which the official stance afterwards is that "the funds ran out so we are no longer doing it."

Fortunately, we not only helped spark and launch Project Impact in Polk County, Iowa but also were party with Superintendent Ralph Norris and his staff three years later in transferring this Title III federally financing on local taxpayers' money. An initial organized opposition (desiring to drop the program) arose against this proposed transition. But this brought about an even more vigorous counteraction—a loud voice from those who had participated in and experienced the merits of this productive thinking program. Some of the opposition spokesmen even started to back off from their initial stance when they heard the points made during the counteraction. The upshot was that the transition to local funding then easily occurred and the program continued to function effectively and spread to adjacent counties.

The reactions of parents in the four talent-focused experimental schools at the Talents Unlimited project in Mobile, Alabama, was interesting. They asked such questions as, "How soon is this program to be expanded to secondary schools and to the entire district?" and "How soon will it become state-wide and nation-wide?" They want their children to have the most up-to-date and the best opportunities that the educational system can provide to help them become more effective, more fully functioning, talented people the rest of their lives.

Teamwork and Coauthorship

We have teamed with others in many ways and settings. One interesting and potentially potent type of teamwork is to have persons join as coauthors and in some cases as the main authors in the venture.

After having an extension class of teachers read "Clues to Creative Teaching," (Taylor, 1963–64), we challenged subgroups to write up how some of these clues could be turned into school activities. This provided a last but crucial linkage in implementing the research findings into classroom practice. Before the teachers realized what we were doing, we picked up two or three of their first crude write-ups of classroom exercises and took them to another room, where they were typed and reproduced in purple dittoed form in about 10 minutes for distribution back to every teacher in every subgroup.[3] In effect, we "published them" immediately for themselves and all the other teachers in the class.

Caught by this surprise step, they listened intently when we asked them to try at least one of these exercises in their classrooms during the week and report their experiences at the next meeting. They were obviously taken aback by the lack of perfection in their own first draft and by our audacity in reproducing their work in such rough form. Consequently they only tried their own exercises and came prepared next week with improved write-ups. At that next meeting we again promptly reproduced and "published their works" back to the whole class. After a couple of weeks the spirit of tryout and revision and "republication" was established. By then they were also trying each other's classroom exercises and suggesting revisions in them.

Eventually this led to a second stage in which two mimeographed manuals for teachers, a *Productive Thinking Guide* and a *Talent Ignition Guide,* were produced by the Bella Vista staff led by the principal, Gilbert Stevenson, and six main teachers. Eventually as a third stage, these manuals were both expanded and refined and reproduced together in printed form in a single paperback volume entitled *Igniting Creative Potential* (Bella Vista, 1972). This 139-page teacher-authored manual (with our introductory chapter on "Multi-Talent Potential") is our best tool in the hands of teachers for implementing the Multiple Talent Teaching Approach into classrooms.

Teaching for Multiple Talents: A New Student-Centered Approach

The Multiple Talent Teaching Approach has been effectively illustrated by showing the faces of seven students arranged from top to bottom on each of six different talent totem poles (see figure 9.1). Teachers are talent developers, having all students use knowledge to activate and develop a multiplicity of their talents.

Creativity has appropriately created the opportunity for a multiplicity of talents to be added and featured in classrooms. In our multiple talent totem poles we list creativity as the second talent which breaks away from the narrow band, one-talent-only type of classroom and opens the way for at least four or more other heretofore largely neglected talents. Our decision is that it is wiser to add a multiplicity of neglected talents than merely to add creative talent, in spite of its almost pricelessness. In this way, creativity is seen as part of a whole new classroom system. The theory or philosophy of this approach is described in the following paragraphs.

All our research has displayed man's great complexity within his inner processes, his products, his characteristics, and his activities. Instead of hoping for transfer of training effects across such complexity, our talent-focused approach trains directly and separately for each of the talents.

Since intelligence tests miss more than nine-tenths of the 98 important intellectual talents now measurable, the main goal in Multiple Talent Teaching is to have students use many more of these neglected talents—more of their dormant mindpower—than they do at present.

Nearly all students can be above average in at least one of these many intellectual talents which can now be functioning in classrooms. Furthermore, students can use each of these multiple talents to process information across all subject matter areas, also working at the fringe of knowledge and into the unknowns, including projections into the future. Knowledge is therefore a means toward the end of cultivating many high level talents in all students. Students thereby acquire a more lasting, working knowledge instead of knowledge that they merely receive, store, retrieve, and dump (computerlike) on an achievement test—and then forget. At least as much and usually more knowledge is acquired when the goal is a talent-focused rather than a knowledge-focused one.

The Teaching-of-Knowledge Approach has proved to be a less sound educational focus, without yielding its promised by-products. In contrast,

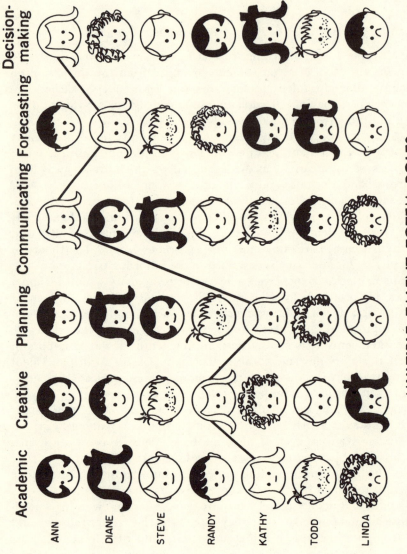

FIGURE 9.1. *Multiple talent totem poles.*

the Multiple Talent Totem Pole Approach moves toward the goal of developing fully functioning, effectively talented people. It enriches and enlivens the students and their teachers and administrators, and thereby humanizes the entire educational process (Hutchinson, 1963; James, 1970; Taylor, 1974).

Instead of conceiving of students as merely subservient learners and reproducers, we esteem them much higher as thinkers and producers, decision-makers, communicators, forecasters, creators, etc. Rather than depriving them of these "adult prerogatives," teachers have them work with knowledge in all these talent ways. The youngest are remarkably ready to function in these adultlike career and life activities. They even become more full-fledged children in the process, being livelier, healthier, happier, and more self-esteemed and self-managed when their natural talent processes are growing and functioning naturally.

The teacher learns to function as a "structure setter"—in fact, as a *multiple structure setter* in order to elicit each type of talent in turn in the students. After setting a particular structure, the teacher then observes students in that talent activity and learns to enter in at times and in ways that will facilitate the functioning of that talent in the students.

Personally it has become more and more painful for us to continue to teach in typical higher educational ways of dispensing knowledge. Consequently, we teach for talents in conducting university classes. We have become effective demonstration teachers, too—ready to be talent developers whenever such opportunities arise.

Analogous to Searching and Processing for Multiple Metals

We can find an analogy in mining for multiple metals. Our largest mine pours a mountainside of boulders through the mills to produce a precious silt stream from which low grade copper ore is extracted. Then the rest of the stream was dumped on the valley floor as waste. Through an unplanned happenstance, someone discovered gold in the silt stream. Much later when the company discovered the discovery, it immediately tested the heretofore waste products for every other known element yet known to man and discovered five other valuable metals besides gold. They now process for seven metals, not just for the copper initially sought, and it doesn't cost much more because the mills exist with the silt stream flowing through.

Similarly, our schools are already set up so we can process not only for the copperlike academic talent, but also for the uraniumlike creative talent, the goldlike decision making talent, and so on. Like the mining specialists we may realize that the waste products we have been dumping out in the streets contain many precious talents of a much larger total value than the ones solely extracted for so long.

Accountability Evidence on Creativity and Multiple Talents

In accountability we are more interested in crude measures of new and important things as yet unmeasured than in more precise measures that already exist for less relevant and less important things.

Our experiences also argue strongly that in working with truly new phenomena, we should not rely solely or very heavily upon existing measures that probably are not well designed for the new purposes.

We are also more interested in working crudely "with no holds barred" to generate new phenomena of important things as yet neglected than we are in working only with precision by retaining entirely the old system or in making only minor though precisely defined changes in the old phenomena.

To us it is also more important to continue to try to create new powerful phenomena until we have successfully done so rather than to rush to build new measuring instruments. Once a sufficiently powerful new phenomenon has been generated—or once a sufficient change has been created—it should stand out sharply and clearly and become quite easily measurable and demonstrable, even by crude measurement techniques—or almost by quick inspection or observation. For example, some visitors to the Bella Vista School very quickly report that "all the vibrations are good."

To some degree every school district (and possibly every school) has individualized its own goals. For sound accountability, tailor-made measuring devices should be built for each district (or school) to assess the outcomes on each of their goals. On measured goals where students fall short of the desired levels, then the district should react to the feedback by trying to create new phenomena so they will better fulfill that goal, or else they could honestly give up or postpone that goal as not yet sufficiently feasible for them.

Consistent with the above thinking, we have looked not only at traditional standardized achievement scores of Bella Vista students (which incidentally are high for their school district) but we have also constructed a new accountability instrument called the Student Activities Questionnaire (SAQ), described earlier, for displaying the new phenomena. We have also used some existing tests of creativity and other neglected talents as well as created some appropriate new tests for these talents.

In their annual Title III evaluation study in 1972, a sample of students in Project Implode at the Bella Vista School were compared to a comparable sample of students from two control schools in a different district. On 58 comparisons against newly selected and constructed yardsticks, the Bella Vista students surpassed the control school students *all* 58 times, with the difference being statistically significant in 42 of the 58 cases. One case of a major difference was on the yardstick of students' experiencing their multiple talents. An average Bella Vista student (at the 50th percentile rank) was found to be at the 83rd percentile rank in comparison with the control school students. And conversely an average student in the control schools was at only the 18th percentile rank in comparisons with Bella Vista students on the Multiple Talent Development yardstick. Nearly as great differences were found on the Career Development yardstick.

On the 1973 data the Bella Vista sample was divided into two subsystems: (1) a first one consisting of teachers who had pioneered the program in the school by teaching for talents for at least four years and by largely authoring *Igniting Creative Potential,* and (2) a second one including other teachers who had seriously started only a couple of years ago to create a second "wave" of change toward talent teaching in that school.

Figure 9.2 shows the control school results versus those for the first Bella Vista subsystem. An average (50th percentile rank) student in the first Bella Vista subsystem would be at the 93rd percentile rank on Multiple Talent Development in comparison with students in the control schools. In the reverse direction, an average student in the control schools would only surpass 8 percent of students in the first Bella Vista subsystem. The average student (50th percentile rank) in the second Bella Vista wave of change surpassed 75 percent of the control students but only 25 percent of the students in the first Bella Vista wave of change. (Almost equally large differences were obtained both years on the new Career Development yardstick, a currently "hot" goal in education.)

This is all very logical in terms of changing a system. The set of Bella Vista teachers in the second wave yielded results that surpassed those in the control schools but their students have not moved as far on the SAQ scores as the first wave of teachers. It is realistic to get only a small fraction of the total system interested initially in implementing research findings. With good experiences and good results together with leader support, this small fraction might be expanded into a wider acceptance in the total system. These small starts are crucial in bringing about change in an established system.

In a follow-through unpublished accountability study reported to the Bella Vista staff, Wesley Craig and his Brigham Young University graduate students recently evaluated the Bella Vista trained students who are now in junior high along with a comparable group of students from another elementary school source. The Bella Vista students won in about 95 percent of the comparisons and tied in another 3 percent of the comparisons (barely losing close contests in the other 2 percent), again with a sizeable number of the positive differences being statistically significant.

The former Bella Vista students performed better but liked junior high less, remembering that Bella Vista had been a better world for them than the junior high. The subgroups who suffered the most in junior high

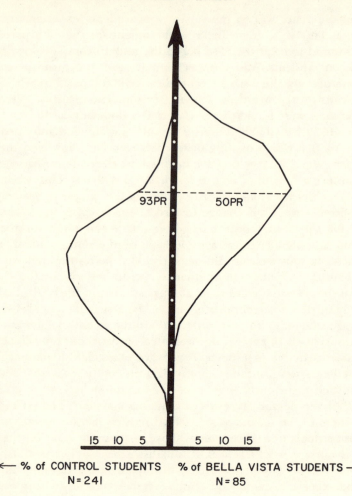

FIGURE 9.2. *Multiple talent development: SAQ scores (1973).*

were the ones who had blossomed and flourished the most during their
Bella Vista experiences, namely girls and "C" students (who were B and A
students in at least some talent activities at Bella Vista).

Beverly Lloyd (1972) recently placed another full class of 26 students on
totem poles. She found all students but one to be well above average on at
least one of the totem poles. The seven highest students on Academic Talents, as a group were compared with the remaining three lower academic
groups on the five other talents. The highest academic group was less
promising than any of the other three groups on the five other (nonacademic) talents where students must function and produce something
of their own rather than "do exactly what the teacher tells them in exactly
the way the teacher tells them to do it."

Clayton Nielsen (1972) in the Granite School District successfully used Multiple Talent Teaching on a group of mentally retarded students and on another group of emotionally disturbed students. Both of these groups flourished more when functioning broadly in Multiple Talent Teaching situations than before under the more narrow band, traditional teaching approach. This was true even against the old yardsticks of standardized achievement tests.

Two summers ago Gilbert Stevenson and the main author worked for only four days with a handful of the "most ready" teachers at the New Hampshire Technical College at Claremont. These teachers then started Multiple Talent Teaching, especially in one program that first year. Their dropout rate changed from one-third to zero in that program and everyone, both students and staff, were very much enlivened by the talent approach and experiences (personal communication over one year later). By becoming multiple talented functioning persons, the students will be more promotable persons in their careers (as well as being initially very marketable from their relevant world-of-work technical training).

The U.S. General Accounting Office, who are responsible for accountability reports to the Congress, now has management persons capable of covering program accountability as well as financial accountability. After examining outcomes from Title I and Title III programs, they had found almost universal instances where more money had "gone down the same old drain"with little or no change in what happens to students in the classroom. About the only oucome had been the discovery of many new "alternatives in education" which do not make the classrooms any worse or any better. When their new specialists heard about our program at Bella Vista, they almost immediately visited the school to see if it was a promising avenue for real educational change that would hold up under their analytical scrutiny. They were impressed during and remained so after the Bella Vista visit. These USGAO people have been kept informed of the accumulating results on the Bella Vista program and have become even more impressed from our latest results presented above (personal communication).

What will persons in educational leadership positions do when they are shown that a major change in classrooms is now possible, based upon these research and development and implementation results? They can either (1) ignore research results as having not been the basis of any of their past decisions, or (2) they can debunk and discard them for other reasons, or (3) they can pay attention to them. This may test them severely.

Some Disappointments

We have often been puzzled at the slow rate and, often to us, almost the absence of progress in implementation. Some in leadership positions are *not* highly "improvement-oriented" but merely keep the operation functioning and tend it carefully. Some others with narrow concepts of efficiency make changes which decrease possibilities for important new things to occur. For example, certain educational leaders are pressing to obtain higher scores on standardized achievement tests. As a bad side-product, teachers tell us that they feel they will get no rewards whatsoever for doing anything else, such as cultivating creativity.

We are still frustrated from not having yet produced more of an impact on the way things are functioning in schools, in organizations, and in life. But we are still trying to learn from our past ineffective attempts, particularly where high hopes have not materialized.

Our greatest single disappointment has been the almost total absence of action by higher education to use the emerging scientific technologies for identifying and cultivating creative students. Being troubled by this point, we took the challenge to speak at a Sigma Xi Distinguished Lecture on our campus on February 22, 1971, on the unusual title "Are Colleges and Universities Obsolete?" Further questions raised were: Is reform enough, or will replacement be required? How are research findings related to what students have been trying to say in the 60's? What is leadership doing about this issue?

Several years ago we helped to sell a wealthy "angel" on the idea of a new type of college for the creatively talented. He then granted a large sum for this purpose to a college that was expanding and becoming a state university. Unfortunately, the anticipated contribution of that Creative College Project toward a rapid world-wide impact on higher education has as yet largely failed to materialize. Nonetheless, at least a dozen colleges are trying to move in new directions, so that other happenings may rescue something from this initial opportunity. In any event, most higher education institutions may be among the slowest to awaken to creativity research findings and may also find difficulties in giving much attention to the many implementation outcomes already occurring, especially in early school years.

The existence of a new type of college for the creatively talented would take away from all secondary schools one main excuse for their not changing toward more creativity in classrooms. They state that they must prepare many students for the almost universal academic pattern in the existing 2,600 colleges and universities. Secondary schools can thus prevent elementary students from continuing to be broadly talented people throughout their high school careers. Gradually, though, some secondary schools are awakening to these new research-based classroom approaches.

The degree of disappointment and impatience is a function of one's idea of what is possible versus what now exists. While impatience can be a motivator toward research-based changes, it can also produce opposition from the unready, as illustrated by Dean Philip Price's recalling a tomb-stone in Western China with the epitaph, "He tried to hurry the Orient."

The Creative Challenge: To Design for People

"Designing for People" is our overall theme as more and more is learned about human beings. Two types of changes should be encouraged: revision and reform of established system plus some total fresh starts that are newly designed and up-to-date with research insights.

We have discovered that if a teacher conceives of students to be learners, this has turned out in practice to be an ill-designed, low concept which students "live down to." Students invariably report that they would much rather be treated as persons (or human beings) than as learners. But if teachers conceive of them highly, as creative thinkers, for example, then teachers more fully join the health delivery system, increasing the level of wellbeing and strengthening the total health of all students who learn to function more fully and effectively. This is why we recommend that schools should move in the direction of becoming better designed to fit the students rather than having the students fit the schools.

Next, we have two specific recommendations: one is a state-wide talent search on a random sample or even a full population of secondary students at one level, using at least the Alpha Inventory which yields equal opportunity, race-unbiased creativity scores. Students so tested at a Utah high school were highly excited if they found that they had a high potential in the uraniumlike talent of creativity. Many seniors were more excited about it than about graduating that week.

As indicated earlier, beginnings are occurring in state-wide testing of applicants for Governor's Schools in both North Carolina and Pennsylvania. Such searches are a fulfillment of the visionary idea of H. S. Richardson, the founder of the Smith Richardson Foundation, that creative and other hidden talents can be found everywhere throughout each state, including the backwoods.

Now that scientific techniques are available, our second recommendation is that all organizations in education, business, and industry should become more active in identifying, developing, and utilizing creativity in their people. To do so, they should establish better climates for creativity. Also, their personnel, training, and other programs must become more aware of and up-to-date with the comparatively recent production of scientific knowledge about creativity.

In summary, our general thesis is that the total research and development effort in creativity could receive its best new burst of opportunities and activities by moving toward working models of creativity in the mainstreams, that is, in the official system in all types of organizations. Undoubtedly there will be complications and rich creative experiences in doing this implementation work. Furthermore, all kinds of exciting new research and other human challenges, as yet largely unmet by creativity workers, will arise as soon as working models of creativity start to function in official systems.

Notes

1. The initial three trustees of this nonprofit trusteeship were Mrs. L. L. (Thelma) Thurstone, Kenneth Beittel, and LeRoy Robertson (our Utah trustee who had won the largest cash award in history ever given to a composer). The first author is the Executive Director of the Institute (IBRIC). After Professor Robertson died, we asked J. P. Guilford and Brewster Ghiselin to be other trustees of that Institute.

2. One of my former supervisors, Roger Bellows, produced possibly the only book, entitled *Creative Leadership* (1959). Since there was very little explicitly on creativity in his book, save the title, the next time I saw him, I asked him why he had used this particular title. He said that the book was on democratic vs. autocratic leadership and he felt that democratic leadership, in action, was essentially creative leadership.

3. My secretary, Connie Jenson, had suggested that she come to the workshop so we could try out this "instant publication" technique.

References

Bella Vista School. *Igniting creative potential*. Project Implode, 2131 East 7000 South, Salt Lake City, Utah, 1972 (2nd printing).

Bellows, R. M. *Creative leadership*. Englewood Cliffs, New Jersey: Prentice-Hall, Inc., 1959.

Bunderson, C. V., Rigby, Janice, and Taylor, C. W. The validity of fellowship selection information. University of Utah Technical Report No. 1, 1963.

Business Week. Good scholars not always best. February, 1962, 77–78.

Ellison, R. L. The relationship of certain biographical information to success in science. Unpublished master's thesis, University of Utah, 1959.

Ellison, R. L. The development of scoring procedures for a biographical inventory to predict various criteria of success in science. Unpublished doctoral dissertation, University of Utah, 1964.

Ellison, R. L., and Fox, D. G. The prediction of academic success and failure. Report submitted to the North Carolina Department of Public Instruction, Part C, 1973. Budget Code 18875, Research Project Funds.

Ellison, R. L., Fox, D. G., Taylor, C. W., and Lacklen, R. J. The development of organizational climate measures: Organizational analysis and supervisory information system (OASIS), on going, U.S. Department of Labor.

Ellison, R. L., James, L. R., and Carron, T. The prediction of scientific performance criteria with biographical information, 1968. Report submitted to Ethyl Corporation, 1968.

Ellison, R. L., James, L. R., Fox, D. G., and Taylor, C. W. The analysis and prediction of Dow scientific performance, 1968. Report submitted to Dow Chemical Company.

Ellison, R. L., James, L. R., McDonald, B. W., and Taylor, C. W. The prediction of scientific and engineering performance with biographical information, 1968, North American Rockwell, Inc.

Ellison, R. L., McDonald, B. W., James, L. R., Fox, D. G., and Taylor, C. W. An investigation of organizational climate, 1968, U.S. Navy Radiological Defense Laboratory. (Published by: Smith Richardson Foundation, P.O. Box 3265, Greensboro, North Carolina, 1969).

Ellison, R. L., James, L. R., Fox, D. G., and Taylor, C. W. The prediction of high level nursing performance, 1969, Contract No. PH-108-66-02, National Institutes of Health.

Ellison, R. L., James, L. R., and Fox, D. G. The identification of talent among negro and white students from biographical data, 1970. Grant No. OEG-8-9-540033-2026 (058) Project No. 9-H-033, U.S. Office of Education, U.S. Department of Health, Education, and Welfare.

Ellison, R. L., James, L. R., Fox, D. G., and Taylor, C. W. The identification and selection of creative artistic talent by means of biographical information, 1971, Grant No. OEG-8-9-540215-4004 (010) Project No. 9-0215, U.S. Office of Education, Dept. of Health, Education, and Welfare.

Eyring, H. B. Comments on creativity by a physical scientist. In C. W. Taylor (Ed.), *The second (1957) University of Utah research conference on the identification of creative scientific talent,* 156–169. Salt Lake City: University of Utah Press, 1958.

Ghiselin, B. (Ed.). *The creative process.* New York: Mentor, 1955.

Ghiselin, B., Rompel, R., and Taylor, C. W. A creative process check list: Its development and validation. In C. W. Taylor (Ed.), *Widening horizons in creativity,* 19–33. New York: Wiley, 1964.

Hoyt, D. P. The relationship between college grades and adult achievement: A review of the literature. Research paper No. 7. American College Testing Program, Iowa City, Iowa, 1965.

Hutchinson, W. L. Creative and productive thinking in the classroom. Unpublished doctoral dissertation, University of Utah, 1963.

Institute for Behavioral Research in Creativity. *Review of activities,* 1417 So. 11th East, Salt Lake City, Utah, 84105, 1973.

Institute for Behavioral Research in Creativity. *Alpha biographical inventory manual,* 1968.

Institute for Behavioral Research in Creativity. *Opportunities for creativity and communications (Teacher's manual).* Salt Lake City: IBRIC, 1417 So. 11 East, 1966.

James, L. R. Development of communication training exercises. Unpublished master's thesis, University of Utah, 1967.

James, L. R. The development of criterion composites for creativity. Unpublished doctoral dissertation, University of Utah, 1970.

Lloyd, Beverly. Required masters project. Department of Education, University of Utah, 1972.

Mooney, R. L. A conceptual model for integrating four approaches to the identification of creative talent. In C. W. Taylor and F. Barron (Eds.), *Scientific creativity: Its recognition and development,* 331–340. New York: Wiley, 1963.

Murray, S. L. An elaboration of the meaning of biographical information. Unpublished doctoral dissertation, University of Utah, 1972.

Nielsen, C. Required masters project. College of Education, University of Utah, 1972.

Price, P. B., Taylor, C. W., Nelson, D. W., Lewis, E. G., Loughmiller, G. C., Mathiesen, R., Murray, S. L., and Maxwell, J. G. *Measurement and predictors* of physician performance: Two decades of intermittently sustained research. Department of Health, Education and Welfare (Grant No. PM 00017), University of Utah, 1973.

Rigby, J., Bunderson, C. V., and Taylor, C. W. The validity of present and potential fellowship selection information. University of Utah Technical Report No. 2, 1964.

Roe, A. Maintenance of creative output through the years. In Taylor, C. W. (Ed.), *Climate for Creativity*, 167–192. Elmsford, New York: Pergamon Press, 1972.

Secrist, G. E. A total environment approach to occupational performance and satisfaction. Unpublished doctoral dissertation, University of Utah, 1974.

Taylor, C. W. A factorial study of fluency in writing. *Psychometrika, 12* (3), 1947, 239–262.

Taylor, C. W. (Ed.). *The 1955 University of Utah research conference on the identification of creative scientific talent.* Salt Lake City: University of Utah Press, 1956.

Taylor, C. W. (Ed.). *The second (1957) University of Utah research conference on the identification of creative scientific talent.* Salt Lake City: University of Utah Press, 1958.

Taylor, C. W. (Ed.). *The third (1959) University of Utah research conference on the identification of creative scientific talent.* Salt Lake City: University of Utah Press, 1959.

Taylor, C. W. The creative individual: A new portrait in giftedness. *Educational Leadership,* 1960, *18* (1), 7–12.

Taylor, C. W. Clues to creative teaching. Series of ten articles appearing in *The Instructor,* Sept. 1963 to June 1964.

Taylor, C. W. (Ed.). *Creativity: Progress and potential.* New York: McGraw-Hill, 1964. (a)

Taylor, C. W. (Ed.). *Widening horizons in creativity.* New York: Wiley, 1964. (b)

Taylor, C. W. Be talent developers as well as knowledge dispensers. *Today's Education,* December, 1968, 67–68.

Taylor, C. W. (Ed.). Educational challenges of creativity. Ninth International Research Conference on Creativity. Held in Buffalo, New York, June 24–27, 1970. Mimeographed.

Taylor, C. W. Developing effectively functioning people—The accountable goal of multiple talent teaching. *Education, 94,* (2), 1973, 99–111.

Taylor, C. W. Multiple talent teaching. *Today's Education,* 1974, 71–74.

Taylor, C. W., Smith, W. R., Ghiselin, B., Sheets, B., and Cochran, J. R. Identification of communication abilities in military situations, (Project 7719); Task 17035) (WADC-TR-58-92), Contract 18(600)-1211, University of Utah, June 1958, Personnel Laboratory, Lackland Air Force Base, Texas, 1958.

Taylor, C. W., Smith, W. R., Ghiselin, B., and Ellison, R. Explorations in the measurement and prediction of contributions of one sample of scientists. (Project 7717, Task 17110) (ASD-TR-61-96), Contract AF-41(657)-158, University of Utah, April, 1961, Personnel Lab., Lackland Air Force Base, Texas.

Taylor, C. W., Ghiselin, B., and Wolfer, J. A. Bridging the gap between basic research and educational practice. *NEA Journal,* 1962, 23–25.

Taylor, C. W., and Barron, F. (Eds.). *Scientific creativity: Its recognition and development.* New York: Wiley, 1963.

Taylor, C. W., Ghiselin, B., Wolfer, J., Loy, L., and Bourne, L. A theory of education based upon psychological and other relevant research findings.

Supported by U.S. Office of Education (HEW), Cooperative Research Project No. 621, University of Utah, 1963. Mimeographed.

Taylor, C. W., Smith, W. R., and Ghiselin, B. The creative and other contributions of one sample of research scientists. In C. W. Taylor and F. Barron (Eds.), *Scientific creativity: Its recognition and development*, 53–76. New York: Wiley, 1963.

Taylor, C. W., Ellison, R. L., and Tucker, M. F. Biographical information and the prediction of multiple criteria of success in science. NASA Research Project, NASA-105, 1964.

Taylor, C. W., Ellison, R. L., and Tucker, M. F. Biographical information and the prediction of multiple criteria of success in science. Greensboro, North Carolina: The Richardson Foundation, 1966.

Taylor, C. W., and Williams, F. E. (Eds.). *Instructional media and creativity*. New York: Wiley, 1966.

Taylor, C. W., and Ellison, R. L. Biographical predictors of scientific performance. *Science*, March 3, 1967, *155* (3766), 1075–1080.

Taylor, C. W., Ghiselin, B., and Yagi, K. *Exploratory research on communication abilities and creative abilities*. U.S. Government Printing Office, April, 1967.

Taylor, C. W., Yagi, K., DeMik, G., Branum, J., Tucker, M. F., and White, A. R. Development of situational tests for the Peace Corps. Supported by Peace Corps, Contract No. PC-(W)-405, University of Utah, 1967.

Taylor, C. W., Nielsen, E., Clark, W. Talent awareness training. *The Instructor*, May, 1969, 61–68.

Tseng, A. T. Biographical inventory—a cross-cultural study. Unpublished doctoral dissertation, University of Utah, 1974.

10. *AHA!*

Sidney J. Parnes

IN THIS CHAPTER I will develop six major themes: (1) an elucidation of Creative Studies as a program that fundamentally concentrates on increasing the probability of more and deeper "aha" experiences for each learner; (2) a historical perspective of my own involvement in this effort; (3) an explanation of the development of a comprehensive, eclectic program at Buffalo; (4) the base of corroborative research for the program; (5) our shift in emphasis toward a strong *balance* between imagination and spontaneity versus judgment and implementation; and (6) the relationship of this "balance" to society's stance toward the present and future.

Increasing the Probability of the "Aha!"

FEELING VERSUS THINKING

In recent years there has been much discussion about the affective versus the cognitive aspects of creativity—the "feeling" versus the "thinking." In preparing for this chapter, however, I have been musing over the idea of talking instead about "deliberate" and "nondeliberate" ways of associating or relating our data. More and more I am seeing these (deliberate and nondeliberate) as the two fundamental ways of looking at the creative process. Another set of relevant terms would be Gordon's "involved versus detached."

Earlier I wrote (1967*a*, 1967*b*):

An individual attempts to make as many relevant associations as possible to the problem at hand. He feeds his associative mechanisms the best fuel for optimum operation, and he defers judgment so as to "remove the brakes." In a sense, incubation is related to both of those endeavors. In order to allow for what is called incubation, the individual must get away from direct involvement in

224

the problem for a period of time. By thus detaching himself, he has, you might say, deferred judgment or closure on the problem. As the problem "simmers" in the back of the mind—"on his back burner"—he attends to other things and allows his senses full play upon his total environment.

With respect to consideration of the problem, it might be reasonable to suppose that the person is in a sort of hypnotic state; that is, he has given himself the suggestion to work on the problem and has then put it out of his consciousness. All input from his environment bombards the fringes of the problem. Suddenly one element connects with an element of the problem and triggers it into momentary awareness. Perhaps this occurs in much the same way as a very remote association is suddenly formed when one consciously attempts to produce ideas under deferred judgment. But note that the idea (as embryonic and fragmentary as it might be) would not occur if the elements needed for the connection were not implanted in the mind prior to incubation. Without the requisite links in my mind, I could be bombarded with apples while resting under a tree, yet never come up with the law of gravity.

Incubation and deferred judgment. We might further relate incubation to deferred judgment as follows: The deferred-judgment principle suggests that when one is working on a problem, judgment is withheld during idea-generation. By deferring judgment we thus increase the time spent in obtaining a variety of perceptions of the problem. Rokeach's (1950) research has shown that increases in the time available to perceive resulted in decreased rigidity in solutions.

Thus we allow free-wheeling to our associative processes so as to produce a large quantity of alternatives. We do this deliberately for a time; then we "incubate." That is, we first involve ourselves deeply and consciously in the problem. Then we detach ourselves for a time while we allow new associative links to be stimulated via new sensory input from the widest variety of sources —as we gain new perceptions of the problem. Thus incubation provides for further deferment of judgment about the problem, and bombardment of the mind with the greatest variety of random input so as to increase the likelihood of a chance connection—a "lucky" observation. (The larger the number of lottery tickets one buys, all other things being equal, the greater the likelihood of holding a winner.)

ESSENCE OF CONCEPT OF CREATIVITY

Let us now examine this concept more closely. Perhaps we might say that there are really not even *two* basic ways of relating, but only *one*—but that this one way is used at a variety of speeds or tempos. Suppose we started with the idea that the essence of the concept of creativity is the fundamental notion of the "aha"—meaning the fresh and relevant association of thoughts, facts, and ideas, into a new configuration which pleases, which has meaning beyond the sum of the parts, which provides a synergistic effect. Let us assume that the new connection, association, or relationship that you make is harmonious, relevant, valuable, satisfying, pleasing, etc., to *you*. It might be something as simple as moving the body or the parts of the body in a spontaneous new way, in response to a sound or rhythm that you hear. The "aha" may be implicit in even such a momentary, fleeting relationship of elements as in that little spontaneous dance routine that so many of us have experienced.

"AHA" EXPERIENCE

The typical "aha" experience may be considered to be the result of the new connection of elements residing inside our mind and/or within our perceptual field. This new and relevant connection or *new and harmonious* connection often "just happens," accidentally or serendipitously. In earlier days, it was frequently thought that this was the *only* way it could happen—accidentally—that is, one had to just wait and let it happen, like the famous "Eureka!" of Archimedes in the bathtub. However, what research of the last 25 years has made increasingly clear is that there are many processes a person can use to help increase the *likelihood* that the chance connection will take place. Notice that I do not say processes that will *make* the connection happen, but only that will increase the *likelihood* or *probability* of its occurring.

ETHICAL CONSIDERATIONS

I will not even attempt at this point to get into the ethical considerations of the use of creativity—that is, whether the resultant ideas of an individual's creative process will be "good" for society. We cannot guarantee this, any more than we can guarantee the "best" use of technological advancements. Without delving deeply into this crucial philosophical and sociological aspect of creativity, let me at least point out and acknowledge the challenge it presents, and emphasize that we hope the new connections, associations, relations that people generate will be helpful, valuable, satisfying, harmonious, etc., to themselves *and* to others in society; or at *least* that they will not be *harmful* to others. Harmonious for the individual *and* for society is probably the key point here.

RELATIONSHIPS IN FACT

In getting at the heart of the "aha" experience, let me explain and illustrate how fundamental it can be to all learning. Before preparing for this chapter, I had always spoken of an idea as being the interconnecting of two facts that had not been associated that way before. But the very facts which interconnect to form an idea are *also* relationships, or interconnections of their *own* elements. Even something so basic as a speck of sand is, of course, a relationship of the elements that make it up; likewise with an atom.

I then realized that a fact might really be defined as "a relationship that is *observed* and *agreed upon*." This made me ask myself if there is any such thing as a fact unless more than one person is involved. I derived this answer: until it is *agreed* upon, it is probably only an individual's observation. Then I puzzled, what if one person makes the same consistent observation of this phenomenon? I concluded that this, then, might constitute the meaning of the word "fact" to an *individual*. A fact, then, might be considered an *observation* that is *consistent* to an individual *and/or agreed upon* by two or more persons.

Note how a young child learns the meaning of the word "dog." If he had observed several sizes of dogs and had heard them all called "dogs" before he had seen other animals, he might call horses, cows, pigs, cats, and dogs all "dogs." As his experience grows, he begins to make finer distinctions in the *relationships* of elements he observes and begins to understand "dogness" as something different than "horseness." When he first makes this discovery or, as we say, "gets it," it is an "aha" experience for him. When he finally "closes in" on the concept of "dogness," it is somewhat like Helen Keller finally understanding "water."

Now, let me come to a key point of what excited me about these ideas I am discussing. I had heard Bert Decker say many times that "learning is creating and creating is learning." I intuitively believed this but did not really fully understand it. I kept asking myself, "If learning is creating and creating is learning, then why isn't a lecture that 'teaches' just as effective as 'discovery-type' learning that I had always been favoring?"

I saw the answer in two expressions that popped into my head. The expressions are "*Got* it!" and "I *get* it!" Let me explain. Suppose I say to a child, "The sum of four and four is eight. *Got* it?" He might repeat, "Got it!" He might have a visualization in his mind of eight objects, grouped into two clusters of four each. Perhaps it is that "mental picture" that prompts the "*Got* it!" response. But suppose I then go on and say, "One-half of eight equals zero; got it?" Perhaps the child might say, "No; I don't *get* it!" Suppose I next went on to explain, "Well, picture the figure 8 in your mind; now cut it in half horizontally and look at the top half or the bottom half; isn't it zero?" The child might "light up" and exclaim, "Oh yes, I *get* it!"

Let's analyze what happened. If your thought processes paralleled what I just described, then you were helped by me to see a new relationship in elements associated with the concepts eight, 8, zero, 0, one-half, and so on—a relationship or viewpoint that you had not thought of before. When you "see" it, with my prompting, you say, accompanied by a sort of "aha," "I *get* it!" The learning that took place was your observing and understanding a new relationship that had meaning, relevance, harmony, etc. This may have "tickled" or delighted you, once you saw it. This is what generally happens when you hear a good joke or see a funny cartoon.

The jokester or cartoonist presents a situation that can be viewed two ways; it is the sudden "getting" of the second relationship or viewpoint that makes it funny. No one tells you what to look for; he just presents the data in a clever way so that you almost automatically generate another way, beyond the obvious one, of interconnecting the data presented; it surprises and delights you and probably results in a laugh. For example, in one "Family Circus" cartoon, two small boys are standing in front of a gum-ball vending machine. One has his hand on the release handle. He hands a penny to his companion and says, "Here, you put the penny in and I'll flush it." The new association of the word "flush" to the given situation, as against the more obvious association of flushing a toilet may stir the "laugh-aha" in you. It is what Arthur Koestler (1964) speaks of as bisociative thinking. It is the recognition of "appropriate incongruity," as someone once defined *humor,* or of "appropriate strangeness," or "harmonious novelty," as we might define *creativity.*

What I am beginning to see is that when someone gives a good lecture, he probably brings together elements into interrelationships and associations that are both new as well as relevant or harmonious to the listener. In other words, the good writer or lecturer (or "teacher") *helps* the learner to see relationships that he might otherwise miss—relationships that are both *new* and *interesting, valuable, satisfying, relevant* and/or *harmonious.* He thus provides a setting for many "aha" feelings as the person examines these new relationships for the first time.

In light of the above, I then asked myself, what is it that a good creative problem-solving instructor or "facilitator" does over and above a good "teacher"? I suddenly saw the difference. The former does everything that the good "teacher" does, *plus* getting the learner to "generate" a lot of "ahas" on his own—"ahas which the facilitator would not necessarily be able to predict.

Let's look at another example, but this time from the behavioral realm. A transfer-pupil finds himself in a classroom with a very stern teacher. Another child warns, "Watch yourself in here; she's a pill! *Got* it?" The new pupil might respond, "Yep, *got* it!" Suppose, after watching her stern look and behavior all morning, he hears another child at lunch say, "She's the nicest teacher in the school." The new youngster might be confused and say to himself, "I don't *get* it!" On the other hand, if he approached the teacher for the first time with a problem, and suddenly recognized through the stern exterior the gentleness and understanding inside, he would probably get a real "aha" from this new and relevant relationship that he himself discovered—probably a more exciting "aha" than if someone had simply explained all of this to him.

INTERPERSONAL "AHA"

In our interrelationships with other people, we see only an infinitesimal part of a person's behavior pattern every time we make an observation. If we have seen particular behaviors that provide us with the consistent relationship or the "fact" that someone is a "pill," but if we then make an additional observation that is quite inconsistent, we may react by feeling, "I don't get it!" But if this inconsistent bit of behavior then suddenly connects up to a much broader realm of behavior that we *do* understand, but had failed to sample at all in our former experience, we then have a kind of "interpersonal-aha," where we suddenly "see" the other person in an entirely new light. The inconsistent bit of behavior is no longer an isolated piece of behavioral experience, but part of a broad pattern which had not been seen.

The "intelligent" person observes and stores relationships that are brought to his attention; he understands them and appreciates their value, and he calls them into play constantly in meeting his problems and his challenges. The "creative" person does all of this, but goes the next step—that of *extending* these relationships through the generation of new and more encompassing ones for every initial relationship that is brought to his attention by a "teacher,"—a book, or a lecture.

GENERATING NEW INSIGHTS

How can we deliberately extend the value of a "good" lecture or "good" book—that is, one which, as described above, provides for the viewing of many new and relevant relationships for the listener or reader? My answer is to constantly ask the listener or reader to make some new connections, thereby extending the relationships that he has been helped to see. We can ask the learner always to take it the next step—connect it up with other elements of unique experience and data within himself, as well as with other new data that is constantly being assimilated into his mental computer; he may then generate many new and worthwhile connections and relationships beyond those already provided. What does all of this suggest to you, the reader, in relation to all of your unique experiences? Can you relate aspects of what I have written thus far so as to go beyond anything I am presently suggesting? Can you generate "ahas" (*new insights*) as a result?

I wonder what would happen if, from the earliest days of formal "teaching," the teacher or parent, after presenting a new bit of learning (that is, some new "relationship" for the child), would invariably ask next, "How might you use this bit of information? What new ways might you connect this up with something else you know? What else might you look for today to relate to what I have just taught you? How many ways could you and your friends put this new bit of information to use? How many things that you already know can you connect this with?" I would predict that by this one deceptively simple tactic, we might launch the next generation into a completely new level of mental power, almost beyond our own limited comprehension from where we stand now.

RELATIONSHIPS

All people form relationships among the elements of their sensory input. However, I suggest that everyone may be "programmed" to form more as well as deeper, broader, and more all-encompassing relationships; or at the least they may be helped from being "programmed" *against* generating these kinds of relationships.

I think that infants and young children experience so much joy because they are constantly generating new relationships by their manipulations, their experiments, their play, their random interaction with their environment, their risk-taking. As they get older, we ply them with "facts," *showing* them all the relationships faster than any they can generate themselves. Learning by discovery gets them to generate the relations. When they learn *how to learn*—how to *generate* new and harmonious relationships—they can do this all their lives, in all the new circumstances they encounter. They can learn to cope with whatever life brings them, using their own resources.

CREATIVE PHILOSOPHY OF LIFE

Life's meaning might be defined as the joy or satisfaction of successfully meeting each obstacle or challenge—of overcoming, developing, growing, achieving—constantly drawing on and extending one's resources. This might be viewed as a creative philosophy of life. This philosophy may be increasingly insignificant in the world's present state of what Alvin Toffler (1970) refers to as "future shock." As I wrote earlier:

> Change is bewilderingly rapid in our nuclear and space age—more rapid than ever before. The discoveries and innovations of the next 20 years will probably make the previous 100 years seem to have progressed at a snail's pace. As one medical professor tells his students at the close of his course, "Within five years, over half of what I've taught you will prove to be wrong or not worth a darn; and my biggest dilemma is that I can't even tell you which half is which!"
>
> Therefore, a person cannot foresee exactly what knowledge he will need five or ten years from now to meet life's problems. He can, however, develop attitudes and abilities that will help him meet *any* future challenge creatively by finding better solutions to problems. The objective of the creative problem-solving course is to help the student do just that. He learns to associate in new ways the knowledge and experience he possesses, as well as the new knowledge and experience he acquires throughout his education and his life. Thus he becomes better able to apply his learning to problems he meets as he progresses through school and into the future. [Parnes, 1967*b*]

The general assumptions underlying our conceptual systems in Creative Studies are that each individual has many potentials that he has failed to recognize or tap—be he retarded or genius—and that these potentials, once recognized, sampled, and cultivated, can trigger a lifetime of new meaning and joy for a person. When someone once asked Leonardo da Vinci what his greatest accomplishment was, he replied, "Leonardo da Vinci."

Sometimes I "let myself go" to some tune—all by myself—just because I feel the impulse. I let my body move spontaneously with the music, and I feel *joy* in the experience. Its only significance is to *me* and for *that moment*. It is *that* significance of the creative process or creative experience that I am talking about. We so often look at creativity from the standpoint of the *product* of the poet or the painter. But cannot the poet or the painter create for the sheer joy of the process in the same way the dancer does in the example above? It is in this same sense that a problem-solver can experience the joy of ideation or of a brainstorming session, irrespective of whether there is any implementation of the ideas later. A child behaves this way much of the time—releases spontaneity—experiences *joy;* but unfortunately, most adults seem to do this less and less as they "grow up."

History of Effort

Over the past 20 years I have been asked many times how I got started in this new, intriguing field of Creative Studies. The genesis is quite specific, and I'm happy to have this opportunity, commemorating the 1950 inaugural address of J. P. Guilford as president of the American Psychological Association, to recount in writing how my own life work developed in this way.

It began for me specifically in 1955, when I received the announcement of the first annual Creative Problem-Solving Institute conducted by the University of Buffalo, with the cosponsorship of Alex F. Osborn's Creative Education Foundation. Alex Osborn had written several books, including the widely-known text *Applied Imagination* (1963), and had developed interest at the University in courses and institutes on the subject. The courses had begun as early as 1949 in the extension division, then called Millard Fillmore College; however, it was not until 1955 that these programs in creative problem-solving were called to the attention of people throughout the nation. Such wide announcement was provided through the first Creative Problem-Solving Institute in June of 1955, to an audience of several hundred people from all parts of the nation, all of whom were interested in the nature and curriculum of this newly evolving program of study.

The brochure explaining the Institute immediately captured my interest. It looked like something for which I had been groping all of my life; I had always thought I was a "loner" in my philosophies. However, when I attended the program, along with several hundred kindred individuals, I was ecstatic to find this philosophy of education and life being expounded and discussed by so many diverse individuals, many of whom were actively involved in helping cultivate this type of creative behavior and creative thinking in their schools, industries, or governmental organizations. At that time there was much greater involvement in business and industry than in education, as is frequently the case with educational innovation. Perhaps only 10 percent of the participants were from the field of education. (I am happy to point out, however, that today more than half of the persons attending our Institutes are from the field of education; these individuals are involved in studying and applying these processes and programs throughout the nation and the world. Our annual Institutes are scheduled in Buffalo each year, with extension programs in regions from coast-to-coast.)

I had driven to the Buffalo Institute from my home in Pittsburgh, and as I drove back I cannot remember how many times I pulled off the road to write voluminous notes that had been triggered in me as a result of the sessions that I had attended. I became more and more excited about the idea of becoming totally involved with this kind of work. By the time I returned to my desk the next week, I had already added numerous ideas through incubation and by brainstorming with my wife.

REVAMPED CURRICULUM

As the first step in my plan of action, I proposed and gained acceptance for the idea of conducting a first Creative Retailing Institute at the School of Retailing of the University of Pittsburgh, where I was then a member of the faculty. Over the summer period, I revamped the curriculum for each of the courses that I was teaching in the adult distributive education field (including management development, group dynamics, human relations, and methods of teaching). I incorporated the concepts that I learned at the Creative Problem-Solving Institute into all of these programs for the following academic year. As a result of all of this activity I was called upon the next year by Alex Osborn and Dean Robert Berner of the University of Buffalo to assume the position of the first full-time director of the University of Buffalo's Creative Problem-Solving program, which had been handled with part-time faculty until that time.

But what had brought me to the point where I became so engulfed in this program in Creative Problem-Solving? Here the history goes back much farther. Until my graduate work, I had always disliked school, and had considered it, as do many students today, irrelevant to my life. Without doubt the most meaningful and valuable part of my first 12 years of education was my work with the high school newspaper. I served as a reporter, news editor, and then editor-in-chief. This provided me with knowledge, experience, and insights that have been useful and important to me throughout my life. In my undergraduate work, I found that you either read the text or you went to classes, but that there was not much point in doing both, for the one merely repeated the other. I am sure I would never have gone through this college experience without parental urging.

Concurrent with all of my formal education beyond the elementary school, I had been working in various kinds of jobs, from door-to-door selling, to general assistance in a small community newspaper, and in a family business. These and my World War II army experiences provided me with my greatest understanding of people, relationships, problem solving, and all the skills that seem to be required in everyday living.

After graduating from college, I went to work in a large department store. I had felt I wanted to get into some sort of personnel work, but didn't really know too much about the field. I ended up in an assignment as a training supervisor. As soon as I began helping to instruct employees, I became very curious about the way people learn, and wondered whether I was going to be guilty of the same unchallenging teaching that had bored me so much during my own education. I therefore determined to probe into the problem. I enrolled in graduate courses in education and, in spite of frequent reports berating educational courses, found these graduate courses to be both stimulating, relevant, and very helpful—both in my work and in my formation of a more complete educational and personal philosophy. For the first time I could see real connections between what I was learning and what I was doing, and I determined that this kind of education needs to be provided from the cradle to the grave.

I completed and then taught courses in applied educational psychology and applied industrial psychology—courses which proved invaluable to me and to managers I taught in my adult education programs. One of these courses especially emphasized problem-solving processes; another emphasized conference-leadership methods for improving the productivity of meetings.

After later joining the faculty of the University of Pittsburgh, I enjoyed most the teaching of courses which were designed to help instructors find ways to make their courses more relevant and more useful to the students who were taking them. I felt that this could be done with any course, given enough determination and imagination on the part of the instructor.

MEETING ALEX OSBORN

From the vantage point described above I fell into the fortunate discovery of the creative problem-solving processes that had been devised and outlined by Alex Osborn. It was an "aha" experience, where all of the old as well as the new bits and pieces suddenly fit together for me in a new, synergistic way. Furthermore, I found in Alex Osborn someone who not only believed what I believed about the learning process and the problem-solving process, but who had spelled it out in detail, quite beyond the point to which my own thinking had progressed. It was through participation in the Creative Problem-Solving Institute that I first began *really* to understand and appreciate the tremendous potential of the imagination. With this new insight, I could see ways to make my problem-solving course many-fold more effective, even though I had always considered it the best and most important course I had ever taught. The problem-solving process per se is not substantially different in our Creative Studies program—in terms of its steps or logical processes—from those of John

Dewey, Graham Wallace, or any of the well-known problem-solving models, historic or modern. However, the added ingredient that Osborn introduced was the deliberate and exaggerated use of the imagination; this provided a powerful force when effectively harnessed within a total problem-solving model.

Development of Eclectic Program

Over the years, since first encountering Osborn's program, I have tried to establish an eclectic approach to the development of the most comprehensive program possible for nurturing creative behavior. Starting with Osborn's well-known model, I have tried to synthesize with it relevant and important parts of all the existing theories and programs we could uncover, as well as the many new approaches that were being developed concurrently over the past 20 years. Fundamental principles of Osborn's model involve combining, adapting, and modifying, and we have tried to apply these principles as fully as possible. While some individuals or groups have constructed a particular program and developed it extensively in an almost independent manner, ours has been at attempt to study and relate—even to "force" relationships—with all areas and approaches, to incorporate and synthesize as much as possible from the growing body of research and development over the past 20 years.

For example, Synectics is a well-known program whose developers are represented in this volume among the pioneers in the creativity field. I have tried over the years to study and understand their processes as fully as possible, and to adapt and utilize these processes within our own program. William Gordon and George Prince have cooperated fully in our efforts; as a result, we have built into our basic programs aspects of what Synectics has learned from many years of research. We have also developed advanced areas of our courses and institutes dealing specifically with synectics processes—helping people to gain a greater grasp of the power of the metaphor and of the metaphorical approaches of the basic Synectics course, as stressed in the title of Gordon's book, *The Metaphorical Way of Knowing and Learning* (1971).

As another example, Albert Upton's work in creative analysis (1963) and its research-substantiation became widely disseminated in the 1960s. After careful study of his theories and his unique set of mental exercises, we collaborated with him and one of his disciples in integrating these materials into our advanced programs of our institutes and creative studies courses.

SENSITIVITY PROGRAMS

Almost concurrently with our own program development came the sensitivity programs, with National Training Laboratories (NTL) providing the strong initial thrust in this direction. As these programs grew and spread, there occurred a focus on the entire area of human-potential development exemplified by the National Center for the Exploration of Human Potential, the Esalen program, and the multitude of "Human Growth Centers." Some of my colleagues and close friends cautioned me about this development. There had been adverse publicity because of some poorly led programs and unfortunate incidents. But in this emerging movement I saw close parallels and factors that could strengthen our own courses and institutes. Hence we began to research this field—first through the literature, then through involvement in order to experience what these programs had to offer. Gradually we modified and adapted aspects of these approaches in ways that have helped to strengthen our total program of Creative Studies (Parnes and Noller, 1973).

Viktor Lowenfeld (1970) first caught my attention among the scholars on creativity in *the arts*. His research aroused by curiosity and led me to exploring relationships between artistic creativity and creative problem solving. We began to introduce art experiences into our creative problem-solving programs, first with fear of "turning off" the businessmen, engineers, and other "practical" members of our institute body. I will never forget the reaction of one very indignant engineer during the bus ride to the Albright-Knox Art Gallery, where we had scheduled, for *all* participants, a session on artistic creativity and the artistic creative process. He complained about the "nonsensical" idea of bringing this whole group to a modern art gallery for a session which had nothing to do with creative problem solving. At that session an artist painted while simultaneously explaining his thought processes. A photographer, who was also a school administrator, related those processes to the ones used in creative photography and in creative problem solving in administration. Then the audience strolled through the gallery and discussed the modern art products on display. After the session, the engineer sought me out to tell me that this experience alone had been worth his entire trip to Buffalo—that he, for the first time, saw how important it was to understand and relate creative processes to all aspects of a person's being and living.

CREATIVE EXPERIENCES

From that point on we began to introduce "creative experiences," as we call them, in a variety of areas, all the way from creating music, art products, or drama, to creating "things" such as new toys. One such session was led by a member of the music department of the State University of Buffalo. Participants were people who had never played an instrument. The leader got everyone involved, and actually had them play together as an orchestra before the end of the evening. As I was walking across campus after the session, I happened upon a woman who looked as though she were in a trance. When I asked if she was all right, she exclaimed, "I'm ecstatic! I played in an orchestra! And I had never touched an instrument before in my life!" This is how deeply an individual can be moved when he begins to experience his creative potentials in new and untried areas.

We began to introduce experiences with body movement and body awareness—with fantasy, both guided and undirected, with Eastern philosophies and practices such as meditation and yoga—as well as experiences involving general semantics, bionics, and many other relevant areas. All of these processes are related to a heightened self-awareness and awareness of the environment, to increased associations of both stored knowledge and new sensory input for the solving of human problems—probems in art, in music, in business, in science, in education, in the home, in government, or in whatever area of life one finds himself at any particular time.

Thus the problem-solving process becomes one of opening up the self to the fullest possible awareness of the storehouse of energy and resources within oneself—in his vast mental library of life experience—as well as in the vast data of the external world. Problem solving becomes the task of finding the greatest number of interconnections and interrelationships among these vast resources, including the layer upon layer of primary information stored in our brain cells from birth and even from embryonic states. One searches for the kinds of synergistic connections that he can make toward the solution of his problems, his goals, his wishes, his aspirations, his hopes, his dreams—for himself, his family, his group, his society, his world, his universe.

LIFELONG PROCESS

Our programs change each year because of the eclectic approach we use. We are researching, learning, adapting, and synthesizing constantly, epitomizing the expression that one student used to summarize this kind of lifelong process: "Nuttin's final!"

At our Institute this year I will attempt to display this ongoing synthesis in a general session. I will try to capsulize the kind of interactive programming we have created between synectics, sensitivity, art, fantasy, meditation, body awareness, and so on, in one session that will experientially provide the participants with a montage of what their week-long program is designed to accomplish. The Institute itself, with its multilevel advanced programs, serves as a compressed-in-time version of our two-year Creative Studies program, designed to extend and advance the individual's concern for creative process and product for himself and mankind.

Research Base

Over the years of our efforts in Buffalo, continuing research has accompanied the development of new approaches, processes, and programs. It is not the purpose of this chapter to recount the details of research completed or under way; however, it will help place my explanations in focus by summarizing briefly the results of our research to date.

Research and development in creativity at the State University of New York at Buffalo from 1949 to 1956 was concerned with pilot experimentation and the development of courses, programs, and methods designed to stimulate creative behavior in students. Experimentation was first conducted in the evening division of the University and later in the day division. Constant revision, adaptation, and improvement resulted from new insights gained through each experimental course and program.

After this period of preliminary exploration, we began an extensive research effort in 1957 to evaluate scientifically the results of these methods and programs. During the next eighteen years, as new knowledge was gained, intensive development activities paralleled the research efforts.

Research for the first ten years dealt with: (1) the effects of a semester's program in deliberate creativity-stimulation; (2) the relative effects on creative ability of a programmed course used alone or used with instructors and class interaction; (3) the effects of extended effort in creative problem solving; (4) the effectiveness of the specific creative problem-solving principle of deferred judgment. (This principle calls for deliberate deferment of judgment during idea-finding to avoid hampering imagination, with judgment being applied *after* a wide variety of alternatives is listed. It is equally applicable to individual idea-finding effort and to group collaboration. Studies covered its use in both situations.)

Major findings were as follows:[1]

(1) The semester programs resulted in significant increments on the two measures of quantity of idea-production, and on three out of the five measures of quality of the ideas produced. In general, these increases in creative productivity remained evident in another group of students who were tested from one to four years *after* taking the course. A significant increment on the California Psychological Inventory Dominance Scale also resulted from the program.

(2) In the study regarding the programmed course, on almost every test the experimental students made greater gains than did the control students. On almost all the measures, the gains of the instructor-taught programmed groups were significantly superior to those of two control groups. Students in groups who took the program alone were significantly superior to control students in gains on most tests, but less so than the instructor-taught programmed groups. In other words, the instructor-taught groups tended to be more markedly and consistently superior to the control groups than program-taught students who had no instructor.

(3) Extended effort in idea-production resulted in a greater proportion of good ideas among the later ideas produced.

(4) Significantly more good-quality ideas were produced by individuals under deferred judgment instructions than under concurrent-judgment

instructions. (Criteria included uniqueness and usefulness of ideas.) The subjects trained in a creative problem-solving course emphasizing the principle of deferred judgment produced a significantly greater number of good-quality ideas when using the technique than did the untrained students. (The same criteria were employed.)

Groups producing ideas on a creative problem-solving task produced more good-quality ideas when adhering to the deferred-judgment principle than when employing the more conventional discussion methods which entail concurrent evaluation of ideas. Groups which adhered to the deferred-judgment principle when generating ideas were likewise more productive of good-quality ideas than the same number of individuals working independently under conventional methods, with concurrent evaluation.

CREATIVE STUDIES PROJECT

Following the ten years of research and development efforts described above, we then launched a comprehensive longitudinal investigation at the State University College at Buffalo. This ongoing study is called the Creative Studies Project. Specific hypotheses tested in the project were as follows: Students who complete a four-semester sequence of Creative Studies courses will perform significantly better than otherwise comparable students on: (1) selected tests of mental ability, problem solving, and job performance; (2) tests of creative application of academic subject matter; (3) nonacademic achievement in areas calling for creative performance; (4) certain personality measures associated with creativity. Further hypotheses for the longitudinal study are currently being formulated.

A very brief capsulization of the results is as follows:

(1) The course students show significantly better performance than comparable controls in ability to cope with real-life situational tests, including not only the production of ideas, but also their evaluation and development.

(2) They perform significantly better than comparable controls in applying their creative abilities in special tests given in English courses.

(3) They perform significantly better than the comparable controls on the semantic and behavioral half of J. P. Guilford's structure of intellect (SI) model, including three of five of his mental operations—cognition, divergent production, and convergent production; they show no significant accomplishment over the controls in the symbolic and figural half of Guilford's model, nor in his memory or evaluation operations.

(4) Most course students report large gains in their own productive, creative behavior; they rate the program as quite helpful in their other college courses and their everyday lives. In the second year, there is a significant increase in the percentage of students who report large gains in ability to cope with problems and to participate actively in discussions.

(5) Test results bear out their significant year-to-year improvement over comparable controls.

(6) Course students show a growing tendency (not yet attaining statistical significance) to become more productive than comparable controls in their nonacademic achievement in areas calling for creative performance.

(7) The data show consistent positive movement on personality measures by course students compared with their controls, although not significant on any single scale. One coping instrument, as well as the course students' own questionnaire responses, provided further significant evidence of gains of personality dimensions.

(8) As to generalizability, it was concluded that, for a group comparable to our total sample of experimentals and controls who started such a two-year program of Creative Studies—and this would very likely include a portion of the student body at most colleges and universities—the gains in the study relative to time spent in courses would be expected for those continuing with the program.

Shift in Emphasis

There has been a significant shift in my focus on creativity and its development. When I first began with Osborn's concepts in 1955, I had been fascinated with the potential in recognizing, understanding, and using one's imagination. I felt that this was what had been missing in my own education over the years. It may have been implicit in what I had been taught; but it never had come through as it did at the Creative Problem-Solving Institute. Since judgment and logic had been emphasized so strongly in my own education, to the relative exclusion of imagination, I erroneously generalized that our efforts should concentrate almost solely on stretching the imagination in students. So I began my efforts accordingly rather than in the context of a total creative problem-solving process. Through a few unnerving experiences, I soon learned that not all individuals had acquired the judgment needed to deal with an unleashed imagination.

I then began to see the necessity of unleashing the imagination gradually, and of strengthening judicial abilities concurrently so as to deal with the torrent of ideas that the imagination can generate. But I also came to see how the imagination could be used very constructively in the evaluation process itself, as well as in the development and implementation process. For example, the more imagination a person calls forth, the more potential consequences, repercussions, and effects he can see of ideas that he might want to put into action. Obviously any new idea will have repercussions. Often the reason ideas fail is that people are insensitive to the impact of their ideas on others and on the environment.

As our institutes and courses evolved over the years, there was a steady growth toward more emphasis on imaginative exercises in evaluating ideas or in implementing ideas and developing plans of action. We practiced more and more the stretching of the imagination in these phases of the problem-solving process rather than mainly in the idea-generation stage itself. In the matter of problem definition, we likewise devote a great deal more effort now than earlier to using the imagination for acquiring a multiplicity of viewpoints of the problem.

In summary, we found that we were able to do the necessary imagination-stretching—the core of our program—in *all* stages of the creative problem-solving process rather than emphasizing it only for idea-generation as such.

The impact that this has had may be understood from this comment written by a student: "When Criteria is so drummed into you, you make a habit to judge items on certain bases, before you decide."

Thus, in our programs we are *practicing* creative skills just as much as in our earlier programs, but we are practicing them within all stages of problem solving, with much more emphasis on the difficult evaluation, development, and implementation stages. We still feel as Guilford (1952) did when he said: "Like most behavior, creative activity probably represents, to some extent, many learned skills. There may be limitations set on these skills by heredity; but I am convinced that through learning one can extend the skills within those limitations."

DEVELOPING A BALANCE

In adapting all of the evolving programs that we have been able to synthesize with our creative problem-solving courses and institutes, we have been trying always to develop a balance between the judgment and the imagination, as well as between the open awareness of the environment through all of the senses and the deep self-searching into layer upon layer of data stored in the memory cells, between the logic and the emotion, between the deliberate creative effort and the incubation, and between the individual working with the group and his working alone. The longer I work in this field the more the underlying problem seems to become one of developing this balance between these extremes, by *strengthening* the weaker aspect, not by stunting the stronger side.

STAY-INS VERSUS DROP-OUTS

In our latest research efforts, we have been discovering interesting related facts about the nature of the students who stayed with the program of Creative Studies as against those who dropped out after one or more courses in the series of four. When comparing pretest data on the stay-ins versus the drop-outs, significant and interesting differences were found in both experimental students who took the courses and their comparable controls. Dr. Mazie Wagner of the Counseling Center reported (Wagner and Schubert, 1973), that, according to analyses of the Minnesota Multi-phasic Personality Inventory (MMPI) data (Hathaway and McKinley, 1951), both experimental and control drop-outs *as a group* (not necessarily true for each individual) tended to be somewhat more depressive, hysteri-cal, and more directed toward deviancy and toward culturally disapproved behavior; appeared to be more impulsive, quicker to "take off" rather than stick with something, in closer contact with their "primary processes," "freer," more compulsive, obsessional, ruminative; showed less potential for "above-average achievement," less likelihood to succeed in college, more likelihood to drop out, to fail out or to get lower grades, and tended to be less responsible and more anxious. She reported that the above pat-terns were reinforced by the repeated instances of significant differences also found between the stay-in groups and drop-out groups on Adjective Check List (ACL) scales (Gough and Heilbrun, 1965) as follows: stay-ins significantly exceeded drop-outs on Total Adjectives Checked, Self-Con-trol, Nurturance, Deference, and Welsh's Low Origence, High Intellec-tence;[2] drop-outs significantly exceeded stay-ins on Lability, Aggression, and Change.

Heist (1968) reported on studies regarding the frequency of the more creative students dropping out of college. He found that:

> Observations in seven quite dissimilar schools indicated that the proportions of identified creatives withdrawing ranged from approximately 50 percent to 80 percent. In five out of seven of the particular institutions included in these analyses, a significantly higher proportion of the creative students on each campus left than did drop-out students not identified as creative. The major conclusion to be drawn from the data is that the students who are ranked as creative or identified by measured characteristics of creativity either leave some colleges more frequently than or as frequently as all other students not so identified.

Our study may throw some light on the reasons for this as well as what might be done about it; for the drop-out from our project and the drop-out from our college turn out to exhibit the same general personality syn-drome. As a matter of fact, 45 percent of the course drop-outs also left the college by the end of the sophomore year.

In discussing the above findings, it will be useful to introduce a brief discussion from an earlier publication (Parnes and Noller, 1973):

> There's a delightful little book entitled *The Dot and the Line* by Norton Juster (1963). (It has also been made into a film produced by Metro-Goldwyn-Mayer.) Essentially the book portrays the trials and tribulations of a very straight, rigid line as he attempts to become more free and open, more uninhibited and spon-taneous, in order to win the love of a dot. We have found that the story has deep meaning for those interested in the study of the creative process and the creative person. The line in the story learns to bend and twist into all forms of complex and versatile shapes and structures, including complex ellipses, tetragrams, etc.

He breaks the rigidity in his being—in his structure—into dazzling and profound displays of form that have not only *uniqueness* but also *relevance* and *harmony*. This, of course, is the true nature of the creative process—creating new relationships that are not only unique but relevant and harmonious.

The line's rival in the little parable is an unruly, wild squiggle (scribble), who is undisciplined, unconventional, uninhibited, etc. In Juster's story, the squiggle loses out in his competition with the line after the line has learned to merge his innate freedom and spontaneity with his learned self-discipline and responsibility so as to produce *"channeled freedom."* The squiggle does not know how to direct and channel his freedom, and goes on being only a wild and unkempt bit of anarchy.

Historically, our Creative Studies courses were developed to help the "line" capture the "squiggliness" within himself, and to build the "squiggliness" into relevance in terms of his overall goals, as did Juster's "line" in his story. Thus, neither the self-control of the line nor the originality and spontaneity of the "squiggle" are considered sufficient for fully achieving one's purposes in life—for meeting one's challenges and problems. Both qualities need melding for full self-actualization.

The findings of our study regarding the personality of the drop-outs have made us aware that we may need to design programs especially to help the "squiggles." Ten years ago, we rarely encountered a student like this, but today it seems that about one-third of each Creative Studies class is made up of such students. Many of them presently experience great frustration because they are unable to harness and channel their spontaneity toward their life purposes as they see them. On the other hand, those "squiggles" who *do* stick with the program seem to learn to better channel their freedom by means of the "structured" problem-solving processes, with strong emphasis on implementation of ideas, following through with the development of plans of action, etc. Thus, our overall program is now attempting to create the necessary "balance" between the two extremes—freedom and self-discipline—so that one achieves a truly "channeled freedom." And it is important to emphasize that we do not want to achieve this balance by reducing "squiggliness"; rather, we want to *strengthen* the self-discipline while maintaining and even extending the originality and spontaneity of the "squiggles."

One current student put it this way: "Just like the movie we saw in class about the straight, rigid lines versus the squiggly line: A person has to find a happy medium in order not to be too extreme, or what Maslow considers 'sick.' "

We say that people should learn to "stay loose" in their stance toward life and in their mental processes, but, of course, the question becomes, "How loose until one falls apart?" And by the same token, "How tight can one remain before he freezes up?" This helps to portray the type of "balance" we feel is needed for one to be able to exercise his creative potential productively in our society. Our hypothesis is that the "drop-out syndrome" represents a stance that is "too loose."

It is worth noting that we are using the word "balanced" in this sense in quite a different way than the word "balanced personality" is usually construed. We do not equate our term "balanced" with the term "normal," which more often implies the "conventional" type of individual in our society. Visualize instead a sling-shot. If one side of the elastic is weaker, it will not have full power and cannot be aimed for maximum accuracy. With two equally "balanced" elastic sides, the force and accuracy of propelling will be the greatest. So it is, we hypothesize, with the forces of our spontaneity and of our self-control as they mutually aid us in propelling ourselves toward our goals. If one force is weaker than the other, we may be weakened and/or misdirected. Utilizing these two complementary forces effectively is what Alex Osborn meant when he quipped, "Don't drive with your brakes on (1963)." This metaphor introduces the important elements of sequencing and timing that are not inherent in the sling-shot analogy. The gas pedal represents a tremendous force; when used by a skillful driver, it is "balanced" with appropriate sequencing and timing with the brake pedal, with its equally powerful capability. One likewise can learn to develop and use productively these two forces in his personality through effective sequencing and timing.

With respect to this question of "balance," we have countless data from the comprehensive testing of the Creative Studies Project, and are beginning to look more deeply into some of it. The P-J scale of the Myers-Briggs Type Inventory (Myers, 1962) is involved. It measures emphasis on perception—"processes of becoming aware"—versus judgment—"coming to conclusions about." In our project report, we mentioned that a preliminary study of the MBTI data did not show any differences between the experimentals and the controls. However, the Inventory is scored in such a manner that each subject turns out to be either "P" or "J", followed by a number indicating the strength of the P or the J. Hence the people who score lowest—P1 or J1—would be very close to being "balanced" between these two scales. Persons who score highest—P61 or J55 (highest scores attainable on the respective scales) would tend to be at the extremes. An analysis of the number of students falling into the *bottom* third of the scores on either P or J (meaning the students who were closest to zero or "balance" between the two scales) showed 47 percent of students completing the two years of Creative Studies to be in this "balanced range," as compared to 28 percent of the control students. The difference between the two groups was even more pronounced when the smaller number of males was dropped. As to the experimental students who dropped out after one or more courses, only 20 percent were in the "balanced range."

We will be testing these differences for significance, and also examining pretest data for these subjects to make certain that the subgroups that completed this questionnaire were initially comparable as were the total experimental and control groups in the experiment. The initial finding, however, is quite encouraging; it is what we hypothesized in light of the "balance" theory that I have been discussing. We are planning to do a number of other analyses of some of the data on the Adjective Check List in order to see whether further evidence can be discovered supporting this theory. In many cases, standardized personality tests such as the ACL have been used to measure characteristics of highly creative, accomplished individuals who often score high on traits associated with spontaneity, impulsivity, and disinclination to socialize. But these individuals usually show other characteristics, such as strong determination, that enable them to harness their talents. In assessing a program like ours, it may be important to look for "balance" in overall profiles rather than examining unitary traits.

One might reasonably conjecture that many people have developed traits like "disinclination to socialize" because society tends to ostracize the "original" or "deviant" individual, or to reject his ideas so frequently that he finds group efforts nonproductive for him. Of course, some of these highly creative people may be accepted in spite of eccentric traits because they have demonstrated their creativity in their achievements. And others may develop their "antisocial" traits as a self-defense against spreading themselves too thin as they concentrate intensely on their creative efforts —or for other possible reasons.

ORIGINALITY REFINED

But we are not trying to teach people to become the kind of individual who has great originality combined with other qualities that are less acceptable in our society. Instead, we are trying to teach people how to extend their originality and spontaneity gradually, within the framework of a total creative problem-solving context, including the gaining of acceptance for and implementation of their ideas. This involves making their ideas relevant to society's needs as well as their own. In our course, we provide a climate that encourages the original, spontaneous behavior, but we unite this with an emphasis on the self-discipline required to bring originality to creative fruition. Many students who cannot "limit" their freedom and spontaneity tend to drop out of the course. Those who remain learn to extend their freedom and spontaneity, but in a self-controlled, relevant way. They show traits somewhat analogous to those assessed by the Rorschach "O+" originality measure, which is concerned with productive, purposeful, goal-oriented originality, as against "O−" which measures bizarre, meaningless originality. The "squiggle" tends to fail to distinguish between the "O+" and the "O−." We will undoubtedly be struggling with this problem for some years, with the help of our students and our research, as we continue developing and adapting our programs to the needs of the "squiggles" as well as the "lines."

The "Squiggle" and Society

When a person's spontaneity takes over, allowing free reign to his emotions, this probably results in reducing his inhibitions. But if overcoming my inhibitions frees me to punch you in the nose, most of us would probably be opposed to *that* kind of *uninhibitedness*. At the other extreme, if I am so inhibited that I am afraid to express an idea in a discussion, most of us would probably be against *that* kind of *inhibition*. But what about the gray areas in between? For example, what about the "psychological" punch in the nose? For one person it might be hearing abusive, foul language. Another might be able to withstand the foul language without psychological harm, but might be very uptight, for example, if a person were to enter a classroom without any clothes on.

It has been said that one person's freedom begins with the edge of another person's nose. That physical edge is much easier to define than is the psychological edge. What would constitute a psychological punch in the nose for you? I suppose that some psychological jabs, perhaps a little stronger each time, may be needed to shake us loose from some of the cultural and societal restraints that have no meaning other than pure convention. Many extremists would remove all those psychological, cultural blocks in one "revolution." On the other hand, most of us seem to behave as though this can be an evolutionary process. I personally am willing to work within the system, gradually helping people to see how much they are being inhibited and constrained unnecessarily from full realization and from fruitful interrelationships. For example, I know one person who is so offended by "four-letter words" that this person will not attend a classroom where such language is used. This to me is being psychologically strait-jacketed, and is one example of many ways in which individuals become "blocked" from the free flow of ideas, interconnections, and associations that allows for the greatest probability of new "aha" relationships to occur. Some of the emphases in the Creative Studies and Human Development programs are best understood in this light—as attempts to "break a person loose" from some of this inhibiting influence.

I have been haunted by the last paragraphs of an article in *Life* on "The Other Culture," by Barry Farrel:

> There are few painters and sculptors in the Underground, and not many writers of prose. It is performers' turf—poets, happeners, actors, showmen, musicians. The best means of judging them is by their intentions; and the best way to understand them is to think of them as cultural revolutionaries.
>
> The one universal intention of Underground artists is to open new areas of perception by clearing away taboos, to make the secret psychic drama the collective experience. This is their revolutionary proposal, and it should be taken seriously as such; it is a utopian dream and people are jumping the wall to embrace it.
>
> Whether or not you approve depends, of course, on who you are and how well you like the life you're leading. Meanwhile, an alarm bell is ringing, and we're deep in our beds, complaining about its vulgar, brutal tone. [*Life* Magazine, Copyright 1967, Time, Inc.]

My own concern regarding some of the extreme programs is that they "dump" people back into the same society from which they came—a society which is completely unready and unwilling to accept or tolerate the kind of behavior that may be the most natural and the ideal. Even in our own much less extreme programs, we spend considerable time helping people to analyze how they might function most effectively outside the Creative Studies atmosphere.

Recently I have been talking with various students about the results of our Creative studies Project, and particularly about the findings regarding the stay-ins versus the drop-outs, the latter group of which seems to contain many of the "squiggles." Each time I have discussed this with students, they have asked whether I would rather not see "squiggles" in our society. I emphatically point out that I *do* want to see "squiggles," but *self-disciplined* "squiggles." And I want to see this for the "squiggle's" own sake as well as for society. I feel that the "squiggle" is cheating himself (as well as society) in terms of the accomplishments and satisfaction that he could experience from achieving more of his creative potential, rather than from concentrating only on his imagination or spontaneity.

GREATER SELF-ACTUALIZATION

The "squiggle" to me represents the person whose "squiggle" side is out of balance with his "line" side or "self-discipline" side. I do not wish to concentrate on making his "line" side so long that it is correspondingly out of balance with his "squiggle" side. My thesis is that a person has the greatest potential for self-actualization when he develops to his fullest capability both sides of his personality—both the "line" and the "squiggle." If either side is shorter than the other, he may be like the "out-of-balance" sling shot of my earlier analogy; this can reduce both his strength and his direction.

Some students stress that the "squiggle" is needed in society to prevent stagnation and to bring about change and development. I wholeheartedly agree, except that I would express it this way: society needs a great deal of "squiggliness" to accomplish just what the students emphasized. It does *not* need "squiggles" *per se;* that is, it does not need unbalanced people, but needs "squiggliness" that is *channeled* through *self-discipline.*

The "squiggle" might be very effective in certain rather unique situations in our present society. If an organization, for example, can afford to have a person whose sole function is to produce ideas which others then develop and implement, then the "squiggle" might operate largely with his imagination and let others carry his ideas to fulfillment. However, I contend that even if the "squiggle" is fortunate enough to find and hold such a position, he may lose a great deal of the self-fulfillment that can come from seeing an idea to fruition. It may be somewhat like the difference between the sex act alone as against sex concomitant with conceiving and giving birth to a child. In the first instance there may be joy and ecstacy connected with the creative process; but in the second case, this joy and ecstacy culminates in a "product" that can provide a wealth of self-realization and fulfillment to the creator. By analogy, I am suggesting that the "idea-originator" can have a great deal of joy and satisfaction from generating ideas, but he may be missing the totality of fulfillment brought about by the development and implementation of an idea—*in spite of* the "birth pains" that usually go along with it.

Thus, my concern is to develop both the freedom and the self-discipline in people, as though each were one leg of their bodies. We want both legs to be of equal length, and we want both to be full-length and strong. The so-called "squiggle" represents to me the person whose "squiggly" leg is much longer than his self-disciplined leg. This hampers him in his personal and societal efforts just as much so as his counterpart, the "straight line," whose self-disciplined leg out-distances his "squiggly" stump.

When I point out the large number of "squiggles" in my classes, I do not do so in alarm; I do so with great hope and anticipation, for I feel that it is the "squiggle" in our culture who has blazed the trail in terms of calling our attention to needed change in society. The "squiggles" have currently evolutionized many of our cultural behaviors, almost to the point of revolution. If I had to choose between the "good old days" or today in this respect, there would be no question in my mind which I would prefer. I would live with the "squiggles" and today's breaking of taboos. But I am not talking about yesterday versus today; I am talking about today versus tomorrow, for tomorrow I see the possibility of a great surge forward toward positive change, far beyond what we have witnessed today, but in a more directed sense—almost like a guided missile as against a missile out of control. If we can help people become fully aware of their total potential—both their "squiggliness" and their self-discipline—I feel certain that we can increase each person's creative productivity, for both his own self-fulfillment as well as for the benefit of society.

Notes

1. Summaries of the detailed findings and procedures regarding these studies may be found in Volume I, Nos. 1 and 2 of the *Journal of Creative Behavior*.

2. High scorers on this scale tend to be individuals whose responses are intellectualized and who seldom act impulsively (Welsh, 1969).

References

Gordon, W. J. J. *The metamorphical way of learning and knowing.* Cambridge: Porpoise Books, 1971.

Gough, H. G., and Heilbrun, A. B., Jr. *The Adjective Check List manual.* Palo Alto: Consulting Psychologists Press, 1965.

Guilford, J. P. Some recent findings on thinking abilities and their implications.

248   SIDNEY J. PARNES

TA&D informational bulletin, directorate, Deputy Chief of Staff Operations, Hq. ATRC, Scott AFB, Illinois, Fall 1952, *3*(3), 48–61.

Hathaway, S. R., and McKinley, J. C. *Manual for Minnesota Multiphasic Inventory.* New York: Psychological Corp., 1951.

Heist, P. *The creative college student: An unmet challenge.* San Francisco: Jossey-Bass, 1968.

Hertz, M. R. *Frequency tables for scoring responses to the Rorschach Inkblot Test.* 3rd ed. Cleveland: The Press of Western Reserve University, 1951.

Juster, N. *The dot and the line.* New York: Random House, 1963.

Lowenfeld, V. *Creative and mental growth.* 5th ed. New York: Macmillan, 1970.

Myers, I. B. *Manual (1962) for the Myers-Briggs Type Indicator.* Princeton: Educational Testing Service, 1962.

Osborn, A. F. *Applied imagination.* New York: Scribners, 1963.

Parnes, S. J. *Creative behavior guidebook.* New York: Scribners, 1967. (*a*)

Parnes, S. J. *Creative behavior workbook.* New York: Scribners, 1967. (*b*)

Parnes, S. J. *Creativity: unlocking human potential.* Buffalo: D. O. K., 1972.

Parnes, S. J., and Noller, R. B. The creative studies project: raison d'etre and introduction. *Journal of Research and Development in Education,* 1971, *4*(3).

Parnes, S. J., and Noller, R. B. *Toward supersanity: channeled freedom.* Buffalo: D. O. K., 1973.

Rokeach, M. The effect of perception time upon rigidity and concreteness of thinking. *Journal of Experimental Psychology,* 1950, *40*, 206–216.

Toffler, A. *Future shock.* New York: Random House, 1970.

Upton, A., and Samson, R. W. *Creative analysis.* New York: E. P. Dutton, 1963.

Wagner, M. E., and Schubert, D. S. P. College drop-outs from a program for training in creativity. Manuscript in preparation.

Welsh, G. S. Relationship of personality and classroom performance in talented students. Proceedings of the Twenty-First Annual Special Education Conference, North Carolina Department of Public Instruction, Charlotte, N.C., November 1969.

11. Creativity, Self, and Power

George M. Prince

FOR A NUMBER of years—certainly from 1950 to 1957—my interest in creativity was peripheral. I was in the advertising business and while there is a great need for ideas in advertising, these are only one element in a complex campaign or plan of action.

Now, in 1973, after I have devoted many years to understanding the creative process and where it fits in the human scheme, I have broadened my definition of it. I see all problem solving as creative. I believe learning is much the same as problem solving and that both learning and problem solving are necessary for achievement which in turn is necessary to human satisfaction and self-esteem. This, of course, boils down to: creative activity is necessary to self-esteem.

However, if in 1950 a reporter had asked me what my underlying assumption about creativity was, I don't believe I could have told him. I had observed that one copywriter seemed to get better ideas than another and yet even this was a matter of opinion. I believed my own ideas (I was an ex-copywriter) were often better than anyone else's. Retrospectively, I might say "creativity seems to be a gift and one tends to exaggerate the extent of that gift in one's self—and at the same time is secretly afraid he does not have it." In the next few years—1952 to 1957—my views of creativity were focused by a series of events. First, I was put in charge of the company's creative departments: art and copywriting. My mandate was to make these operations more creative. Second, I went into psychoanalysis. And third, I came to know and work with Mark Wiseman, a skilled analytical thinker and experimenter in advertising effectiveness. He believes that a methodology can be devised for any task.

This combination started lines of thought and experiment that continue today. My thinking revolves around three needs that seem necessary to health: to problem solve, to be confident that one can do it repeatedly, and to continually build one's self-esteem. These three needs were not then clearly connected (in fact, they were not clear at all), but they proved to be recurrent themes in my work.

I was not naïve about the unconscious, but until psychoanalysis, I had not knowingly observed myself being the victim or beneficiary of it. This experience gave me an appreciation of the personal powers in all of us of which we are not only unaware, but often deny. I am not thinking only of the special unconscious which Freud made famous (or vice versa). I am thinking of the more commonplace unawareness like the completeness of our recall, the astounding perceptiveness and lightning speed of our powers of observation. In the early 1950s I did not wholly appreciate these faculties. Indeed, I am not certain I do now, not because I don't wish to, but because they are unbelievable to me due to my lack of referents and my cultural tendency to require logical explanations before acceptance.

But from 1952 to 1957, I was getting glimpses into some of these capacities: the feats of observation demonstrated with the tachistoscope in which a subject responds with a measurable skin resistance change to a dirty word flashed on a screen for a fraction of a second, does not respond to a clean word, and is unable to consciously read or recall either; the experiments with subliminal advertising in which a message like "you are thirsty, go get a Coke" was flashed on movie screens so rapidly it is not perceptible (results inconclusive).

While I found those experiments interesting and suggestive, I believed it would be more useful to understand the unconscious motives I was newly learning to experience. I was an early champion of something called motivational research. An example will clarify my thinking then. We had a bank as a client. I asked a psychologist to conduct interviews to determine how people *really* felt about banks in general and our client in particular. It will surprise no one now to learn that banks are hated, feared, and associated with stern unforgiving parents. At that time it was a surprise—at least so they told us—to the bankers.

Our copywriters and artists, known in the agency business as the creative people or, for short, creatives, took these findings and devised a series of advertisements that said, in effect, "We know you hate to come to us for money. We understand and will be easy on you." They even thought of having a small advertisement in the paper that said, "You don't have to ask us for money, just bring this advertisement and we will know." This was a successful campaign. Many people brought in the advertisement.

I believed that a person would be better able to get good ideas (be more creative) if he could get in closer touch with his own unconscious storehouse. To that end, since fortunately I was unable to persuade everyone to go into psychoanalysis, I exposed the men and women in my departments to a random set of experiences that I thought would put them in closer touch with the unknown in themselves. These ranged from talks by one of the psychologists who worked on the Kinsey reports to individual discussions between each person and a very skillful psychologist involved in market research.

At the same time that I was tentatively exploring the little-known inner man, I was, with Mr. Wiseman's help, setting up some objective, analytical procedures to help the creative people tackle their problems with a methodology. These consisted mainly of systematic series of questions which, if answered, would better define the problem. I saw no reason, then, to question the wisdom of the old rule of thumb, "When one has really defined the problem, it is 90 percent solved."

The third area I interested myself in was validation. We availed ourselves of every opportunity to test our advertisements. Sometimes we could test for readership, compared to other advertisements in the same magazine or newspaper. Other times, as in the bank advertisements, or in mail order advertising, we could get a more accurate evaluation of the effectiveness of our creativity.

Validation of the quality of ideas proves to be a sticky business, as does any evaluation of a creativity system. While I did not see it at the time, I had set up in my department a crude creativity system complete with the following characteristics: the ability to be objective to understand the problem, to look inward and use the nonlogical, and finally, a feedback mechanism that could tell us when we were being effective and when we were not. The system appeared to work. We consistently won more readers than competing advertisements. Our few mail order accounts had excellent cost per order records. Among the business people in the agency the consensus was that we *were* more creative than we had been. We prospered.

Among the creative people there was less joy. Most resented the methodology. Most resented the motivation research. This second resentment I now understand better. I believe that one characteristic that set the creative people apart from the businessmen was their intuitive appreciation of motivation. It damaged their magic to have this information out in the open for all to interpret.

This dissatisfaction raised an issue with which I am still struggling. In our usual hierarchical organization much of the creative problem solving is done by managers. How does the subordinate maintain his or her self-esteem in this situation?

In that case we were a small group—perhaps twenty people—and we were friends. We had a lot of meetings regarding what to do about resentments. No real agreement was reached and we continued to use the loose system that had apparently produced results. We were all willing to change the system but none of us knew how to go about it. My real and obvious concern about their dissatisfaction, the frequent meetings, and the friendship preserved the status quo. I suspect it cost us all a lot in satisfaction.

During this period I was enormously impressed with brainstorming. Within the loose, larger system we saw this as an exciting way to cooperate in problem solving. At the time it was the only well-defined, repeatable idea-getting strategy I knew. I still see the separation of evaluation from idea generation as one of the great breakthroughs in learning about the engines that move creativity. It was oversimplified and incomplete, but it remains a giant leap toward understanding. I believe that brainstorming has not been given its due. It was the first organized system for producing ideas. The very fact that Osborn invented a system that could be readily invoked by any group demonstrated to all of us that systems for increasing creativity are thinkable.

Another system I learned about was that of our copy chief. I believe now that every person has his own internal system, but Grantly Wallington could describe and demonstrate his before my very eyes and no one else could or would do that. His system was deceptively simple. First, he looked over the analysis to get the problem in mind. For example, in one case the problem was to emphasize the fine detail captured by a professional photographic paper. With the problem in mind he would take *The Saturday Evening Post* and leaf through it looking idly at the headlines, captions, and pictures. He stopped at a caption that said "It is wise to skirt the white water."

"That gives me an idea," he said. "We will take a picture of a complicated plaid skirt and we will magnify part of it to show how the detail comes through. We might even play around with Scotch and money savings in the headline."

I considered Mr. Wallington's system interesting. He could repeat it nearly at will and I found it impossible to evaluate. How good were these ideas he produced so easily? He could not explain exactly how he got from one thought to another, so his system appeared operational only for him. I understand it better now, and we regularly teach an idea-getting strategy that uses association and imaging as he did then. It turned out that to use the system required a loose, disciplined tolerance that is rather difficult to maintain.

During this same period I became a member of the management team of the agency. It was an experience that was quite different from my expectations and it had far-reaching effects. As a young man working my way up in the world after World War II, I had assumed that in every successful company there was a management team that really knew the answers. I also assumed that when I was taken into the fold, these experienced heads would help me learn the answers. This was not the case. No one knew for sure what the answers were and most of us were not even sure of the questions.

There were always urgent problems, and I was again impressed with the interplay of the need to problem solve, to understand how we were doing it, and to recognize that we were not each dependably logical and cooperative. Because I had been thoroughly indoctrinated in the need for methodology by Mr. Wiseman, I was sensitive to the fact that there was very little method to our management, but I had no idea what to do about it. We observed the structures, had executive committee meetings, and made decisions. Each meeting was an improvisation where opinions were freely given and rediscussed and reacted to, and we would seemingly drift into a position. In spite of this we were a rapidly growing, well-managed company, well regarded by clients and competitors. Much of our success grew out of the president's mode of operating. Charles Rumrill was a paradoxical mixture of easygoing, power sharing, and quietly determined to be successful. He was one of the most experimental, open-minded people I have ever known. I now realize that his willingness to share power encouraged each of us to problem solve and feel good about it.

Mr. Rumrill's style was important to my present thinking because as the company grew and each of the members of the management team was responsible for larger groups of people, much of the former excitement and satisfaction disappeared. We believed that in order to avoid errors and continue to be effective we must institutionalize what was successful. Because we had not studied our processes, we really did not know what to make rules about. We made them anyway, as we thought good managers should. In retrospect, this transition from easy power sharing toward greater control presents an interesting paradox. As we managers held power more closely, one would have thought we would do more creative problem solving and feel a greater sense of accomplishment and healthy self-esteem. This did not seem to be the case. The more control-oriented we became, the less was the sense of excitement and accomplishment.

I now believe we would have continued the excitement and sense of accomplishment if we had institutionalized Mr. Rumrill's easygoing power sharing and open-mindedness. These are difficult capabilities, or talents, to spread, yet the rewards for learning how to do so are great.

It was at this transitional time in 1957 that I read an article entitled "Operational Creativity" by William J. J. Gordon (1956). Mr. Gordon claimed to have devised a new systematic way to produce good ideas. It was the first new system I had heard of since brainstorming, and I was fascinated by the article. I was not able to apply the steps outlined in the article, but I apparently sensed their importance because I clipped the article and started a file on operational creativity. That is a file that has become very thick, for that was the seed thinking that led to the synectics process. From 1958, when I joined Mr. Gordon, to 1965, we were collaborators both in developing the process of synectics and in starting the company, Synectics, Inc.

The business of Synectics, Inc., was invention. We had three basic activities. In one we would invent for a company a new product to meet its specifications. For example, the Veeder Root Company wanted new uses for the counters with which most gasoline pumps are equipped. We conceived the idea of a pump that would dispense several octane blends of gasoline. Sunoco now uses this device.

A second activity was teaching small groups from other companies our system for invention and implementation. We trained groups for such companies as Kimberly-Clark, Johns Manville, Singer, and Whirlpool Corporation.

The third activity was to invent products ourselves which we sold to appropriate companies to make and market. Two examples were: a tampon that reduces menstrual pain, which we sold to Lehn and Fink; and a method of explosively forming metal fibers and other material into sheets, which was purchased by the Rohr Division of Brunswick.

While all these activities proceeded, we continued our research into the creative process. Our major research tool was the tape recorder. We did much problem solving in groups and we recorded these meetings. When the meetings produced results, we could go over the tapes and discover what modes of thinking were successful and learn how to repeat them.

In the agency business I was only faintly aware of process and peripherally interested in creativity. From 1958 to the present my main interest has been the process by which people cooperatively accomplish something that gives them satisfaction. And as time has passed I have become more and more interested in the importance of this process and its effect on a person's sense of self and the effect of this in turn on ability to learn, change, and grow. Early in that period the focus was narrowly on creative problem solving. Out of that joint work came Mr. Gordon's book *Synectics* (1961), and much later my own book *The Practice of Creativity* (1970). Briefly, the synectics process focuses on two basic and interrelated approaches: first, procedures that aid imaginative speculation, and second, disciplined ways of acting so that speculation is not reduced but valued and encouraged.

By 1965 Mr. Gordon's attention was shifting to children and the use of metaphor to help them learn. He started to design a series of metaphorical work books. The first was completed in 1967 and when Harper & Row contracted to publish this series titled *Making It Strange* (Synectics, Inc., 1968), Mr. Gordon left Synectics and started his own company to produce the series. My own understanding of our business was changing at this time also. I saw the synectics set of procedures as quite useful in helping people to produce novel ideas. However, the process was difficult to learn and even when learned the decay rate was rapid after the student returned to his post in industry. This and other observations about the effectiveness of our services led to a gradual change in our activities and in my own view of what we could and could not do.

An experience that has had great influence on my thinking occurred in the early 1960s. A division of one of the large automobile companies came to us for an invention. The need for the specialized components they made was diminishing and they wanted something new. We met with the general manager and his second in command. We ran a long and systematic meeting to discover opportunity areas that would be acceptable to them. One was carburetion (I am altering the fact as the real invention remains wrapped in secrecy). They said that if we could give them a really new carburetion system, they would be happy. We went to work. Four months later we had conceived of an electrically driven gas vaporizer and system for delivery to each cylinder that showed great promise. The general manager and his assistant were excited by the enormous volume implied by our device. They were concerned over the crudeness of the model and the need for further invention and perfection. They wanted their chief engineer to come and see if it really did what we thought it did.

The chief engineer came and said yes, he thought so, but that he would like an outside opinion. A consultant came and said yes, it really does what we think it does. There was a month of silence from the client. I called him finally and arranged a meeting. He really did not want to commit himself to the next phase of development. I said, "If you could have anything you wanted right now, what would you want? You take over development? Get your money back? [His investment at this point was about $30,000.] Stop everything?"

He asked if I would excuse him while he huddled with his assistant. On his return, he said he would like his money back. Within a couple of days I found a buyer who was a supplier to the automotive industry. When I reported this to our client he decided not to sell. Nor did he wish to proceed. The carburetion system went on the client's shelf.

This was the first of a series. A client would pay us to invent something. We would do it. It would then languish with little or no further action.

In contrast, the groups we worked with who did their own inventing would overcome one monstrous difficulty after another until they had a marketable product. The lesson gradually came clear to me: to change anything, to learn anything, to turn an idea into a product or process demands enormous and continuing energy and commitment. Unless one has some authorship, the lackey effect robs him of energy. If one is simply carrying out the ideas of others, this damages self-esteem, and no one needs that. So we redesigned that service to conform with people. We help with process, but the client and his people solve their own problems. This has become a successful service called a Problem Laboratory.

From 1964 to the present, Problem Laboratories gave me the opportunity to work with many hundreds of problem solvers on a vast number of real problems ranging from highly technical, such as devising a more efficient way to acidize oil-bearing limestone strata, to very people-oriented problems such as determining ways to help a new salesman move more quickly from being an expense to making a profit.

Our training services changed also. We shifted emphasis from small groups of five people from the same company working with us for several months to larger groups of up to sixteen spending a week with us. Members come from different companies and institutions: schools, hospitals, communes. Each brings several real problems and the groups take turns working on each other's problems. We videotape these working sessions and a member of our staff reviews the tape with the participants.

Since 1964 this has provided me with the opportunity to study thousands of meetings and the actions of many different people. In the early sixties I looked mainly at idea-getting strategies. We made heavy use of analogy and metaphor to help people see problems in new ways. We also developed various ways to handle differences in a constructive way. We identified the key roles that are played in any meeting. All of this is described in detail in *The Practice of Creativity* (Prince, 1970).

Between 1967 and the present I gradually became convinced that we were overdoing our emphasis on idea-getting strategies. Getting good starting ideas appeared to be something just about everyone does well. The data that led me to this conclusion came at first from Problem Laboratories. The format of a two or three day Lab is quite standard. The opening hour and a half is devoted to an experiment with the eight members of the client team. We give them a problem unconnected with their business. We videotape ten or fifteen minutes of their meeting and then examine the tape with them. The purpose of this experiment is to increase the probability they and we will be successful in our work together. We use the tape to prove that they are able to work together. We use the tape to prove that they are able to get good ideas, that they quite naturally use something we call imaging (pictures in the mind's eye), that they are good at building on a starting idea, and that they are easily evoked into overcoming obstacles. They also see and hear that they tend to have several conversations at once, put ideas and each other down, lose ideas, get defensive, and as a result have some problems cooperating. We further identify the roles we will all be dealing with for the duration of the Problem Laboratory, which are the Leader, the Client, and the Participants. The Leader is in charge of process. It is his job to see that no thought or idea gets lost, that only one person talks at a time, that no idea or person gets put down and so on. The Client of the Laboratory is that person who will get his hands dirty implementing the possible solutions that may come out of the Laboratory. He is in charge of content, though he also contributes thoughts and ideas. He evaluates ideas and decides whether they meet his specifications. He may consult other members of his team who have special expertise, but he basically governs the content. Participants are all the other members of the group, and we ask them to agree to go along with the Leader's decisions on process and the Client's decisions on content. This agreement is not difficult to obtain after people have seen the taped experiment of themselves and understand that we are not being arbitrary.

During the next two hours of the Problem Laboratory we go to work on the Client's problem. The role of Leader is taken by a member of our staff. Two or three other staff members are participants. It is unusual for these two hours not to produce some useful material for the Client. Our leaders employ no idea-getting strategies during this period. They protect ideas, welcome any sort of thinking, and encourage a lot of wishing about outcomes. A client almost never brings a brand-new problem to us. Typically he and his group have been working on it for several months—sometimes several years. Nevertheless, in their first two hours of work with a skilled leader who pays close attention and values individual thinking, the group nearly always produces one or two complete possible solutions and many beginning ideas. I suspect that very often the possible solutions that emerge this early are partially or even wholly formed in prior thinking. The supportive atmosphere brings them out.

The point that is important to me here is that I see a lot of solid examples of inherent creativity in Problem Laboratories and courses. Everyone who tries at all is good at getting ideas and at solving problems.

It was difficult for me to see this because we were in the business of teaching creativity and I had a built-in bias that influenced my observation. Without being aware of it, I was convinced that people tended to come to us weakly creative and leave strongly creative. Our function was to strengthen and add to the students' idea-getting strategies. The first chink in this bias came when I was examining the role of speculation in idea getting. I believe that one makes ideas happen through speculation. Any activity that increases speculation will increase the probability of getting ideas. Whatever decreases speculation decreases probability.

In my observation I realized that in a given meeting people are willing and able to speculate until they are punished for it. Punishment may seem too strong a word because the action nearly always appears innocent of malice and even rational. For example: You and I have a flat tire and no jack. It is a cold, icy day and there are chunks of ice at the side of the road. You speculate, "How about using chunks of ice to prop the car up while we change the tire?" I reply, "I don't see how that will work because we don't have any way to get the car up on ice in the first place."

After watching thousands of exchanges like this and seeing the consequent reduction in speculation, I began to wonder if perhaps the real culprit in low creativity was high skill in discouraging speculation. Some examples of this skill are obvious, like my rejection of the ice idea. Others are not so easily recognized: Such seemingly acceptable actions as close questioning of the offerer of an idea, good-natured kidding about someone's idea, or ignoring an idea. Any action that results in the offerer of an idea feeling defensive will tend to reduce not only his speculation but that of others in the group. The combination of all these actions and responses creates the climate of the meeting, or, in a larger sense, of the company.

In about 1967 I began to identify and evaluate every action and response I could spot by watching videotape and live action meetings. My thought was to eliminate by legislation the responses and actions that reduce speculation. For the next few years this occupied much of my attention. When speculation-reducing actions are [re]eliminated, there is no question that idea production and problem solving increase—and so does accomplishment and satisfaction. The real difficulty was and is to get the speculation-enhancing behaviors to persist. Take the tendency to reject ideas and find flaws in them illustrated by the flat tire exchange above. The flaws are generally real; unless corrected or overcome the idea will not solve the problem.

The rational way out of this dilemma is to say, "We are all mature people here. We must recognize that negative information is valuable and intended to help and should be perceived that way. Accept it and use it." This is the way the world ought to be but reality is quite different. Time after time we would see A point out a valid flaw in B's idea. B might even thank A. Later in the meeting A starts an idea and before he can even be clear what it is, B interrupts to say, "That will be too expensive." Or B will oppose a procedure A recommends, or start a conversation across A, or ignore him. There are an infinity of variations. We have become so familiar with this phenomenon that when we are sitting in a meeting with a client group and A puts B down in some even slight way, we can predict that there will be destructive consequences. If we have the permission of the group to lead the meeting, we can usually intervene, repair the damage, and prevent the destructive consequences.

We have had at different times on our staff two skilled sensitivity-group trainers. Each explained to me that the problem is one of lack of trust and not inability to level with each other. We experimented with fourteen different groups who had been through extensive sensitivity training (two weeks). They tended to be more open and outspoken in their put downs of each other and also more open and outspoken in their revenge reactions. Each of our National Training Laboratory (NTL) trainers became persuaded that learning to level is not the answer to this problem.

This pervasive sensitivity to hurt feelings is real. We see clear evidence of it among top, middle, and lower level executives as well as among underprivileged young people and blue collar workers. The reason I consider it a serious problem is that it appears in our culture wherever

I have had a chance to observe. But it is not generally visible. Few people believe it is a real factor until they have observed a number of instances on tape.

It is even more alarming because most of us in our culture appear to be programmed to diminish our fellows whenever we can. There are two behaviors which are indicative of the faulty assumptions that decrease creativity. The first assumption is that as a mature person I seldom get my feelings hurt. The second is that my intentions toward other people are generally fair and friendly. Given these assumptions, I had a lot of trouble explaining the way people repeatedy acted to reduce speculation in meetings. It is interesting to turn those assumptions around and lead a meeting where the leader does not permit people to act in any way to hurt the feelings of anyone and insists that each member is fair (if not friendly) to ideas and people. The contrast between this and a traditional, chaired meeting is startling. In both satisfaction and accomplishment, the chaired meeting tends to be far less productive. I have not been able to validate this in any scientifically acceptable way. Any member of our professional staff can demonstrate it. Businessmen and faculty members who know our process are nearly all persuaded of its validity in fact.

The symptoms of aggressiveness and hurt were clear to me, and I needed some hypotheses to help me understand them. I decided that the aggressive, combative behavior could be explained by the competitiveness that is such an important part of our culture. I believe that each of us views his own relationships with others as generally helpful and cooperative. At a deeper level, perhaps largely below our awareness, we feel in a win-lose competition with each of those around us. For example, I ask a couple of friends for help on a problem. X gives me an idea. My rational self says "Good; here is some possible help." But another element of self feels the threat of being a loser. This threatened self undertakes a defensive (aggressive) action. This would partly explain why so often we hear, "Yes, that's a good idea but . . ." even when the idea has much going for it.

Whenever I hear someone put another person in a win-lose position, I know that there is going to be a bad outcome for someone—and later a get-even action. We have all learned subtle ways of competing and also getting even, ways that are perfectly acceptable in our culture. A few examples are: disagreeing, nitpicking, sulking, asking the penetrating question, questioning assumptions, correcting, and so on. In every situation there is a rationalization for the behavior, yet if it is studied in context there is evidence of a nonrational motive. Recently a participant, Y, in a meeting I was videotaping, crossed his arms and closed his eyes for about five minutes. Some earlier actions of his suggested that he was sulking. In any case, it was a fairly gross nonverbal signal. When we were examining the tape, I stopped it on a view of Y apparently asleep. "What is happening here?" I asked.

There was a burst of laughter. Someone said, "Y is making a commentary on our meeting."

"Not at all," said Y, "I was meditating."

The victim of the win-lose or competitive posture is always speculation, and therefore idea production and problem solving. When one speculates he becomes vulnerable. It is too easy to make him look like a loser.

The problem of competition proved complex, and I tried a number of hypotheses to make it visible so people could deal with it. One line of thought was: competition in meetings is mostly out of one's awareness. By being aware that one may slip into it, one can avoid it. Further, it is a mistake to assume that because Z has an idea I am losing. Both of these were of some use, but were not entirely satisfying. For example, as some middle managers pointed out, they really *are* competing with each other for promotion. An answer I used was that one will probably get more promotions by putting oneself up than by putting others down. This made some sense, but, like an exhortation, it was not operational.

One of the tantalizing elements of this problem was that in Problem Laboratories (led by our staff) and with course groups after three days (of the five) we routinely develop noncompetitive climates. The acceleration in the production and use of ideas is quite exciting. Participants are persuaded that the noncompetitive climate is splendidly productive. The problem is: how to implement this climate back home on the job.

A second hypothesis, useful to me for a while, was that a person normally uses two strategies in his interactions with others (and himself). One strategy is aimed at getting ideas, the other strategy is aimed at getting and maintaining power over a situation. Going back to the flat tire example, the idea-getting strategy might have been one called looking for parallels. One thinks, "We want the tire off the ground. Where have I seen tires off the ground without a jack?" I remember a car up on blocks. I see some ice "blocks." The strategy produces an idea. When my friend presents the idea to me, I can join him in idea-getting strategies or I can go into a power strategy. If I join to get ideas and solve the problem, my response might be, "OK, let's figure a way to get the car up on the ice." If I go into a power mode my response is quite different. I make judgments and point out flaws.

This hypothesis has been particularly useful in understanding that there are real differences and that few of us are aware of slipping from one mode to the other. Confusion about this has serious consequences.

A third line of thought I experimented with is the redefinition of an idea. If we could make explicit the true nature of an idea, we could enjoy each other's ideas much as we appreciate a joke. (Koestler [1964] establishes a close connection between an idea and a joke in *The Act of Creation*.) I believe there is some good in this way of thinking. An idea is too often treated like a monolithic, final, unalterable proposal. We believe we must accept it or reject it. In reality I believe an idea is more like a brief, tentative position paper. It is a compressed communication device I use to tell you in an open way where I am in relation to the problem we are working on. It is more akin to an expression of taste than to a fact. A yes or no is not appropriate because there are too many implications to even the simplest idea. If we see an idea as a communication device, it changes our value system surrounding ideas. For example, in order for my idea to be successful, it must help you to learn. My notion here was to change the perception of an idea so that it could not threaten anyone with losing.

In 1969 I read Dr. Harris's *I'm OK, You're OK* (1969). As a result I attended some Transactional Analysis workshops, and by 1970 we had a full-time professional doing TA workshops and working with us on synectics developments. It appeared to me that many of the hypotheses of transactional analysis could be used to understand the problems of aggression, competition, and hurt with which I was having such difficulty. "Transactional Analysis, compared to psychoanalysis, puts less emphasis on probing the dark places of the psyche and more emphasis on understanding the personality as it reveals itself in social situations, or transactions" (Lamott, 1972).

With our videotape instant replays, this was exactly what we were doing: analyzing transactions. Our purpose, rather than therapeutic, was to help people transact in ways that would foster their own creativity and that of others. TA looks at transactions to learn what is going on within the transactors.

Transactional Analysis was originated by Dr. Eric Berne (1966) and draws heavily on the innovative thinking of Dr. Harry Stack Sullivan (1953). Berne believed that each of us has some deeply ingrained assumptions about himself and that these continually affect the way we behave toward ourselves and others. These assumptions about self, comparable to Sullivan's idea of self-concept, start to develop when we are born. "The nature of a child's self-concept will be determined by the balance of approval and disapproval in his existence" (Elkind, 1972). Berne and his followers believe that self-concept need not be static. Dr. Robert and Mary Goulding with their redecision theory (in Kaplan and Sager, eds., 1972) hold that everyone can reexamine the early decisions made at two to ten years of age upon which self-concept largely depends and remake those decisions in the present when one has more realistic data. For example, a decision made at three in an effort to comply with mixed signals from parents might be a generalized "Try hard but don't make it." Since this decision is an operating guide for the young person, it has an obvious effect on his competence and on his accomplishments—and on his self-concept. The Gouldings believe that such a person can, by documenting the effects of that early decision, discover what it is and change it. This changes his transactions with himself and others and allows him to work toward accomplishments and a healthier self-concept.

Basically Berne says that each of us is capable of displaying three ego states—Parent, Adult, and Child (P, A, C)—in our dealings with other people as well as in our internal dialogues. The Parent in us tends to consist of directives we received while we were young—from 0 to 10 years old or so. The directives are of two kinds. Some are negatives and forbidding. "See, you have done it wrong again." The others are nurturing and supportive. "Good boy. I can always depend on you." The Adult in us tends to be reality-oriented and is developed as we grow up. It is the decider and the doer in us. It is influenced overtly by the P in us and less obviously but just as strongly by the C. The Child is our feeling both loving and rebellious— also our sense of fun, enjoyment, and exploration. There are several books (e.g., James and Jongeward, 1971) that give a clear and complete explanation of TA. I introduce this brief discussion above as background to help you understand how it has been useful to me.

We have worked with people of quite diverse backgrounds. Our objective was usually to help them learn creative problem solving. We have had courses for black high school drop-outs, blue collar workers, ministers and priests (many of whom tend to leave the problem solving to God), as well as with managers of every level. I am continually looking for patterns that might help me explain what I see happening. A pattern that is emerging (which TA helped me see) is a basic difference between the haves and the have nots in our culture. There is wide agreement among transactional analysts that nearly all of us as children decide we are not OK. I believe that the socialization or civilizing process used by parents has perhaps 80 percent negative to 20 percent positive input. These figures are unsupportable, but the proportion of negative to positive is high. I imagine myself as a three or four year old always being corrected and told not to do this or that (and my parents were about average). At some point I say, "Something is *wrong* with me. I am obviously not living up to specs. My parents, who know everything, would not have unreasonable specs. So it must be me."

I believe nearly everyone goes through some experience like this. A very depressing business.

At five or six I go out in the world to kindergarten and first grade and so on. I continue to get put down by my teachers and also by my peers because that is the only way we know how to act. An eye-opening experiment is to watch and listen to a group of eight to ten year olds playing an unsupervised game of baseball or football. The murderous tones, vituperation, naked anger you see is their replay of the Parent in their heads. That is the Parent with whom they carry on internal dialogues. It gives one pause.

However, the game does go on and in school and at play and in church and Sunday school some fascinating things happen. I learn by observing (no one explicitly tells me this) that I live up to specs about as well as the rest. I begin to have success experiences. I pass into third grade. I get some Bs. I get elected to bring the milk in for the class. I don't really believe this data until there is a lot of it—ten or twelve years of success experiences —and I begin to believe that I am probably capable. I can accomplish things. When I get a job I get things done. I am one of the fortunates and my cross section looks like this:

Layers of confidence that I can
accomplish what I want to

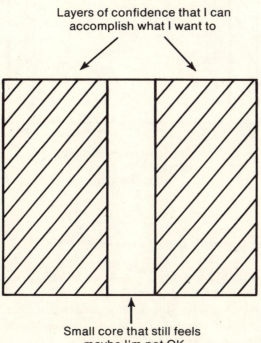

Small core that still feels
maybe I'm not OK

FIGURE 11.1.

The unfortunates have the same early experiences, but because they are poor or because their parents are particularly tough they don't have the success experiences in enough quantity to give them confidence. Their cross section looks more like Figure 11.2 (see next page).

The effect of these cross sections on behavior are considerable. Any action that I perceive diminishing me reverberates in that core of me that believes maybe I'm not OK. I feel it as a threat to my self-esteem. I feel anxious and I react with defensive maneuvers (from Sullivan). A very small input results in a disproportionate output. While the output mas-

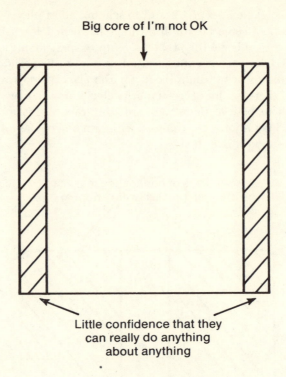

Big core of I'm not OK

Little confidence that they
can really do anything
about anything

FIGURE 11.2.

querades as Adult it will actually be from my Child or my Parent. For example:

My friend, Joe, and I are meeting to have lunch together.

Me: "Joe, let's go to Chez Jacques."

Joe: "The food there is terrible. Let's go somewhere else."

If I am feeling perfectly OK I can perceive this as an Adult-to-Adult exchange and we can problem solve about lunch from there. If, however, I am not feeling OK, I can perceive Joe's words as meaning: "George, you are stupid about food." I then go into a defensive maneuver to avoid the threat to my self-esteem. One way that may appear to help is to diminish Joe. "You don't know what you are talking about." Another is to establish Chez Jacques' food as excellent. Neither of these will really make me feel OK, but I don't know that.

What is important here is to recognize that there is a continuing, more or less blind struggle to feel OK, to avoid the anxiety when one's self is threatened. TA makes visible some of the dynamics.

For example, if Joe were knowledgeable about TA and synectics he would know that in TA terms his statement "The food there is terrible," is sweepingly judgmental and Parental. From synectics he would know that his response to my suggestion implies that it has no value. To avoid the possibility of misunderstanding he might say, "Jacques is a nice guy and the place is right around the corner [your suggestion, George, has valuable implication]. I don't like the food there [he's speaking for himself, not the whole world]."

I would like now to bring up again the three lines of thought that I have been pursuing in a rather scattered way since 1951. I am fascinated by the interplay between three human needs: the need to produce possible solutions to fit a given situation—that is, to accomplish objectives; the need to do this in some understandable, repeatable way—that is, to believe in one's competence; the need to be in touch with one's own nonlogical urgings, feelings, and anxieties.

The work we have done in creative problem solving and the examination of transactions between people, together with the remarkable work of Sullivan, Berne, the Gouldings, and Harris that has produced TA suggest a coherent hypothesis about cooperative accomplishment.

Hypotheses

Each person's most fundamental enterprise is the development, enhancement, and protection of his or her self-concept.

One's self-concept has some stability. It is gradually developed and changed through transactions with other persons, and it remains dependent to a large extent on the reflected appraisals of other persons.

Self-esteem is the unstable component of self-concept.

Threats to self or self-esteem are experienced as anxiety and result in defensive maneuvers.

To the degree that one is able to create a climate that (1) makes stimulating demands without threat and (2) explicitly appreciates process (e.g., wishing, imaging), those in the climate including oneself will flourish and grow as problem-solvers, learners, and accomplishers.

TA and Synectics provide concrete behavioral tools to establish such a climate. They are appropriate for use with family, friends, co-workers—in virtually any encounter with anyone. They are particularly valuable practiced on oneself.

Further, the tools are realistic. They make possible delegation, cooperation, and decision making without expedient use of power over others and the consequent usurping of autonomy and threat to self.

This has implications for nearly every activity that one person undertakes with another—from learning and teaching, to marriage, to work, to inventing a new product.

Below are some examples of a mode of operating to effect this climate.

Creating a solution to a problem is, I believe, exactly like learning. Here is a step-by-step reconstruction of solving a problem.

My wife, Mardi, enjoyed baking bread. I sometimes helped her knead it, a boring job. One morning she said, "I wish I could get the dough to knead itself when I tell it to."

A picture formed in my mind's eye (we call this imaging). The dough in my picture was having a convulsion. A second image formed of an old-fashioned package of white margarine being kneaded in its plastic bag with the yellow color pellet. I put that image aside for the moment and said, "How can we make the dough laugh itself into being kneaded?"

Mardi heard me say "lap" instead of "laugh" and the image that formed in her mind was of a wave lapping on the beach. When she said that, I could not see the connection and so said, "Keep talking about the wave and how it will help."

"It tumbles over and over on itself and so it would be kneaded."

I pictured the dough in a wave being tumbled.

Mardi said, "I was thinking of the dough as the wave."

I put aside my dough in a wave picture and saw the dough tumbling over itself like a breaker. I described my image of the breaker.

"How could we get it to tumble over like that?" I said.

Mardi imaged the breaker curling over and tumbling down. The image suddenly changed to sneakers tumbling and thumping (like she thumped the dough on the counter?) in the clothes dryer. The ridges in the rotating drum carry the sneakers up the wall and drop them back to the bottom. In her image she changed the sneakers to dough. She said, "I could put the dough in the dryer and let *it* do the kneading."

"Yes! And put it in a plastic bag so it won't spread flour."

"And I can turn it to no heat so the dough won't cook."

(The possible solution, when tested, worked. It is even better to put the dough in a cloth bag within the plastic bag.)

Then I asked Mardi where she got her wave image from. How did it connect with "laugh." She said, "Oh, I thought you said 'lap.' "

Misunderstandings like this happen far too often, it has seemed to me, for them not to be purposeful. There are many ways to be purposeful in addition to misunderstanding. The important process point here is the willingness to pursue temporarily *any* line of speculation however unconnected it seems to be.

Earlier I mentioned some remarkable personal powers of which we are unaware. One example is the way we somehow learn to make damaging, limited assumptions about our power to recall useful things from our past experiences. The same applies to our power of observation. These assumptions are self-fulfilling prophesies. Because we do not trust our recall and our abilities to "read" a situation or understand a complex problem, we cannot. Imaging and wishing are tools to help you tap your recall.

There is a vast store of experience, feeling, knowledge, and intuition in each of us. We begin to pack it in as soon as we are born. Much more of it than we are aware of is available. With a problem in mind, when one is loose—relaxedly stimulated—and letting the images happen as of their own volition, one's mind chooses interestingly and purposefully. The connections won't always be clear nor always valid. They will always be interesting. Delightful even. One of the important benefits of reaching into one's self for these riches is that it increases one's self-esteem.

Imaging is as natural as breathing. A child images long before talking. He also learns wishing very early. Just as imaging helps you tap your vast storehouse of knowledge and experience, so does wishing help you become focused and purposeful and positive. Imaging and wishing are the two most basic tools of problem solving and, therefore, I believe, of learning.

Dr. Sullivan holds that "the child's sense of self evolves gradually during the first year of life, primarily as a consequence of the ministrations of the person who takes care of the child. If this caretaker is loving, comforting, and meets the infantile needs, the infant has a generalized feeling of "good me." On the other hand, if the caretaker is anxious, tense, and rejecting, this too is communicated to the infant, who experiences a generalized feeling of 'bad me' " (Elkind, 1972).

I believe the generalized feeling of "good me" comes to the child, partly at least, through his or her own efforts, and these efforts consist of problem solving or learning. For example, I can imagine myself at three weeks or a month feeling hungry, wishing a bottle (or breast) would appear. I image it. I wiggle for it. That does not work. I yell for it. That doesn't work. I cry for it. That works. I enjoy not only the bottle but the fact that I learned a way of getting it—solved a problem. This need—to learn, to solve problems, to accomplish—never leaves us. One's sense of "good me" depends on it and, of course, so does self-esteem.

Imagine the sense of self and self-esteem a child gets from learning the incredible art of walking and later talking. What happens to this enormous talent for problem solving? A parallel to what happens is described in Dr. Elkind's (1972) article about Sullivan. "If, for whatever reason, a child in our society is not reading by the end of first grade, he already begins to feel that he is a 'flop' in life. More and more, reading comes to be associated with the anticipation of negative self-appraisals. It is not long before anything connected with reading arouses anxiety and, to protect the self, reading is avoided. . . . In helping such children, the major task is not to teach them to read but to refurbish their self-concept."

In the case of wishing and imaging the extinguishing mechanism is much the same. Here is an example of imaging to acquire information or to learn about an idea. We were working on a child-proof package for poison household liquids.

TOM: "I wish we could teach a poison bottle to be invisible to a child and visible only to a grown-up."
HARRY: "That gives me an idea."
LEADER: "Let's hear it, Harry."

HARRY DESCRIBING HIS IDEA
"You know those snap-up bottles?"

MY IMAGING
At this point I have very little data from Harry. So most of my image comes from my own store of information and imagination. I picture a bottle that bends in the middle and snaps up

Bent   **Snapped up**

FIGURE 11.3.

"It has a sort of thing that goes in and out."

and my picture instantly changes to a bottle with an unrolling party favor I believe is called a dragon.

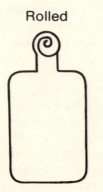

Rolled

FIGURE 11.4.

"When it is in, it is closed. When out it is open."

When I squeeze the bottle the dragon unrolls.

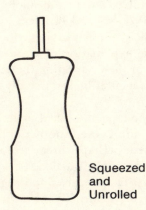

Squeezed
and
Unrolled

FIGURE 11.5.

"They use them on Elmer's glue and Ivory liquid detergent."

I image the Ivory bottle that Harry had in mind.

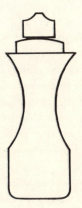

FIGURE 11.6.

"Well, let's control that opening not from the top but from some place invisible to the kid."

I image my squeeze activating Harry's closure.

GEORGE: "I think I know a way to do what Harry wants to do."
LEADER: "Good. What have you got?"
GEORGE: "We can mold ridges into the side of the plastic bottle. They are too stiff for a kid to press together but an adult can. When she squeezes, that pushes the snap top up and it is open.

This idea still needed help and the other members of the group used their imaging to build the idea to acceptability.

As the idea of imaging evolved and became more and more useful to us, I questioned people in both courses and Problem Laboratories. During the initial experiment when the group is working on a problem we give them, there is always at least one explanation of an idea that brings images to mind. I would replay one of these, stopping the tape after a few words to ask if anyone had formed a mental image. Usually one in eight has started to (or will admit it).

I play a little more of the tape and ask if anyone else has begun to see a picture of the idea in his mind's eye. Another of the eight says yes. When the whole incident is played, perhaps three to four of the eight will talk about their images. The others look puzzled.

When the first person says he has started to image, I ask him to describe his image or picture. Almost invariably he says, "Well, my image was wrong but what came to mind was . . ."

In many other experiments in helping people to relearn to image, there is reluctance to form images until the person is reassured that there is no right or wrong to it. Most young (6 to 8) children love to be asked the same sort of questions, and they give wonderfully imaginative, detailed descriptions of their images.

I believe that what happens is that as a child listens and images, the early pictures like my bent bottle prove to be off target. He begins to make judgments about his wrongness. When he is "wrong" he makes a negative self-appraisal. Before long he is avoiding imaging much like the slow reader avoids reading. This does not mean imaging stops. I believe it continues but below awareness, and the only image he permits himself to "see" is the correct one. You can see how this impoverishes him. If I had repressed my first three images in the poison bottle example, I would simply have understood the snap-up closure. As it was, I was able to add to it from my image material.

Wishing, which is so intimately entangled with imaging that often it is hard to know which comes first, suffers an even worse fate. It appears that people stop wishing except in daydreams, and even daydreaming is in bad repute. This is unfortunate because a wish is an unfettered, speculative way to define an objective. It was a result of seeing the power of wishing to lead to new perceptions and ideas that I began to question the wisdom of the saying, "When a problem is clearly defined it is 90 percent solved." Because a wish can make free with reality, it gives license to think without debilitating concerns about practicality. Neither of the wishes in my examples would be admissible into regular, serious meetings. What do you mean, "have the dough knead itself?" How can you teach a bottle anything—let alone how to be invisible?

Yet, one of the reasons children learn and problem solve at such fantastic rates from 0–3 is that they are relatively free to wish and image in seemingly irresponsible ways. What the wishing and imaging hypotheses suggest is a much more participative and less rigorous approach to teaching children, one that would explicitly value their imaging and wishing capabilities.

Adults, as each learns to value and use his images even though "wrong" and rediscovers how to wish for outrageously satisfying outcomes, become better problem solvers and learners. At the same time every such episode builds a stronger self-concept.

In addition to wishing and imaging, there are other synectics devices that increase the probability of success and cooperation. The most important of these is the Itemized Response. Consider the following example.

The finance committee of a graduate school of business was having a synectics session to discover some new ways to get financial support for French students from people in France.

SAM: "Let's run a lottery and the winner gets a French business school graduate." (laughter)

(In a traditional meeting it is probable that this idea would be explored no further. In a synectics meeting the leader sees to it that every idea, no matter how seemingly outrageous, is explored with a presumption of value.)

LEADER: "Sounds like an idea. Tom (Client—the person with the problem), do you understand what Sam is proposing?"
TOM: "Yes, I understand it."
LEADER: "OK, what is useful about this idea?"
TOM: "It would raise money."
LEADER: "Right. What else is going for it?"
TOM: "It is more fun than simply being dunned. Also you have at least a chance of getting a return on your money. Another thing that suddenly occurs to me is that it would attract new people. We only reach our alumni in France now. If we run a lottery, we'll get wider participation in the business community, and the amount from each could be less."
LEADER: "That is a lot on the plus side. Now are there any elements that need more of our work? Will you word these as wishes."
TOM: "I wish we did not have to promise an MBA body as the prize."
LEADER: "Anybody help with this?"
JOE: "Never mind his body, just promise his mind."
LEADER: "Would you say more about what you are thinking, Joe?"
JOE: "I was really just kidding."
DON: "I got an idea from that. When you said 'mind,' Joe, I thought that really is what they want. How about promising consulting time?"

Out of this starting idea developed a possible solution roughly as follows: one or more consulting firms sponsor the lottery and winners from the business community get consulting services at special rates. The sponsors hire the French MBA candidates for summer jobs and presumably would have an inside track for hiring them on graduation.

We developed the Itemized Response originally to avoid the danger of the idea offerer feeling put down and thus going into defensive maneuvers. It has proved to have values far beyond that. In form, Itemized Response is simple. The client (the person who will implement the possible solution) thinks of the idea not as a simple, monolithic thing. He thinks of it as a multiplicity of implications.

FIGURE 11.7.

He exercises his imagination to multiply the useful and acceptable implications and he talks *first* about them. A skilled person discovers unexpected acceptables as Tom did. Next he turns his attention to the implications that need more work and he picks the toughest one. He turns it into a wish. The team works to solve it. If successful, the client brings out any other points that need more work. If the team is not successful the idea does not qualify as a possible solution and is put aside with the understanding that some later thinking may make it acceptable as a possible solution.

I have seen the Itemized Response repeatedly help groups take beginning ideas that would traditionally be ignored or treated as jokes and work them into solid, practical possible solutions—to the great delight of the whole team. Five years of experience with treating ideas this way has convinced me that a negative response to an idea is a bad habit and, more seriously, a defensive maneuver reflecting anxiety about self and self-esteem. It has bad consequences for both the originator of the idea and the negator. An Itemized Response conveys the important information in a way that builds the self-esteem of both parties.

If one examines the transactions in synectics, he will find that the mechanisms like wishing, imaging, and Itemized Response are designed (in P-A-C terms) to keep the members in their creative Child and Adult, although we were unaware of P-A-C when we arrived at the mechanisms. They were simply something that worked.

Another synectics concept that has proven valuable in organizations to make the use of power less destructive to self-concept is that of clientship. We think of clientship in two contexts. One is that of a meeting, which I have already described. I should add that in some meeting cases the client is multiple. An extreme example is when everyone in the meeting has a stake in the possible solution selected. One way we handle this is to rotate the clientship during the meeting. When ideas are evaluated, we ask everyone to join in the Itemized Response. In effect, no idea is accepted as a possible solution until implications that are unacceptable to any member have been overcome.

The other context in which we use clientship is in organizations. We see a marriage or a family as an organization as well as companies and institutions. Here the governing condition is that the person who is responsible for getting the task done and is closest to the front line has clientship. Thus, in a meeting of a company executive committee which includes the president, the marketing vice-president, the sales vice-president, the production vice-president, and the research vice-president, if the problem has to do with production, the production vice-president is the primary client. This concept is akin to delegation and management by objectives, but it has basic assumptions that are different and are made explicit that bear on self-concept.

These assumptions are:

(1) Whenever I turn over clientship to a subordinate there is an automatic predisposition for me to be Parental (judgmental authoritarian) when talking with him or reviewing his progress. There is the same predisposition on his part to be Child (rebellious, resentful).

(2) When I turn over clientship to a subordinate he cannot, by definition, do the job as I want it done because he is not me. In addition, from his point of view I will not treat him the way he wishes I would because I am not him.

(3) Since I am accountable for the way he executes his clientship, it is necessary for us to devise a method of working together that will allow me to know about and where possible to help him with his activities.

It is clear that this complex relationship has a great built-in potential for threats to the self of both the manager and the subordinate. At this stage in my knowledge the best way to handle the turning over of clientship is to explicitly discuss these three assumptions and problem solve together. Some joint wishes (which we translate into How To's) generally are:

MANAGER: "How can I know by E.S.P. when my thinking will be useful to you?"
SUBORDINATE: "How can I take advantage of your experience without having you dominate me?"

MANAGER: "How can I feel comfortable letting you make your own decisions when I am accountable for them?"

SUBORDINATE: "How can I develop in my own way and do the job better than it has ever been done?"

MANAGER: "How can I enjoy your success without feeling competitive and threatened?"

SUBORDINATE: "How can I come to you when I am in trouble without losing stature and without your taking over?"

Out of this session comes an explicit contract between these two people. It is subject to modification whenever the needs of either change. An example of such a contract is:

(1) The words "need a meeting" will be a signal that one of us perceives a problem in this clientship. It also means that we will problem solve rather than dictate.

(2) Either of us can call a meeting.

(3) The subordinate is always the client unless the problem is clearly the manager's and this will be determined by the subordinate.

(4) Itemized Response will be used to make certain that any idea is thoroughly and carefully considered.

(5) Decisions about this clientship will be made by the subordinate.

The words of a contract are more symbolic than definitive. What makes such an arrangement work is the determination on both sides to value each other. By bringing out in the open their recognition of the built-in drawbacks and making their wishes explicit, the two increase the probability that they will cooperatively accomplish and grow in their jobs. An example will help clarify how this approach can work.

In the subject company the advertising manager reports to the sales manager. The sales manager was routinely checking an advertisement aimed at consumers. He believed that the headline might be misinterpreted by the trade.

SALES MGR.: "I need a meeting on this advertisement."

ADV. MGR.: "OK, let's go."

SALES MGR.: "My wish is 'How retain the effectiveness of this advertisement without adverse effect on the trade?' Would you like me to Itemize to the ad as it is?"

ADV. MGR.: "Yes, and I will listen for wishes."

SALES MGR.: "The ad strongly carries out our policy to increase winter usage. The illustration and the headline offer a clear user benefit, and the picture itself is really a nice job. The copy supports the claim and is clear. My wish is 'How to keep the trade from feeling that we are trying to load them up in the off season?' "

ADV. MGR.: "I see what you mean. It is in the headline. I had not thought it came across that way, and now I'll need to think some more about it."

SALES MGR.: Do you want to problem solve on it?"

ADV. MGR.: "Thanks, no, not right now. I'd like to bring the agency into it. You are welcome to come to that meeting, though.

SALES MGR.: "If you'll let me know, I'll see if I can."

In the meeting with the agency, clientship shifted to the agency people. They are charged with writing the advertising. The agency chose to rewrite the headline on the spot and developed four alternative new headlines. Three of these survived the Itemized Response—that is, three of them were acceptable without concerns to the advertising manager or the sales manager. The advertising agency then decided which of the three to use.

The important element here is that traditionally, from the hierarchical view, the most powerful people would make the decision and quite probably word the headline. In the clientship model above, the alternatives must be acceptable to the people accountable, but the decisions are made by the person who does the actual work.

The first response of most managers to the above clientship system tends to be an unitemized, "For God's sake! Life is too short!" I sympathize. This procedure seems, and sometimes is, cumbersome and also confusing. As two people work with it, their skills increase and it becomes less so. I believe that better, more streamlined procedures will be invented, and in the meantime it is a useful way to help keep reality out in the open where it can be dealt with.

The accounting side of an organization presents an interesting parallel to the human side. Most accounting procedures are elaborate, complex, and effective. Nearly everyone accepts their importance and learns to conform to their necessary rules. In contrast, the human relationships in an organization are governed by power which is applied using the seat-of-the-pants judgment. To compound the possibility of misunderstanding, each manager operates with his own set of assumptions which are seldom articulated to his subordinates or even examined by himself. The cost in energy and time spent in defensive maneuvering has to be very high.

Earlier I said that I am concerned about the destructiveness to self of many of our habitual modes of transacting with others. Because most of us are unaware of our impact on other people, we feel no need to change. We are somewhat more aware of the impact of others on ourselves, but we are conditioned not to admit even to ourselves the extent of the threat to self. It seems weak to do so and we are oriented from birth to becoming powerful. "The full development of personality along the lines of security (avoidance of anxiety caused by threat to self) is chiefly founded on the infant's discovery of his powerlessness to achieve . . . with the tools . . . at his disposal." Unfortunately, our models of the acquisition and use of power are nearly all authoritarian. This leads to a difficult confusion. To develop a healthy self-concept I must manifest power. Power in this sense is the ability to accomplish. I equate this with power over other people. There is enough truth to this equation—that power over other people means I have the power to accomplish (and therefore have a healthy self-concept)—that it is extremely hard to see that this is not the only truth. In fact, exercising power over people has side-effects that are incalculable because the cause and effect is seldom visible. In our experimental environment we have been able to trace some of the effects of power strategies. We have also experienced the remarkable effect of careful power sharing.

This leads me to believe that it is vitally important that people in general be given education in how to interact with others in more rewarding ways. There is little doubt that education is needed: "Dr. Paul [psychiatrist, Harvard University] observes that very few human beings in our culture have . . . an objective consciousness-of-self. All people live under the mistaken belief that they are fully conscious and aware of themselves. This in spite of the fact that hardly anyone knows how his speech sounds to others, how his behavior affects others, what he looks like to others, and so forth" (Lederer, 1973).

The pay-off from becoming skillful in power sharing can be very great for the person who does so. To a much greater degree than most of us know, our own self-concepts depend upon the people we interact with. Sullivan holds that self-concept is "entirely interpersonal in origin and is gradually elaborated out of the reflected appraisals of other persons" (1953). My observations suggest to me that most people operate according to the principle of: "Don't get mad, get even." If I am skillful in my power sharing and in my transaction, the people I interact with have less need to "get even." Even more important is the posture I internalize. Instead of a predisposition to perceive interactions as threats to my power, I tend to see them as presentations of problems that invite me to *use* my creative power to help.

To summarize, in this time when we are becoming more aware of the importance of the human equation in family and business life, it is useful to attend to the fundamental enterprise in the forefront of everyone's mind—the development, enhancement, and protection of one's own self-concept.

By using the explicit tools of Transactional Analysis and those of synectics one can develop an "objective consciousness-of-self" and, therefore, change and become a person for whom it is possible to share power without in any way being powerless. The consequences of this self-interested sharing are enormously rewarding in increased capacity to be creative, to learn, to grow; in short, to cooperatively accomplish. And from accomplishment comes success in the enterprise dearest to each of us: a healthy and continually enlarging self-concept.

References

Berne, E. *Principles of group treatment.* New York: Grove Press, 1966.
Elkind, D. "Good me" or "Bad me"—the Sullivan approach to personality. *New York Times Magazine,* September 24, 1972, p. 18.

Gordon, W. J. J. *Synectics*. New York: Harper & Row, 1961.

Gordon, W. J. J. Operational approach to creativity. *Harvard Business Review,* November–December, 1956, *34* (6) .

Harris, T. A. *I'm OK, you're OK*. New York: Harper & Row, 1969.

James, M. and Jongeward, D. *Born to win: Transactional analysis with Gestalt experiments*. Reading, Mass.: Addison-Wesley, 1971.

Kaplan, H., and Sager, C., (Eds.). Redecisions in transactional analysis—creating an environment for redecision and change. In *Progress in group and family therapy*. New York: Brunner-Mazell, 1972.

Koestler, A. *The act of creation*. New York: Macmillan, 1964.

Lamott, K. The four possible life positions: 1. I'm not OK—you're OK; 2. I'm not OK—you're not OK; 3. I'm OK—you're not OK; 4. I'm OK, you're OK. *New York Times Magazine,* November 19, 1972.

Lederer, W. J. Videotaping your marriage to save it. *New York Magazine,* February 19, 1973, p. 40.

Prince, G. M. *The practice of creativity*. New York: Harper & Row, 1970.

Sullivan, H. S. *Conceptions of modern psychiatry*. New York: W. W. Norton, 1953.

Synectics, Inc. *Making it strange*. New York: Harper & Row, 1968.

12. Creativity Research in Education: Still Alive

E. Paul Torrance

INCREASINGLY I AM BEING advised by well-meaning colleagues that creativity research in education is a dead issue and admonished to shift my research and development efforts to something that will make more of a difference in education. They remind me of the devastating pronouncements in the 1960s of such notable and revered scholars as Sir Cyril Burt (1962), Robert L. Thorndike (1963), Ernest Newland (1963), Quinn McNemar (1964), Philip C. Vernon (1964), Michael Wallach and Nathan Kogan (1965), and others. My colleagues also quote today's younger scholars who quote as authorities these older scholars. They point to the even more devastating 1973 pronouncements of such powerful figures in educational psychology and research as Robert L. Ebel, president of the American Educational Research Association, and Robert M. W. Travers and George J. Mouly, popular textbook writers in educational psychology. They point also to the fact that almost no creativity research in education is now being supported by the United States Office of Education, the National Science Foundation, the Institute of Health, or large foundations.

If I were a more authority-accepting person, I would probably accept these bitter pronouncements and proceed to what are regarded by authorities as "greener fields." Even so, my own perceptions of reality are challenged and I must ask, "Have I deceived myself?" In this chapter I shall try to look as objectively as possible at these pronouncements and try to weigh the evidence as I know it. First, let us review some of the newer statements that pronounce creativity research as dead.

One of the more damaging of these statements occurred in the presidential address of Robert L. Ebel at the 1973 annual meeting of the American Educational Research Association. This statement is as follows:

Those who try to teach people to be creative in general, or test for creativity in general, seem to me to be chasing a will-o'-the-wisp. I know of no good reason to believe that those who excel in creative accomplishments owe their success to a superabundance of general creative ability or talent. Creative achievement seems always to depend on special abilities, on special opportunities, on special effort. [Ebel, 1973, p. 10]

In the third edition of his popular textbook, *Psychology for Effective Teaching,* George Mouly (1973) similarly sounds the death knell of creativity in education and devotes only two of his 560 pages to the topic of creativity. His death pronouncement reads as follows:

The concept of creativity has had a rather hectic existence during the past decade. After a period of almost complete neglect going back practically to the Renaissance, creativity had a tremendous surge in the early 1960s, only to return to a more passive status as evaluation of the early data revealed major weaknesses in creativity as a construct. . . . The point that probably more than any other caught the imagination of the profession as well as the lay public was the claim that creativity was relatively independent of the traditional IQ. . . . Enthusiasm subsided when further analysis (e.g., Thorndike, 1963; McNemar, 1964; Wallach, and Kogan, 1965*a*) showed that creativity and traditional IQ were not independent as originally postulated, and further that creativity was not a unitary trait. [Mouly, 1973, p. 379]

Robert M. W. Travers (1973) in his new textbook, *Educational Psychology,* devotes only two pages of 448 to the entire topic of creativity and makes the present author the prime target of his death pronouncement of creativity in education. His pronouncement reads as follows:

The writings on creativity most familiar to teachers are those of Torrance (1965), who has reported some classroom experiments on the rewarding of aspects of creative behavior. Although these experiments are superficially convincing, just what learning they demonstrate is hard to say. . . . The technique proposed by Torrance is virtually that of operant conditioning, though he makes no reference to Skinner in his entire book. Those who read the book and similar books should also be cautioned that colorful anecdotes do not provide the evidence needed to set up a program to help children to become more creative. A much more substantial basis for such programs is needed. [Travers, 1973, p. 182]

Those of you who are familiar with the facts about creativity research in education can spot immediately the subtle, if not outright, fallacies in these pronouncements. Yet I would be willing to predict that these statements will be widely quoted during the coming decade. They will be taught as facts to thousands of young people now in teacher education programs. These future teachers will not be taught the truth that the skills of creative thinking are teachable (Torrance and Torrance, 1973) and that they can even be applied to problems of teaching. They will not be taught that to be useful these skills must be practiced. They will not be taught that the abilities measured by tests of creative thinking are not heritable in the sense that Jensen's Levels I and II abilities are heritable (Pezzullo, Thorsen, and Madaus, 1972), that there is little or no racial or socioeconomic bias in such tests (Torrance, 1971), and that performance on such tests taken during the high school years are significantly related to the creative achievements of young adults twelve years later (Torrance, 1972b). They will not be taught that creativity has long been of concern to educational psychologists and that not even Getzels and Jackson (1962) and Torrance (1962) maintained that creativity was separate and distinct from intelligence. Many of these young teachers will not find out that a major thrust of Guilford, Calvin Taylor, Getzels, Jackson, Torrance, and others has been to expand, not reduce, the concept of intelligence or mental functioning. They will not learn the important differences between behavior modification and the variety of methodologies for encouraging creative thinking and teaching the skills needed for a higher level of creative problem solving.

Contradictory Evidence?

RESEARCH ON CREATIVITY IN EDUCATION

To accept the harsh verdict that creativity research in education is a dead issue, one would need to establish the fact that there is a definite decline in research concerned with creativity and that the influence of the research on educational practice has diminished. Let us examine some of the facts.

I have just completed the compilation of a bibliography of research on the *Torrance Tests of Creative Thinking* (1967b). If this can be used as an index of research interest, there are no real signs of death. Counting only publications in professional journals, books, and dissertations, the distribution of publications on the TTCT by years is as follows:

Year	Count	Year	Count
1961	12	1968	53
1962	22	1969	68
1963	37	1970	64
1964	51	1971	65
1965	60	1972	57
1966	46	1973	57
1967	59		

It will be noted that the only year in which there has been a marked drop was in 1966, the year I moved to the University of Georgia and the year in which the tests were published.

There is no question in my mind but that it has become increasingly more difficult to get acceptance by journals of research with the TTCT in spite of the fact that the predictive validity evidence has become more compelling. For example, a student of mine recently had an article using the TTCT rejected by one of the APA journals, with a reviewer's comment that read somewhat as follows:

> Although the article is well written and organized and deals with an important problem, I recommend that it be rejected because of the questionable validity of the instrument used. I know that there have been several publications using the Torrance tests but a recent article by O. J. Harvey casts doubts upon their validity.

Instead of several articles there have, of course, been several hundred publications of studies using the TTCT. The Harvey, Hoffmeister, Coates, and White (1970) study, which is rapidly becoming the most frequently quoted study in the literature, attributes a number of assumptions to me that are the obverse of which I have clearly stated from the very outset of my work with the instrument. They sought to validate the TTCT with a group of 64 educators (male and female) against criterion measures of Supernaturalism, Moral Relativism, Dictation of Classroom Procedures, Need for Structure-Order, Dogmatism, Authoritarianism, Curricular Traditionalism, Disciplinarianism, Encouragement of Student Exploration, Concreteness-Abstractness of Beliefs, and Belief System Classification. These investigators ignore the fact that the criterion measures are quite unrelated to the theoretical rationale of the TTCT and that they were correlating personality variables with mental ability variables. Even so, it is interesting to note that they obtained significant positive relationships between the creativity measures and Moral Relativism, Fostering Student Independence, and Fostering Exploration and significant negative relationships between creativity measures and Supernaturalism, Dictation of Classroom Procedure, and Need for Structure-Order, precisely what I would have predicted.

SPACE IN EDUCATIONAL PSYCHOLOGY TEXTBOOKS

One index of the influence creativity research is having on education may be found in the amount of space devoted to this research in educational psychology textbooks. Is the situation any different now from what it was in 1950 when Guilford made his APA presidential address? To check on this I analyzed 9 commonly used educational psychology textbooks in 1950 and 9 commonly used at the present time. (See Appendix for list of textbooks used in this survey.) The textbooks in use in 1950 ranged from 0 to 39 pages with a mean of 10.6 pages compared with a range from 13 to 47 pages with a mean of 27.8 for the textbooks now in use. The difference in means is statistically significant at the better than the .02 level (t-ratio =

2.81). With the appearance of the Mouly and Travers books in 1973, it is possible that this picture may be changed within another year.

EMPHASIS ON CREATIVITY IN ELEMENTARY AND
SECONDARY TEXTBOOKS

Another index of the influence of creativity research might be derived from an analysis of the textbooks and teachers' manuals in use in elementary and secondary schools. Although I have made no systematic comparison of the textbooks and teachers' manuals in use in 1950 and in 1973, casual examination of a large number of textbooks at both the elementary and secondary levels has convinced me that there is no question but that an enormous change has occurred in the direction of more creative activities, more open-ended questions that cause children to examine information in different ways, and the like.

I have had the very gratifying experience of working with authors, editors, artists, and others in the Ginn Reading 360 Program, Elementary Social Studies Program, and the Urban Reading Program. Deliberate efforts were made to build into these programs in a thoroughgoing manner features that will facilitate creative growth and the development of creative thinking skills. Contrary to Travers (1973), important skills are involved in creative thinking, and these skills have to be developed through meaningful practice. Some of the stories, reading materials, illustrations, and graphic elements of the books themselves motivate readers to think creatively. The teachers' editions have a great variety of suggestions for such practice. In addition, exercises in the skills practice books are also designed to develop important skills in creative thinking.

For authors, editors, and others, I prepared two types of guidance: (1) developmental information about the hierarchy of creative thinking skills and (2) information about teaching methods and strategies for use before, during, and after a lesson. In my book, *Encouraging Creativity in the Classroom* (1970a), I attempted to generalize these materials for subject matter other than reading and social studies, and I have demonstrated to my own satisfaction that even relatively inexperienced teachers can use this guidance in teaching.

Nash and Torrance (1970) conducted a rather systematic and thorough evaluation of the use of the Reading 360 Program in two first grade classes with quite positive results. The creative growth and creative functioning of the children experiencing the program exceeded that of their controls on both individual and small group measures of creative thinking. Other independent evaluations have had similar positive tones, as illustrated in the following quotation from a field test report in *The Creative Teacher* (Plooster, 1972):

> These are only a few of the many activities that the Reading 360 Program initiated for these first graders. The children became very enthusiastic about

securing information for so many things that they were taking 4–6 library books per week from the school library plus those they found in the public library. This reading program never ended at any one time period. Instead, it acted as a springboard for daily, weekly, and yearly class activities in all subject areas. [p. 5]

What we have described here is precisely what we have known all along will happen if children are involved creatively in their learning and the very opposite of what Travers (1973), Wallach (1973), and other critics of creativity research in education have accused us of fostering. Children so involved will be motivated to want to know and as a consequence will read books, ask questions, conduct experiments, and the like.

EMPHASIS ON CREATIVITY IN MAGAZINES FOR TEACHERS

Still another index of the extent to which creativity is alive in education might be obtained by analyzing the contents of magazines used by large numbers of teachers. To obtain such an index, my wife made a careful analysis of the contents of the *Instructor* magazine for 1950 and 1972. This magazine was chosen because it has one of the largest readerships among magazines for teachers and has always had a lively interaction between the staff of the magazine and its readership. Thus, it reflects a great deal of what is happening in schools. During the mid-1960s the *Instructor* ran monthly features on creativity four years in succession by Elliott Eisner, Calvin W. Taylor, E. Paul Torrance, and Richard J. Suchman. No such series, however, was active during either 1950 or 1972.

The 11 issues of *Instructor* in 1950 carried a total of 33 items on creativity or a mean of 3 items per issue compared with 101 or a mean of 10.1 items in the 10 issues appearing in 1972. The difference in means is significant at better than the .01 level. Even a casual glance at the contents of current issues of the magazine makes obvious many changes in education conceivably related to increased and continuing interest in creativity. More products of children's creativity are in evidence, especially visual art and literary products. Advertisers are sponsoring creative writing and other contests of creative achievement and describe a great variety of books, films, recordings, games, and other materials designed to facilitate creative learning and teaching. There are evidences that creative thinking has become an integral part of almost every area of the curriculum and methods of implementing the curriculum. There are also evidences of a creative interaction between the school and community. Not only has the school gone into the community; increasingly the community is going into the school.

What Do We Know about Creativity in Education?

Let us assume that Travers, Mouly, Wallach, and the other critics of creativity in education are correct and the death knell of creativity in education has been sounded. What, if anything, have we accomplished since 1950 that will stand the test of time and go down in history as contributions to knowledge?

CREATIVITY TESTS

First, I would like to tackle the matter of testing, since some critics maintain that the experimental and evaluative studies are invalid because they rely upon so-called creativity tests for which there is no evidence of validity. A major criticism of tests of creative thinking ability and the TTCT in particular is that there is no evidence of a link between performance on test tasks and real-life achievements.

Recently, I (Torrance, 1972a) reviewed thirteen predictive validity studies of the TTCT which I believe do link test performance with real-life behavior. In a long-range predictive validity study involving high school students tested in 1959 and followed up in 1971, a canonical correlation of .51 was obtained for the combined scores on the creativity test battery to predict the combined creative achievement criteria in the total sample of 236. For men, the canonical correlation coefficient was .59 and for women, .46. The following additional findings provide encouraging support:

1. The class of 1960 was followed up both in 1966 and in 1971, and there was a consistent trend for the validity coefficients to increase from 1966 to 1971. Using the measures of Fluency, Flexibility, Originality, and Elaboration and measures of Quantity and Quality of Creative Achievements and Creative Motivation, the mean validity coefficient was .40 for 46 subjects in 1966 and .51 for 52 subjects in 1971.

2. The present and projected occupations of 252 respondents were classified as conventional or unconventional according to criteria developed by Getzels and Jackson (1962). Using a median split within grade and sex on the original population, 113 subjects were classified as high creatives and 138 as low creatives. Sixty-two or 55 percent of the high creatives and 13 or 9 percent of the low creatives were in unconventional occupations in 1971. When projected occupations or future aspirations were classified, 71 percent of the high creatives and 32 percent of the low creatives chose unconventional occupations.

3. The measures of creativity are significantly and positively related to number of different jobs held since high school graduation. A greater percentage of the high creatives (29 percent) than the low creatives (14 percent) have studied or worked in foreign countries.

4. Creative achievements in writing were most easily predicted, followed by creative achievements in science and medicine and in leadership, perhaps because the criteria in these areas are clearer and more obvious than in such fields as business, music, art, and the like.

5. Almost twice as many of the high creatives as the low creatives re-

ported three peak creative achievements while three times as many of the low creatives as the high creatives described no peak achievements.

6. Significantly more of the high creatives than the low creatives reported peak achievements in the areas of writing, style of teaching, research, musical composition and performance, human relations and leadership, and medical discovery.

7. The low creatives tended to report as peak achievements what appear to be "cop-out" or "drop-out" experiences unaccompanied by constructive action, while many of the high creatives reported withdrawal experiences either for periods of renewal or for creating a more humane style of life.

At this point, one must ask what are reasonable and acceptable standards of validity for tests of creative thinking ability. Some critics (Crockenberg, 1972; Baird, 1972) have stated that the problem is not a lack of validity data on the TTCT but that these data are weak. When confronted by the fact that creative functioning involves a variety of phenomena which occur simultaneously and interact with one another, how much weight should we expect measures of general creative abilities to carry? Research evidence indicates that the motivation of the subject, his early life experiences, the immediate and long-range rewards, the richness of the environment, and other factors are all important enough to make a difference in creative functioning and furthermore that these phenomena interact with one another.

When we found that the women in the long-range prediction study were less predictable than the men, we confronted this matter to some extent and tried to obtain responses to the Alpha Biographical Inventory for as many of the women respondents as possible. With a sample of 45 of these women, we (Torrance, Bruch, and Morse, 1973) combined the creativity score of the Alpha Biographical with the originality score and a composite creativity score derived in 1959 (which did not include a measure of originality). A canonical correlation of .60 resulted. The coefficients of correlation between the Alpha Biographical Creativity Scale and the criteria of creative achievement are .38, .39, and .37; the mean coefficients of correlation for the creative ability tests and the criteria are .37, .45, and .36; and the mean coefficient of correlation between the Alpha Biographical score and the creative ability measure is .15.

To correct a number of misconceptions in the literature, I would like to review some of the history and characteristics of the TTCT. Five years of rather basic research preceded the selection of tasks or activities for the TTCT and four years of additional research preceded their publication in 1966. This research has been continued and much of its results will be reflected in the revised technical-norms manual that I hope will be off the press soon. I shall summarize here the major considerations that guided this process.

No claim has ever been made for the unidimensionality of the TTCT, contrary to assertions of critics. On the contrary, I have always maintained that a person may be creative in a great variety of ways and that the problem of assembling a test battery is to sample this universe as well as possible within the constraints of requirements in practical, educational situations. The TTCT tasks were devised so that they reflect different aspects of creative behavior; that is, kinds of cognitive-affective functioning that facilitate effective creative behavior. This was accomplished primarily by (1) analyzing the behavior of eminent creative people as recorded in autobiographies and biographies as well as studies of the creative problem-solving process and trying to identify the most important composite skills and (2) subjecting scores derived from a wide variety of test tasks to factor analyses and selecting tasks that are factorially different. In summary, the criteria for selecting specific tests and testing materials are as follows:

1. They must have relevance to creativity theory.
2. They must have relevance to adult creative behavior.
3. They must sample different aspects of creative thinking.
4. They must be attractive alike to children, adolescents, and adults.
5. They must be open-ended so that a person can respond in terms of his experiences whatever these may have been.
6. The instructions and response demands must be adaptable to the educational range from kindergarten through graduate school and professional education.
7. They must yield data that can be scored reliably for such qualities as fluency, flexibility, originality, and elaboration.
8. The testing materials, instructions for administration, time limits, and scoring procedures must be such that the use of the standard batteries in schools is feasible.

Long before the initial publication of the TTCT, many of the matters that were made issues by Wallach and Kogan (1965) had been tested out with reasonable care as a part of the routine developmental work. For example, we had experimented with variations in time limits as well as with unlimited time. We had found that instructions to produce responses that "no one else in the class will think of," not only resulted in greater originality but was obviously more fun than instructions without such an admonition. In thousands of administrations, we observed none of the stress that Wallach and Kogan (1965) and Kogan (1971) have been so concerned about.

Since the publication of the TTCT, research to improve the tests in the light of the above criteria have focused primarily on the following:

1. Warm-up conditions immediately prior to the administration of the tests.
2. Variations of the setting (contents of the testing room) in which the tests are administered.
3. Variations in time limits, including the use of "take home" test procedures.
4. Applications to cultures outside of the United States.
5. Bases for determining statistical infrequency in guiding the scoring of originality.

RELATIONSHIP OF CREATIVITY TO INTELLIGENCE

Wallach (1968, 1970, 1973) has repeatedly made an issue of the fact that the TTCT is not clearly distinguished from intelligence tests and asserts that it is only another intelligence test. I would certainly agree that I have never tried to make a clear distinction between intelligence and creative thinking, as separate variables, because I believe that they are interacting variables and that to try to force clear distinctions between the two types of measuring instruments would be to create false distinctions that do not exist in reality.

Wallach (1970) is fairly correct in concluding that both divergent and convergent thinking are parts of the process implied by the TTCT and that the way I define creativity seems to be "a general intelligence concept liberalized by the addition of references to a problem-solution phase in which it is useful for thinking to go off in different directions" (p. 1224). I believe that the creative problem solving process as described by Osborn (1963), Parnes (1967), Guilford (1967), and others involves both divergent and convergent processes as well as continuous resort to memory and at least periodic resorts to evaluation. At least Wallach shows more insight in making this observation than do those who insist that the term "divergent thinking" rather than "creative thinking" should be applied to the TTCT.

Although there have been published thousands of coefficients of correlation between measures derived from the TTCT and measures of intelligence, many critics select only those correlation coefficients that satisfy their biases, rather than looking at the larger picture. In a 1967 publication, I summarized a total of 388 such correlations from a great variety of dissertation studies and published studies. The median of 114 coefficients of correlation involving figural measures was .06; for the 88 correlations involving verbal measures, the median was .21; and for the 178 correlations involving both verbal and figural measures combined, the median was .20. Even in my 1962 book, *Guiding Creative Talent,* I reported a wide range of coefficients of correlation between intelligence and creativity measures. All along the data have seemed to support the conclusion that these two variables are related only moderately. The relationships were especially low in samples consisting predominantly of high ability children or adults. They were highest in samples consisting largely of low ability students where motivation and test taking attitudes and skills rather than intelligence and creative ability were perhaps the common factor.

I still believe that the degree of differentiation between the TTCT and measures of intelligence is best described by a generalization of mine criticized by McNemar in his 1964 presidential address before the American Psychological Association in the following terms:

> The argument against the IQ is now being reinforced by the claim that the selection of the top 20% on IQ would mean the exclusion of 70% of the top

20% on tested creativity. This startling statistic, which implies a correlation of only .24 between IQ and creativity, is being used to advocate the use of creativity tests for identifying the gifted.

The correlations in the samples from which this generalization was derived were in fact somewhat less than .24. In none of these discussions back in the early 1960s was there any advocacy on my part for replacing measures of intelligence with measures of creativity. My whole plea, as was the case with Calvin Taylor (1968) and others, was to consider a wider range of abilities both in identification and in program development.

Perhaps the most serious oversight of those critics who maintain that there is no distinction between creativity and intelligence or between the abilities assessed by the TTCT and measures of intelligence is a failure to recognize the differences in the ways scores on the two kinds of measures behave. I shall review a few of these.

LACK OF RACIAL AND SOCIOECONOMIC BIAS

Whether one agrees or disagrees with the conclusions reached by Arthur Jensen (1969) and his followers on matters of intelligence, race, and socioeconomic status, the fact remains that there are racial and socioeconomic differences in measured intelligence and that these differences are fairly consistent. In another source, I (Torrance, 1971) summarized the results of 16 different studies conducted in different parts of the United States to study racial and/or socioeconomic status differences on the TTCT. In some of these studies, there were no racial or socioeconomic differences on either the verbal or figural tests. In others black children excelled white children on certain tasks and white children excelled blacks on others. The same was true where socioeconomic status differences were studied. Overall, there were no racial or socioeconomic differences. A major reason for this, of course, is that the creativity test tasks are open-ended and a child may respond to them in terms of his own life experiences, whatever these may have been. This is not true of intelligence tests.

Since my review published in 1971, a number of additional studies have reported essentially the same verdict of no racial or socioeconomic bias. It is true that these studies have been relatively small (about 100 subjects) or moderate (around 700) in size. Efforts have been made to secure support for a larger, more definitive study with broader sampling, but these efforts have not been successful.

HERITABILITY OF CREATIVE ABILITY

A recent study by Pezzulo, Thorsen, and Madaus (1972) found no evidence of hereditary variation in either the figural or verbal forms of the TTCT. Their subjects were 37 pairs of fraternal and 28 pairs of identical twins carefully tested. These investigators found that short term memory (Jensen's Level I abilities) has only a moderate index of heritability, .54;

the general intellective factor (Jensen's Level II abilities) has a relatively high index of heritability, .85. The heritability index for the figural and verbal measures of the TTCT approached zero. Another twin study by Richmond (1968) similarly found no evidence of heritability for the abilities assessed by the TTCT. Davenport (1967), using the Getzels and Jackson (1962) measures, did find weak evidence for heritability on most of these measures of creativity. The indications were so weak, however, that Davenport concluded that there was a wide margin in which experience could influence the creative thinking abilities.

An important implication of the finding that creative abilities are not heritable is that educators can expect to be able to do more to modify the creative abilities than they can the abilities assessed by intelligence tests. Thus, educational programs that build competencies in creative thinking and build upon the creative positives of disadvantaged children are likely to be more successful than are those programs that seek to improve intelligence and compensate for deficiencies in this area.

There are, of course, strong indications that many of the influences in disadvantaged groups encourage creative behavior (Torrance, 1972c). In addition to my own work, that of Susan Houston (1973) supports this conclusion. Houston has identified a number of reasons why poor black children customarily get lower scores than white children do on scholastic and verbal-intelligence measures. She maintains that their creativity actually interferes with their success on such tests. In her studies of poor black children in the South who lacked material playthings, Houston found that they engaged in constant language play and verbal contests. They placed high value on creativity and giftedness, and Houston rates the stories they told her as highly imaginative. She also found that the poor black children interacted more with one another and developed skills in group interaction which far excelled those of other groups of children of the same age. They also supported or encouraged one another more.

Thus far, the findings concerning the lack of heritability of creative abilities and the lack of racial and socioeconomic bias have stimulated no visible enthusiasm. This is in spite of the potentcy of the implications of these findings and in spite of the great attention that has been given to the Jensen debate, the Coleman Report (Coleman et al., 1966), and the Jencks Report (Jencks et al., 1972). In fact, these findings are particularly relevant to some of the criticisms of critics of the Jencks Report, particularly the black critics (Edmonds et al., 1973). These black critics maintain that the school environment has been culturally responsive to the affluent and is actually antipoor. Further, they assert that "compensatory education doesn't work because it doesn't make the school responsible for teaching in the ways that children are prepared to learn" (p. 81). They argue that people vary in their cognitive styles and "that until schools learn to recognize this and plan different ways of teaching the same requisite skills to all children, they will not come close to providing equality of educational opportunity" (p. 83).

Although there have been some brilliant examples of successes with programs that build upon the creative positives of disadvantaged children (Clary, 1970; Shepherd, 1972; Witt, 1971), little enthusiasm has been generated for them. From George Witt's long-range experiment, for example, we know that it is possible to develop high levels of both academic achievement and creative achievement among black, disadvantaged children identified as gifted solely on the basis of the TTCT. All that it took was to give them a chance to build upon their exceptional creative abilities. Practically all of these children selected in 1965 at the time they were in the second and third grades have distinguished themselves in one or more of the creative arts. Some of them, however, have also shown brilliant promise in the sciences and at the junior high school level most of them are succeeding in first-rate private schools in New England.

Socialization and Creative Growth

Creativity research in education has opened up for scientific investigation a number of fundamental problems that have persisted in education for many years. One of the more intriguing of these issues is concerned with the role of socialization training in creative functioning and development. Early in my research it came to my attention that there are disturbing drops in creative functioning at about ages 5, 9, and 13—at times when there are customarily increased socialization pressures in the dominant, affluent culture of the United States. Most people argued that socialization training is necessary and that there are no better times for intensifying socialization training than at ages 5, 9, and 13.

First, I became interested in the decline which occurs at about age 9 when the child enters the fourth grade, going from the primary school to the intermediate school. When I began studying this development in other cultures (1967a), it seemed fairly clear that drops in creative functioning occurred in almost all cultures whenever and wherever there are increased socialization pressures and sharp discontinuities. No drops occurred, however, in a black, segregated school in middle Georgia and in schools in Western Samoa. Response to this finding was that the culture of Western Samoa and the black, disadvantaged culture of middle Georgia simply failed to socialize its members during these periods and that we certainly could not accept them as models.

Next, my associates and I (Torrance and Gupta, 1964) developed instructional materials and teaching procedures that we believed would facilitate continued creative growth in the fourth grade in white, advantaged cultures. Field tests were arranged in a Minneapolis suburb, some all-white schools in south Georgia, and some suburban schools in South Dakota.

In all three settings, creative growth and functioning were maintained apparently with no violence done to socialization training. At least fewer of the children in the experimental groups hated school and a greater proportion of them were present for the post-test than was true of the controls. Furthermore, they learned as much as the controls as measured by tests of reading, arithmetic, and the like.

When I moved to Georgia in 1966, I changed my focus first to the preschool years and the socialization pressures of five-year olds (1970b).

During my first three years at the University of Georgia, I had the opportunity to evaluate the creative development resulting from the application of the Creative-Aesthetic and Structured-Cognitive approaches to preprimary education. During the second and third years I had unprecedented opportunities to experiment with materials and procedures to improve the quality of both the socialization and creative skills within the Creative-Aesthetic program. From the results obtained at the end of the first year, it was obvious that five-year-old children participating in this program attained unusual heights in originality of thinking. They showed enormous growth on pre- and post-tests of creativity, both verbal and non-verbal (Torrance, 1968). They excelled their controls on every measure of originality we had devised and also on those developed by Starkweather (1965). Their mean originality score at the end of the school year was 1.1 standard deviations above the mean of our fifth-grade norm group, actually a rather superior group by national standards (Torrance, 1966). On the measure of elaboration which requires considerable intellectual discipline, however, their performance placed them a full standard deviation below our fifth-grade norms. There were also some indications that their socialization skills did not equal those of children in the traditional kindergarten program. Furthermore, children in the Structured-Cognitive preprimary model achieved a higher degree of elaboration (Torrance, 1968).

During the next two years, I began experimenting with materials and procedures that I hoped would increase socialization skills and ability to elaborate without causing a reduction in originality. By the third year, many of these materials and procedures had been tested experimentally and had been incorporated into the curriculum of the two classes of five-year olds enrolled in the Creative-Aesthetic approach to preprimary educational stimulation. The originality scores at the end of the second and third years were at about the same high level as at the end of the first year. Fluency and flexibility also were at about the same level as in the first year. Elaboration, at the end of the third year, however, was about 1.36 standard deviations above that attained at the end of the first year. Similarly, studies of group functioning on creative tasks showed a higher level of organizing and cooperating behavior than was found during the second year. (No objective studies of group functioning were made during the first year.)

The major emphasis of my developmental work to refine certain aspects of the Creative-Aesthetic model (Fortson, 1969) was focused on experimentation with factors influencing interaction processes and the development of assessment procedures to evaluate the outcomes of these experiences. The pervasive objective was to facilitate simultaneously the socialization and creative processes. We were able to test rather carefully through experimental studies some of our hypotheses and I reported these results at the 1970 creativity research conference at Buffalo-Niagara Falls. To me, the indications were clear that it was indeed possible simultaneously to facilitate socialization and creativity.

I was really delighted with what happened during the fourth year of our longitudinal evaluation of the Cognitive-Structured model to preprimary education. At this time there were no longer any funds to keep the Creative-Aesthetic model going but many of the critical elements of the Creative-Aesthetic model had been added to the Cognitive-Structured program. When I went into the first grade rooms near the end of the year when we were doing our post-testing, I was amazed at what I saw. Here were six-year olds who had entered the program at age three. Now they were practically managing their own learning. They were working quietly as individuals, in dyads, and in small groups. There was no bickering, fighting, pushing, and screaming—the kinds of behavior I find in most of the first grade classes I visit. I was almost afraid to administer the tests of creative thinking. Although I knew that socialization is possible without sacrificing creativity, this seemed almost too orderly. Surely children who behaved in such a disciplined manner must have had their creativity "beat out of them." To my delight, we found that these children produced far more original ideas on both the verbal and figural measures of creative thinking than did their controls.

From my research and experience with young children, the evidence seems compelling that creative activities facilitate socialization and that healthy socialization facilitates creative functioning. Psychologsts, psychiatrists, and educators are only now beginning to grasp the real promise of creative activities for psychotherapy as well as socialization. Regularly I receive reports of children who ceased being discipline problems when given chances to learn in creative ways. A challenging future task for research and development is to translate the creative problem solving model into learning activities for preprimary and primary children. It has been demonstrated that stories in beginning reading books can describe how children can solve problems creatively and that enjoyable learning activities in day care centers and nursery schools can be used to teach creative problem solving skills.

Conclusions

Although barriers to creativity research in education are likely to continue to be very great, there is much that is healthy about creativity research on the educational scene. There are enough anticreative leaders in education and psychology to exercise sufficient power to deny financial support to such research, to prevent the publication in certain journals of such research once it has been executed, and to disapprove dissertation proposals for such research. Although these barriers will deter completely many young researchers, there are enough determined young scholars who will persist, execute meaningful research, and keep creativity research alive.

The field of gifted education may provide a good index of what has been happening and is likely to happen in creativity research. The older leadership in this field has tended to be committed to the Terman approach to the identification and encouragement of intellectual giftedness. This group of older leaders has discouraged and disparaged creativity research and in numerous instances they have succeeded in denying support and dissemination of such research. They have applied tactics of both hostile attack and ignoring. However, many of the younger leaders have not been deterred and the national climate for creativity research in this field is favorable. Four of the national presidents of the Association for the Gifted of the Council for Exceptional Children, including the current president and the president-elect, have been associated with creativity research. The Office of the Gifted and Talented of the Office of Education under the leadership of Harold Lyon has been friendly to programs designed to encourage creative giftedness. The National Association for Gifted Children and its journal, *Gifted Child Quarterly*, has given a place of real prominence to this aspect of giftedness. Several states have recently approved the use of creativity tests in identifying gifted students in state-supported programs.

Perhaps the most encouraging sign of the health of creativity research is to be found at the "grass roots" level. More and more elementary, high school, and college textbooks are being rewritten to encourage creative thinking. There is an increased flow of supplementary curriculum materials at all educational levels designed to encourage creative thinking and problem solving. The older teachers' magazines such as the *Instructor* continue an emphasis on creative teaching and new ones like *Learning* and *Early Years* have an even bolder emphasis. During 1974 I have had more requests than ever before to conduct summer workshops on creativity for teachers or to recommend someone else who might do so. These are only a few of the more obvious and visible signs that creativity research has made a difference in educational practice and is still alive.

References

Baird, L. J. Review of "The Torrance Tests of Creative Thinking." In O. K. Buros (Ed.), *The seventh mental measurement yearbook,* pp. 836–838. Highland Park, N.J.: Gryphon Press, 1972.

Burt, Sir C. The psychology of creative ability. *British Journal of Educational Psychology,* 1962, *32,* 292–298.

Clary, D. Music and dance for the disadvantaged. *Instructor,* 1970, *79* (6) , 58–59.

Coleman, J. S. et al. *Equality of educational opportunity.* Washington, D.C.: U.S. Government Printing Office, 1966.

Crockenberg, S. B. Creativity tests: A boon or boondoggle for education. *Review of Educational Research,* 1972, *42,* 27–45.

Davenport, J. D. A study of the performance of monozygotic and dyzygotic twins and siblings on measures of scholastic aptitude, creativity, achievement motivation, and academic achievement. Doctoral dissertation, University of Maryland, 1967. (University Microfilms Order No. 68-3350).

Ebel, R. L. The future of measurements of abilities II. *Educational Researcher,* 1973, *2*(3), 5–12.

Edmonds, R. et al. A black response to Christopher Jencks's *Inequality* and certain other issues. *Harvard Educationaal Review,* 1973, *43,* 76–91.

Fortson, L. R. A creative-aesthetic approach to readiness and beginning reading and mathematics in the kindergarten. Doctoral dissertation, University of Georgia, 1969. (University Microfilms Order No. 70-10, 187) .

Getzels, J. W., and Jackson, P. W. *Creativity and Intelligence.* New York: Wiley, 1962.

Guilford, J. P. *The nature of human intelligence.* New York: McGraw-Hill, 1967.

Guilford, J. P. Creativity. *American Psychologist,* 1950, *5,* 444–454.

Harvey, O. J., Hoffmeister, J. K., Coates, C., and White, J. A partial evaluation of Torrance's tests of creativity. *American Educational Research Journal,* 1970, *7,* 359–372.

Houston, S. H. "Black English." *Psychology Today,* 1973, *6*(10), 45–48.

Institute for Behavioral Research in Creativity. *Alpha Biographical Inventory.* Salt Lake City: Prediction Press, 1968.

Jencks, C. et al. *Inequality: A reassessment of the effect of family and schooling in America.* New York: Basic Books, 1972.

Jensen, A. R. How much can we boost IQ and scholastic achievement? *Harvard Educational Review,* 1969, *39,* 1–123.

Kogan, N. Is all thinking creative? *Contemporary Psychology,* 1971, *16,* 463–464.

McNemar, Q. Lost: Our intelligence? Why? *American Psychologist,* 1964, *19,* 871–882.

Mouly, G. J. *Psychology for effective teaching.* 3rd. ed. New York: Holt, Rinehart and Winston, 1973.

Nash, W. R., and Torrance, E. P. *A preliminary evaluation of the effects of reading 360 on creative development and functioning at the first grade level.* Athens, Ga.: Georgia Studies of Creative Behavior, 1970.

Newland, T. E. A critique of research on the gifted. *Exceptional Children,* 1963, *29,* 391–399.

Osborn, A. F. *Applied imagination.* 3rd ed. New York: Scribner's, 1963.

Parnes, S. J. *Creative behavior guidebook.* New York: Scribner's, 1967.

Pezzullo, T. R., Thorsen, E. E., and Madaus, G. F. The heritability of Jensen's level I and II and divergent thinking. *American Educational Research Journal,* 1972, *9,* 539–546.

Plooster, B. Pilot reading program (Ginn 360). *Creative Teacher,* 1972, *4*(3), 4–5.

Richmond, B. O. Creativity in monozygotic and dyzygotic twins. Paper presented before American Personnel and Guidance Association, Detroit, April 1968.

Shepherd, J. Black lab power. *Saturday Review,* August 5, 1972, *55*(32), 32–39.

Starkweather, E. K. An originality test for preschool children. Stillwater, Okla.: Oklahoma State University, 1965. (Mimeographed)

Taylor, C. W. Be talent developers as well as knowledge dispensers. *Today's Education,* December, 1968, *57*(9), 67–69.

Thorndike, R. L. The measurement of creativity. *Teachers College Record,* 1963, *44,* 422–424.

Torrance, E. P. *Guiding creative talent.* Englewood Cliffs, N.J.: Prentice-Hall, 1962.

Torrance, E. P. *Education and the creative potential.* Minneapolis, Minn.: University of Minnesota Press, 1963.

Torrance, E. P. *Rewarding creative behavior.* Englewood Cliffs, N.J.: Prentice-Hall, 1965.

Torrance, E. P. *The Torrance tests of creative thinking: Technical-norms manual.* Research edition. Lexington, Mass.: Personnel Press, 1966.

Torrance, E. P. *The fourth grade slump in creative thinking.* (Final Report of USOE Cooperative Research Project 994) Washington, D.C.: United States Office of Education, 1967. (*a*)

Torrance, E. P. The Minnesota studies of creative behavior: National and international extensions. *Journal of Creative Behavior,* 1967, *1,* 137–154. (*b*)

Torrance, E. P. Must pre-primary educational stimulation be incompatible with creative development? In Williams, F. E. (Ed.), *Creativity at home and in school.* St. Paul, Minn.: Macalester Creativity Project, Macalester College, 1968.

Torrance, E. P. *Encouraging creativity in the classroom.* Dubuque, Iowa: William C. Brown, 1970. (*a*)

Torrance, E. P. Achieving socialization without sacrificing creativity. *Journal of Creative Behavior,* 1970, *4,* 183–189. (*b*)

Torrance, E. P. Are the Torrance tests of creative thinking biased against or in favor of disadvantaged groups? *Gifted Child Quarterly,* 1971, *15,* 75–80.

Torrance, E. P. Predictive validity of the Torrance tests of creative thinking. *Journal of Creative Behavior,* 1972, *6,* 236–252. (*a*)

Torrance, E. P. Career patterns and peak creative achievements of creative high school students 12 years later. *Gifted Child Quarterly* 1972, *16,* 75–88. (*b*)

Torrance, E. P. An alternative to compensatory education. *Educational Horizons,* 1972, *50,* 176–182. (*c*)

Torrance, E. P., Bruch, C. B., and Morse, J. A. Improving predictions of the adult creative achievement of gifted girls by using autobiographical information. *Gifted Child Quarterly,* 1973, *17,* 91–95,

Torrance, E. P., and Gupta, R. *Programmed experiences in creative thinking.* Washington, D.C.: United States Office of Education, 1964.

Torrance, E. P., and Torrance J. P. *Is creativity teachable?* Bloomington, Ind.: Phi Delta Kappa Educational Foundation, 1973.

Travers, R. M. W. *Educational psychology.* New York: Macmillan Company, 1973.

Vernon, P. C. Creativity and intelligence. *Educational Research,* 1964, *6,* 163–169.

Wallach, M. A. Review of Torrance tests of creative thinking. *American Educational Research Journal,* 1968, *5,* 272–281.

Wallach, M. A. Creativity. In P. H. Mussen (Ed.), *Carmichael's manual of child psychology.* 3rd ed., Vol. 1. New York: Wiley, 1970.

Wallach, M. A. Ideology, evidence, and creativity research. *Contemporary Psychology,* 1973, *18,* 162–164.

Wallach, M. A., and Kogan, N. *Modes of thinking in young children.* New York: Holt, Rinehart and Winston, 1965.

Witt, G. The life enrichment activity program: A continuing program for creative, disadvantaged children. *Journal of Research and Development in Education,* 1971, *4*(3), 14–22.

*Appendix**

Sample of Educational Psychology Textbooks Used in 1950

Boynton, P. L., Charles, J. W., Harriman, P. L., Powers, F. F., Ryan, W. C., Witty, P. A., and Wrightstone, J. W. *Elementary educational psychology*. New York: Prentice-Hall, 1946. (10 pages)

Cole, L. E., and Bruce, W. F. *Educational psychology*. Yonkers-on-Hudson, N.Y.: World Book Company, 1950. (39 pages)

Gates, A. I., Jersild, A. T., McConnell, T. R., and Challman, R. C. *Educational psychology*. Third Edition. New York: Macmillan, 1948. (17 pages)

Guthrie, E. R., and Powers, F. F. *Educational psychology*. New York: Ronald Press, 1950. (7 pages)

Mowrer, O. H. *Learning theory and personality dynamics*. New York: Ronald Press, 1950. (6 pages)

Rasey, M. I. *Toward maturity*. New York: Hinds, Hayden & Eldridge, 1947. (0 pages)

Simpson, R. G. *Fundamentals of educational psychology*. Chicago: J. B. Lippincott Company, 1949. (0 pages)

Trow, W. C. *Educational psychology*. Second Edition. Boston: Houghton Mifflin, 1950. (15 pages)

Woodruff, A. D. *The psychology of teaching*. New York: Longmans, Green & Company, 1948. (2 pages)

Sample of Educational Psychology Textbooks Used in 1973

Biehler, R. F. *Psychology applied to teaching*. Boston: Houghton Mifflin, 1971. (29 pages)

Charles, C. M. *Educational psychology: The instructional endeavor*. St. Louis, Mo.: C. V. Mosby, 1972. (17 pages)

DiVesta, F. J., and Thompson, G. G. *Educational psychology: Instructional and behavioral change*. New York: Appleton-Century-Crofts, 1970. (47 pages)

Eson, M. E. *Psychological foundations of education*. Second Edition. New York: Holt, Rinehart and Winston, 1972. (17 pages)

Klausmeier, H. J., and Ripple, R. E. *Learning and human abilities: Educational psychology*. Third Edition. New York: Harper & Row, 1971. (31 pages)

Lefrancois, G. R. *Psychology for teaching*. Belmont, Calif.: Wadsworth Publishing Company, 1972. (41 pages)

Loree, M. R. *Psychology of education*. Second Edition. New York: Ronald Press, 1970. (13 pages)

Sawrey, J. M., and Tellford, C. W. *Educational psychology*. Boston: Allyn and Bacon, 1973. (42 pages)

Staats, A. W. *Child learning, intelligence, and personality*. New York: Harper & Row, 1971. (14 pages)

* Page citations in parentheses refer to number of pages devoted to creativity research; see page 281.

13. An Emerging View of
Creative Actions

Irving A. Taylor

THIS CHAPTER WILL summarize cumulative results of some twenty years of investigation of creativity and related behavior. The thrust has been toward viewing creativity less as a singular concept but increasingly as a complex multidimensional set of related components or areas interacting to produce various patterns or styles of behavior that can be called creative. Increasingly, creativity has been seen as a function of different personality dispositions in interaction with various types of climates or environments. Within this interaction, problems are selected and formulated, cognitive processes come into play by transforming these problems into products or creative outcomes. These several processes, including the interaction between the person and the environment, combine to produce different forms or systems of creativity.

Background

In this context, five important areas emerged as foci for investigating creativity: the person, the problem, the process, the product, and the climate. The goal was to determine the nature, variety, and interaction of these five areas in a conceptual model of creativity which would provide a basis for systematic research.

The starting point which served as a background for these studies originated in several earlier investigations of extreme social attitudes. In one study (Taylor, 1960e), the extreme authoritarian personality was found to be similar to the extreme egalitarian personality in terms of perceptual closure and various demographic characteristics. In a subsequent study (Taylor, 1962b), similarities between the extremes were found for perceptual contrast and constancy. One important part of the earlier findings

(Taylor, 1960*e*) was the observation of a discernible but not significant tendency for students with "concrete majors" (such as physics, chemistry, engineering) to increase in conservative social attitudes and, conversely, for the number of students with "abstract majors" (such as philosophy, art, humanities) to increase in liberal social attitudes. Also, an inverse correlation was found in an unreported part of the study between extreme and conservative social attitudes and ratings of creativity. An examination of creativity (reported by Riessman, 1962, pp. 77–78) in children of contrasting socioeconomic classes indicated a greater number of signs of creativity or creative potential in disadvantaged children than in middle-class children. Disadvantaged children appeared more creative nonverbally. They were also found to be more creative on a word-distance scale. A later study in empathic communication through nonverbal symbols (Taylor, 1960*d*) indicated that nonverbal forms of communication may be more effective in transmitting human thoughts and feelings than the familiar verbal and formal types.

Interest in creativity investigation was further stimulated by several years of research in the psychology of music reported in a paper on current theory and research in the effects of music on behavior (Taylor and Paperte, 1958). After reviewing several theories of emotional induction, concepts were developed as to how music shapes behavior. It was stated that "common to . . . these theories is the principle of *emotional induction,* based on the observation that music produces changes in behavior by stirring up emotions directly or indirectly" (p. 252). The review of several other theories led to an *isomorphic* principle of emotional induction, which states that "music sounds the way emotions feel in that music indirectly embodies and resembles the formal characteristics of inner-dynamics. . . . If these two principles [emotional induction and isomorphism] are combined into a single theoretic framework, the following picture emerges: *when the structural dynamics of the music is similar to the structural dynamics of the emotion, sympathetic unison of the two results and any changes of the former will produce corresponding changes in the latter"* (p. 253). These formulations, and studies of the authoritarian personality led to the formulation of *personality transaction* in which the person shapes some significant part of his environment, rather than being shaped by the environment.

Early involvement with the general semantics movement and communication studies in general suggested the importance of problem formulation in creativity, as indicated in a recent paper on patterns of general semantics, perceptions, and creativity (Taylor, 1972*b*). The idea of a basic or generative notion in which certain fundamental assumptions or ideas are formulated which trigger a large number of derivative ideas was described by Langer (1942).

Several years of teaching the psychology of art produced a broader basis for understanding creativity in relation to other psychological functions of art. These functions were seen as five areas: perceptual organization, emotional expression, symbolic communication, art appreciation, and aesthetic creation. Perceptual organization was viewed developmentally (Taylor, 1960*a*, 1960*c*) as being initially oceanic or diffuse, evolving toward differentiation and articulation in accordance with Gestalt principles of perception and resulting in a highly organized synthesis of elements. As Arnheim (1969) pointed out later, "Once it is recognized that productive thinking in any area of cognition is perceptual thinking, the central function of art in general education will become evident. The most effective training of perceptual thinking can be offered in the art studio" (p. 296).

Expression by the artist through nonverbal forms was examined (Taylor, 1964) to determine the degree of empathy of subjects rated by instructors as creative or noncreative. The creative group was able to identify the nonverbal message "embodied" in the forms constructed to depict various emotions to a significantly greater extent than the noncreatives. Weber (1969) has noted "that art is expression, but expression not of reality but of ideality, not of concrete and experienced feeling, but of the life of those images in which reality and unreality merge. In a word, art is not a dream or a daydream; it is the expression of the dream of the artist" (p. 108). From the point of view of the receiver, art is symbolic communication (Taylor, 1960*d*), although the artist may not intend to communicate with others. He may, through expression, "effect communication, and this is not by external accident—but from the nature he shares with others" (Dewey, 1934).

Another function of art is appreciation. The observer in viewing art creates his own experience, and his appreciation of the art product consists of "a series of responsive acts that accumulate toward objective fulfillment" (Dewey, 1934).

Attempts at formulating concepts in creativity as an art function resulted in the development of creative personality dispositions (Taylor, 1960*b*). Sessions (1954) has indicated that "art is a function, an activity of the inner nature—that the artist's effort is, using the raw and undisciplined materials with which his inner nature provides him, to endow them with a meaning which they do not of themselves possess—to transcend them by giving them artistic form" (p. 39). Subsequent investigation was on the origins of creativity (Taylor, 1973*b*) as indicated by various individuals and investigators. Some of these origins include: (1) *vitalism,* in which creativity has a theistic or mystical source (Künkel and Dickerson, 1947; Rothbart, 1972); (2) *nativism,* or the belief that the origins are rooted in genetics (Galton, 1870, 1911; Hirsch, 1931; Kretschmer, 1931); (3) *empiricism,* the view that creativity is essentially learned, held by a number of investigators (Hutchinson, 1949; Osborn, 1953; Torrance, 1962); (4) *emergentism,* the view that creativity emerges as a synthesis of hereditary and environmental forces (Arnheim, 1954; Wertheimer, 1945); (5) *cognition,* creativity resulting from thought process (Guilford, 1968; Hersch, 1973; Mednick, 1968; Wallas, 1926); (6) *serendipity,* the notion that creative discoveries are accidental although the person may be prepared for a sudden insight (Cannon, 1940; McLean, 1941); (7) *romanticism,* the belief that creativity originates through unanalyzable inspirations and that examining the illusory roots of creativity will destroy it (Agha, 1959); (8) *physiology,* the contention that creativity is rooted in the biology of the human organism (Eccles, 1958; Gutman, 1967; Mumford, 1970; Sinott, 1959); (9) *culture,* or the determination of creativity by the historic Zeitgeist (Durkheim, 1898; Stein, 1967); (10) *interpersonal relations,* or creativity resulting from or being triggered by group interaction as in brainstorming or synectics (Anderson, 1959; Gordon, 1961; Parnes, 1962; Prince, 1970); and (11) *personality,* or the contention that the sources of creativity are understandable by examining the development of personality either psychoanalytically (Freud, 1908; Jung, 1928; Rank, 1945) or through self-actualization theory (Goldstein, 1939; Maslow, 1959; May, 1959; Rogers, 1954). This led subsequently to the concept of personality transaction (Taylor, 1971) and creative transactualization (Taylor, 1972c).

THE CREATIVITY PROGRAM

The development of a theoretic framework evolved during the past several years in the Creativity Program of the Center for Creative Leadership (Taylor, 1972c). The program was initiated to develop such a framework and to subsequently link it with leadership theory toward the development of a theory of creative leadership. A general research program was consequently planned to evaluate the various hypotheses derived from this theory and to explore the use of various creativity assessment techniques, developing new instruments where the field was found to be lacking. The program also initiated a series of training and development projects, some in conjunction with the center, which allowed us to modify, expand, and generally evaluate the creativity model. Finally, an attempt was made to develop a coherent conceptual framework which would lend itself to a theory of creative leadership.

Transactualization

THEORETIC BACKGROUND OF TRANSACTUALIZATION

Searching for an explanatory or descriptive concept for creative behavior has led to many theoretic concepts including sublimation (Freud, 1948b), compensation (Adler, 1917), restitution for destructive impulses (Sharpe, 1930; Fairbairn, 1938), regression in the service of the ego (Kris, 1952; Schafer, 1958), structure of the intellect (Guilford, 1968), and self-acualization (Jung, 1928; Goldstein, 1939; Maslow, 1954), to cite a few.

Transactualization is largely an extension of theories of self-actualization rooted in the works of Jung and Goldstein, particularly as developed by Maslow (1962), and in Rogers's (1963) conception of the "fully functioning" individual; self-actualization from these perspectives is related to creativity. From a humanistic viewpoint it is the most fully developed framework for understanding creativity as resulting from the full development of personality potentials. One of the limitations of self-actualization theory as a basis for understanding creativity development is that it is essentially psychological, that is, it is limited to the boundaries of personality growth. It does not easily lend itself to a psychosocial system for understanding the effects of psychological creativity on organizations and society, or indicate the nature of the influence of the person in shaping the external environment. It focuses heavily on self-shaping and development.

Self-actualization accounts for growth within the person toward his outer personal boundaries. Although the implication for external development is implicit, what is needed is an explicit formulation of the relation of the person to external shaping and developing, particularly in accordance with internal controls and direction and self-actualizing tendencies.

RELATION BETWEEN SELF-ACTUALIZATION AND TRANSACTUALIZATION

As conceived here, transactualization involves a person-environment system in which the person alters the environment (rather than being altered by it) in accordance with self-actualizing forces. Therefore, transactualization is an extension of self-actualization in which the person's growth has not only been extended to its personal limits but extended to shape the "potentiality" of the environment.

It is conceivable that transactualizing can occur without self-actualization, in which case there are three possibilities with implications for creativity and creative leadership. First, there can be a highly self-actualizing person with minimal transactualization. Although the person's potentials are fully developed, little if any effects are produced in the environment by the person in the way of environmental change, as is the case with many solitary artists, philosophers, historians, and businessmen. This type of person-environment relation has implications for "laissez-faire" creativity or creative leadership; that is, the person is concerned with self-direction and not with the control and direction of others.

As indicated, it is possible to be highly transactualizing with minimal self-actualization. This kind of person-environment relation has implications for "authoritarian" creativity and creative leadership in which there is minimal self-development but much external shaping.

When there is both highly developed self-actualization and transactualization development, the creativity and creative leadership behavior in the resulting person-environment relation may be "egalitarian," that is, highly developed forces of self-worth are extended to others.

COMPONENTS OF TRANSACTUALIZATION

This theory of creativity, as indicated, involves five essential interacting and interfacing components. These include the person, the problem, the process, the product, and the climate. I describe a creative person as being essentially *transactive* in the sense that his motivations which are autonomous are directed toward designing or shaping the external environment. The problems with which a creative person is generally concerned we describe as *generic,* or basic to other problems. That is, they underlie those phenotypic problems which exist as symptomatic manifestations of these underlying generic problems. The creative process is essentially one of *transformation,* which involves both perception and communication. It is a process in which the individual is exposed to both the external situation and internal experiences and transforms these into creative expressions; he reshapes problems into fruitful forms that allow for solution. The resulting creative outcome, or creative product, can be characterized as *generative,* since a creative product usually ushers in a host of new outcomes. The environment which facilitates creativity is one that is *stimulating,* one that initiates behavior toward unpredictable and unique out-

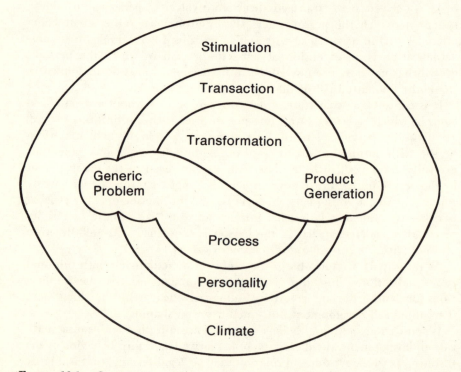

FIGURE 13.1. *Components of Transactualization and Their Interrelations.*

comes. Therefore, creativity as a system is viewed as involving a transacting person who transforms basic or generic problems into creative outcomes or products in a stimulating environment. These components and their inter-relations are depicted in figure 13.1.

IMPLICATIONS OF TRANSACTUALIZATION THEORY

The implications of transactualization are largely psychosocial. Creativity as a psychological process is thereby brought into relationship with social forces. Transactualization relates creativity as a psychological system to social systems relevant to leadership, especially creative leadership. Through transactualization, creativity in organizations is developed with a balance of consideration and structure for each person rather than in the more customary and noncreative practice of superimposing external controls. Finally, it suggests a concept of "creatorship," bringing the creator into relation with the appreciator.

Personality Transaction

THEORETIC BACKGROUND OF TRANSACTION

I have used *transaction* (Taylor, 1971) to describe behavior directed at transforming or reorganizing portions of the environment in accordance with the creative person's internal system. Seward (1963) has called similar behavior "exogenous." Central to the concept of transaction is the idea, "Perceiving is that part of the process of living by which each one of us, from his own particular point of view, creates for himself the world within which he has his life's experiences and through which he strives to gain his satisfactions" (Ittelson and Cantril, 1954). The general psychological implications are embodied in Dewey and Bentley's (1949) early formulation of "transaction," and again in the interpersonal psychiatry of Sullivan (1953). It is implied in Stein's (1956) conceptualization of creativity as a transaction.

PERSONALITY-ENVIRONMENT SYSTEMS

Creativity as viewed here is fundamentally a *transaction* system as opposed to a *reaction* or *interaction* system. The essential characteristic of a *transaction* system is that the source of action originates from within the person (O-R-S) rather than from the environment (S-R-O) or as an interplay between the person and the environment (S-O-R). Also, in a transaction system, the behavioral process as well as the end product is defined by the preexisting internal state or motivational character of the person, while this is untrue in a *reaction* system, and only partly true in an *interaction* system where the behavioral processes and products are largely defined by the environment.

The environment may trigger or facilitate creativity in a transaction system as, for example, with stimulation. But the environmental stimulation is neither necessary, generating, nor defining in transaction as it is in reaction and partially in interaction. In transaction, the response corresponds to the internal perceptions and motivations of the person, while in reaction, the response corresponds to the nature of the environmental stimulus, and for interaction, the response is a function of both the organism and the stimulus. Creativity is an integral part of transaction; conformity, imitation, and reflex type behavior are related to reaction; and functional adaptation is related to interaction. From one point of view, these levels of social action can be described as behavior (reaction), becoming (interaction), and being (transaction).

The transactive personality, therefore, stands in sharp contrast to the reactive personality. In *transaction* the person shapes the environment, while in *reaction* the environment shapes the person. Differences between reactive and transactive persons, of course, are a matter of degree rather than of kind. When both the person and the environment are involved and contribute to the shaping of resulting behavior, *interaction* has occurred. Transaction probably never occurs continuously in a person nor completely in any given instant. Reaction or interaction on the other hand occurs to a much larger extent. The view here is that whereas not all transacting people are creative, all creative people are transacting.

This does not rule out the operation of environment in transaction, but only the ordering relationship between the person and his environment. In transaction, the environment is converted into a form different from its original state.

TRANSACTIONAL MOTIVATION

Creative motivation is seen as a form of perceptual transaction in which the environment becomes altered or reorganized in accordance with personal perceptions. Personal perceptions are viewed as comprising all of the individual's needs, judgments, hypotheses, or perceptually organizing forces that actively exist within the person which can be described as "autonomous motivation" (Lee, 1961).

It was suggested (Taylor, 1971) that initially there is a discrepancy between the inner world of personal perception and the perception of the outer world, between the psychological and the "veridical" environment, especially the social environment. The disparity of the two produces a state of organismic tension which can be reduced in at least one of two ways: either the person alters his personal perceptions to correspond with the external social environment, or the person alters or reorganizes the environment congruent with his personal world resulting in a new environmental organization. The former results in social conformity for the majority largely because of the threat of the social environment. The latter may result in creativity. At least one necessary condition is fulfilled, that of perceptual independence.

We can hypothesize that one of the factors of creative transaction is that the "inner environment" is perceived as being more stable and organized than the "external environment," and in seeking psychological unity, the person is compelled to project his inner world onto the outer world. This assumes the necessary energy and internal resources to effect personal closure in the environment.

Formulating creativity as a perceptual transaction system brings more sharply into focus the person's motivation system. What is creative is not the solution of the problem so much as the reorganization of the environment in accordance with personal patterns of perceptions and motivations. It explains the creative conceptualizations of Einstein, for example, who reputedly said that his theory reflected the way he saw the universe before he learned to speak. It brings the relationship between the individual and the environment into clearer focus, since the attribution of creativity has to take into consideration the person's beliefs, hypotheses, and needs with regard to the environment. Most important, it implies that the person in the Leibnitzean tradition has his own maps, dispositions, and perceptions rather than following the Lockean "empty box" tradition where creating is either serendipitous or produced through external reinforcement schedules.

It is necessary to assess the person-creating-in-the-environment rather than to assess either the creative person or the environment conducive to creativity. From this, also, can be derived differentiated forms of creativity, creative processes, and criteria for identifying creative behavior. The creative person is described here as essentially transactive, that is, capable of actualizing transformation of environmental problems into products compatible with his disposition style. These dispositions include *expressive, technical, inventive, innovative,* and *emergentive* creativity, which are viewed here as perceptual or motivational hypotheses similar to Klein's *Anschauung* (1951).

CREATIVE DISPOSITIONS

The term "creativity" is a highly multiordinal concept, ranging from the spontaneous, expressive drawings of children to the scientific and artistic formulations of Einstein and Picasso. Therefore, conceptually and for research purposes, it is necessary to distinguish between different creativity dispositions, levels, states, or life styles. In an overview of creativity (Taylor, 1960b), five distinct psycholinguistic clusters of usage of the term "creativity" emerge, each involving different psychological processes. Each of these clusters or usages seemed to relate to a different developmental level of creativity, each sufficiently different to suggest that very different processes are involved. Transactional dispositions to creativity include:

Expressive creativity. The first level can be called expressive creativity, the most fundamental form involving independent expression skills. Originality and quality of the product are unimportant. The spontaneous drawings of children are examples of expressive creativity. The important characteristics are spontaneity and freedom which form the foundation upon which more creative talents develop. This form of creativity is generally involved in spontaneous finger painting, free dance, spontaneous writing, and impromptu talks. It is generally the kind of creativity Moreno spoke of in psychodrama or that displayed by Louis Armstrong as an expressively creative musician. Expressive creativity is largely somatic, as in spontaneous dancing, where

> the ideas of the dance come both from the movement, and are in the movement. It has no reference outside of that. A given dance does not have its origin in some thought I might have about a story, a mood, or an expression; rather, the proportions of the dance come from the activity itself . . . so in starting to choreograph, I begin with movements . . . and from that, the dance continues. [Cunningham, in Rosner and Abt, 1972, p. 175]

Technical Creativity. This style, which was earlier termed "productive," is characterized by proficiency in creating products and is essentially at the technical production level. The emphasis is on skill at the expense of expressive spontaneity. It is not essentially concerned with novelty, although it does involve the achievement of a new level of proficiency by the individual. "The astounding productive capacity of this almost utopian nation has filled the pipelines of consumer needs and wants. . . . For business managements have applied the full measure of creativity to production" (Harris, 1959, p. 146). Stradivarius is an excellent example of a technically creative person.

Inventive Creativity. The inventive level is characterized by a display of ingenuity with materials. It involves insight into unusual combinatory relationships between things previously separated, for the purpose of solving old problems in new ways. Creativity at the inventive level does not result in new basic ideas but in new uses of old parts and new ways of seeing old things. Inventive creativity is reflected in the development of novel plots, cartoons, and occurs in all of the typical classical inventions of Edison, Bell, Marconi, and others. In this type of creativity, "the creative product is unrelated to the creator as a person, who in his creative work acts largely as a mediator between externally defined needs and goals. In this kind of creativity, the creator simply operates on some aspect of his environment in such a manner as to produce a novel and appropriate product, but he adds little of himself to the resultant" (MacKinnon, 1963, p. 168).

Innovative Creativity. At the innovative level basic assumptions or principles are understood so that modification through alternate approaches is possible. Innovative creativity is dependent upon the ability to penetrate and understand basic foundational principles and is exemplified by those innovators who are followers of established schools of thought, as exemplified by Jung and Adler, who innovated on Freudian psychology. Another example is Copernicus, who, as Koestler (1964) has pointed out "was neither an original nor even a progressive thinker; he was, as Kepler later remarked, 'interpreting Ptolemy rather than nature.' He clung fanatically to the Aristotelian dogma that all planets must move in perfect circles at uniform speeds; the first impulse of his long labours originated in his discontent with the fact that in the Ptolemaic system they moved in perfect circles but not at uniform speed. It was the grievance of a perfectionist—in keeping with his crabbed, secretive, stingy character (which every Freudian would gleefully identify as the perfect 'anal' type). Once he had taken the Ptolemaic clockwork to pieces, he began to search for a useful hint how to put it together again; he found it in Aristarchus's heliocentric idea which at that time was much in the air. It was not so much a new departure as a last attempt to patch up an outdated machinery by reversing the arrangement of its wheels" (p. 677). Ghiselin (1958) speaks of a level of creativity which brings "further development to an established body of meaning through initiating some advance in its use" (p. 150).

Emergentive Creativity. The most complex form of creativity is considered to be emergentive creativity, involving the most abstract ideational principles or assumptions underlying a body of art or science. In rare instances, an entirely new principle or assumption, around which new schools flourish, emerges at a most fundamental and abstract level. Thus, this highest form of creative power I have called emergentive creativity. The scope of the formulations at this level are reflected in the works of Einstein and Freud in the scientific field, and Picasso and Wright in the field of art. Most people have this level in mind when they speak of creativity, although it represents the smallest but most influential group in the history of the world. What is involved is an ability to absorb the experiences which are commonly provided and from this produce something that is quite different. Wertheimer (1945) described Einstein's conflict in developing the theory of relativity: "In appraising these transformations we must not forget that they took place in view of a gigantic given system. Every step had to be taken against a very strong Gestalt—the traditional structure of physics, which fitted an enormous number of facts, apparently so flawless, so clear that any local change was bound to meet with the resistance of the whole strong and well-articulated structure. This was probably the reason why it took so long a time—seven years—until the crucial advance was made" (p. 232). Emergentive creating is largely individualistic, manifesting itself in highly generative insights.

CREATIVITY STYLES

The creative styles may manifest themselves in various segments of the creative process. This may involve the actualizing ability to initiate a creation, but not develop it further. Many organizations have a small share of "originators" of problems which are left to others to solve. I have termed the initiation of ideas as *endogenous creativity* because the ideas originate from within a person.

Others may be lacking in basic origination of ideas, but once articulated, they can develop these ideas more fully. These are essentially the "development" men of an organization manifesting *epigenous creativity,* or creativity which expands on that which is already created.

Finally, there are those whose actualizing talents lend themselves neither to initiating nor developing but to applying, manifesting originality in the practical utilization of developed ideas or products. I have characterized such persons as exemplifying *exogenous creativity,* or creating upon external sources.

The characteristics hypothesized to be related to transaction include: openness to both the inner and outer world (Rogers, 1954), a highly developed internal system (Klein, 1951), drive (Roe, 1953), internal resources (Guilford, 1968), internal control (Rotter, 1966), and courage (McClelland, 1963).

IMPLICATIONS OF PERSONALITY TRANSACTION

The most important derivative of transaction is the emphasis it places on allowing for the development of autonomous self-regulation. It provides a basis for encouraging the development of authentic individuality with accompanying feelings of self-worth and possibly empathy and tolerance for the transactional fields of others.

Generic Problem

Generally ignored, but considered here to be as important as any part of the creative processes, is the question of the kinds of problems which creative people identify or select. Obviously, they are problems which are keys to larger problems that, if identified, would result in much productive investigation. Therefore, creative problems are strategic, and, if resolved, would be avenues to unlocking other problems or problem areas. They are frequently unrecognized or unstated problems for which an uncanny sensitivity is needed. They are problems which are inherently challenging, puzzling, or formidable. They may be gamelike in nature, solutions of which bring intrinsic pleasure. They are problems that have been avoided, neglected, or rejected. They may be instigated by the presence of contradictory facts, or may involve areas that have never been completed or thoroughly organized. They are important problems for which there is no suitable methodology for investigation.

Creative problem discovering is seen as an abductive ability (Fann, 1970) about which little is yet known. It is suggested here that creative people tend to gravitate toward or formulate strategic questions or problems that may have been neglected or overlooked by others. Probably, the ability to recognize a potentially rich problem area that will open the door to larger problems is a *generic* approach to problem discovery or creativity, that is, an approach that generates additional ideas wherein fruitful outcomes may result. From this point of view, the creative person chooses a problem as a point of departure for fruitfully investigating much larger problems. Going beyond the limits of a problem to solve larger ones may be disturbing to those who like to confine their logical analysis of a problem within boundaries, but it is probably one of the major styles of creative problem formulation. Such problems are generic because they may become seminal to a host of problems that generate from them.

THEORETIC BACKGROUND OF GENERICS

Interest in what we have called generic problems stems from few sources. Charles Peirce (Fann, 1970) worked for twenty years on abductive logic, working backward for an explanatory concept which he felt was the heart of creativity, rather than inductively or deductively forward in merely testing a hypothesis or problem once stated. This ability to "catch" a hypothesis rather than merely test it is generally ignored in the training of most scientists, as noted by Getzels and Csikszentmihalyi (Getzels, 1964; Getzels and Csikszentmihalyi, 1967; Csikszentmihalyi and Getzels, 1971). The general semanticists (Korzybski, 1941; Hayakawa, 1964; Johnson, 1946) have strongly emphasized the important but neglected role played by the "formulation of a problem." Langer (1942) noted that in every era there are "generative" notions which are developed by the very few and which provide a fountain source of generation for most of the resulting ideas of that era.

One way of looking at the formulation of generic problems is by analyzing underlying assumptions popular at various historical periods from the point of view of the complexity of reduced structural factors underlying proposed concepts (Taylor, 1962a). Early "Greco-Roman-Christian" concepts are *monial* attempts to reduce world events to a single "ideal" factor—for example, truth, beauty, power, atom—or to Aristotelian *summum bonum* values. From this we get the quest for the single answer, value element of all things or things at hand. The Renaissance period used a more complex *binial,* or two-point system, usually interaction, such as in Cartesian dualism or Newton's thermodynamic law of force-counter force. The conceptualizations embody knowledge or events as containing rivalry or counteracting "ideal" and "real" forces. The current, or modern, period perhaps ushered in by Hegel assumes a more complex, *trini*al, or three-point base. The idea of thesis, antithesis, and emergent synthesis is clearly contained in the "constructs" work of Marx, Darwin, Freud, and Einstein. The transition has been, therefore, from idealism to realism to construct synthesis.

The relation of the underlying generic formulation to manifest problems is seen here as having the same relation and fruitfulness of the formulation of Lewin (1935) of problems into genotype and its phenotypes. The analogy can be made to the medical model of cause and symptoms, where the cause is the genotype or is generic to the symptoms. It is hypothesized that creative persons tend to focus on generic problems, or conversely, the more generic the problem, the more potentially creative the outcome.

Several essential factors are seen as related to generic problem formulation. These include parturiency, articulation, heuristics, radicality, disparity, and synthesis.

IMPLICATIONS OF GENERICS

The implications of fostering a generic approach to the creative formulation of problems include effective and efficient identification of key problems avoiding the waste of dealing with manifest superficial problems. Generic formulation transfers emphasis from industrial technology to humanistic problems since most problems at a generic level are humanistic or psychological.

Transformation Processes

THEORETIC BACKGROUND TO TRANSFORMATION PROCESSES

The underlying question concerns the nature of the creative process. Even though creativity may be manifest in various forms, is there an underlying pattern? A process can be deduced from a transactional approach which is somewhat similar to Wallas's (1926) early description of the creative process which writers have either accepted, rejected, or modified. Patrick (1937) later attempted empirical verification of Wallas's stages but with little if any success. Important transformation development programs have been instituted by Gordon (1961), Torrance (1962), and Parnes (1971).

DIRECT PROCESSES COMPARED TO TRANSFORMATION PROCESSES

It can be asserted that only simple problems lend themselves to direct solution processes. Complex problems require complex solution processes, or processes which transform these problems into forms that allow for solution. Transformation processes as approaches to rendering problems soluble include reversals, lateral thinking, contrasting, analogy and meta-phor, transpositions, remote associations, and divergent thinking.

SEQUENTIAL CHARACTERISTICS OF TRANSFORMATION

The creative process involves an *exposure* or initiating phase in which the person is perceptually open to the environment and to his thought processes; a *predivergent* phase in which the inputs are directed toward a central reformulation in accordance with transactional forces; a crucial *conversion* phase in which the structure of the inputs is reformulated or converted into a new configuration, the moment of insight; a *postdivergent* phase in which the new organization is revised, elaborated, and developed into a tangible form; and finally, an *expression* or terminating phase in which something new is formulated and released.

The general character of the creative process depends on the degree of initial openness to the environment in the exposure phase, and the degree of transactional manipulation. In general, it is hypothesized that the greater the openness, the greater the creative production. The creative process characterized here is essentially a conversion or conservation process in which environmental inputs are transacted and transformed into environmental outputs. In the following section, the initial exposure phase and the final expression phase will be emphasized as the important terminals of the creative processes.

Exposure Phase. The initial phase can be described as *exposure,* a period in which the environment is perceived, similar to Rogers's "openness." Sensory stimulation to the point of saturation, for example, may be one way of producing psychological openness and initiating the creative process. Exposure is essentially characterized by high receptivity of raw sensory data, deferred judgment, or a posture of open acceptance to infor-mation, cognitive complexity, and a set for unexpected or serendipitous findings.

Principles of perceptual organization (Taylor, 1959, 1960c, 1960d) can be utilized both to understand and to permit increased exposure by avoid-ing premature closures and "hardening of the categories." These principles are largely rooted in the works of Gestalt psychologists (Wertheimer, 1945; Köhler, 1929; and Koffka, 1935). Openness and the ability to assimilate large amounts of complex information can be enhanced if these is a suit-able framework for receiving information. The information will be openly received if it flows into a state of *perceptual homogeneity or grouping, perceptual differentiation or separating,* and *perceptual integration or relating* of information.

Predivergent Phase. The exposure phase is followed by *predivergence,* where the inputs are divergently "imploded" at a relatively rapid rate into a central reformulation. During this phase, the person may no longer be open to environmental perceptions since the assimilation may require the greater psychological portion of the person's capabilities. The phase is characterized by a natural interaction of data, unconscious incubation, induction, and possibly an experience of being overwhelmed with information.

Conversion Phase. A moment of *conversion* follows where insight or perceptual transaction occurs. This phase in which perceptions of the external world are transformed is at the very heart of perceptual transaction and is creative to the extent that the reorganization of the environment is congruent with personal perceptions. This is the "Eureka" phase or moment of reformulation in which reversals, using opposites, lateral thinking, analogies, and metaphors (Dreistadt, 1970) may occur; the suddenness or flash of new ideas in which the familiar may become unfamiliar, and the unfamiliar, familiar.

Postdivergent Phase. Prior to the articulation of the finished product, the new transactional perception is subject to modifications and elaboration, additional personal organizations, or a *postdivergent* phase involving release, formulation, development, and fluency toward restatement. This is a period in which ideas have freedom to take form through deductions and inferences or idealized extrapolations.

Expression Phase. Finally, *expression*, related to communication, implementation, and actualization, terminates the process with, at times, the creative "explosion" of something new. This period of composition generally involves tension, and may require painstaking work. Outputs are generated at an increased rate.

The same processes may be involved in various forms of creativity but with different phases emphasized. For example, expressive spontaneity may emphasize the postdivergent and expressive phases but not so much exposure or conversion; while emergentive originality may emphasize to a larger extent the exposure or openness phase. However, certain processes may be involved in all creativity, for example, psychological openness, divergent thinking ability, field-ground reversal facility, and inner orientation. This phase is enhanced if there is minimal fear of criticism in which partial ideas can be expressed and bounced off people as sounding boards, especially if there is little censorship. It is a period of creative communication, and the principles of general semantics (Korzybski, 1941; Hayakawa, 1964; Johnson, 1946) seem especially relevant to the creative processes as well as to all the components of transactualization (Taylor, 1972b).

IMPLICATIONS OF TRANSFORMATION

There are several implications in the utilization of transformation processes. Complex, basic, and generally ignored problems lend themselves to solution only by transformation where direct approaches are not tenable. Transformation requires greater problem latitude, thereby encouraging divergency and cross-fertilization from other fields. It emphasizes the feasibility and potency of bringing together highly diverse people into effective creative leadership processes in organizations.

Product Generation

The creative product may be as tangible as an invention or as intangible as an idea. The essential question of a creative product is that of criteria. Product criteria can be described in terms of the product itself as an entity, the problem which it resolves, the field in which it is presented, and its out-of-field effects. Of the various qualitative criteria we have used to identify a product in each of these ways, probably the most important is *generation*, or the amount of subsequent research and activities the product engenders.

THEORETIC BACKGROUND OF PRODUCT GENERATION

The most frequently used standards or criteria of creativity include statistical deviations of scores on tests (Terman, 1925; Guilford, Christensen, and Merrifield, 1958; Torrance, 1966; Mednick, 1968), number of citations or number of lines devoted to "famous people" in the literature (Cattell and Butcher, 1968; Galton, 1870), judgments of professionally qualified people (Roe, 1951; Stein, Heinze and Rodgers, 1958; MacKinnon, 1962), generally acknowledged eminence (Freud, 1948a), number of products defined as creative (Rossman, 1935), pursuit of activities assumed to require creative talent (Eiduson, 1958; Rosen, 1955), peer ratings, supervisor ratings, promotion rate, number of patents, and number of publications (Lehman, 1953; Dennis, 1958).

OBJECTIVE PRODUCT CRITERIA AND QUALITATIVE PRODUCT CRITERIA

Creativity criteria of products, one of the more important problems in creativity investigation, most frequently rely on objective product criteria —count, ratings, or judgments. These focus largely on extraproduct considerations, eminence of the person, and quantity of production. What is needed is a qualitative analysis of the creative attributes of the product itself and the effects of the product (Taylor and Knapp, 1971; Taylor and Sandler, 1972).

A CREATIVE PRODUCT INVENTORY

The term product is used in the broad sense which includes the concrete product itself, the effects of the product on the problem, the effect of the product on the field, and its out-of-field or social effects. An inventory of seven clusters of product attributes was developed for use in the evaluation of any creative product. Within each of the criteria, the product is evaluated for degree of effective creativeness (1) as a concrete product, (2) as related to the problem, (3) as related to the field, and (4) for its out-of-field effects. The criteria considered relevant include (somewhat in order of importance) generation, reformulation, originality, relevancy, hedonics, complexity, and condensation. The reliability for evaluating products in terms of these qualitative criteria has been high with trained observers. As summarized in Table 13.1 these seven criteria, each at four levels, were separately named, in some cases arbitrarily, for purposes of assessing products with the use of a Creative Product Inventory (Taylor, 1973a; Taylor and Sandler, 1972) as follows:

1. Generation. Generation refers to the degree to which the product initiates activity in oneself or others as an effect of the product; that is, the extent to which it generates or produces new ideas. Generation, in terms of a concrete product, was described as its *germinal* potential; in terms of the problem, its *fruitfulness;* in terms of the field, its *fertileness;* in terms of out-of-field effects, the amount of *cross-fertilization* it produces.

2. Reformulation. Reformulation refers to the extent to which the product introduces significant change or modification in oneself or others. Reformulation, in terms of a concrete product was related to its *asymmetry* (which empirically produced generative changes); in terms of the problem, the degree of *alteration* to the problem; in terms of the field, the amount of change or *restructuring* it produces; in terms of its out-of-field effects, the degree of *reorganization* that results.

3. Originality. Originality, considered here as less important than generation or reformulation, is evaluated as to the degree of the product's usefulness, uncommonness, or statistical infrequency. Originality for a concrete product was described as its *uniqueness;* as to the problem, its *remoteness* in terms of the solution; as to the field, its *novelty;* and as to its out-of-field effects, its *diffusion* impact.

4. Relevancy. Relevancy has to do with the extent to which the product satisfactorily provides a solution to a problem. In regard to the concrete product, relevancy was described and considered to be inherent in its *functional* potential; in regard to the problem, its *appropriateness;* in regard to the field, its *utility;* and in regard to its out-of-field effects, its general *value.*

5. Hedonics. Hedonics refers to the valence or degree of attraction the product commands. The hedonics of a concrete product was described as its *elegance;* its relation to a problem, its *appreciation;* its relation to the field, its *impact;* and its relation to out-of-field effects, its *popularity.*

TABLE 13.1. Criteria for Evaluating the Creativeness of a Product at Four Different Levels: The Product Itself; The Product's Relation to the Problem; The Effects of the Product in a Field; and The Product's Effects Out-of-Field.

Criteria	Product	Product-problem	Product-field	Product-out-of-Field
1. Generation	Germinal	Fruitfulness	Fertileness	Cross-Fertilization
2. Reformulation	Assymetry	Alteration	Restructuring	Reorganization
3. Originality	Uniqueness	Remoteness	Novelty	Diffusion
4. Relevancy	Function	Appropriateness	Utility	Value
5. Hedonics	Elegance	Appreciation	Impact	Popularity
6. Complexity	Completeness	Adequacy	Comprehensiveness	Universality
7. Condensation	Compactness	Reduction	Integration	Unification

6. Complexity. Complexity refers to the degree of range, depth, scope, or intricacy of the information contained in the product. Complexity in terms of a concrete product was described as its relative *completeness,* related to information quantity; in terms of the problem, its *adequacy;* in terms of the field, its *comprehensiveness;* and in terms of its out-of-field effects, its *universality.*

7. Condensation. Condensation refers to the degree to which the product simplifies, unifies, and integrates. The condensation of a concrete product was described as its *compactness;* in its relation to the problem, the amount of *reduction;* in its relation to the field, its degree of *integration;* and in its out-of-field relation, the amount of *unification* it produces.

IMPLICATIONS OF PRODUCT GENERATION

The most immediate implication is that the creativeness of a product and its effects are evaluated rather than the person's eminence or amount of productivity. The emphasis is on the qualities of the product itself rather than the quantity of production or fame of the creator. It allows for an evaluation of the outcome of new products.

Climate Stimulation

The environment of the creative person, including his personal, organizational, social, and cultural climate, is characterized by high and unusual sensory stimulation. This raises the problem of what kind of climate will facilitate creativity.

The effects of sensory stimulation (Taylor, 1970a, 1972a) can be contrasted with those of sensory deprivation (Zubek, 1969), which have been intensively studied. One of the effects of a creative product is to produce stimulation in the environment. Such motion or stimulation produces an attraction or novelty for others and may facilitate their creativity. Stimulation is not as necessary for creative transactualization as transaction, generics, transformation, and generation, but it facilitates these processes. There are several reasons why transactualization occurs best in an environment which is stimulating. First, it is easier to redesign an environment that is in motion. Second, such an environment allows transformations to occur. Finally, stimulation is congruent with change.

THEORETIC BACKGROUND OF CREATIVE CLIMATES

The following is a partial list of conditions in the environment which are reported in the literature as tending to induce or facilitate creative behavior: (1) reduction of frustration-producing factors in the environment; (2) elimination of win-lose competition; (3) provisions for support; (4) encouragement of divergent thinking; (5) emphasis on problem solving and working through of conflict rather than on generating a harmonious atmosphere; (6) general maintenance of an open environmental structure; (7) minimization of coercion; (8) minimization of enforcement of behavior norms; (9) elimination of environmental threats; (10) provision of encouragement; (11) aiding the person to understand himself and his divergence; (12) allowing free communication; (13) acceptance of fantasy; (14) withholding of frustration at unusual questions; (15) exposure to the risk-taking opinion of others; (16) group discussion and comparison of ideas; (17) homogeneous grouping of individuals for group interaction; and (18) competent group leadership.

The importance of environmental stimulation has been emphasized by Berlyne (1960), Denenberg and Bell (1960), Murphy (1951), and Fiske and Maddi (1961). My research has indicated that *stimulation* is an important phenomenon in inducing openness and creativity in a person (Taylor, 1970a, 1972a). In these studies environmental stimulation, consisting of several minutes of simultaneous sensory stimulation, was produced in a laboratory. Comparison of before and after drawings and a creativity test (the Guilford Consequences Test) showed that following stimulation the subjects' drawings were more open, aesthetic, and creative.

STIMULATION COMPARED WITH REINFORCEMENT

It is important to compare and contrast the effects of stimulation with reinforcement theory. In reinforcement contingency schedules, the outcomes of behavior are usually predictable and specifically shaped. In stimulation, behavior is initiated with unpredictable but possibly creative outcomes. Both stimulation and reinforcement involve creative use of the environment for producing novel behavior. In the latter, predictable outcomes are achieved through rewards; in the former, the purpose is to arouse, initiate, and facilitate organismically-directed behavior that will actualize unique potentials. The problems concerned in fully comparing reinforcement and stimulation as creative uses of the environment go beyond the scope of this chapter and therefore will not be pursued further at this time.

IMPLICATIONS OF CLIMATE STIMULATION

The fundamental implication of stimulation is that it releases, triggers, or initiates creativity in individuals. What is initiated is person-directed behavior or transactional motivation.

Transactualization and Creative Dispositions

We have defined creative transactualization as involving a person who transacts or designs his environment by transforming generic problems into generating products in a stimulating climate. The dispositions to creativity

TABLE 13.2.   *Relation Between Creative Dispositions and*
Transactualization.

Creative Transactualization				
Creative Personality Transaction	Creative Problem Generics	Creative Process Transformation	Creative Product Generation	Creative Climate Stimulation
1. Expressive	Somatic	Spontaneity	Motor	Sensory
2. Technical	Skill	Refinement	Craft	Resource
3. Inventive	Combinations	Ingenuity	Utility	Enrichment
4. Innovative	Implication	Flexibility	Subsystem	Development
5. Emergentive	Assumption	Originality	System	Ideation

include expressive, technical, inventive, innovative, and emergentive. The relationships between each of the dispositions and the transactualization components are indicated in Table 13.2. We have recently developed an instrument, The Creative Behavior Disposition Scale, which correlates with various other creativity tests as well as various parts of the Personal Orientation Inventory, which measures aspects of self-actualization (Taylor, 1973a). From this it is possible to measure five distinct forms of creative transactualization dispositions:

1. Expressive Transactualization. The disposition to creative expressive transactualization involves designing one's environment by spontaneously transforming problems at a somatic level into motor products stimulated by sensory inputs. This level of creative transactualization is exemplified by Isadora Duncan dancing spontaneously to music.

2. Technical Transactualization. The disposition to creative technical transactualization involves designing the environment by transforming problems through repeated refinement into a crafted product or outcome stimulated by resources such as good materials or equipment in the environment. This level is exemplified by a musician such as Nicolo Paganini seasoned by many rehearsals.

3. Inventive Transactualization. The disposition to creative inventive transactualization involves designing the environment by ingeniously transforming materials through various combinations into utilitarian products stimulated by enriched facilities. An example of a creative person at this level is a conductor such as Arturo Toscanini who combined the various elements of an orchestra into a unique symphonic rendition.

4. Innovative Transactualization. The disposition to creative innovative transactualization involves designing the environment by flexibly transforming the implications of a problem into subsystem products in an environment that supports development. Arnold Schoenberg is an example of a composer at this level whose atonal compositions were an innovation to the world of music.

5. *Emergentive Transactualization.* The disposition to creative emergentive transactualization involves designing the environment through original transformation of basic assumptions into products in the form of a system in an ideationally stimulating environment. This level is exemplified by a composer who originated a new form of music, such as Beethoven or Bach.

Creative Leadership Transactualization

A creative leader is one who strives with his followers to produce social changes characterized by outcomes which will be described shortly. He is creative in the same way or ways that others are creative, but the creativity is expressed through leadership rather than, for example, in science or art. A leader stimulates and manipulates followers, but a creative leader's manipulations are directed toward social changes in the environment or some organization of human endeavor in a way that is uncommon or unique; he solves problems effectively, and transforms some part of society. The utilization of others to effect creative outcomes is regarded here as a *social transaction* (Taylor, 1970*b*).

CREATIVE LEADERSHIP

We have recently developed a theoretic model of creative leadership which allows us to understand the basic components involved in transforming a psychosocial situation into creative leadership. Initially there is a creative leader who has a highly formulated internal system as to how things ought to be. He is immediately confronted by a myriad of conventional obstacles which prevent the externalization of this internal system into the psychosocial environment. It is necessary, therefore, first to identify the underlying *un*creative generic problem which holds all of these psychosocial obstacles together. Following this, the *un*creative psychosocial generic problem underlying these obstacles is transformed by identifying a creative generic problem or notion (such as passive resistance). This generic problem subsequently generates a new and creative psychosocial system, allowing for the externalization and realization of the initial internal system.

The climate for investigating creative leadership contrasts with the general theoretic tendency of psychology to study the effects of the environment on the person. From the point of view of transactualization, it is more appropriate to view the direction from the person to the environment, to understand the effects of behavior on the environment. From the point of view of leadership, the emphasis would be on the persons involved— the leaders and followers—who produce social changes rather than the environment.

Creative change is produced by reversing the direction of effect from person to environment rather than from environment to person. It is posited here that products having creative characteristics resulting from creative processes initiated by creative problems are formulated and identified by creative persons who produce forces that lead to creative social change. When the processes of transactualization are understood, the manner in which changes in society come about through creative leadership will be understood.

IMPLICATIONS OF CREATIVE LEADERSHIP TRANSACTUALIZATION

Creative leadership transactualization is a dynamic synthesis of creativity and leadership. The inherent value involved in creative leadership is the assumption of responsibility for creatively solving problems in the environment or for creatively changing social organizations. The goal is to unleash creative ability for resolving stressful environmental problems including ecology, population, and interpersonal relations. Transactional creative leadership provides society with mechanisms for producing environmental design and effective organizational change. The direct implication is that creative leadership transactualization increases the creativity of followers and organizations and establishes a basis for "creatorship."

PHASES OF CREATIVE LEADERSHIP

More recently, creative leadership has been formulated in terms of actual creative leadership behavior (Dorn, Taylor, and Sandler, 1973). This involves developing behavior in the following eight phases: (1) *assessment* of relevant information in regard to an initial situation; (2) *problem formulation* or the search for generic problems; (3) *problem transformation* or reformulation of the problem into a form that allows for creative solutions; (4) *goal setting* or statement of objectives and purposes; (5) *planning and organizing* which is a consideration of resources, alternatives, constraints, and system factors; (6) *evaluation and control* emphasizing feedback systems and methods of measurement; (7) *implementation* of the plans to bring the task at hand to fruition; and (8) *reassessment* in which the success of the outcome is evaluated to determine if the cycle needs to be repeated.

Summary

Although research in creativity has increased over the past several decades, stimulated by Guilford's early paper, many obstacles still exist, both in society and in conventional psychology. There is a need for systematic creativity investigations. A systematic approach to creativity, involving personality transaction, generic problems, transformation processes, product generation, and environmental stimulation, has been examined in a theory of creativity described as transactualization.

Each of these creativity areas—person, problem, process, product, and climate—has many levels and many characteristics, but it is suggested that they operate as a system of interconnected, interfaced components with important interaction effects. For example, transaction, which is organismically directed behavior, may be triggered by environmental stimulation; and the creative process may be triggered by the discovery of a creative problem.

The major hypothesis of the research now in progress is that creativity occurs to the extent that the components of transactualization occur. Our definition of creativity as a system is that *creativity involves a transacting person who transforms generic problems into generating products, facilitated by a stimulating environment.* Although the theory is conceptualized in relation to creativity, it is also relevant to creative leadership processes.

References

Adler, A. *Study of organ inferiority and its psychical compensation.* New York: Nervous and Mental Diseases Publishing Co., 1917.

Agha, M. F. The mechanics of creativity. In P. Smith (Ed.), *Creativity: An examination of the creative process.* New York: Hastings House, 1959.

Anderson, H. H. Creativity as personality development. In H. H. Anderson (Ed.), *Creativity and its cultivation.* New York: Harper, 1959.

Arnheim, R. *Art and visual perception: A psychology of the creative eye.* Berkeley: University of California Press, 1954.

Arnheim, R. *Visual thinking.* Berkeley: University of California Press, 1969.

Berlyne, D. *Conflict, arousal and curiosity.* New York: McGraw-Hill, 1960.

Cannon, W. B. The role of chance in discovery. *Scientific Monthly,* 1940, *50,* 204–209.

Cattell, R. B., and Butcher, H. J. *The prediction of achievement and creativity.* Indianapolis: Bobbs-Merrill, 1968.

Csikszentmihalyi, M., and Getzels, J. W. Discovery-oriented behavior and the originality of creative products: A study with artists. *Journal of Personality and Social Psychology,* 1971, *19,* 47–52.

Denenberg, V. H., and Bell, R. W. Critical periods for the effects of infantile experience on adult learning. *Science,* 1960, *131,* 227–228.

Dennis, W. The age decrement in outstanding scientific contributors: Fact or artifact. *American Psychologist,* 1958, *13,* 457–460.

Dewey, J. *Art as experience.* New York: Minton Balch, 1934.

Dewey, J., and Bentley, A. F. *Knowing and the known.* Boston: Beacon Press, 1949.

Dorn, R. C., Taylor, I. A., and Sandler, B. E. Eight phases in the creative leadership cycle. Unpublished manuscript, Center for Creative Leadership, Greensboro, N.C., 1973.

Dreistadt, R. Reversing, using opposites, negativism, and aggressiveness in creative behavior in science and philosophy. *Psychology*, 1970, 7, 38–63.

Durkheim, E. Representations individuelles et representations collectives. *Rev. de Metaphysique*, 1898, 6, 274–302.

Eccles, J. C. The physiology of imagination. *Scientific American*, 1958, 199, 135–146.

Eiduson, B. T. Artist and non-artist: A comparative study. *Journal of Personality*, 1958, 26, 13–28.

Fairbairn, W. R. D. Prolegomena to a psychology of art. *British Journal of Psychology*, 1938, 28, 288–303.

Fann, K. T. *Peirce's theory of abduction*. The Hague: Martinus Nijhoff, 1970.

Fiske, D. W., and Maddi, S. R. *Functions of varied experience*. Homewood, Ill.: Dorsey Press, 1961.

Freud, S. *Leonardo da Vinci*. Translated by A. A. Brill. London: Routledge and Kegan Paul, 1948. (*a*)

Freud, S. The relation of the poet to day dreaming (1908). In *Collected papers*. Vol. 4. Translated by J. Riviere. London: Hogarth Press, 1948. (*b*)

Galton, F. *Hereditary genius: An inquiry into its laws and consequences*. New York: Appleton, 1870.

Galton, F. *Inquiries into human faculty and its development*. New York: E. P. Dutton, 1911.

Getzels, J. W. Creative thinking, problem-solving, and instruction. In E. Hilgard (Ed.), *Theories of learning and instruction*. 63rd Yearbook of the N. S. S. E., Part I. Chicago: University of Chicago Press, 1964.

Getzels, J. W., and Csikszentmihalyi, M. Scientific creativity. *Science Journal*, Sept. 1967, 80–84.

Ghiselin, B. Ultimate criteria for two levels of creativity. In C. W. Taylor (Ed.), *The Second (1957) University of Utah Research Conference on the Identification of Creative Scientific Talent*. Salt Lake City: University of Utah Press, 1958.

Goldstein, K. *The organism: A holistic approach to biology: Derived from pathological data in man*. New York: American Book, 1939.

Gordon, W. J. J. *Synectics: The development of creative capacity*. London: Collier-Macmillan, 1961.

Guilford, J. P. *Intelligence, creativity, and their educational implications*. San Diego: Robert K. Knapp, 1968.

Guilford, J. P., Christensen, P. R., and Merrifield, P. R. *Consequences: Manual for administration, scoring, and interpretation*. Beverly Hills, Calif.: Sheridan Psychological Services, 1958.

Gutman, H. The biological roots of creativity. In R. L. Mooney and T. A. Razik (Eds.), *Explorations in creativity*. New York: Harper & Row, 1967.

Harris, R. A. Creativity in marketing. In P. Smith (Ed.), *Creativity: An examination of the creative process*. New York: Hastings House, 1959.

Hayakawa, S. I. *Language in thought and action*. New York: Harcourt, Brace, & World, 1964.

Hersch, C. The cognitive functioning of the creative person: A developmental analysis. In M. Bloomberg (Ed.), *Creativity: Theory and research*. New Haven, Conn.: College & University Press, 1973.

Hirsch, N. O. M. *Genius and creative intelligence*. Cambridge, Mass.: Science-Art Publishers, 1931.

Hutchinson, E. D. *How to think creatively*. New York: Abingdon-Cokesbury, 1949.

Ittelson, W. H., and Cantril, H. *Perception: A transactional approach*. Garden City, N.J.: Doubleday, 1954.

Johnson, W. *People in quandaries.* New York: Harper, 1946.

Jung, C. G. *Two essays on analytical psychology.* Translated by H. G. and C. F. Baynes. New York: Dodd, Mead, 1928.

Klein, G. S. The personal world through perception. In R. R. Blake and G. V. Ramsey (Eds.), *Perception: An approach to personality.* New York: Ronald Press, 1951.

Koestler, A. *The act of creation.* New York: Macmillan, 1964.

Koffka, K. *Principles of Gestalt psychology.* New York: Harcourt, 1935.

Köhler, W. *Gestalt psychology.* New York: H. Liveright, 1929.

Korzybski, A. *Science and sanity: An introduction to non-aristotelian systems and general semantics.* 2nd ed. Lancaster, Penn.: Science Press, 1941.

Kretschmer, E. *The psychology of men of genius.* Translated by R. B. Cattell. New York: Harcourt Brace, 1931.

Kris, E. *Psychoanalytic explorations in art.* New York: International Universities Press, 1952.

Künkel, F. and Dickerson, R. E. *How character develops.* New York: Scribner's, 1947.

Langer, S. *Philosophy in a new key.* Cambridge, Mass.: Harvard University Press, 1942.

Lee, D. Autonomous motivation. *Journal of Humanistic Psychology,* 1961, *1,* 12–22.

Lehman, H. C. *Age and achievement.* Princeton, N.J.: Princeton University Press, 1953.

Lewin, K. *A dynamic theory of personality: Selected papers.* New York: McGraw-Hill, 1935.

MacKinnon, D. W. The personality correlates of creativity: A study of American architects. In G. S. Nielsen (Ed.), *Proceedings of the XIV International Congress of Applied Psychology.* Vol. 2. Copenhagen: Munksgaard, 1962.

MacKinnon, D. W. Identifying and developing creativity. *Journal of Secondary Education,* 1963, *38,* 166–174.

Maslow, A. H. *Motivation and personality.* New York: Harper & Row, 1954.

Maslow, A. H. Creativity in self-actualizing people. In H. H. Anderson (Ed.), *Creativity and its cultivation.* New York: Harper, 1959.

Maslow, A. H. Lessons from the peak-experiences. *Journal of Humanistic Psychology,* 1962, *2,* 9–18.

May, R. The nature of creativity. In H. H. Anderson (Ed.), *Creativity and its cultivation.* New York: Harper & Row, 1959.

McClelland, D. C. The calculated risk: An aspect of scientific performance. In C. W. Taylor and F. Barron (Eds.), *Scientific creativity: Its recognition and development.* New York: Wiley, 1963.

McLean, F. C. The happy accident. *Scientific Monthly,* 1941, *53,* 61–70.

Mednick, S. A. The Remote Associates Test. *Journal of Creative Behavior,* 1968, *2,* 213–214.

Mumford, L. *The myth of the machine: The pentagon of power.* New York: Harcourt Brace Jovanovich, 1970.

Murphy, G. *An introduction to psychology.* New York: Harper, 1951.

Osborn, A. F. *Applied imagination: Principles and procedures of creative problem solving.* (Rev. ed.) New York: Scribner's, 1953.

Parnes, S. J. Do you really understand brainstorming? In S. J. Parnes and H. F. Harding (Eds.), *A source book for creative thinking.* New York: Scribner's, 1962.

Parnes, S. J. Creativity: Developing human potential. *Journal of Creative Behavior,* 1971, *5,* 19–36.

Patrick, C. Creative thought in artists. *Journal of Psychology,* 1937, *4,* 35–73.

Prince, G. M. *The practice of creativity: A manual for dynamic group problem solving.* New York: Harper & Row, 1970.

Rank, O. *Art and artists.* Translated by C. F. Atkinson. New York: Knopf, 1932.

Riessman, F. *The culturally deprived child.* New York: Harper & Row, 1962.

Roe, A. A psychological study of eminent physical scientists. *Genetic Psychology Monograph,* 1951, *43,* 121–239.

Roe, A. *The making of a scientist.* New York: Dodd, Mead, 1953.

Rogers, C. R. Toward a theory of creativity. *ETC: A Review of General Semantics,* 1954, *11,* 249–260.

Rogers, C. R. The concept of the fully functioning person. *Psychotherapy,* 1963, *1,* 17–26.

Rosen, J. C. The Barron-Welsch Art Scale as a predictor of originality and level of ability among artists. *Journal of Applied Psychology,* 1955, *39,* 366–367.

Rosner, S., and Abt, L. E. (Eds.) *The creative experience.* New York: Dell, 1972.

Rossman, J. A study of the childhood, education and age of 710 inventors. *Journal of the Patent Office Society,* 1935, *17,* 411–421.

Rothbart, H. A. *Cybernetic creativity.* New York: Speller, 1972.

Rotter, J. B. Generalized expectancies for internal versus external control of reinforcement. *Psychological Monographs,* 1966, *80*(1, Whole No. 609).

Schafer, R. Regression in the service of the ego. In G. Lindzey (Ed.), *Assessment of human motives.* New York: Rinehart, 1958.

Sessions, R. The composer and his message. In B. Ghiselin (Ed.), *The creative process: A symposium.* Berkeley: University of California Press, 1954.

Seward, J. P. The structure of functional autonomy. *American Psychologist,* 1963, *18,* 703–710.

Sharpe, E. F. Certain aspects of sublimation and delusion. *International Journal of Psychoanalysis,* 1930, *11,* 12–23.

Sinott, E. W. The creativeness of life. In H. H. Anderson (Ed.), *Creativity and its cultivation.* New York: Harper & Row, 1959.

Stein, M. I. A transactional approach to creativity. In C. W. Taylor (Ed.), *The 1955 University of Utah Research Conference on the Identification of Creative Scientific Talent.* Salt Lake City: University of Utah Press, 1956.

Stein, M. I. Creativity and culture. In R. L. Mooney and T. A. Razik (Eds.), *Explorations in creativity.* New York: Harper & Row, 1967.

Stein, M. I., Heinze, S. J., and Rodgers, R. R. Creativity and/or success: A study in value conflict. In C. W. Taylor (Ed.), *The Second (1957) Research Conference on the Identification of Creative Scientific Talent.* Salt Lake City: University of Utah Press, 1958.

Sullivan, H. S. *The interpersonal theory of psychiatry.* New York: Norton, 1953.

Taylor, I. A. Psychological roots of visual communication: Research into the properties of visual symbols. *Journal of the American Society of Training Directors,* 1959, *13,* 34–42.

Taylor, I. A. Creative perception in art education. *NYSATA Newsletter,* 1960, *10,* 5–6. (*a*)

Taylor, I. A. The nature of the creative process. In P. Smith (Ed.), *Creativity: An examination of the creative process.* New York: Hastings House, 1960. (*b*)

Taylor, I. A. Perception and visual communication. In *Research principles and practices in visual communication.* Publication of the Dept. of Audiovisual Instruction. Washington, D.C.: NEA, 1960, 51–70. (*c*)

Taylor, I. A. Psychological aspects of visual communication. In E. Whitney (Ed.), *Symbology: The use of symbols in visual communications.* New York: Hastings House, 1960. (*d*)

Taylor, I. A. Similarities in the structure of extreme social attitudes. *Psychological Monographs*, 1960, *74*(2, Whole No. 489). (*e*)

Taylor, I. A. Creativity research for future creativity. Conference proceedings. In J. L. Steinberg, (Ed.), *Implications of creativity research*. Los Angeles: Los Angeles State College and Chouinard Art Institute, 1962. (*a*)

Taylor, I. A. Further studies in the similarities and structure of extreme social attitudes. Paper presented at the meeting of the California State Psychological Association, San Diego, December, 1962. (*b*)

Taylor, I. A. Emphatic communication through nonverbal symbols in creative and noncreative subjects. Paper presented at the meeting of the American Psychological Association, Los Angeles, 1964.

Taylor, I. A. Creative production in gifted young adults through simultaneous sensory stimulation. *Gifted Child Quarterly*, 1970, *14*, 46–55. (*a*)

Taylor, I. A. In search of creative leadership: Creative leadership as social transaction. In B. J. Gantz (Chm.), Creative leadership in organized human endeavor. Symposium presented at the American Psychological Association, Miami Beach, September, 1970. (*b*)

Taylor, I. A. A transactional approach to creativity and its implications for education. *Journal of Creative Behavior*, 1971, *5*, 190–198.

Taylor, I. A. The effects of sensory stimulation on divergent and convergent thinking. *Abstract Guide of XXth Congress of Psychology*, Tokyo, 1972. (*a*)

Taylor, I. A. Patterns of general semantics, perception, and creativity. *ETC: A Review of General Semantics*, 1972, *29*, 123–132. (*b*)

Taylor, I. A. A theory of creative transactualization. *Creative Education Foundation*, Buffalo, N.Y.: Occasional Paper, 1972, No. 8. (*c*)

Taylor, I. A. The measurement of creative transactualization: A scale to measure behavioral dispositions to creativity. Paper presented at the meeting of the Southeastern Psychological Association, April, 1973. Published by *The Journal of Creative Behavior*, 1974, *8*(2), 114–115. (*a*)

Taylor, I. A. Psychological sources of creativity. In Z. A. Piotrowski (Chm.), Psychological origins of creativity: A clinical analysis. Symposium presented at the meeting of the American Psychological Association, Montreal, August, 1973.

Taylor, I. A., and Knapp, M. W. Creative artistic production of chronic schizophrenics through simultaneous sensory stimulation. *Proceedings of the 79th Annual Convention of the American Psychological Association*, 1971, *6*, 411–412.

Taylor, I. A., and Paperte, F. Current theory and research in the effects of music on human behavior. *Journal of Aesthetics and Art Criticism*, 1958, *17*, 251–258.

Taylor, I. A., and Sandler, B. E. Use of a creative product inventory for evaluating products of chemists. *Proceedings of the 80th Annual Convention of the American Psychological Association*, 1972, *7*, 311–312.

Terman, L. M. Genetic studies of genius. *Mental and physical traits of a thousand gifted children*. Vol. 1. Palo Alto, Calif.: Stanford University Press, 1925.

Torrance, E. P. *Guiding creative talent*. Englewood Cliffs, N.J.: Prentice-Hall, 1962.

Torrance, E. P. *Torrance tests of creative thinking: Norms—technical manual*. Princeton, N.J.: Personnel Press, 1966.

Wallas, G. *The art of thought*. New York: Harcourt, Brace, 1926.

Weber, J. P. *The psychology of art*. Translated by J. A. Elias. New York: Dell, 1969.

Wertheimer, M. *Productive thinking*. New York: Harper, 1945.

Zubek, J. P. (Ed.) *Sensory deprivation: Fifteen years of research*. New York: Appleton-Century-Crofts, 1969.

14. Creativity: Prospects and Issues

J. W. Getzels

WHATEVER THE PROSPECTS and issues in the field of creativity, there is one issue on which there is general agreement: creativity is a subject deserving the most vigorous systematic inquiry. As Terman said in the opening paragraph of his monumental *Genetic Studies of Genius* in 1925, "The origin of genius, the natural laws of its development, and the environmental influences by which it may be affected for good or ill, are scientific problems of almost unequaled importance for human welfare" (p. VII). A quarter century later Guilford directed his influential address on creativity at the American Psychological Association toward disputing Terman's conceptual and methodological assumptions, but he too insisted on what hardly needs insistence any longer: "the importance of the quest for knowledge about creative disposition" (1950, p. 446).

The investigation of creativity may be divided historically into three overlapping periods, each period marked by a salient emphasis: "genius," "giftedness," and "creativity." Systematic work on the problem was initiated in 1869 by the publication of Galton's *Hereditary Genius: An Inquiry into Its Laws and Consequences.* In the hundred years since then the inquiry shifted from the study of genius defined, as Galton had, by recognized achievement to the study of giftedness defined by mental tests, and from study of giftedness to the study of creativity defined by a wide range of criteria including recognized achievement and mental tests.

The investigation of genius persisted into the first part of the twentieth century; it is reflected in the nearly hundred studies on the subject in the six years following the reissue of *Hereditary Genius* in 1914 (Getzels and Dillon, 1973). With the increasing popularity of the intelligence metric and the publication of Terman's studies of highly intelligent children in the 20s, the research emphasis turned from genius to giftedness. By

World War II, genius ceased to be a major focus of inquiry and was replaced by a vast amount of work on highly intelligent children. Although, as Miles (1954) pointed out, the essential portrait of such children had been drawn by 1925–1930 and was not changed substantially thereafter, a multitude of investigations continued to discover and rediscover what had already been known for a generation.

In the 1950s the research emphasis shifted once more—from giftedness as measured by the intelligence test to creativity. While six percent of the references in a bibliography on giftedness for 1950–60 (Gowan, 1961) dealt with creativity, its successor for 1960–1964 (Gowan, 1965) listed fifty percent of its titles under creativity. The shift was prepared for by a number of circumstances, among which were the redundancy of the work with the intelligence metric, the needs of science, industry, business, and the arts, and the appearance of several provocative clinical studies of scientists and artists (such as Roe, 1946, 1953). But it was undoubtedly Guilford's address reformulating the problems of creativity and offering new methods for its study that sparked the explosion of work. Issues that had long lain dormant—issues of definition and criteria, theory and procedure—were opened to exploration; almost as many studies appeared in an eighteen month period a dozen years after the address as had appeared altogether in the quarter century before.

Definitions and Criteria

There is no universally agreed upon definition of creativity—any more than there is of intelligence. In general, the most widely applied conceptions are of three sorts, depending on the relative emphasis given to the product, the process, or the experience (Getzels and Madaus, 1969). Thus some definitions are formulated in terms of a *manifest product,* which is novel and useful. MacKinnon (1962), for example, suggests that the criterion is a statistically infrequent response or idea that is adaptive and sustained to fruition. Other definitions are formulated in terms of an *underlying process,* which is divergent yet fruitful. Ghiselin (1952) speaks of creativity as a process of change and development in the psychic life of an individual leading to invention. Still other definitions are formulated in terms of a *subjective experience,* which is inspired and immanent. Maslow (1963), for one, insists on the importance of the flash of insight—the transcendent sensation itself—without reference to whether it will ever result in anything tangible. Creativity resides not in the "inspired product" but in the "inspired moment." Getzels (1964) has attempted to deal with creativity along somewhat different lines, giving primacy to the nature of the problem rather than the solution. The significant element in creative performance is the envisagement of the creative problem, for it is the fruitful question to which the novel solution is the response.

None of these conceptions of creativity is immune from the objection that each omits some characteristic vital in the others, and so an omnibus definition has been proposed: thinking may be called creative if (1) the product has novelty and value either for the thinker or the culture, (2) the thinking is unconventional, (3) it is highly motivated and persistent or of great intensity, and (4) the problem was initially vague and undefined so that part of the task was to formulate the problem itself (Newell et al., 1962). An omnibus definition has the advantage of inclusiveness but the disadvantage of being an inventory without a unifying rationale.

The criteria and measures of creativity are as varied as the conceptions and definitions. To be sure, during the past quarter century the conceptions and definitions, the criteria and the measures, have both been broadened and sharpened. Nonetheless, the diversity of definitions and criteria represent a critical issue. What *is* an appropriate index of creativity? Among the most commonly used criteria (Getzels and Csikszentmihalyi, 1966) are:

Achievement. An attempt is made to identify achievements that are manifestly creative. The Nobel Prize or some other mark of outstanding accomplishment is taken as an index that hardly anyone would dispute (Ghiselin, 1952).

Rating. It is assumed that a person who has had an opportunity to observe another person can provide a sound judgment of his inventiveness and originality, and so evaluations by peers, supervisors, and teachers have been used as a criterion of creativity (Drevdahl, 1964).

Intelligence. Performance on intelligence tests is the most widely used and best validated index of mental functioning. Since creativity is a mental function, a superior IQ has been taken as a criterion (Terman, 1925).

Personality. Characteristics of personality are evaluated in relation to an empirically derived or a priori profile of the "creative personality," and the closeness of fit is used as a criterion (Cattell and Drevdahl, 1955; Domino, 1970).

Biographical correlates. Certain descriptive items in a person's history are related to his creative performance and are then used to predict others' future performance (C. Taylor and Ellison, 1964; Schaefer, 1969).

Creativity Tests. Although attempts to assess aspects of creativity through tests have a long history, Guilford's divergent thinking instruments inspired a variety of devices. Among the many tests are: Remote Associates Test (Mednick and Mednick, 1964), Ingenius Solutions to Problems Test (Flanagan, 1958), A. C. Test of Creative Ability (Buhl, 1960), Torrance

Tests of Creative Thinking (Torrance, 1966) and numerous other devices like ink-blots, drawings, thematic apperception tests, and so on.

The variety of definitions and criteria is at once a bane and a virtue. On the other hand, the diversity instigates observations of such different kinds and the communication is in such different vocabularies that work in the field is fragmented. But on the other hand, the diversity of conceptions and methods opens to exploration aspects of creativity which might otherwise be shut from view by premature closure on a single conception and method.

Theories and Procedures

Perhaps the fundamental and most critical issue throughout the course of inquiry into creative thinking has been the problem of theoretical and procedural strategy. The issue may be raised most briefly in dichotomous terms, although this runs the danger of oversimplification which should be avoided.

There are those who begin from the premise that the focus of effort must be on the collection of reliable observations and data. The formulation of theory is as yet premature and diversionary, and in any case cannot be done without a base in data. And there are those who begin with the opposed premise that the focus of effort must be on theoretical work in the construction of heuristic conceptions. The collection of data without a base in such conceptions leads only to "blind" empiricism, as they say, and in any case data cannot be collected without recourse to *some* framework.

The first group points to the possible biases of current theories. They agree with MacLeod's (1949) general position regarding research procedures, urging the "deliberate suspension of all implicit and explicit assumptions . . . which might bias our observation" (p. 194). The question that must be raised regarding creativity is "What is there?" without regard to Why, Whence, or Wherefore. To proceed otherwise is to invite biases from theory which predetermine what is seen.

Several of MacLeod's categories of theoretical bias are illustrative of the more general point. There is, for example, "the organism centered bias" where the determinants of behavior are defined as conditions of the organism or as forces like needs, attitudes, or dispositions. Why is one creative? Because one has a disposition for curiosity. There is "the genetic bias" where a present activity is sought in the forces which operated at an earlier period rather than those operating at the time of the activity. The question, Why is one creative?, is answered by a "because" pointing back to early childhood. There is "the sociological bias" where the human activity becomes defined by a set of institutional structures having reality for the scientific observer but not necessarily for the individual observed. The question, Why is one creative?, is answered by a "because" of a presumed situational condition.

The second group does not deny the possibility of bias. They maintain that conceptual and theoretical bias is inevitable. The observing, perceiving, thinking organism cannot proceed without an assumptive base. One cannot look at everything, and so one must select what to look at on some grounds. If one set of assumptions is suspended, another set will sneak in anyway, unbeknownst to the observer. From this point of view, instead of suspending theory, which is impossible—the language one chooses to use is itself already "theoretical"—one should proceed within the framework of consciously held theory. In Neal Miller's words,

> Pure empiricism is a delusion. A theorylike process is inevitably involved in drawing boundaries around certain parts of the flux of experience to define observable events and in the selection of events that are observed. Since multitudinous events could be observed and an enormous number of relationships could be determined among all of these events, gathering all the facts with no bias from theory is utterly impossible. Scientists are forced to make a drastic selection, either unconsciously on the basis of perceptual habits and the folklore and linguistic categories of the culture, or consciously on the basis of explicitly formulated theory. [1959, p. 200]

The juxtaposition of the two views probably draws the issue too sharply, but that the issue exists is certain. In any event, whether one holds to the one view, to the other, or as is more likely to some uneasy view between them, there is no dearth of theories of creativity, which presents an issue in itself. Even when there is agreement by observation on what constitutes an act of creative thinking, there is the widest disagreement among theories to account for that act. Among the more widely held conceptions or theories are those deriving from such diverse sources as logic or philosophy, learning theory, Gestalt principles of thought, psychometrics, psychoanalysis, and social perception (Getzels and Jackson, 1962).

Traditional logic holds that thinking is concerned with truth, and being true or false is a quality of assertions and propositions. Certain combinations of propositions make possible *new* propositions, and reason establishes the correctness of the "creative" conclusion. Allied to this "rational-philosophical" approach is Dewey's (1910) famous formulation of the five "logically distinct" steps in the "act of thought": a felt difficulty, its definition, suggestion toward a solution, development by reasoning of the bearings of the suggestion, and observation and experiment leading to its acceptance or rejection. Although Dewey himself was at some pains to point to nonlogical "playfulness" in thought, the "logically determined" five steps with the apparent focus on "reasoning" has been taken as an emphasis on the central role of logic and rationality in creative thinking.

For learning theorists like Thorndike and the associationists, habit and past experience—associations rather than reason—are the essential factors in thought. A novel solution is the outcome of conflicting action tendencies from past associative learning and consists of selecting previous associations to try out in the new situation. All thought no matter how apparently "novel," "insightful," or "creative" rests ultimately on associative stimulus-response principle. As Thorndike said, "A closer examination of selective thinking will show that no principles beyond the laws of readiness, exercise, and effect are needed to explain it; that it is only an extreme case of what goes on in the associative learning as described under the 'piecemeal' activity of situations" (1922, p. 190).

Wertheimer and the Gestaltists propose a formulation that differs from the traditional logic and classical association points of view. The thinking process does not proceed either by the piecemeal operations of logic or the piecemeal connections of associationism but through the "structurization" of Gestalten. There is first the problem situation in which the process starts, and then through a series of perceptual organizations and reorganizations a second situation in which the process ends, a solution reached. In productive or innovative thinking the problem situation, which is structurally incomplete involving a "gap" or "structural trouble," is altered into a solution situation which is in these respects structurally better, the gap is filled and the structural trouble has disappeared. In Wertheimer's words, "When one grasps a problem situation, its structural features and requirements set up certain strains, stresses and tensions in the thinker. What happens in real thinking [as against piecemeal 'ugly' thinking] is that these strains and stresses are followed up, yield vectors in the direction of improvement of the situation, and change it accordingly" (1954, p. 195).

A fourth and very different conception derives from the psychometric tradition, and involves two points of view within that tradition. On the one hand there is the straightforward identification of creativity with intelligence, the intelligence test being held a measure also of creative potential. On the other hand, there is the analysis of intellectual behavior into component more or less independent factors. Although there have been many factor analyses of intellectual behavior, Guilford focused specifically on the problem of creativity. The analysis distinguished between convergent and divergent mental processes, the former pertaining to new information that is more determined by known information, the latter pertaining to new information that is less determined by known information. In the one, the requirement is for a simple or already ascertained right response. In the other, a variety of responses involving "fluency," "flexibility," "originality," and "elaboration" may be called for. Divergent thinking is an essential substratum for creative performance.

A different conception of creativity yet has its roots in psychoanalytic theory. Here as elsewhere psychoanalytic theory is too complex to lend itself to brief summary without risk of misrepresentation. Nonetheless, several relevant points may be outlined if only to suggest its unique flavor. There is a cleavage in all human thought between two fundamental processes, an unconscious *primary process* and a more conscious *secondary process*. The interaction between the two processes is conflictual, involving repression and defense. Creative thought derives from an elaboration of the "freely rising" primary process fantasies and ideas related to daydreaming and children's play. The creative person accepts the freely rising ideas, the noncreative person does not. It is when these unconscious forces become "ego-syntonic" that the occasion exists, in Freud's words, for "achievements of special perfection" (1949, p. 127), that is, creativity.

It is impossible here to do justice to the psychoanalytic view; a fuller discussion of the points outlined here is given elsewhere (Getzels and Jackson, 1962). Recently there has been a shift of emphasis from id to ego processes and a concomitant shift of interests from the role of the unconscious to that of the conscious in creative thinking. Kris (1962), for example, suggests that the ego may voluntarily gain access to primary process thought by way of the preconscious, and that many creative products from wit to art derive from acts of regression in the service of the ego. Kubie (1958) puts the issue more sharply. He argues that where conscious processes predominate, thinking is rigid since the conscious symbolic functions are anchored in literal relationships to reality. Where unconscious processes predominate, there is an even more rigid anchorage in an unreality which has been rendered inaccessible to conscious introspection and the corrective influence of experience. The source of creativity is in the preconscious, which mediates between the conscious and the unconscious.

Finally, a social and perceptual point of view may be mentioned as illustrative of a rather more humanistic set of theories of creativity. Schachtel (1959) proposes that what psychoanalytic theory refers to as primary process thought may be the appropriate concept for daydreams, reveries, and idly wondering thought. It is not appropriate to creative thought where the play of ideas is due not to instinctual drives, regression, or defense but quite contrary to the openness of the human being to the world around him. Openness in the encounter with the world means that one's sensibilities are more freely receptive to new reflections of one's self and the environment in their varied aspects. Creativity is not referable to a "drive discharge function" but to a perceptual "openness in the encounter with the world."

This brief review of theories is obviously not exhaustive. Yet it is sufficient to suggest the wide range of competing conceptions underlying work in creativity, and to expose in systematic terms numerous of the issues—perhaps better, paradoxes—in the field.

Theoretical Paradoxes: Impulse and Control, Stimulus Reducing and Stimulus Seeking

One apparent paradox recurring through virtually all formulations may be stated most briefly as follows: Despite the self-evident need for strenuous effort, reflection, and rationality in problem solving, creative thinking entails, at least in some degree, surrender to freely rising playfulness, impulse, and a-rationality (Getzels, 1964). Hadamard in his treatise on *The*

Psychology of Invention in the Mathematical Field (1954) cites the relevant distinction between "cogito" meaning originally to "shake together," and "intelligo," meaning originally to "select among." Cogitation and intelligence: the one refers to letting ideas, memories, impulses, fantasies rise freely; the other refers to the process of choosing among the combination those patterns which have significance in reality. The "cogito" component of creative thinking seems predominantly an impulsive, sub-conscious, playful, divergent process, the "intelligo" component predominantly a reflective, conscious, directed, convergent process.

This dual process is well illustrated in Einstein's famous letter describing his own thinking: ". . . combinatory play seems to be the essential feature in productive thought—before there is any connection with logical construction in words or other kinds of signs which can be communicated to others. . . . Conventional words or other signs have to be sought for laboriously only in a secondary stage, when the mentioned associative play is sufficiently established and can be reproduced at will" (Hadamard, 1954, p. 142).

Two features of this and other such accounts are notable. One feature is the similarity of description in the arts and the sciences (Bronowski, 1956, pp. 30–31). The second feature is the insistence upon the presence of spontaneous and almost involuntary imagination and of conscious and rational reflection. Sometimes the process begins with a conscious effort as in the case of Poincaré, who struggled for years on a mathematical problem without avail, only to have the solution appear effortlessly one day as a "sudden illumination" (Hadamard, 1954, p. 14); sometimes as in the case of a poem by Housman, the process seems to begin with a suddent illumination, which is then worked out by conscious effort (Ghiselin, 1955, p. 91). But invariably there seems to be an alternation between a subconscious sphere, or what Galton called the "antechamber" of thought, and the conscious sphere or what Galton called the "presence chamber" of thought (Hadamard, 1954, p. 25).

Prevailing theories of creativity deal with this phenomenon by emphasizing one process or the other, some placing the essential source of the creative achievement in the "antechamber" or "cogito" component, other theories placing the essential source of the achievement in the "presence chamber" or "intelligo" component. Such solutions have not resolved the issue; the one group charges that failure to control the freely rising ideas leads to bizarre thought fatal to creative achievement, and the other group charges that control (censorship) of the freely rising ideas leads to sterile thought fatal to creative achievement. An obvious alternate solution is to postulate that both impulse and control are necessary in equal proportion. But this does not resolve the issue, for it is not clear that what follows from this kind of compromise is fruitful conceptually or methodologically.

There is another paradox recurring in the formulations. The drive to creative endeavor is seen by some as emanating from psychic conflict having its roots in childhood experience. A parallel is drawn between conflict as the genesis of neurosis and of creativity. Deutsch, for example, states this position directly, "As the instinctual pressure rises and a neurotic solution appears imminent, the unconscious defense against it leads to the creation of an art product. The psychic effect is the discharge of the pent-up emotion until a tolerable level is reached" (1960, p. 34). The material for working out the conflicts is founded in the experiences of childhood; adult creative imagination is rooted in psychic conflict and childhood experience. In Freud's words: "You will not forget that the stress laid on the writer's memories of his childhood, which perhaps seems so strange, is ultimately derived from the hypothesis that imaginative creation, like daydreaming, is a continuation of and substitute for the play of childhood" (1949, pp. 181–182).

But there are those who take a contrary view. The child is not a helpless repository of experience, adult thinking is not rooted in childhood events, imagination is not a defensive outcome of psychic conflict, creative achievement is not explicable as a discharge of pent-up instinctual pressure. On the contrary, to use Schachtel's formulation, which holds for others as well, "The infant is not entirely helpless but shows from birth on steadily increasing capacities for active searching for satisfaction and for active discovery and exploration and that it enjoys these active capacities" (1959, p. 5). The developmental movement by virtue of this boundless human exploratory drive is toward increased "openness" and "objectification" in the perception of the world during adolescence and adulthood. The mature perceiver approaches the object actively—inquisitively—and in doing so either "opens himself toward it receptively or, figuratively or literally, takes hold of it, tries to 'grasp' it" (Schachtel, 1959, p. 83). Far from being conflictual and defensive, the motivation underlying creative behavior is constructive and active in the highest degree. In Schachtel's words, "The main *motivation* at the root of creative experience is man's need to relate to the world around him. . . . This need is apparent in the young child's interest in all objects around him, and his ever renewed explorations of and play with them. It is equally apparent in the artist's lifelong effort to grasp and render something which he has envisaged in his encounter with the world, in the scientist's wonder about the nature of the objects around him . . ." (1959, p. 241).

From this point of view, the core of creativity is not in the unconscious or "regression to primary process thought," even in the service of the ego. It is not in withdrawal from the world; it is in openness to the world. The root of creative endeavor is not the discharge of id drives by the path of fantasied or hallucinated wish fulfillment in order to reach a tensionless state; it is the centering on the multiple aspects of an object, an idea, a problem, an enigma which goes beyond the closed, the familiar, the already-labeled.

As has been remarked, where the one set of theories attempts to account for creativity as due to a "drive discharge function," the other set of theories attempts to account for it as due to an "openness in the encounter with the world." To put the issue in extreme form, for the one creative behavior is seen as a tension or stimulus reducing activity, for the other, as a tension or stimulus seeking activity.

Facilitating Creative Behavior: The Process of Thinking and the Content of Thought

Methods for teaching and facilitating creative behavior rest on the assumption that the *process* of thinking can be separated from the *content* of thought, so that one can learn a general cognitive strategy outside the confines of a particular structure of knowledge. Or put another way, it is possible at least in theory to learn a way of thinking that cuts across the subject matters to be thought about.

This assumption raises a problem of fundamental importance both to conceptual and applied work in the area: Is separation of the process of thinking and the content of thought possible? There are those who aver that this is possible; they point to the construction of tests of thinking and to methods for teaching higher mental processes that have produced successful results. Indeed, they contend that it is not only possible but desirable, and argue that the generalized process should be given priority over particularized content in the cultivation of intellect and the objectives of education. But there are those who assert that not only is such priority not desirable but the separation itself is impossible (Ebel, 1974).

Among the methods for teaching, facilitating, or at least liberating creative thinking are the "reinforcement of original behavior" (Mearns, 1958), "brainstorming" (Osborn, 1953), "synectics" (Gordon, 1961), "training for originality" (Maltzman et al., 1960), "auto-instructional programs" (Covington and Crutchfield, 1965), "evaluationless classroom atmospheres" (Torrance and Myers, 1970). Evidence has been reported for the efficacy of each method. For example, subjects who had taken courses in brainstorming subsequently produced significantly more imaginative ideas than those who had not (Parnes and Meadow, 1960, 1963); subjects trained in originality, that is, in producing responses low in the response hierarchy, increased in the novelty of associations (Maltzman et al., 1960); subjects taking auto-instructional programs for stimulating originality were markedly superior to controlled subjects in criterion problem-solving and creativity measures (Covington and Crutchfield, 1965). These results are not without challenge (e.g., D. Taylor et al., 1958). Nevertheless, a review of the research in deliberate methods for facilitating creative behavior concluded that creative ability, as measured by tests, can be increased through instruction (Parnes and Brunelle, 1967).

Two issues pertinent to the separation of the process of thinking and the content of thought may be posed. The first issue is: What is the relative merit of the process and the content emphases in facilitating creative behavior? Without adducing evidence other than personal anecdote and predilection, some assert, "Emphasis on the process of thinking rather than its content grossly undervalues the essential and predominate contribution of knowledge to cognitive development. It is far less necessary and far less possible to teach a person how to think than to give him something that is true and useful to think about" (Ebel, 1974, p. 488). Without derogating the value of knowledge, others nonetheless assert the contrary view. They point to the bibliographers, pedants, and persons with perfect recall who seem to "know" everything yet create nothing. The issue is not likely to be settled by opposing assertions, however plausible they seem.

The second issue is: Do people with good performance in tests of creativity and originality, presumably measuring the process of thinking rather than any particular content, behave in more creative and original ways than those with poor performance? Some systematic attempts to answer this question have been made. One longitudinal study, for example, found a relationship between performance on a test of creativity administered to teacher-trainees in their junior year of training and creative behavior in the classroom six years later when they were actually teaching (Torrance et el., 1970). But the work in this area is still scant, and the results even when positive cannot be taken as a conclusion of a more general order. The relation between the process of creative thinking and the content of creative thought, between theories and methods emphasizing cognitive strategy and theories and methods emphasizing the structure of knowledge, remains an important issue for inquiry.

Prospects and Issues for Inquiry

Conceptions of creativity are so varied and the consequent definitions and criteria so diverse that it is impossible to order the issues in any conceptually systematic way. There is no single prospect, as it were, from which to see the field as a whole and to organize the issues in relation to each other. It is of course possible to compose inventories or "laundry lists" of issues—say, alphabetically or by a miscellany of topics like measurement, family influences, cross-cultural differences and such ad infinitum. But the organization of such lists is arbitrary and does not provide a rational framework for selecting the issues or for seeing relationships among the issues.

From one point of view this may be an advantage, for it permits the inclusion of the widest diversity of problems. From another point of view this advantage becomes a severe disadvantage, for the lack of any conceptual restriction may result in only a grab-bag of odds-and-ends of issues without rationale or relation to each other.

We are then faced with a choice in the field of creativtiy as in other fields without theoretical or methodological consensus: to pose any issues that seem in some wise interesting or relevant, or to attempt to formulate an explicit scheme that would provide at least a modicum of order to guide the selection of topics for inquiry and possibly reveal relationships among the topics, even though matters of relevance may be omitted because they do not fit into the categories given by the scheme. My inclination is in the latter direction, despite the self-evident risks involved (Getzels, 1969).

At the most general level individual and group behavior—whether creative or conformist—may be seen as embedded in a social system. We may think of a social system as involving two classes of phenomena which are at once analytically independent and phenomenally interactive. There are, at one level of analysis, institutions with certain roles and expectations that will fulfill the goals of the system. Behavior and its products may be seen as a function of the institutionalized roles and expectations; this is the sociological level of analysis. There are at another level of analysis, flesh and blood individuals with certain personalities and dispositions inhabiting the system. Behavior and its products may be seen as a function of these individualized personalities and dispositions; this is the psychological level of analysis. More integratively, at an interdisciplinary level of analysis, behavior and the products of behavior may be thought of as the outcome of the interaction between individuals and institutions, personalities and roles, idiosyncratic dispositions and normative expectations. All professors, for example, profess but no two profess quite the same way. All writers write but no two write quite the same way.

Like all analytic frameworks, the present one is an abstraction and as such an oversimplification of "reality"; some factors have been brought to the foreground, others relegated to the background. By focusing on the sociological and psychological dimensions, we have omitted other factors contributing to behavior. Three additional dimensions must be mentioned, although they do not of course exhaust the possibilities, which are in a sense inexhaustible (Getzels and Thelen, 1960).

There is first the obvious constitutional or biological dimension. Just as we may think of the individual in personalistic terms, we may also think of him in organismic or constitutional terms. The individual's personality whether creative or not is embedded in a biological organism with certain constitutional characteristics and potentialities. The dispositions of personality are surely related in some as yet unknown ways to these constitutional characteristics and potentialities. In this sense, it must be borne in mind that underlying the psychological dimension is a biological dimension, although the one is not reducible to the other. In addition then to the familiar psychological issues of creativity—the motivations, cognitive styles, and so on—there are also biological issues of creativity.

Second, there is what may be called the cultural or anthropological dimension. Just as we may think of institutions in social terms, we may also think of them in cultural terms, for the instituitons are embedded in an ethos with certain mores and values. The expectations for the institutional roles—whether military or artistic, conformist or creative—must in some way be related to the ethos or cultural values. One need but consider the values placed upon originality and secularism in medieval art and in modern art. In this sense, it must be borne in mind that interacting with the sociological dimension is an anthropological dimension, although again the one is not reducible to the other.

Finally, there is a group or social-psychological dimension, mediating between the institutional expectations and the individual dispositions. No person is without membership in some face-to-face or reference group. The group can support institutional expectations for normative behavior, and it can support individual dispositions for idiosyncratic behavior. Even the most independent of pure scientists and fine artists publish or exhibit their work; they become liable to group influences from peers and critics, academies of science and galleries of art. In this sense it must be borne in mind that in addition to the other dimensions, there is a group or social-psychology dimension, which is pertinent to the understanding of creativity.

From the point of view of the social systems framework we have sketched here, creative behavior and its products may be seen as a function of these interactive elements, which may be studied separately or in combination through the relevant concepts and methods: organismic constitution, individual personality, social institution, group influence, and cultural values. The dimensions of the framework may serve both to suggest and to order problems and issues for inquiry, among which the following are illustrative.[1]

ORGANISMIC CONSTITUTION

The work here is so scant that it is not clear how to formulate the issues other than to raise the general problem: What factors are part of the biological basis of creativity? A number of tentative approaches to this issue may be suggested, none with any confidence. One approach is through the detailed study of the very earliest exploratory movements of infants and the development of such exploratory behavior. Another approach is through the study of monozygotic and dyzygotic twins. Yet another approach is through biofeedback methods. More directly, it might be possible to study individual differences in basic levels of brain activity to observe any variabilities between creative and noncreative subjects. It might also be possible to obtain the cooperation of truly creative individuals, and study the relation of fallow periods and productive periods as measured by alpha and other brain activity indices. These are of course beginnings toward the formulation of issues rather than statements of formulated issues. Perhaps the chief value of including this dimension is in pointing out that this is a domain where inquiry is needed, and in calling attention to recent advances in research in brain functioning which may possibly be applied to work on creativity.

INDIVIDUAL PERSONALITY

By far the greatest effort has been devoted to this dimension; the very promise of the results points to deeper issues in this domain. More needs to be known about the obscure dispositions that drive—literally force—an individual into the strains and risks of creating when about him are individuals enjoying the ease and safety of conforming. A distinction has been made between "deliberate" and "nondeliberate" creative processes. Is such distinction valid? Is the creative work of the psychologically "sick" and tortured person the same or different from that of the psychologically "sound" and placid person? Are there different kinds of imagery, metaphor, and sensitivity to problems in different kinds of creative endeavor by different types of creative individuals? We need to study the relation between the more conscious ego functions and the more primitive layers of personality and the relation of this interaction to creative processes. This is not easy—not as easy as giving tests and administering questionnaires. It might be possible to examine the relation of dream content over time to the vicissitudes of the creative process. And it might be possible to find highly creative persons who would be willing to introspect upon their ongoing creative processes and allow clinically trained personologists to inquire into aspects of the processes upon which they themselves might be unable to report. The investigation of the phenomenon of incubation in creative work has barely been started. Several issues may be stated in the form of illustrative hypotheses. The incubation period permits the operation of certain "unconscious" processes; the incubation period permits "unfreezing" of a fixated way of perceiving the problem and its elements; the incubation period permits the "retrieval" of information from memory storage; the incubation period permits the "transformation" of material that is memorized or perceived in established ways into novel patterns.

SOCIAL INSTITUTIONS

Although more has been done here than in the biological domain, less has been done than in the psychological domain. We must investigate the societal as well as the individual and the face-to-face group conditions that serve as a stimulus or incubus to originality. What are the social properties of a particular period in time than encourage creative production? Are there institutional structures that facilitate the translation of new, potentially useful ideas into innovative tangible outcomes? The historic differences in scientific and artistic creativity between males and females are surely due more to social conditions than to biological potentialities. What are the effects of institutionalized expectations on the creative processes of particular gender, ethnic, race, or age groups? Is the following a tenable formulation? The conflict between social-structural opposition to change and individual tendencies toward change can be stimulating, enlivening, and challenging; this effect is rendered likely if one not only expects the conflict, but looks forward to it, as a kind of world view and opportunity for self-fulfillment. More generally, what is the interaction between institutional and personalistic forces over time, that is, longitudinally, facilitating or hindering creative behavior?

GROUP SETTINGS

We need to study the effect of group settings on the development and expression of creativity. What kinds of family interactions, for example, will generate and nurture creative individuals? With the earlier and earlier attendance of children in schools, more must be known about the effects of different kinds of classrooms on the development of styles of thinking including originality. And of course the same issues are germane to the higher levels of education, including specialized schools of art and laboratories of science. We need to round out the picture of creativity by studying creative performance not only in organizations directed toward scientific, aesthetic, and technological ends, but in organizations directed toward commercial, political, social, and religious ends as well. We need to know more about "creative leadership"—leadership that is not only inventive in itself but facilitates invention in others. It seems clear that certain organizational "climates" promote health and others illness—are there certain organizational climates that promote creativity and others conventionality? We need to study the "official" or "formal" structure of an organization or group, its "unofficial" or "informal" structure, and the interaction between the two to determine the circumstances stimulating or suppressing creative behavior.

CULTURAL VALUES

Over and above the biological, psychological, societal, and group contexts of behavior is a cultural context composed of characteristic values. This is not the place for a disquisition on culture and values. Yet clearly there are patterns of values that distinguish one people from another, or the same people in one era or another. For example, different cultures have been said to reflect Apollonian or Dionysian values. Two different eras of American culture have been said to reflect "inner-directed" or "other-directed" values. More specifically, distinctions have been made between peoples or periods dominated by a pattern of values composed of "the work-success ethic," "future-time orientation," "individualism," and "Puritan morality," or a pattern of values composed of "an ethic of sociability," "present-time orientation," "togetherness," and "moral relativism." The consideration of values raises a number of issues with respect to creative behavior. What are the pervasive philosophies of life in different cultures or at different periods that influence the magnitude and character of the creative work that will be undertaken? What kinds of values contribute to what kinds of creativity in what types of individuals in what places during what historic periods? If the fullest possible answers to questions of this order are to be found, the study of creativity will have to become more cross-cultural (less time-bound and less place-bound) than it has been.

These problems are of course illustrative and the framework only one form of generating and organizing pertinent issues and indicating relationships among them; other potential factors like economic and political variables, for example, have been omitted. As has been suggested, it is possible as well to raise pertinent issues in a more phenomenological mode. Ultimately, the most productive work will probably be forthcoming not within any single mode but across a variety of modes.

Significant problems may also be derived topically: problems of definition and criteria, theories and procedures, the paradoxes of impulse and control, of stimulus reducing and stimulus seeking, the facilitation of creativity through the process of thinking and the content of thought. The specific issues may be posed in the terms given by Dewey, Freud, or Schachtel, by Galton, Terman, or Guilford, or in a combination of these, others, and those not presently envisioned.

But three implications from the perspectives included in this volume are clear: First, fruitful issues can be raised and productive work can be done, and has been done, from a variety of perspectives. Second, in Gordon Allport's words, "Our [strongest] censure should be reserved for those who close all doors but one. The surest way to lose truth is to pretend that one already wholly has it." Third, whether one is concerned with the timeless dilemmas of individual fulfillment or the existential requirements for social amelioration, with understanding the products of mankind's highest aspirations or the processes of mental functioning in more mundane pursuits, creative thinking is a subject of study of almost unparalleled significance for human welfare.

Note

1. The issues are drawn from those mentioned at the symposium on the Future Implications of Creativity Research at the Center for Creative Leadership. Present at the symposium were F. Barron, J. W. Getzels, J. P. Guilford, D. W. MacKinnon, S. R. Maddi, S. P. Parnes, G. M. Prince, C. W. Taylor, I. A. Taylor, and E. P. Torrance. My debt to the symposium is gratefully acknowledged.

References

Bronowski, J. *Science and human values.* New York: Harper & Row, 1956.
Buhl, H. R. *Creative engineering design.* Ames: Iowa State University Press, 1960.

Cattell, R. B. and Drevdahl, J. E. A comparison of the personality profile (16 PF) of eminent researchers with that of eminent teachers and administrators, and of the general population. *British Journal of Psychology*, 1955, *46*, 248–261.

Covington, M. V. and Crutchfield, R. S. Facilitation of creative problem solving. *Programmed Instruction*, 1965, *4*(4), 3–5, 10.

Deutsch, F. Mind, body, and art. *Daedalus*, 1960, *89*, 34–45.

Dewey, J. *How we think*. New York: D. C. Heath, 1910.

Domino, G. Identification of potentially creative persons from the adjective check list. *Journal of Consulting and Clinical Psychology*, 1970, *30*, 48–51.

Drevdahl, J. E. Some developmental and environmental factors in creativity. In C. W. Taylor (Ed.), *Widening horizons in creativity*, pp. 170–186. New York: Wiley, 1964.

Ebel, R. L. And still the dryads linger. *American Psychologist*, 1974, *29*, 485–492.

Flanagan, J. C. Definition and measurement of ingenuity. In C. W. Taylor (Ed.), *The second (1957) University of Utah research conference on the identification of creative scientific talent*, pp. 109–118. Salt Lake City: University of Utah Press, 1958.

Freud, S. The relation of the poet to day-dreaming. *Collected papers*. Vol. 4, pp. 173–183. London: Hogarth Press, 1949.

Freud, S. The unconscious. *Collected papers*. Vol. 4, pp. 98–136. London: Hogarth Press, 1949.

Galton, F. *Hereditary genius: An inquiry into its laws and consequences*. London: Macmillan, 1869.

Getzels, J. W. Creative thinking, problem-solving, and instruction. In E. R. Hilgard (Ed.), *Theories of learning and instruction*, The Sixty-third Yearbook of the National Society for the Study of Education, Part I, pp. 240–267. Chicago: University of Chicago Press, 1964.

Getzels, J. W. A social psychology of education. In G. Lindzey and E. Aronson (Eds.), *Handbook of Social Psychology* (2nd Ed.). Vol. 5, pp. 459–537. Reading, Mass.: Addison-Wesley, 1969.

Getzels, J. W. and Csikszentmihalyi, M. The study of creativity in future artists. In O. J. Harvey (Ed.), *Experience, structure, and adaptability*, pp. 349–368. New York: Springer, 1966.

Getzels, J. W. and Dillon, J. T. Giftedness and the education of the gifted. In R. M. W. Travers (Ed.), *Second handbook of research on teaching*, pp. 689–731. Chicago: Rand McNally, 1973.

Getzels, J. W. and Jackson, P. W. *Creativity and intelligence: Explorations with gifted students*. New York: Wiley, 1962.

Getzels, J. W. and Madaus, G. F. Creativity. In R. L. Ebel (Ed.), *Encyclopedia of educational research*, pp. 267–275. New York: Macmillan, 1969.

Getzels, J. W. and Thelen, H. A. The classroom as a unique social system. In N. B. Henry (Ed.), *The dynamics of instructional groups*. The Fifty-ninth Yearbook of the National Society for the Study of Education, Part II, pp. 53–82. Chicago: University of Chicago Press, 1960.

Ghiselin, B. (Ed.) *The creative process*. New York: New American Library, 1952.

Gordon, W. J. J. *Synectics: The development of creative capacity*. New York: Harper & Row, 1961.

Gowan, J. C. *An annotated bibliography on the academically talented*. Washington, D.C.: National Education Association, 1961.

Gowan, J. C. *Annotated bibliography on creativity and giftedness*. Northridge, Calif.: San Fernando Valley State College Foundation, 1965.

Guilford, J. P. Creativity. *American Psychologist*, 1950, *5*, 444–454.

Hadamard, J. *The psychology of invention in the mathematical field.* New York: Dover Publications, 1954.

Kris, E. *Psychoanalytic explorations in art.* New York: International Universities Press, 1962.

Kubie, L. *Neurotic distortion of the creative process.* Lawrence: University of Kansas Press, 1958.

MacKinnon, D. W. The nature and nurture of creative talent. *American Psychologist,* 1962, *17,* 484–495.

MacLeod, R. B. The phenomenological approach to social psychology. *Psychological Review,* 1947, *54,* 193–210.

Maltzman, I., Simon, S., Raskin, D., and Licht, L. Experimental studies in the training of originality. *Psychological Monographs,* 1960, *74*(6), 1–23.

Maslow, A. H. The creative attitude. *Structuralist,* 1963, *3,* 4–10.

Mearns, H. *Creative power: The education of youth in the creative arts.* 2nd, rev. ed. New York: Dover Publishers, 1958.

Mednick, S. A. and Mednick, M. T. An associative interpretation of the creative process. In C. W. Taylor (Ed.), *Widening horizons in creativity,* pp. 54–68. New York: Wiley, 1964.

Miles, C. C. Gifted children. In L. Carmichael (Ed.), *Manual of child psychology,* pp. 984–1063. 2nd, rev. ed. New York: Wiley, 1954.

Miller, N. E. Liberalization of basic S-R concepts: Extension to conflict behavior, motivation and social learning. In S. Koch (Ed.), *Psychology: A study of a science.* Vol. 2, pp. 196–292. New York: McGraw-Hill, 1959.

Newell, A., Shaw, J. C., and Simon, H. A. The process of creative thinking. In H. E. Gruber, G. Terrell, and M. Wertheimer (Eds.), *Contemporary approaches to creative thinking,* pp. 63–119. New York: Atherton Press, 1962.

Osborn, A. F. *Applied imagination: Principles and procedures of creative thinking.* New York: Scribner, 1953.

Parnes, S. J. and Brunelle, E. A. The literature of creativity (Part I). *Journal of Creative Behavior,* 1967, *1,* 191–240.

Parnes, S. J. and Meadow, A. Evaluation of persistence of effects produced by a creative problem-solving course. *Psychological Reports,* 1960, *7,* 357–361.

Parnes, S. J. and Meadow, A. Development of individual creative talent. In C. W. Taylor and F. X. Barron (Eds.), *Scientific creativity: Its recognition and development,* pp. 311–320. New York: Wiley, 1963.

Roe, A. The personality of artists. *Educational and Psychological Measurement,* 1946, *6,* 401–408.

Roe, A. A psychological study of eminent psychologists and anthropologists, and a comparison with biological and physical scientists. *Psychological Monographs,* 1953, *67*(2), 1–55.

Schachtel, E. G. *Metamorphosis.* New York: Basic Books, 1959.

Schaefer, C. E. The self-concept of creative adolescents. *Journal of Psychology,* 1969, *72,* 233–242.

Taylor, C. W. and Ellison, R. L. Predicting creative performances from multiple measures. In C. W. Taylor (Ed.), *Widening horizons in creativity,* pp. 227–260. New York: Wiley, 1964.

Taylor, D. W., Berry, P. C., and Block, C. H. Does group participation when using brainstorming facilitate or inhibit creative thinking? *Administrative Science Quarterly,* 1958, *3,* 23–47.

Terman, L. M. *Genetic studies of genius. Vol. 1. Mental and physical traits of a thousand gifted children.* Stanford, Calif.: Stanford University Press, 1925.

Thorndike, E. L. *Psychology of arithmetic.* New York: Macmillan, 1922.

Torrance, E. P. *Torrance tests of creative thinking, Manual.* Princeton, N.J.: Personnel Press, 1966.

Torrance, E. P. and Myers, R. E. *Creative learning and teaching.* New York: Dodd, Mead, 1970.

Torrance, E. P., Tan, C. A., and Allman, T. Verbal originality and teacher behavior: A predictive validity study. *Journal of Teacher Education,* 1970, *21,* 335–341.

Wertheimer, M. *Productive thinking.* New York: Harper and Brothers, 1954.

Name Index

Subject Index

Perspectives in Creativity
edited by Irving A. Taylor and J. W. Getzels

Alexander J. Morin, *Publisher*
Ann Waters, *Manuscript Editor*
Georganne E. Marsh, *Managing Editor*

Designed by Aldine Staff
Composition by Typoservice Corporation,
Indianapolis, Indiana
Printed by American Publishers Press,
Chicago, Illinois
Bound by Brock & Rankin,
Chicago, Illinois

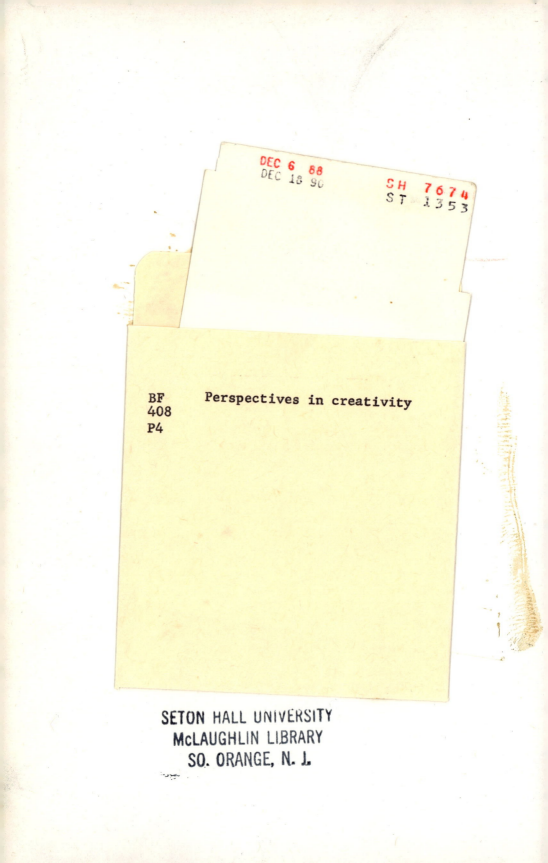